AF437718

The Woolems
of Averlune

by Matt Pelicano

Written by Matt Pelicano
www.mattpelicano.com

Illustrated by Sandra Stanton

Averlune Press, Inc.
www.Averlune.com

Summary: Annelyse Bellamy thought she knew her mother well. But, when unimaginable tragedy strikes, and a mysterious young man plants questions in her mind, everything Annelyse ever took for granted is cast into doubt.

Tracing a path outlined for her by a cryptic poem, Annelyse sets out on a journey to discover the truth about the mythical creatures called Woolems, and to find answers to the questions clouding her mother's past.

Along the way, she learns a valuable lesson: that there is no more-foreign country through which to wander than Grief, but the way back to all that she once held dear lay hidden where least expected.

1. YOUNG ADULT FICTION / Social Themes / Death, Grief, Bereavement
2. YOUNG ADULT FICTION / Coming of Age
3. YOUNG ADULT FICTION / Fantasy / Epic

ISBN/SKU: 9798218090180
ISBN Complete: 979-8-218-09018-0
Publication Date: 10/22/2022

The Woolems of Averlune/Matt Pelicano. -- 1st ed.
ISBN 979-8-218-09018-0

For my children who have suffered great loss and yet
continually mine the dark depths of grief for the riches of
kindness, generosity, gratitude, and love. I could not be
prouder of the people you have become.

"No one ever told me that grief felt so like fear."

-C.S. Lewis

For a Map of Laprofonde
visit www.Averlune.com

Table of Contents

Preface

Denial, Anger, Bargaining, Depression, Acceptance. These are traditionally understood to be the five stages of grief, as defined by Dr. Elisabeth Kübler-Ross. Though a useful starting point for navigating common methods of coping with loss, recent studies have led to a much more complex understanding of grief. For example, denial is now understood to include such reactions as avoidance, confusion, and fear. Anger might manifest itself as irritation or anxiety. Bargaining can often be displayed as an attempt to find meaning or a desire to reach through to the other side and touch the loved one lost. It appears that there are endless roads down which the heartsick might wander.

The reality marring any definition of the grieving process is that grieving is not a process at all. Processes are usually clearly defined and linear. If this were true of how people grieve, then the grief-stricken might expect to pass from one clear-cut stage to the next in a steady progress toward healing.

But this is not how it happens; grief is not linear. In fact, grief is a sort of circular madness. I say madness because those grieving seem to get trapped in emotional eddies, retracing old ground - over and over and over again – in the hope of finding a different outcome. But it would be madness to think that any attempt to deny undeniable facts could ever change the reality of loss. It is unrealistic to believe that any degree of anger could ever wrest control away from the obstinate hands of fate. And no amount of bargaining could possibly ransom those held captive by death. Such notions are not rational, but then neither is death.

Denial, anger, and bargaining are all impotent, and still, we wield these wooden swords in the face of a deadly foe. In times of tragedy, any lifeline appears comforting at first, no matter how ineffective it proves to be in the end. And so, we grasp at imaginary ropes, while the whirlpool of emotion holds us in its grip.

No, grief is not a linear process outlined by clearly marked milestones; it is a messy operation of sifting through the rubble of a life demolished. Hidden among the wreckage, memories and emotions like *grief snipers* take aim at vulnerability where and when we least expect it. Things we have always treasured become the enemies of our fragile hearts. The result is a writhing separation of ourselves from everything that had once helped to define us and the life we knew. Everything, including our own selves, becomes unfamiliar. Indeed, there is no more-foreign country through which to wander than Grief.

In time, inevitably, the grief-stricken is presented with a choice. He can choose to freefall into the internal abyss consuming his life or turn his eyes outward in an effort to rediscover that which still remains. This book is, in part, an exploration of that choice.

The Woolems of Averlune began its life as something somewhat humbler than a novel. Setting for myself the goal of writing a rhyming poem that featured alliteration using every letter in the alphabet required that I employ some poetic license. The end result was a poem which spoke of an enchanting little girl and mythical creatures inhabiting fictional lands.

Unsure of precisely what the poem was about, the geographic imagery I employed was the first thing that fired my imagination. From the poem's text, I drew a map of the locations it mentioned. The western coastline is loosely based upon the coast of France near Bordeaux. I'd always been fascinated by the keystone-shaped landscape between Arcachon and Soulac-sur-Mer, and so it became the coastline of Averlune. I allowed myself to indulge in flights of fancy, filling out the rest of the map, much of which receives little more than a glancing mention in the story.

I never dreamed when I wrote the poem that it would grow from 221 words to over 138,000; but it obviously had far more to say than I'd anticipated. Perhaps, it would be truer to confess that something in me had found its voice in that little poem, and it needed to speak its mind fully.

The result is an extended allegory, *The Woolems of Averlune*, a journey through grief. In the pages of this passion play, I was able to explore those things I had held dear prior to the events that *killed what was most precious inside of* me, before the time of great suffering. In the thoughts, experiences, and footsteps of Annelyse and Edward, I was able to rediscover so much of what I had lost or simply cast aside.

To be human is to suffer. At some point in our lives, we all experience loss. It is unavoidable. But, even though universal, individual suffering cannot be compared. It is as unique as the heart it breaks. Nonetheless, I think we can learn from each other's experience of suffering and grief. I think the best use pain can be put to is alleviating the suffering of others. This is but one more of my aspirations for this work of fiction.

I have suffered. I have grieved. In those dark moments, I discarded so much of what I'd always held dear. I cast off faith, hope, and even the possibility of love. I traveled the well-worn, circular paths of the Five Stages of Grief and explored all of their tributaries. I was the target of *grief snipers*. I turned my eyes inward, let go, and watched it all slip over the edge of the abyss. I let painful events *kill what was most precious inside of me*. And I did all of this utterly alone, while trying to help my children through their own grieving.

And then, I slowly began to turn my eyes outward. What I found was not the emptiness of loss, but a gratitude for everything from sunsets to the sweet smile of a long-ago friend - and healing soon followed. In its wake, I rediscovered faith; I tasted the fruits of hope; I found love to make sense of life's lights and darks; and I started to understand that one brush stroke, no matter how grim, cannot obscure all the colors of a life fully lived.

But my rebirth began with this poem, this little girl, and the mysterious Woolems inhabiting my inner landscape. This is my hope for you, too.

When titling the chapters, I took a somewhat unorthodox approach. I outlined a possible talk I might give on the subject of grief, and then used each bullet point as a chapter title. The title summarizes a theme being illustrated by the corresponding chapter, however subtle.

Regardless of the efforts I always put into descriptive narrative, many details of my story escape my own imagining. So, it should not come as a surprise when I say that I had no idea what a Woolem looked like until Sandy conceived and drew one. The moment I saw her drawing, I knew she had achieved a clearer vision of Woolems than I had. Despite our intention to leave as much to the reader's imagination as possible, I felt strongly that her depiction of a Woolem should be included in this edition. And so, it is.

Throughout the course of this project, I have enjoyed the collaboration of several gifted people. This was a lesson I learned long ago, to surround myself with people more talented than myself and let them enrich not only the end result, but the process, as well. My heartfelt thanks go to Rikson Stanton, Megan Pelicano, Joey Pelicano, and Andy Pelicano for their work in creating the theatrical trailer used in marketing the release of this novel. From the original score and superb vocals to the 3D-printed props and stunning videography filmed on location in Iceland, these four young artists exceeded expectations in both professionalism and proficiency. I could not be more pleased.

I enjoy incorporating into my novels those whom I

love and those who have made an impact on me by the grandeur of their personality. This book is no exception. Thank you to Mia Cotter for lending her name and exuberance to the role of the young river otter. Thank you also to Pat Arre, Halla Walton, Kendra Herron, and Isaiah Weaver for gracing me with their friendship and kindness. I hope you will forgive any license I took with your fictional selves; it was all done with the highest regard.

Lastly is she who has contributed the most, Sandra Stanton. Thank you for your partnership in bringing to life my world and the characters who call it home. Your illustrations adeptly highlight the tone my writing tried to establish. Sharing the process with you, almost from Day 1, was invaluable and wonderfully enjoyable. Thank you for all the ways you so gracefully move my heart and mind to see deeper and discover more. I have loved you from the beginning and I will love you 'til the end.

As I look out my window at the black, volcanic sand beach skirting the southern shore of Iceland, and the North Atlantic that batters it day and night, I'm moved to thought. This awe-inspiring spectacle was here before I arrived, and it will be here long after I'm gone. In an endless succession of birth, death, and rebirth, waves form, exhaust themselves, then disappear. But they are no less magnificent for the brevity of their lives. In some mysterious way, they are more so – as are we all.

Vík í Mýrdal, Iceland   *M.R.P.*
October 1, 2022

CHAPTER ONE

Loss is Estrangement

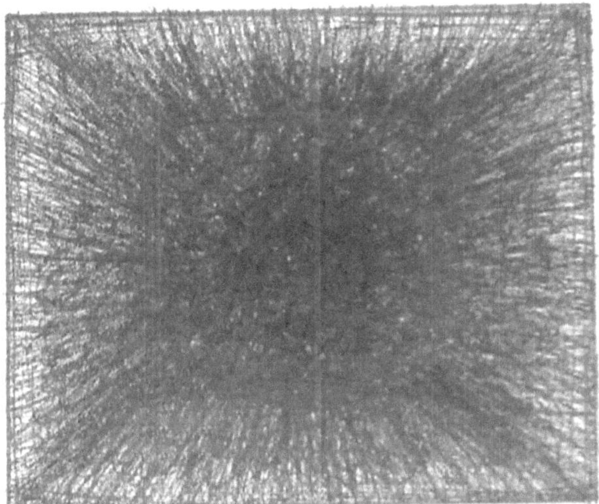

Annelyse sat on the edge of her bed, staring into the darkness. With the toes of her right foot, she'd been digging at the heel of her left shoe for the better part of an hour. Scuffing and scratching at the stiff leather as if picking at a scab, she was hardly aware of what she was doing.

In a bruised corner of her heart, she hid a silent desire to punish something for all that had gone wrong recently, and tight shoes were as good a scapegoat as any. She was angry, but her anger had not yet bobbed to the surface of her thoughts. Like a bitter, black fruit, it needed time to ripen. For now, she was mostly just irritated.

Freeing her foot at last, her shoe slipped off and fell through the dark, striking the bare floor with a rudeness that sent shudders up Annelyse's spine. Sitting there with one shoe on and one shoe off, she stretched her toes and breathed a long sigh of exhaustion. Her cramped feet had not been allowed to move so freely since early that morning.

The entire day had felt like a cruel punishment; but for what offense, she didn't know. It reminded her of the times as a child when she'd misbehaved and been forced to stand in a corner. It made no sense; it was a pointless punishment that had nothing to do with the crime. That's what today had been, pointless beyond all proportion. Annelyse now felt her anger detach itself from the bottom of her heart and bubble to the surface. Clenching the bedsheets in her fist, she set her jaw in defiance.

Wiggling her foot, Annelyse reached down and pulled-off her long, white sock. With bare toes, she loosened the strap of her remaining shoe. Then, flicking her ankle, she sent the white, leather instrument of torture sailing through the air. With a dull thud, it landed on the floor beside its mate. Normally, the fact that her two shoes were not perfectly arranged side-by-side and stored in their proper place would have bothered her to no end. Under any other circumstance, she would have gotten up without hesitation and set the situation right. But, in a world where so much was out of place, disheveled shoes were right at home.

Her left sock had fallen down around her ankle early on in the day, causing her a great deal of annoyance. The more she pulled at it, the more stretched out of shape it became. Finally, she just gave up and let it slide down on top of her foot. There it sat, like a saggy innertube, ringing her ankle. All she had to do now was give her foot a good shake, and the sock sloughed off in a lazy heap.

Her year-old dress still fit her just fine, since her big

growth spurt had ended a few months before her mother had made it for her. But her feet had continued growing, even after the rest of her had slowed. As a result, her shoes were now about a year too small for her and pinched the little toe on each foot mercilessly. She was glad to finally be rid of them – for good, she hoped.

She was still dressed in the clothes she'd been wearing all day. There just hadn't been much of a reason to change. Even discomfort hadn't been enough to motivate her. By the time she returned home that evening, she was so completely wrung out that she lacked the energy to care how uncomfortable she'd become. The thought of changing her clothes was more than she could handle.

Since early in the evening, one question had been gnawing circles in Annelyse's mind: when was the last time she'd been forced to wear her *good clothes*? They were always reserved for happy occasions like holidays or birthday parties; but at the moment, she couldn't remember ever having been happy before. Not today, she couldn't.

Whenever the last formal occasion had been, it really didn't matter all that much. She never intended to wear *good clothes* again, whatever the event. They were ridiculous and altogether impractical. Besides, after today, dressing up would forever hold new meaning for her – a meaning she didn't care to think about again.

Alone in the dark, her room felt like a foreign country. Everywhere she looked, she failed to find the meaning and significance that had once lived there. Somehow, the whole house seemed deserted beyond explanation.

Her heart had been so full of emptiness, lately, that it had overflowed into her surroundings. Now, even the cozy assurance of her bedroom was awash in cold discomfort. The keepsakes on her dresser, once precious reminders of joyful times, dripped with absurdity. The hope chest at the foot of her bed, once filled with treasures and mementos, now looked like nothing but a crate for useless clutter.

Everything that had ever been important to her had been stolen away. It was as if the good things in life had never really existed at all; happiness had been just one, big lie. She might as well have been living someone else's life, her own was nowhere to be found.

She now occupied a world that was completely different from the one she'd always known. Everything she'd taken for granted, everything that had once been rock-solid-certain was now irretrievably lost. In its place, there was only the swirling confusion of her life going down the drain. Trying to make sense of it all, she began to retrace the events of the day in her mind.

It was a Friday, and morning had come long before the sun. Her father, who had always been an early riser, barely had the motivation to rouse himself let alone carry the weight of waking Annelyse, too. She'd seen it in his tired eyes, and she felt guilty for adding to his burden.

"Leesy, it's time to get up," he said, his weary face appearing at the top of the ladder that joined her loft to the rest of the house. "Let's eat something before getting dressed. It's gonna be a long day."

Climbing back down the ladder, Annelyse's father disappeared from sight, leaving her alone to face the challenge of getting out of bed. She was painfully aware that, today, getting up meant putting out into deep waters. She didn't know exactly what awaited her; but what she did know was enough to make her want to pull the covers back over her head and sink down into the embrace of her mattress.

Then she thought of her father.

He would need her today, of all days. How could any man be expected to weather such a storm on his own? She'd never let him face it alone, no matter how much she wanted to stay in bed and let it all drone on without her.

This was not the day for selfishness. Perhaps, those days were gone forever.

In one great exertion of effort, Annelyse flung the covers off her legs and sat upright. Pushing the long ringlets of gold out of her face, she yawned and rubbed the sand from her eyes. Rising up from the kitchen below her bedroom, she could hear the sizzle of eggs and bacon kissing the cast iron skillet. Breakfast would be ready soon, though she saw little point in trying to eat. Her appetite was still very much asleep.

Digging deep, she struggled to find the strength to leave her bed. There was a battle between dread and willpower raging inside of her, and it wasn't yet clear who would win.

Through the window above her pillow, she could see the flicker of Lower Perigoh Light: a solitary sentry guarding the southern mouth of Perigoh Bay. The lighthouse stood astride Watcher's Island, half a mile from shore. Whenever Annelyse was unable to sleep, she'd lay in bed and stare at the pulsing of the great lamp until drowsiness swept her beneath the waves of slumber. But the previous night – and too many nights before - even the lighthouse had failed to lull her to sleep.

When Annelyse was a child, she'd told her mother that she wanted to be a lighthouse keeper when she grew up. The thought of being surrounded by crashing waves and rocky danger excited her imagination. She could see herself standing beside the mighty lens as it cast its warning out across the bay. She imagined herself holding a spyglass to one eye, searching the salty sea - the last lonely hope of sailors in peril. How many ships would she save from disaster upon the rocks? How many lives would be spared?

Thinking about it now, an ironic smirk crept across her face. If the past few months had taught her anything it was that even in broad daylight some shipwrecks could not be avoided. Lives could not be saved, only prolonged for a while. These thoughts, like Lower Perigoh Light, illuminated the jagged rocks of cynicism hidden beneath the tumultuous surface of her heart. But Annelyse could see no way around them and back to the blissful innocence of youth; she'd drifted too far out to sea.

Swinging her legs over the edge of the bed, she paused a moment before getting up. She'd been clutching her sheets in one hand all night long, and only now had she realized it. Opening her hand felt like letting go of a lifeline. Maybe if she stayed in bed and hid beneath the covers, her father would forget all about her. Maybe if she went back to sleep, she'd awaken to find that nothing had really changed. Her parents would be downstairs engaged in their usual morning routine, and everything would be alright.

"Food's ready, Leesy," her father called from the kitchen, rousing her from this daydream.

Annelyse sighed and slowly opened her hand, leaving her lifeline behind and venturing out into the deep waters of a frightful day.

"Coming," she called in a weak voice, as she wrapped her grey, woolen bathrobe around her shoulders.

Descending the narrow ladder, she turned to find her father seated alone at the kitchen table. He looked smaller than usual. Or maybe the table had somehow grown too big. It had always seemed just right, before.

On the plate in front of him, one fried egg sat beside a fragment of stale bread. Annelyse thought there was far too much empty space and not enough food on her father's plate. She was certain that, unlike the table, the size of the plate was not to blame. He never had much of an appetite anymore.

Holding his tea in both hands, Mr. Bellamy looked up to see his daughter standing at the foot of the ladder.

"Come, eat while it's still warm," he said, with a feeble smile.

Annelyse walked over and kissed her father on the cheek, then took her seat on the long side of the table. On her plate, two fried eggs, three strips of bacon, and a piece of buttered bread awaited her. Ignoring the food altogether, Annelyse reached for her teacup, cradling its soothing warmth in her chilly, stiff hands. The scent of orange peel and cinnamon filled her mind, lifting her spirits in a moment of welcome forgetfulness. She took a sip, then looked over at her father who sat expressionless across from her.

All of a sudden, he looked old to her. His unruly mop of sandy-brown hair hadn't been touched in months. He'd never exerted much effort in taming it before, even less so lately. As a result, the thick, heavy locks now framed his face and concealed his ears altogether. Annelyse noticed a sag in her father's shoulders, as if he were unable to hold up his head beneath the weight of all that hair. Or perhaps it was that his thoughts had become too heavy. Once a strong man, her father now looked broken.

He'd always been clean-shaven, though not by choice. His was a naturally smooth, almost baby-face. But now deepening lines splayed out like fingers from the corners of his eyes. And his forehead was as furrowed as a newly plowed field. Even his cheeks had wasted away to hollow, sunken caverns, surely a symptom of his diminishing appetite.

Most distressing of all, Annelyse saw in her father's eyes a sadness deeper than the black waters off Wastrel Grugh. It crushed her to see his shattered heart so clearly. Edward Bellamy had aged a lifetime in the span of a few short years, and one could easily read the story of it all written on his face.

Turning to Annelyse with concern, he noted, "You're not eating."

She just shrugged her shoulders and sipped her tea. Bracing herself, she expected her father to insist that she take a bite.

"I don't blame you," he said, much to her surprise. "Seemed like a good idea at first, but now that it's staring up at me…"

Mr. Bellamy interrupted himself midsentence to finish his tea. Standing, he picked up his plate and fork, then looked long at Annelyse. She shook her head slowly, dropped her eyes, and returned to what was left of her own tea. Her father quietly stacked his plate on top of hers then carried them over to be scraped into the bucket reserved for the pigs. The effort had been valiant, but there would be no breakfast in the Bellamy home this morning.

"We'll leave, soon as you're ready," her father said, without looking up from washing the dishes.

Annelyse made no answer but stood and carried her cup over to the sink. Placing it down on the counter beside him, she rested her forehead against her father's shoulder. With soapy hands, he paused a moment, then lowered his cheek until Annelyse felt the weight of his head atop her own. No words were spoken; none were needed. They were both thinking the same thing.

"Need me to dry?" she whispered, breaking the long silence.

"No. I'm glad for the distraction. You get ready. I'll finish up."

Annelyse turned and walked over toward the ladder leading up to her room.

"Good clothes, I'm afraid," her father called out, shooting an apologetic glance in her direction.

Annelyse wrinkled her face in reply, then climbed the seven rungs to her bedroom. A few minutes later, she emerged wearing the dress her mother had made for her the previous year.

It was navy blue and white, reaching down to just below her knees, and reminded Annelyse of something a sailor might wear - if the sailor were a fourteen-year-old girl. Maybe that's why her mother had made it for her, she knew how much Annelyse loved the sea. In fact, Mrs. Bellamy and her daughter were very much alike, in that regard.

As a child, Annelyse accompanied her mother on her daily walks along the Averlune peninsula. From the sloping cliffs above Perigoh Bay, they could clearly see the lighthouse half a mile to their west. On a clear day, even the faint, chalky coastline of the Wandering Isle was visible, just south of Averly Point. The moment they stepped outdoors, a world of wonder opened up as immense as the unbroken horizon. Everything they saw piqued their curiosity and filled them with awe.

The Averlune peninsula turns sharply north after jutting westward from the mainland. To the east, the southern stretch of Perigoh Bay is enclosed on three sides by a semicircular coastline. Following the coast around Windy Point toward the northeast, one soon encounters the mouth of the Perigoh Fair.

The widest and longest of all the rivers in Laprofonde, the Perigoh Fair cannot be crossed for many miles inland. Its estuary is so broad that it behaves less like a river and more according to the whims of the sea. Strong tides and waves stir and churn the turbulent mixture of salt and freshwater. It isn't until the river passes the Fenneleen Stream and finally narrows at Pebble Ford - 93 miles inland - that the Perigoh becomes less fierce and more Fair.

Bordered by the mouth of the mighty river to its north and the Great Sault Sea to the west, this northernmost part of the territory of Averlune is cut off from its more southern neighbors by two geographic oddities.

The first is Mount Averly. Vaulting up toward the sky, with one foot on dry land and one in the sea, Mt. Averly is a single, stony peak that has no business standing where it does. The mountain rises to a height of 918 feet, without the benefit of any other peak or mountain chain within two hundred miles. At high tide, the western foot is completely submerged in saltwater. At low tide, the saltwater turns to saltmarsh and quicksand. No better fortress could be conceived or constructed. Mt. Averly is a conspicuous giant with its feet in the sea and its head in the clouds.

The second geographic oddity is the Fenneleen Stream. More like a short river, the stream finds its source among the craggy heights of Mt. Averly and rushes headlong toward Mydland Dells, before turning northward and emptying itself into the Perigoh Fair. Its descent is so nearly vertical that the white waters of the Fenneleen reach breakneck speeds.

For centuries, it has carved-out its path to the Perigoh among jagged boulders and tumbling stones, until its depths delved far beyond fathoming. The locals say that the stream is so deep that its bed cuts straight through to the center of the Earth. But it's no mere myth to say that many a careless fisherman has lost his footing and been consumed by the rapid current never to be seen again. It's true, the treacherous Fenneleen has a reputation for taking and never giving back.

Sheltered by Mt. Averly to the south and watered by the frigid flow of the Fenneleen to the east, upper Averlune has ever looked westward across the Great Sault Sea and the rich waters of Perigoh Bay. For ages beyond remembrance, the people of this region have made their living in and around boats, sending the fruits of their labors upstream to Pebble Ford, the Mydland Dells, and beyond. Though certainly not the only fishing community on the coast, upper Averlune and the village that bears its name are among the most prosperous.

Upper Averlune is also home to the northernmost reaches of the Fäerie Fields. A wide-open prairie stretching from just south of the town of Prennel all the way to the foot of Mt. Averly in the north, the Fäerie Fields occupy much of central Averlune.

The local farmers pasture their livestock throughout this richly beautiful area without the use of fences. Though vast in size, the prairieland is enclosed by natural boundaries, and entirely free from large predators. As a result, cows, sheep, goats, and rabbits roam freely throughout the lush, green fields. Able to flourish untroubled, it is often said that there are more sheep than people in Averlune, and it just might be true.

Indeed, down through the ages, there have been many more wondrous creatures making their homes in the Fäerie Fields; but these have been largely forgotten by most of the inhabitants of the region. Most, but not quite all. Legends of mysterious animals echo throughout the poetry, songs, and lore of Averlune; but few put much stock in such stories. As years lengthen and generations pass, memory grows thin and, with it, credulity.

An abundance of hay, alfalfa, clover, and grasses of every kind have earned Averlune the nickname *Greenfields*. But when these grasslands spill over the Fenneleen Stream to the north, the Fäerie Fields become wildflower meadows as far as the eye can see.

Strolling through these same wildflowers overlooking the shore, Silloah Bellamy would often braid daisies into a crown for her young daughter to wear. Saving one daisy for herself, she'd place it in her own flowing hair.

Annelyse loved to see her mother with daisies in her hair, though she didn't know exactly why it pleased her so. Perhaps it was her mother's beauty that made such an impression on the little girl. Maybe it was the unspoken connection between the two symbolized by the shared flowers. Most likely, it was her mother's playfulness. Annelyse was in awe of the noble woman who could be so perfectly childlike without ever dulling the luster of her dignity. It would be many years before Annelyse understood this, an opinion already shared by everyone who knew her mother.

Silloah sang to Annelyse during their walks, spinning together tales of the places and animals they encountered with melodies of her own making. Hers was a happy heart and even the creatures of field and fen delighted in her company. Hedgehogs, squirrels, otters, and field mice were unafraid to approach the gentle Silloah. They were drawn by her sweet singing and the warmth of her kindness.

Annelyse recalled how her mother would lead her - barefoot and giggling - over the smooth, egg-shaped stones on the shore. The sound of the waves rushing up the beach reminded the child of the hiss of a great snake. Mother and daughter would always clasp hands and, laughing, run headlong into the foam before the tide receded back out to sea. All the while, Silloah sang songs of the kitebirds that fly over Killoughee, or the cherry blossom breezes of Inidyllique Isle. Hand in hand, they splashed in the surf, until both were so thoroughly soaked, they'd end up swimming in their clothing.

Most of all, Annelyse remembered the sound of her mother's laughter. Carried on the ocean breeze, it was like the merry chime of tiny bells. In truth, Annelyse could hardly separate the sound of her mother's laughter from the voice of the sea itself. She would forever blend the scents and sounds, images, and emotions of these early years into one poignant memory of innocence and happiness. So much had been learned during those walks; so much joy had blossomed; so many precious secrets had been shared between mother, daughter, and the Great Sault Sea.

The two of them would often stay out from morning through afternoon and on into evening, sometimes returning home just before dark - much to Mr. Bellamy's dismay. Though he might greet them with a raised eyebrow and a frown of disapproval, he never really worried for their safety. Edward Bellamy was very proud of the fact that his wife could walk the length and breadth of Upper Averlune blindfolded.

Enthroned in his heart, he called her his Queen of Averlune. And, like an observant princess, Annelyse came to know every nook and dell between her home and the fathomless Fenneleen, just like her mother. A lively spirit of adventure was born inside the child. Passed on from Silloah's own curiosity and daring, it would one day serve Annelyse well.

But for now, here she stood in the blue and white dress her mother had sewn for her over a year earlier. She felt as far away from adventure and exploration; as far from joy and daring; as far from her mother as she had ever felt before in all her life. Maybe that's why, on this particular morning, she made one small addition to her outfit.

With her tight-fitting shoes in one hand, she held a dry circlet of pressed daisies in the other.

"What do you have?" her father asked, although he already knew the answer.

"I'm gonna wear it," Annelyse replied, with uncharacteristic shyness.

Her father nodded, a loving softness in his sad eyes. He understood the impulse to hold on to what little remained.

"Can you help me with this?" he asked, holding up a black necktie with both hands, a look of helplessness on his face. "I never quite got the knack of it."

Annelyse placed the crown of daisies on the table then, dropping her shoes on the floor, took the necktie from her father. As she did, she noticed that his hands were trembling. Looking into her father's eyes, she saw a man who - before meeting his match in the form of a necktie - had never before been powerless to do anything. It wasn't frustration or irritation that she now saw in his eyes. It was fear. Annelyse wasn't the only one who had been forced to let go of her lifeline.

"Mom always…" he began, falling silent.

"I know, Daddy. But I was watching, too."

Annelyse wrapped the tie around her father's neck, produced a perfect knot, then straightened both tie and collar like a pro. She *had* been watching her mother. She'd learned that all-important skill, how to tie a proper necktie. Her father was relieved.

"You look nice," he said, almost by way of an apology for having made her wear her *good clothes.*

"Thanks," she replied, accepting her father's veiled apology, but still annoyed by the ridiculousness of her outfit. "And you look…"

"As silly as I feel," Mr. Bellamy interrupted, then added with a sheepish smile, "Maybe sillier." Becoming serious, he whispered, "It'll all be over soon. We just need to get through this day."

The morning sky had paled from dark purple to a faded blue, by the time Annelyse and Mr. Bellamy stepped outside. Spring had finally gained a foothold against the chilly westerlies blowing in from the sea. The morning breezes came more from the south, now, and with them a heavy fog. Neither Annelyse nor her father had thought to bring a coat for the short walk into town. They both tended to urge the warmer weather on by a show of faith. If they dressed for a warm day, maybe Spring would deliver, just so it wouldn't look foolish.

There were several paths leading into town from which they might choose. Feeling far less sociable than usual and trying to conserve their smiles and hellos for when they'd really count, they chose the least-traveled path.

The two sullen Bellamys walked along in silence. There was nothing to talk about. Mr. Bellamy had summed it all up when he said, "We just need to get through this day." As far as Annelyse was concerned, that's precisely what she was doing.

She'd turned off her feelings, weeks ago. So, there was very little danger of becoming overwhelmed by emotion, even today. She'd always been good at mustering a smile or a sincere sounding thank you on cue. She felt confident she'd be able to deliver when called upon. Even her overactive brain had finally settled-down into a zombie-like trance, and it wouldn't restart its incessant thinking, wondering, questioning, and arguing until after she'd returned home that evening. For now, she was as ready as she'd ever be.

The dense fog created the illusion of invisibility that both Annelyse and her father found comforting. They didn't want to be seen. They didn't want to be recognized. Not yet. It was too early to deal with everything *that* would entail. They needed to "get through this day," but they didn't want the unpleasantries to begin any sooner than necessary.

Unfortunately, by the time they reached the village, the sun had begun to burn-off the comforting cover of fog. There was nowhere to hide anymore. The full light of day was upon them, and soon everyone would see the "poor Bellamys." The unpleasantries would start when the first smile or thank you was required of them. Once begun, all they could do was soldier-on as best they could until the last well-wisher had gone.

And so, it began.

Annelyse resolved to keep count of how many times she heard the phrases, "I'm sorry," "We're thinking about you," "How are you holding up?" and her least favorite of them all, "If there's anything I can do, don't hesitate." But she lost track half an hour into it all.

It's not that she doubted the sincerity of the people speaking these lines (most of them, anyway), it's that she knew better than anyone just how weak and feeble these phrases really are in such circumstances.

She didn't want people to be sorry. It wasn't their

fault, why should they be sorry? She didn't want people wasting their time and energy thinking about her. How could that possibly help? And asking her how she was "holding up," the painfully practical Annelyse thought, was just a dumb question and should be torn from the pages of grief etiquette books.

What bothered her most of all was the fact that the people saying, "If there's anything I can do, don't hesitate," had no idea *what* they could do. Most of them didn't bother to ask.

The truth was, the only thing Annelyse wanted anyone to do was simply do it all *for* her. Don't speak, just take charge. Speaking added to her burden by requiring an answer from her. Make it all go away, the way her mother used to do when the young Annelyse fell and scraped her knee. Her mother would kiss it and make the hurt disappear. She never asked what she could do, she just took charge; and it never failed to fix what needed fixing.

But now, if the only things people had to offer were their words, Annelyse thought it best that they just keep to themselves. In the absence of real help, anything less than helpful is insulting.

It was around this time that Annelyse's left sock first fell down around her ankle.

"Great," she thought to herself, "They're a pair, aren't they? Then why aren't they the same size?"

Between hellos, smiles, and thank yous, she began fidgeting with her unruly sock.

"What? Is my right leg bigger than my left? This is stupid."

Lifting her leg and reaching down with one hand, she discretely pulled the offending sock back into place; but it just slid back down the moment she stood up straight. Over and over, Annelyse repeated the same hopeless drill:

Smile.

Say, "Hello."

Lift her left leg.

Respond, "Thank you very much."

Reach down, yank sock, stand up straight.

Then, without fail (or rather, without success), the sock would slide back down around her ankle.

If anyone had been paying attention, it would have looked like an intricate dance. As it was, Annelyse was becoming more and more annoyed. She was one hour into a long day, and she couldn't feel the small toe on either foot anymore. She felt like a wind-up toy, repeating her repertoire of *Smile, Hello, Thank You* for strangers she'd never seen before and would surely never see again. She was convinced that she looked like a stuffed sailor doll in her dress, and now her sock refused to cooperate. She couldn't imagine anything more irritating.

It was getting harder and harder to "just get through this day," when, without warning, things got much worse.

"Oh, what a pretty crown of daisies," the woman said, then made the mistake of adding, "Too bad they're all ugly and wilted."

That's it. Annelyse's eyes squinted. Her fists clenched. She set her jaw, ready for battle.

"They're **not** ugly and they're **not** wilted," she shot back at the woman. "They're **perfect**." Taking a step closer and leaning in close to the woman's wrinkled face, Annelyse let her have it, "What do *you* know about anything, anyway?"

At the sound of his daughter's tone, Mr. Bellamy broke off his conversation with the woman's husband, reached one hand down to take hold of Annelyse's arm (before she lobbed it at the clueless woman), and intervened.

"Thanks for coming, Mrs. Whitford. Always nice to see you. You know, we were talking just this morning about those cranberry scones you brought by last week. Delicious. Thank you so much."

It was the old *Thank, Flatter, Deflect and Distract* routine that Mr. Bellamy had perfected over the past fourteen years as Annelyse's father. She'd provided him with plenty of practice; he knew the warning signs, by now. As it always did, the routine worked this time, too. Mrs. Whitford grinned a clueless grin, moved through the line of well-wishers, and fluttered out the door like a pudgy, clumsy butterfly. The following week, there'd be more cranberry scones, further proof of just how effective *Thank, Flatter, Deflect and Distract* was at providing damage control.

Without saying a word, Mr. Bellamy squeezed his daughter's arm, then returned to greeting the long line of well-wishers filing past them. It wasn't a warning sort of squeeze. It wasn't even a squeeze of disapproval. It was a sympathetic squeeze, the kind that said, "I know. I understand. I'm here." It was exactly the sort of squeeze Annelyse needed.

It dawned on her that, if all these people would just walk in, give her and her father a sympathetic squeeze, then leave without a word, the whole nonsense might be more bearable. In fact, it might be more meaningful and even helpful. But everyone seemed to feel compelled to say something - and they all chose from one of the four dreaded phrases. Some refused to limit themselves to just one of the four. They were the most tiresome of all.

Annelyse was beginning to realize that funerals are for others, not for the family, and certainly not for the deceased. She and her father were there to reassure the well-wishers that they had succeeded in bringing consolation, when in fact they had not. In a world where good intentions are often the best we can hope for, the well-wishers had achieved success. But, in reality, there was no consolation anyone could bring to Annelyse and Edward Bellamy.

When the last of the mourners had filed out the

door, Annelyse and her father found themselves awkwardly alone in a group of four. The third member of the group looked on in respectful silence, which was more than just a little awkward. After a day of enduring their pain on parade, even this final moment came with an unwanted chaperone.

The curate stood with his hands folded and head tilted, wearing his best sorry-for-your-loss face. His lower lip was forced upward, causing the lines on either side of his mouth to collapse into craters. He looked like a ventriloquist's dummy, in every creepy and expressionless way possible.

"Take your time," he said, though it was clear from his body language that he had better things to do.

Mr. Bellamy made no reply.

The fourth member of the group remained entirely silent. Nothing could have been more out of character and, as a result, stranger than that. The silence that Annelyse now experienced was so profound that it was more like absence. This created a confusing situation.

Annelyse could see her mother, but her mother was not there. Her laughter was gone. Her smile was rigid and unnatural. The caress of her soft hands had ceased altogether. It all reminded Annelyse of some of the seashells she used to collect during their daily walks along the peninsula. The shell looked like an oyster, but the oyster was gone. There in front of her, laid out in a long, narrow box, was her mother's shell. But her mother was gone. More to the point, her mother was missing.

It wasn't sadness Annelyse was feeling. It was panic, the panic she used to feel when her mother's hand slipped from her own as the waves rushed toward the shore. She had put out into deep waters and lost hold of her mother's hand. What was worse, her mother no longer reached for her. Annelyse was far from land and drifting further out to sea.

No, it wasn't sadness that she felt, it was a panic laced with growing anger and disillusionment. Her mother had always been one of her two biggest and most important rock-solid certainties. But certainty had turned to sand in the receding tide. Annelyse was awkwardly and tragically alone, and so was her father. Both of them together. And both of them lonely.

Annelyse detected an alarmingly unexpected feeling growing inside of her. Looking down into the box, she felt only revulsion. But it wasn't a morbid revulsion or a feeling of disgust in the presence of a dead body. The word "gross" never crossed her mind.

Her revulsion was intense animosity. She loved her mother more than any other person in her life, the same way she loved her father more than any other person in her life. They were Mom and Dad. They were beyond comparison. Yes, she loved her mother, but she hated that thing in the box.

That was not her mother. It was the enemy. It was the *thing* that had taken her mother away. If that wretched thing hadn't gotten sick, her mother would still be there now. All she wanted to do was be rid of it, and the realization was both horrific and liberating.

Mr. Bellamy turned his head without taking his eyes off the coffin.

"Are you ready?" he asked, under his breath.

Annelyse just shrugged her shoulders. Her father looked up at the curate (whose changeless expression appeared glued to his face like some sort of ghoulish mask) and mumbled something inaudible. The curate unfolded his hands with overwrought solemnity and approached the coffin with an obvious air of relief.

Fumbling with the lid, he lost his grip an inch or two above the top of the box. With a loud slam that echoed stupidity against the bare stone of the church's interior, Silloah Bellamy was hidden from view for all eternity.

The curate then pushed the wheeled contraption bearing the coffin down the center aisle and out the front door where the crowd of mourners had gathered. Front and center, there stood Mrs. Whitford, who made a point of looking directly at the crown of daisies ringing Annelyse's head. Annelyse just pursed her lips and glared back at her.

The procession came to a disheveled halt beside a perfectly excavated, rectangular hole in the ground. The mourners fanned out, surrounding the gravesite, four or five people deep, like players on a stage. Without hesitation, the curate began to speak. After all, he did have better things to do that morning.

As the monotonous voice oozed platitude after platitude, Annelyse grew distracted by an unusually large flock of birds singing with unabashed merriment in the trees. In stark contrast to the black-clad murder of mourners below, the birds appeared to be a contingent of representatives from every colorful species in Averlune.

Blue jays, cardinals, goldfinches, and orioles, even seagulls and kitebirds from the coast had come out to sing. There was no taint of sadness in their songs, only an orchestra of melodies that harmonized with all of nature. Up above it all, the sun was dressed in its Sunday best, and a clear, blue sky smiled down on the scene taking place graveside. Somehow, Annelyse thought, nature's funerary rites were much more fitting.

She now caught herself searching the faces of those standing around the grave. Annelyse was unwittingly frantic to find her mother's smile in the crowd. Her eyes moved first to her father beside her, then around to her right. But only empty space gaped back at her from where her mother used to be. Everywhere she looked, her mother was missing. It made no sense, but then, neither did death. She was beginning to think that the sooner she stopped trying to make sense of everything, the happier she'd be.

Her attention returned to what was going on around

her, where the curate's voice droned-on and on through the late afternoon. His storehouse of cliches was inexhaustible. Still, he was determined to exhaust everyone within earshot by exploring each and every one of them. Before she knew what was happening, Annelyse's mouth opened, and a most out-of-place (though entirely understandable) sentiment escaped her lips.

"Come *on*..." she complained, loud enough for her father, the curate, and Mrs. Whitford to hear and react - each in their own characteristic way.

Her father wrapped his arm around her shoulders and drew her close to himself. The curate cleared his throat and kept right on droning, while Mrs. Whitford rolled her eyes and let out a "Pfft" sufficiently loud for Annelyse to hear and promptly ignore.

"...and so, we commit the body of our sister, Shiloh..."

"Shiloh?" Annelyse thought to herself. "He can't even get her name right. *Enough*, already!" She was becoming more irritated by the second.

"Why all the ceremony?" she thought. "It's not *her*. She's not here. It's just a box of..."

Annelyse stopped herself. She wasn't sure how to finish her thought. All she was sure of anymore was that her mother was gone forever, and with her all the love and joy Annelyse and her father had ever relied upon.

"Amen," punctuated the end of the curate's droning, at last. It was long overdue, according to Annelyse and, undoubtedly, many of the others present.

Slowly, the box was lowered down into the hole prepared for it. Annelyse fully-expected the curate and his helpers to fumble this task, much the same way he had fumbled the closing of the coffin lid.

Her father stepped forward and bent down to pick up a handful of earth from the mound beside the grave. Raising his hand to his lips, he kissed it before tossing the dirt carefully into the hole. He stood there, quietly speaking words that only he and Silloah could hear – and wishing he had been allowed the privilege of solitude for this final moment in his wife's company.

When, at last he returned to his place beside Annelyse, she saw tears in his eyes and a tremor in his lower lip. He was quickly approaching the limits of his self-control.

Now, it was Annelyse's turn.

Walking over to the side of the grave, Annelyse looked down at the coffin. She felt nothing, just numbness. It was not at all how she'd expected to feel, and she didn't know what to make of it. But today was not for figuring things out, it was for letting go. What else could she do?

Taking the crown of pressed daisies from her head, she held it in her hands a moment. She remembered the last time her mother had been well enough to walk out into the wildflower meadow behind their house. Silloah leaned on her husband's arm and shuffled from daisy to daisy, with great difficulty. She'd been determined to weave one last crown for her daughter. Exhausted by the effort, she sat on the old stump her husband used for chopping wood and carefully plaited each daisy into a perfect circlet.

"Annelyse. Come here, my love," Silloah called with a smile. "I must crown you."

Annelyse walked over and knelt before her mother, as she always did when receiving her crown from the hands of the queen. She loved how her mother always took seriously the business of having fun.

"Annelyse Bellamy, I crown thee Lady of Laprofonde and Guardian of the Fäerie Fields."

Then placing the circlet of flowers on her daughter's head, Silloah bowed, saying, "Arise, princess of Averlune."

Annelyse stood, as her mother placed one remaining daisy in her own hair. Then, struggling to her feet, she wrapped her arms around Annelyse and kissed her cheek.

Resting her forehead against her daughter's, she whispered, "Remember this, my child. I have every reason to believe that my love for you will not die with my body. Do not let the events to come kill what is most precious inside of you."

Annelyse felt a great wave swell within her. Holding onto her mother with frail desperation, she wept to be rid of all sorrow.

Now, standing at the side of her mother's grave, she pulled one flower from the circlet of daisies and placed it in her hair the way her mother had done. Letting go of the rest, she watched as the last crown her mother had woven for her fell through the open hole in the ground and came to rest on top of her mother's coffin.

Still, she felt nothing.

Was there something wrong with her, she wondered? Instead of a feeling of separation and finality, she felt phony - like a bad actor going through the motions. Nothing she could do could possibly touch her mother, and that's all she wanted to do. With every drop of her strength, that's all she wanted. What good was anything else?

After a moment, she turned to rejoin her father. As she did, she glanced over at Mrs. Whitford in time to see her avert her eyes. The old woman finally understood, and her fat face flushed with shame. Annelyse found herself hoping Mrs. Whitford tasted every ounce of embarrassment her shallow heart could hold. Disgusted with herself for letting grief smolder with such fire, Annelyse drew herself up short and looked away.

Mr. Bellamy took his daughter in his arms, "It's done," he said softly. "Let's go home."

Without another word, father and daughter simply walked away, leaving behind the curate; Mrs. Whitford; the crowd of well-wishers; the hole in the ground; the box; and the shell that was not their wife and mother.

The chorus of colorful birds that had been singing all throughout the graveside service now took to the sky in a pixelated rainbow of rapturous flight. Climbing into the limitless blue, the enormous flock of birds flew over the heads of the mourners, like a color guard paying its last respects. Beneath the tree in which the birds had been sitting, Annelyse thought she spied the figure of a man, his head bowed in sadness.

Father and daughter made no eye contact as they left the crowd behind. There would be no more smiles, hellos, or thank yous. They had done their duty. There would be no more rounds of "I'm sorry," "We're thinking about you," "How are you holding up?" or the dreaded, "If there's anything I can do, don't hesitate." Not today, anyhow. They had answered them all with a pasted-on smile.

They'd made it through this fearful day, as they'd set out to do, and there was a great deal of relief involved in knowing that it was over. But even their relief was tainted by a pang of guilt. Was it wrong to be glad it was all behind them? Was it a lack of love or an excess of selfishness to be happy to see the end of this day?

It would not be the last time they'd have to wrestle with irrational fears. For, if the day was over, their grief had just begun. They would soon learn that grieving begins in earnest with the return to "normal life." But they'd also learn that there really is no way back to normal. There is no returning. There is no getting over it. There is only moving on.

By the time they got home the sun had begun to set. Neither Mr. Bellamy nor Annelyse felt like eating anything, and there was nothing left to be said. The curate had surely said enough for everyone. The day offered nothing more to do but to go to bed and let sleep begin the healing process.

Kissing his daughter on the top of her head, Mr. Bellamy asked with worry in his eyes, "Do you know that I love you?"

"Do you know that I love *you*?" she replied, with equal concern.

"Yes. And so, I think we'll be ok," he said, through his fatigue. "Sleep. Tomorrow's Saturday, and there's nothing to be done."

Smiling as best he could manage, Mr. Bellamy turned and walked into the bedroom he had shared with his wife. Pulling the door closed behind him, he was more perfectly alone than he'd ever known.

Annelyse felt her way up the ladder to her loft, without the aid of a candle. Sitting down on the edge of her bed, she stared into the darkness. Though tired and sore from a day spent standing, the thought of laying down frightened her.

She felt like a suitcase stuffed to overflowing, and she had no idea how to unpack herself. The panic and irritation she'd experienced throughout most of the day had dulled, leaving behind only a sickly sense of turmoil. Her mind was adrift, without the slightest hope of finding calm waters again.

After an hour or more of distracted and disjointed thought, she finally managed to remove her shoes from her swollen feet. It was then that she heard something from her parent's bedroom downstairs. Faint and muffled though it was, she immediately recognized it as the sound of desperate sobbing.

All at once, her heart broke open and a flood of emotion flowed out unencumbered. Burying her face in her pillow, she let go of any attempt to be strong or brave. She cast herself headlong into the storm, unconcerned with what she might find in its depths. At last, she'd begun to unpack her heart with tears. It was the only way she could find "to just get through" this night.

CHAPTER TWO

Everything that Lives Suffers

A light rain had fallen throughout the night, draping a thin veil of mist over the meadow. Every leaf, petal, and cobweb glistened with tiny droplets of water. Down on the beach, seagulls picked through a collection of shells left behind by the outgoing tide, enjoying a hardy breakfast between raucous squawks. Both sea and sky were unblemished and tranquil. It was as pleasant a morning as Averlune had to offer, and that was saying a great deal.

Behind the front door of the Bellamy home, not a sound was heard. The stress and fatigue of the previous day found its outlet, and Annelyse and her father had passed the night fast asleep on tear-dampened pillows.

Mr. Bellamy's bedroom faced east, a fact that contributed to his regular habit of rising early. But, whether due to the drawn curtains or utter exhaustion, the morning sun had failed to awaken him on this particular Saturday.

Annelyse's room faced the sea, only ever seeing the sun's back before setting in the west. Though she would argue that this was the reason she often slept-in past breakfast, the real cause had more to do with her general laziness before 11 a.m. However, thanks to the chorus of kitebirds and seagulls, this morning, Annelyse awoke long before her father.

Upon first opening her eyes, the sight of Perigoh Light rising up from the blue, translucent sea brought a false sense of normality to her mind The wildflower meadows running down to the chalky cliffs; the fishermen preparing their nets on the shore; even the birds at play on the beach; everything appeared to be as it should.

Pushing open the window beside her bed, Annelyse inhaled the morning breeze. A smile of contentment unfolded across her face, as she closed her eyes and stretched her limbs. The scent of rain on green grass was so clean and fresh, she could practically taste the sweetness of the newborn day.

But the moment she realized she was still wearing her blue and white dress, the painful memory of all that had taken place over the last twenty-four hours came crashing down upon her head. Just like the empty oyster shells on the seashore, appearances were deceiving. The world looked the same as ever, but her mother was still gone.

The view from her bedroom window, so beautiful moments before, was now more than she could bear. A sharp, aching pain split her already wounded heart, releasing a slow trickle of tears. Like turning from pitch darkness into the glare of the noonday sun, the contrast was violent. Annelyse drew the covers up under her chin and closed her eyes.

Yesterday had been a new, unpleasant, and uniquely horrible event. But she was starting to understand that it's not the events that are the most difficult; it's the routines of everyday life. Routine is often comforting, because of its predictable familiarity. But when familiarity comes without that which once made it so comforting, the void is filled by unexpected vulnerabilities.

Annelyse was learning that grief comes with an army of snipers, each one hidden beneath the cover of normality and camouflaged by routine. When you least expect it, when your defenses are down, they send a firestorm of emotions and memories. There is no hiding and there is no way to escape. The best you can do is open your eyes and recognize the grief snipers for what they are. You are not the enemy, they are. The beloved lost is not to blame, grief is.

Opening her eyes, Annelyse stared down at the wrinkled dress she'd been wearing for far too long. Taking hold of the collar in her right hand, she tore it from her neck and threw it across the room. She then flung her bedcovers off and began ripping sleeves, bows, hems, and belt until the dress she'd worn to her mother's funeral was nothing but a collection of rags on the floor. She was now quite certain she'd never have to wear her *good clothes* again.

Looking down at the tattered remains of fabric, she felt the same revulsion she'd felt when staring into her mother's coffin. She was glad she'd torn it up. She hated it. She hated it more than reason could explain. It wasn't just a dress, it was all that was left of her mother's funeral, and she never wanted to think about it again. Kicking and sweeping it under her bed with her bare feet, Annelyse buried every shred of her blue and white dress out of sight and well out of mind.

She needed to get out of there. Her room, the whole house had become too full of reminders. Everywhere she looked, she *didn't* see her mother. There were too many places where Silloah *wasn't*. There were too many things she wasn't busy *doing*. Annelyse put her hands to her temples. She felt as if she might lose what was left of her swirling mind. She needed a change of scenery, and she needed it now.

Tiptoeing to the washbasin, she cleaned her face and brushed her teeth. The clothes she'd worn the day before the funeral still hung on a peg beside her mirror. They'd do just fine for what she had in mind. She dressed quickly then eased herself down the ladder. Filling her pockets with a lump of stale bread and a small block of hard cheese, she grabbed a pencil and a piece of paper.

"Gone for a walk. Be back around lunchtime. -A."

Annelyse then placed the salt cellar on top of the note and snuck over to the front door, opening it without making a sound. Holding her breath, she drew the door closed behind her and turned the knob back to its rest position, careful not to awaken her father.

She paused a moment, listening. Nothing. Her father was still asleep, buried beneath a mound of grief and exhaustion. He would not awaken until nearly noon.

Just being outdoors was a welcome change. Everything she'd seen in the last day or so had been small and cumbersome: echoing, stone walls; a narrow box; a hole in the ground; even Mrs. Whitford's pettiness. She missed wide-open things like the ocean; wildflower meadows; unburdened memories; and her mother's laughter. She was intent on somehow finding these things again. An increasingly large portion of her heart was determined to touch her mother any way she could. Reaching through the gaping abyss to feel her mother's presence was becoming an obsession. Annelyse realized this and didn't care one bit.

From the front door, she followed the footpath around to the left and toward the seashore. In the fields running down to the cliffs, wildflowers had begun to bloom, thanks to a warm southerly breeze blowing up from the isles. Among the tall grass, daffodils, primroses, and daisies speckled the fields in white and yellow. They looked like drops of moonbeams and sunlight floating in a sea of swaying green.

Along the path upon which she now walked scruffy tufts of weeds had laid claim to the bare earth. It had only been a few weeks since her mother's feet had shuffled along this same route to the woodchopping stump. But without regular use, even well-worn pathways quickly fade. The second this thought crossed her mind, fear flared inside Annelyse's heart. It was too soon for her mother's footprints to vanish, too soon to face another loss.

Annelyse dropped to her knees and dug the stubborn weeds from the ground using her fingernails. Tugging at the roots, she was careful to leave the intruders no foothold in her mother's final path to the sea. With a strong sense of satisfaction, Annelyse flung the spidery plants – roots, dirt, and all - as far from the footpath as she could. The latest thief hellbent on robbing her of something precious had been defeated.

Walking along, she spread out her arms, running her fingers through the tiger lilies and black-eyed Susans lining the sloping path. Occasionally, a curious grasshopper would spring up out of the feather-topped grass, landing on the ground in front of her. With a short hop it turned to face her before leaping back into the meadow. Hidden in among the thickets, orange-breasted orioles sang their uniquely beautiful songs, careful to avoid being seen. The same joy that Annelyse had experienced with her mother continued to reach out its hand to her now.

A few feet beyond the chopping stump, the path split off in three directions. To the left, it headed southwest toward Watcher's Island, ending at Lightview Overlook. A cliff-head twenty feet above the waves, Lightview is the perfect place from which to survey Watcher's Island and Lower Perigoh Light. Annelyse spent many nights here, wrapped in a blanket, lying on her back gazing up at the stars. Her parents would lay beside her, holding hands and spinning yarns about how the constellations got their names, while the bright eye of Lower Perigoh kept watch over the waves, to the west.

Off to the right, the path turned due north and headed up the peninsula to Windy Point. Here, the swirling sea breeze gets trapped among the cliff walls, as the land curves around the southern bowl of Perigoh Bay. Unable to find its way out again, the wind twirls around and around in a great cyclone of madness, until it plunges headlong into the sea. Even the seagulls find Windy Point too blustery for flight. Instead, they surrender the sky to the nimbler kitebirds and ospreys who glide without effort above the perilous peninsula.

Straight ahead, the path continued downward toward the shore where the chalky cliffs crack and crumble into sharp chasms, opening wide without warning. The sudden drop to the beach below is only a few feet at the path's highest point – high enough to be alarming, but not quite high enough to do any damage. At most, an unsuspecting traveler might find himself caught at the waist, feet dangling above the sand, until he was able to hoist himself back out of the mouth of the crevice.

Annelyse loved these fractures in the earth. They overflowed with hiding places and tall tales of buried treasure. Most of all, she loved to watch the rainwater surge – thick and milky – through the chalky cracks on its way to the sea. She and her mother would make plaster shoes from the white mud left behind by a storm. Plunging their feet into the waves, they would watch it all disappear in a cloud of snowy silt.

As the path crept along the cliff, it gradually descended to the waterline. The last few feet were comprised of stair-like steps that looked as if they'd been carved by hand from the weary limestone. Once the path had reached the shore, it opened-out onto a small beach of black sand sheltered by the cliffs above and a westward-poking finger of land to the south. This is Ruhner's Beach, though few people claim to know the origin of its name. Of those few, Silloah Bellamy held perhaps the most trustworthy claim.

According to Silloah, Ruhner's Beach was not named for any particular person. There was no Abigail Ruhner or Ruhner Jonas from whom the secluded strip of sand got its name. Instead, Ruhner is an intentional misspelling intended to obscure the shameful events that once took place there.

In the rockface beneath the cliffs, caves and tunnels extend inland farther than the fainthearted dare to explore. At high tide, the cave entrances are submerged in the sea. However, their upward slope prevents them from ever flooding, making them excellent hiding holes. Useful only to those hoping to conceal their deeds in darkness, the caves and tunnels of Ruhner's Beach were once employed as storehouses to hide smuggled goods – goods of a sort that many people refuse to believe ever existed.

Long before the first settlers skirted the wide boundary of Worm Canyon and made their way over the Inland Sea from Illyan; ages before they braved the sweltering Wastelands to build their homes in the *Greenfields* of Averlune, pirates from the west pillaged the defenseless coastline from Cor McCrumblin Cove in the south as far north as King's Bay. So foul were the actions of the marauders, that Silloah hesitated to share the details of the story of Ruhner's Beach with her young daughter. But lessons must be taught, both good and bad.

Far to the west, over the Sault Sea, there is a

sprawling collection of rocks called the Isles of Wanton. Whether these windswept stones cast in the middle of the lonesome sea were ever settled by civilized folk, few can say. What is certain, however, is that they served as the launching-off point for the pirate's wicked raids.

At that time, the Lord of Hyland Manor had begun to claim for his own all the lands from the Far Reaches to Mt. Averly. Since much of Wehrle and the Mydland Dells are too vast and lay too far to the east to be easily managed, Hyland Manor focused on consolidating its hold over the untamed coastline and all it contained - especially Perigoh Bay. Controlling the bay meant controlling the Perigoh Fair, the artery upon which the lands to the east depended for their lifeblood. If the Manor wanted to expand its influence eastward, control of the Perigoh river was essential.

The waters in and around the bay teem with fish of every kind, making it a rich prize indeed. The promise of prosperity soon attracted the attention of Hyland farmers who exchanged their stony fields for rickety rowboats and tattered fishing nets. The would-be fishermen came in droves to seek their fortune upon the waves.

In order to provide protection to the growing number of fishermen working the open waters, the Lord of Hyland Manor established a watchtower atop Mt. Averly. From that vantagepoint (over nine-hundred feet above sea level) sentries could easily survey the ocean for miles around. The fishermen now had plenty of advance warning of impending pirate attacks, thanks to Mt. Averly's mastery of the sea.

But it wasn't seaborne attacks against fishermen that the pirates had in mind. It was the establishment of a secret stronghold out of sight of the Mt. Averly watchmen. Ruhner's Beach provided perfect cover, endless caverns for storing contraband, and quick access to the open sea. Here, the pirates would hide and conduct their loathsome activities without fear of discovery.

Since most of the Hyland fishermen focused their labors on the bay to the north, the waters off the lower peninsula were left largely abandoned. With their eyes fixed on the upper Perigoh Bay, the sentries high atop Mt. Averly would easily miss any activity taking place around the foot of the mountain or along the southern shore of the peninsula. Anything too near the mountain went entirely unnoticed, and the pirates were well aware of this fact, exploiting it for their purposes.

The lust in their corrupt hearts was not for the gold and jewels of the mainland, for Averlune possessed very little of such things. What the pirates craved was a much more wondrous treasure; something that could be sold in black markets and underground auctions the world over; something that would bring them more wealth than could be wrested from the vaults of Hyland Manor. The pirates set their sights upon a creature so unique and plentiful throughout the Fäerie Fields that the villains needed only to reach out their hands and seize the fruits of avarice itself.

Lying in wait among the prairie grass, the hunters trapped their quarry using nets and wooden clubs. The poor creatures would panic and quickly become entangled in the pirates' nets, making them easy to subdue. Large enough to kill a man if they had a mind to, these docile beasts refused to use deadly force even in defense of their own lives. Alas, they were too easily captured, too easily enslaved.

Driven on by the sting of a whip, they were forced to ford the icy waters of the Fenneleen where many lost their footing among the slippery stones and were claimed by the deep. Fathomless faces, broken by the thundering current, these were the lucky ones. For, the surviving prisoners were herded in haste around the base of Mt. Averly toward the sea where a life of suffering took its first dreadful steps.

Pushed northward past the modern-day town of

Averlune, they followed many of the same footpaths that Annelyse and her mother explored behind their home. Routes that some thought to be cow paths fallen into disuse were actually widened by the unwilling feet of innocents. In their wake, the captives left behind little more than these ruts in the ground and the frailest of hopes that one day they might return to the Greenfields. But hope, like all small and tenuous things, is easily lost.

Nearing the edge of the land, the prisoners passed down through the broad chasms in the cliffs above Ruhner's Beach. It was there that the slave runners chained the helpless animals to the limestone walls of the tunnels and caves where they were forced to await pirate ships arriving from the south.

Sailing up the shoreline from the murky waters off Wastrel Grugh where they anchored their fleet in secret, the pirate galleons wound their way north completely undetected. Too close to the watchtower of Mt. Averly, the captors worked their evil trade without concern, cruelly filling their holds with living contraband far beyond the ship's capacity and any norms of decency.

Creatures were stacked, one on another, and crammed into dark, dank, odorous spaces once occupied by everything from barrels of ambergris to bundles of narwhal tusks. The swollen pirate ships, too heavy with their cargo, had to put out into deeper water or risk foundering in the rocky shallows.

Long hours were spent beneath the hot sun, the smugglers' ships sweltering in the heat of the afternoon. Down below, soaring temperatures made the air too thick to breathe. There was barely room enough in the overcrowded holds even for desperation, as everyone yearned for the cool dark of night.

When the sun had been swallowed by the sea and the stars were pinpricks in the sky, the pirates set out from Runner's Beach. Employing all hands at the oars, the ships were carefully rowed clear of the shifting sandbars. Once they made open water, sails were unfurled, and the impartial wind carried them across the sea to the Isles of Wanton.

Many innocents died in the dangerous crossing; their bodies thrown overboard. Many others wished they had perished. For once these mythical animals had been deprived of their freedom, their hearts slowly withered. Once they'd been taken from their home in the Fäerie Fields and sold off to foreign lands, their spirits grew thin. Soon, sadness stole from their broken hearts what little the pirates had left them. Tender and sensitive creatures feel all things more acutely, joy and sorrow alike. Nature denies them the protection of a hardened heart.

Ships sailing into the shadowy harbors concealed among the Isles of Wanton sailed behind a wall of mystery. Lies, like contortions posed to avoid the light of day, wove a curtain of dark obscurity around everything that took place in this secluded corner of the world. Those who knew the truth behind the rumors of kidnapping and smuggling were seldom brave enough to bring such wickedness to light. For, only a pure conscience wields perfect courage.

What little is known of these events can be summarized by saying that the creatures taken from the Fäerie Fields were never seen beyond the Fenneleen again. Their enormous size, remarkable strength, and gentle demeanor made them irresistible to those dealing in the slave trade. The unfortunate animals fell victim to the greed of others and the docility of their own hearts. Greed and cruelty often combine to make terrible deeds, and wrongs committed against the innocent are among the darkest shades of scarlet.

As the good people of Hyland and Averlune became more numerous than the pirates of the Isles of Wanton, the marauders sought their ill-gotten gains elsewhere or simply dwindled and died off. Eager to erase the stain upon their land, the people of the peninsula changed the name of Slave Runner's Beach to Ruhner's Beach, thereby burying an unpleasant past.

Stories about the mysterious creatures of the Fäerie Fields quickly passed from history to legend, and from legend to lore. What should have been remembered and healed like a wound was forgotten and left to fester. Rather than coming to terms with their all-to-recent past, those who remained chose to rewrite it by changing one letter and embracing unbelief. And so, Ruhner's Beach was born.

Annelyse remembered every detail of her mother's story. Most of all, she remembered the compassion in Silloah's eyes as she recounted the tale. It was clear, even to the young girl, that her mother keenly felt the loss of these poor creatures. There was a wistful sadness in her voice, as if she had known them personally, as if they had been her friends, or she had played some part in their story. But Silloah would say no more. Some truths must wait for the listener, in order to be heard.

Annelyse now chose to follow the same footpath used by the pirates, as she made her way down to Ruhner's Beach. Leaping over yawning cracks in the ground, she descended the white, stone stairs to the shore. The tide was out, leaving twice the usual distance from cliff wall to waterline. Pools of warm seawater, left behind by the receding waves, rippled in the morning breeze.

Behind her, the cave and tunnel entrances, though long since bricked closed, were still visible in the rockface. The living limestone was slowly engulfing the red bricks, encroaching more and more each year, until several of the openings had been swallowed-up altogether. It's just as well. The sooner the wounds of the past scabbed-over and disappeared, the better, many folks thought.

Annelyse stepped out of her shoes and socks, and let her toes sink into the warm sand. The sea was a pane of glass, silent as the sunrise. Even Perigoh Light stood still above a seamless mirror of saltwater, quietly reflecting upon all it had seen during its years of service.

Scouring her bare feet against the coarse sand, Annelyse felt like she was scrubbing away the thick layer of gloom that had hung heavy on her these past few days. It was what her father would call a *catharsis*… a cleansing of the soul. In the same way that she'd been so ready to close the lid, lower the box, and walk away from it all yesterday, she was more than ready to abandon the gloom and watch it all drift out to sea. The ocean always took whatever she needed to give it. Cleansing waters always made everything new.

After a while spent burying her feet in the tar-colored sand, Annelyse walked down to the waves and let them wash over her bare toes. Inhaling the salt breezes and fishy scents of the blue-green water, she closed her eyes and let it all clear her mind. This was the only thing she wanted to do today. It was the only thing she needed. If the sun traveled the full length of the sky and, looking back over its shoulder before setting, it found her still standing with her feet in the sea, she'd be perfectly content. Time spent at the ocean is never wasted. This was the one remaining truth in which Annelyse still had faith.

In the quiet of the moment, she became aware of a presence. Someone was there on the beach with her. Holding her breath, Annelyse listened with all her might, trying to learn where this other person might be - all without turning around or moving a muscle.

Maybe it was her father come to find his daughter and spend the morning with her. He would have easily guessed where she'd gone. But surely, he would have said something by now. Neither of them would sneak up on or startle the other. Not now. Grief lowers one's tolerance for such things.

Feeling eyes on the back of her neck, she was becoming frightened. She needed to know who this person was, no matter what danger might be involved in learning.

Slowly turning around, she saw the figure of a young man. He was seated on a fallen boulder of limestone which had once been part of the cliff wall. He appeared to be in his late twenties, and his tattered backpack and rugged clothing suggested he might be a vagrant of some kind. She'd never seen him before and, in a town of fewer people than sheep, this was remarkable.

But the moment Annelyse saw his face, her fear and apprehension began to dissolve. There was calmness in his eyes, not at all the look of a madman. Though, it was obvious that he'd been watching her in silence since she'd arrived, somehow, she was certain that it was out of care and concern not some devious intention that he'd taken an interest in her. She relaxed her stance, shielding her eyes from the sun which was just now peeking over the lip of the cliff above the man's head.

In his hand, the stranger held a pencil. On his knee, a leather-bound journal lay open. Before her arrival interrupted his work, the young man had been busy writing something. Now, he gave his full attention to Annelyse who stood speechless on the shore.

Placing his pencil in the crease, he closed the journal and put it in his backpack. He then looked at Annelyse, and with the glow of a warm smile on his face, he said, "There you are."

CHAPTER THREE

Hope Seeks Out the Hopeless

Annelyse was caught completely off guard by the young man's greeting.

"What's *that* supposed to mean?" she wondered to herself.

But, before she could coax the question from her mouth, the stranger (made stranger still by his unexpected salutation) set his threadbare boots aside and joined Annelyse, soaking his feet in the surf.

Feeling that the moment had passed for follow-up questions, Annelyse decided to simply ignore the man's odd greeting and pretend nothing at all had been said. She moved a comfortable distance away as casually as she could, all the while keeping her awkward companion safely in the corner of her eye.

The young man burst out laughing at her wishful attempt to reset the situation.

"I'm afraid it doesn't work that way," he chuckled.

Annelyse was in no mood for much of anything, let alone being laughed at by some weird vagrant. Her temper flared and got the better of her tongue, as it often did.

"What are you talking about?" she snapped.

In barely more than a whisper, the young man replied, "You can't just pretend it didn't happen."

Annelyse was annoyed at being dragged into a conversation. This was *not* what she'd had in mind for the day. She'd come to Ruhner's Beach to be alone. Clearly, her plans were in jeopardy.

"I can't just pretend *what* didn't happen?" she asked, more out of irritation than real interest.

"*Any*thing," the young man replied. "*Every*thing."

Annelyse stared at the stranger with a mix of confusion and derision on her face. She was about to pick up her shoes and socks and head back to the house in a huff when he said it again.

"There you are," he repeated, this time in a more pensive tone.

Without explanation, he was giving her a second chance. He was curious what she would choose to do with it. Standing a few feet away, looking out to sea, there was a mysterious peacefulness about him. He was pleasant and kind, but there was also an edge of something deadly serious about him, like the hard bedrock underlying a merrily flowing stream.

Annelyse could see that this engaging stranger wasn't someone she'd be able to just walk away from. Though she was upset that her morning of solitude had been interrupted, she couldn't help but feel that ignoring the young man would be unwarranted rudeness. A response would have to be given, though she didn't know precisely what to say.

"Here I am," was the best she could manage. It was characteristically sarcastic, and so, quintessentially true to form.

"I was expecting you," he said, still gazing out to sea.

"Were you, now?"

"Yes, I was," he said with firm affirmation, then asked, "Where else would you be?"

Annelyse had no answer. All she had were questions of her own. Who was this man? Why would he be expecting her? What was he getting at? Her irritation was gradually beginning to give way to curiosity. So, she decided to play along.

"Where else would I be?" She repeated, then paused to think. "*Any*where else, I guess."

"Not today," the young man said, turning his eyes westward once more. "Not after yesterday."

"Why? What was yesterday?" Annelyse asked, evading the point he was clearly trying to make, and feeling just a little uncomfortable.

The man looked directly at her again, with compassion in his eyes, and whispered, "Your mother's funeral, child."

At the mention of something so personal and painful, a vicious flame of indignation leapt up from somewhere deep inside Annelyse's heart. She was now in full defense mode.

"What, do you live in the village? How do you know...?"

The stranger ignored Annelyse's questions as being entirely beside the point, and pushed on, saying, "So, I waited here for you. And there you are."

He seemed determined to avoid discussing anything but what *he* wanted to talk about. But Annelyse was determined, too. Spurred on by an increasing tetchiness, she decided that, if she hoped to have any chance of getting some answers, she needed to be more direct.

"Who *are* you?"

"A friend," he replied, without revealing a single thing Annelyse hoped to learn.

"A friend of my father's?" she continued, unwilling to let up.

"I was, yes, though less so."

"Less so than what?" Annelyse's irritation was beginning to spike.

"Less so than I was to your mother," he replied, a knowing grin showing in his eyes.

"You knew my mother? How? I know *everyone* she knew."

"Do you know her grandparents?" the man asked with a sideways glance.

"No, they died before I was born."

"Do you know her teachers from when she was in school?"

"No. How would I?"

"Do you know…"

Annelyse cut him off midsentence, "I get the point."

"Good. A lesson learned is a fault avoided."

Walking over toward the cliff face, the young man sat back down on the boulder and opened his backpack. He removed a canteen and two apples, offering one to Annelyse.

"No, thank you," she said, "I brought some bread and cheese."

Returning both apples to his backpack, he looked up with a glimmer in his eye and said, "Yes, please."

Annelyse raised an eyebrow and let out an incredulous snort. "Greedy beggar," she thought to herself.

"I'm no beggar," the man said, utterly unnerving Annelyse and rousing her from her unkind thoughts. "I just accepted before you offered. It saves time, I find."

"In that case," she snickered, producing the block of cheese and lump of bread from her pockets, "You're welcome!"

"And so are you," he said, handing her his canteen.

Annelyse sat down on the boulder and gave the man half her bread and cheese. Taking a sip of water from the canteen, she handed it back to him with a grateful nod of her head. She was reluctant even to *think* anything in his presence. He seemed to be able to read her like a book. He was unique, no doubt about that. Still, something about him reminded her of someone. She just couldn't put her finger on it.

The sun was warm on their backs, as they sat on the limestone boulder, and a cool breeze had begun to stir the sea. Off to the southwest, a glint of sunlight reflected in the great lens of Lower Perigoh Light. To the north, tiny figures of fishing boats were slowly moving in and out of the bay. Annelyse sighed a long sigh of contentment. No matter what, coming to Ruhner's Beach was always a good idea.

The moment she'd taken the bread out of her pocket, nosey seagulls began circling overhead. Landing by the dozen and sideling up to where Annelyse was sitting, the birds were not at all ashamed to beg.

"Yes, of course, my friends. There's plenty for everyone," the young man said, as he tossed a piece of bread to the seagulls.

Each bird followed the morsel from the moment it left the man's hand until it landed on the black sand. Screeching and squawking they hopped and fluttered until one lucky bird snatched up the bread in its beak and gobbled it down in one gulp. All eyes would then lock back onto the young man's hand, eagerly awaiting the next offering. The game repeated itself - one morsel after another - until the birds had eaten all the man's bread, leaving him only his lump of cheese.

"Here," Annelyse said, handing him her own piece of bread.

"Thank you, child," he replied, as he began tearing and tossing it to the waiting seagulls.

Annelyse chuckled, "I meant for *you* to eat it."

"I'll just have the cheese," he said.

"Looks like we *both* will," Annelyse complained.

As she nibbled on her cheese, she wondered about what the young man had meant when he said he'd been expecting her. She was still confused as to who he was and how he knew her mother (and "less so" her father). The longer she thought about it, the more questions popped up in her mind. Trying to contain her curiosity was like trying to keep the greedy seagulls at bay. She was dying for just one small morsel, and she decided to try again to get some answers. This time, she'd employ a more pointed approach.

Clearing her throat, she began, "Why'd you say you were expecting me?"

"Because I was," the young man replied, matter-of-factly.

"No, I meant…"

"Always say what you mean, child. Anything less isn't worth your breath, and anything more is just decorating the daisy."

"Decorating the daisy?" Annelyse was lost.

"Adorning the azalea. Beautifying the begonia. Or gilding the lily if you prefer. Although, my preference is always for alliteration."

It must have been obvious that Annelyse had no idea what the man was talking about, because he added one last clarification, "Saying more than you mean is just adding decoration to something that needs none. It loses the point you're trying to make. Points are easily lost, after all."

Annelyse felt as if she'd been swept off the beach by a tidal wave and deposited miles out to sea. She now tried to swim back to where she'd been before the stranger had gone off on his flower tangent.

"I meant, why should you expect me, when we don't even know each other?"

"Because I have something for you, and I went where I knew you'd be so I could give it to you."

Reaching down into his backpack, the man pulled out the leather-bound journal in which he'd been writing when Annelyse first noticed him.

"I finally finished it," he said with relief. "Just before you arrived, in fact."

"What is it?"

He looked surprised, as if the answer should have been obvious. "It's a poem, of course."

"You wrote me a poem?"

"I wrote a poem *for* you," he clarified. "But the poem is *about* your mother."

Opening his journal to the page marked by his pencil, he made one small erasure, changed his choice of word, then looked up at Annelyse.

"May I read it to you?"

"Yes, please," she said, shoving the remnants of her hard cheese back into her pocket.

"Thank you," he smiled. Then, stopping himself, he added, "I wanted a challenge, so I wrote forty lines of alliteration using every letter in the alphabet. X and U were the most difficult."

He was clearly pleased with himself.

"Anyway, here it is. I call it, *Silloah*."

Annelyse wasn't sure what alliteration was. But she was duly impressed and made certain to let it show on her face. The young man straightened his journal on his knee and began to read.

Where Woolems wandered, west of Wehrle,
and ambled airy Averlune,
there lived a lovely little girl
with hair of golden June.

She swam the Sault Sea, sun and smile,
while blossom-breezes briskly blew
the Inns of Inidyllique Isle
and glens of Goughlin Grugh.

Fair flowers of the Fäerie Fields
she plaited into petalled pearls.
Her youth and yearning yet would yield
a crown for golden curls.

And dancing sweet while dolphins dream
in undulating undertow,
she jumped and jimbled by the stream
where fern and fennel grow.

For, as a minstrel maiden, mild
who told the Tale of Trinket Trove,
she chirped and cheeped, the chatter-child,
through Cor McCrumblin Cove.

Her voice it vaulted down the vale
like kitebirds over Killoughee,
but faint and quiet, over quail
that slept beside the sea.

For rippling ran her rhymes like rain:
a zillion zigzag, zipping words
'xplored 'xcitedly, 'xclaimed
to squirrels and hummingbirds.

Far north of Narrow Nook there run
the horses of the Hyland herds.
And ere the evening ebb is done,
and ere the morning's stirred,

she'd often, out on Orchard Knoll,
in hazel heather's golden grain
enfold, embracing every foal,
her face in flowing mane.

And where the Woolems wander, wild
and where the western winds did blow
there walked this wise and wistful child
who made fair wonders grow.

When he had finished, he pulled the pages loose from the binding and handed them to Annelyse. Closing his journal, he placed it in his backpack. He then removed the two apples again and handed one to Annelyse.

"Seagulls prefer bread," he said with a wink and a grin.

"It's beautiful," Annelyse whispered, taking the apple from his hand.

"I picked them from Orchard Knoll on my way through last time. The best apples in all of Hyland..."

"The poem," she interjected, correcting his misunderstanding. "The poem is beautiful."

"Art is made more beautiful by its subject," he replied, nodding in agreement with himself.

"You said the poem is about my mother, but it speaks of a little girl."

"Yes, she was a fair child, indeed."

"You knew her when she was little? But how can that be? You're younger than she was."

"I knew her always."

"But... it doesn't make sense. How...?"

"A thing might be true without making sense," he said, looking deep into her eyes.

"But if something is true it *has* to make sense," Annelyse argued.

"Some of the truest things make the least amount of sense," the poet continued. "But it doesn't make them any less true. Your mother chose to suffer more than was necessary, forcing herself out of bed to walk these paths one last time. She did this to weave a final crown of daisies for you. Why?"

Annelyse was dumbfounded. How did this stranger know *that*? With confused wondering and a lump in her throat, she made her quiet reply, "Because she loved me."

"Because she *loves* you. Love is one of the truest things, and it rarely makes sense."

"Loved," Annelyse said, with cold defiance. "Because she *loved* me."

"Child, she loves you still. And that truth makes just about as much sense as love itself."

The young man took a bite of his apple then turned to look westward out over the Great Sault Sea. Annelyse sat motionless beside him, feeling as if she might burst into tears, staring at the waves as they lapped the smooth sand.

She remembered what her mother had said to her after crowning her the last time, how she had every reason to believe that her love would not die with her body. Had her mother somehow shared all of this with the young man? How could he know all that had happened? Her mind was reeling with questions and conflicting emotions.

She remembered the pages she'd been holding in her hand. Letting her eyes come to rest on the text, one word caught her attention.

Breaking the long silence, she asked, "What are Woolems?"

The man leaned over and took a handful of sand from the beach. Letting it sift slowly through his fingers, he answered Annelyse's question.

"You've heard of them before, though perhaps not by name. Their tragic story played out on this very beach."

Annelyse thought for a moment. Calling to mind all that her mother had told her about Ruhner's Beach. She made the connection. The mythical creatures that were kidnapped by the pirates and sold into slavery *must* have been what the poet now referred to as Woolems.

"Then mom told *you* the same story. About the pirates and all. Is that why there are Woolems in your poem?"

"They're in the poem for the same reason kitebirds, dolphins, and quail are. They're all a part of Averlune just like your mother. I write about what is."

"You're not saying that Woolems are *real*, are you?"

"Why write about something that isn't real? Except to tell the truth more truly," the poet replied.

"Huh?" Annelyse couldn't possibly guess what he meant by that.

"The only things worth writing about are things that are real, even if they're better written about in fiction."

Still struggling to understand his meaning, Annelyse tried to pin him down on the one point she cared about.

"So, mom's story about the pirates and Woolems and all that, it was just made up?"

"It was made up of many things," came the exasperating reply.

"Then Woolems *aren't* real," she conceded, somewhat disappointed.

"That's for each of us to decide," the poet said, tossing the last bit of sand into the breeze. "I decided long ago, and now I know the truth of it."

The young man brushed his hands clean then stood, picked up his boots, and slung the backpack over his shoulder. Looking out to sea one last time, he spoke - although Annelyse wasn't sure if it was to her or to himself.

"And there you are," he whispered.

Closing his eyes, he paused a moment on the shore, feeling the breeze at his back and the sun on his hair. Annelyse thought that he looked just as much a part of nature as the boulder, the sand, or the sea. He seemed to be the kind of person who was at home everywhere he found himself, but rarely found himself anywhere for long.

Turning toward Annelyse, he bowed ever so slightly, saying, "I went where I knew you'd be because I had something to give you."

"The poem," she replied, wondering why he felt the need to repeat himself. "Yes, um… thank you very much."

"The poem," he repeated, "And more. But it's yours to discover, now. Yours to decide. Yours alone, but not alone. Never alone."

By now, Annelyse was used to not really understanding what the poet was talking about. She knew better than to try to push him for clarification. That always seemed to muddy the waters further. But she was still so full of questions and so empty of answers.

She could not recall a more dissatisfying and frustrating conversation. And yet, apart from her mother's crowns of daisies, she couldn't recall ever receiving a more precious gift than the poem she now held in her hands.

"Please don't go," she said, surprised by her own words. "Not yet. I still need to ask you…"

"If we decided when others would come and go, we'd strip all comings and goings of meaning. I came when you did not expect me, and I leave now when you do not wish it. I came with a purpose, and now that my purpose has been accomplished, I must leave. Do not stand in the way of true meaning and purpose, or you'll be tempted to invent your own."

"But the poem, the Woolems… you haven't told me

anything."

"I've told you enough, and your mother told you everything else. There's no fairer heart from which to learn than that of Silloah Bellamy."

"Will you at least tell me your name before you leave me?"

"The few who call me anything call me the Poet of Perigoh, and that suits me just fine."

With a smile, he walked over to the limestone steps hewn out of the cliff face. Climbing the stairs, he was soon taken from view by the chalky walls of the crevice. A moment later, his footfalls faded to silence, and he was gone.

On the shore, the seagulls chased the receding tide, pecking at any shell or pebble left in its wake. Annelyse wondered how they could possibly still be hungry after eating so much bread. High overhead, three lonesome kitebirds flew circles around the wispy clouds as the sun rose to its noonday height.

Where only a couple of hours earlier Annelyse had come seeking solitude, the empty beach was now far too quiet for her liking. She didn't want to be alone anymore. She wanted answers to all the questions the poet had planted in her mind. Rereading his poem, she looked for hidden meaning between the words, anything that would help her understand what he'd meant.

Several things the poet had said to her swirled around in her thoughts. How did he know her mother? How did he know Silloah's story of Ruhner's Beach? What are these Woolems, and are they even real? In a burst of annoyance, Annelyse exclaimed aloud, "If it's so important, why not tell me clearly?!"

She was fed up with wispy mysteries that never settle down into solid answers. The only reply she received to her angry demand came from the seagulls on the shore. Cackling like a flock of hecklers, they offered no insight and even less sympathy.

The pages in her hands had nothing more to tell her beyond the words they bore. If there was hidden meaning between the lines, it eluded her completely. She sat there on the boulder just shaking her head, her teeth clenched in aggravation.

Having had her share of riddles for one day, Annelyse intended to place the poem in her pocket (the one empty of cheese) to keep it safe for the walk back. It was nearing lunchtime, the time she'd told her father that she'd be home.

Folding the two sheets of paper in half, she now noticed something written - or rather drawn - on the back of the second sheet. Upon closer examination, Annelyse saw that it was a rough map. She did not recognize the region depicted in the drawing. It was completely foreign to her and of such a scale as to provide her with no reference points.

Inscribed to the left of the drawing were the words, "Maps can't guide you to decision, only your heart can. But this one might start you on your way toward discovery."

Was this the "more" that the poet had alluded to? The "more" she had to discover on her own? If so, it wasn't *much* more, she thought. What could he mean by, "this one might start you on your way toward discovery?" Discovery of what? More riddles? More mysteries? Undoubtedly, and with no more answers than she'd already received. She was flummoxed and needed to settle her brain and take a rest from wondering and questioning for a while.

Getting up, she carefully placed the folded poem in her pocket, walked over to the waterline, and let the cool, blue saltwater caress her feet. Her father would surely be awake, by now, she thought. But the idea of stepping back inside the broken memories of that house filled her with dread. She'd never dreaded going home before; but then, home had never been so empty before. Still, she had no desire to cause her father any worry. It was time to be on her way.

As she returned to put on her shoes, Annelyse caught sight of something peculiar. Resting on top of the limestone boulder where the poet had been sitting there lay a single, white daisy. Stopping dead in her tracks, Annelyse stared in silence at the flower.

She'd set out that morning in the hope of retracing familiar paths, finding healing by the sea, and touching some part of her mother any way she could. In that moment, she realized she'd succeeded in doing just that, thanks to the unexpected presence of a stranger.

Up until her conversation with the poet, she'd always thought that she knew her mother well. But now, mysterious depths began to open up around Silloah Bellamy, and her daughter was resolved to explore them. Perhaps, there was more to her mother than she understood, and somehow the poem, the map, and now this one daisy held the key. Where the doubtful Woolems fit into it all, she did not know.

Picking up the flower, Annelyse held it to her nose and inhaled the wild, sweet scent. In an instant of sudden remembrance, the words her mother had spoken to her echoed in her mind, "Do not let the events to come kill what is most precious inside of you."

But Annelyse wondered, of all the things that had died inside her heart, which of them had been the "most precious?" It was easier to ask, "What still remained?" This she could answer with assurance. All that remained were memories and the certainty that time spent by the sea was never wasted. It certainly hadn't been that morning. These two things would have to suffice for the moment. For, it was early days, still.

CHAPTER FOUR

Tangible Connections

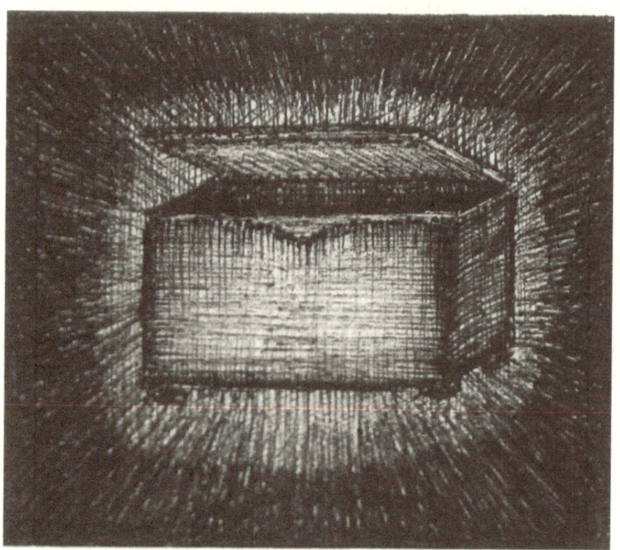

Returning along the same narrow path she'd taken down to Ruhner's Beach, Annelyse followed it through the wildflower meadow and up to the front door of her house. Upon entering, she was greeted by the sight of her father mopping the kitchen floor. From the look of things, he'd been hard at work cleaning the entire house for quite some time.

"I thought we had nothing to do today," she said, chiding him.

"I didn't plan on doing anything," he said, without looking up from his wet floor. "It just kinda happened. I couldn't just sit around idle all day."

Annelyse knew her father. He constantly needed to be busy. If he wasn't weeding the vegetable gardens or pruning the fruit trees, he was tending to the chickens or working in his woodshop. He didn't know any other way to be. Edward Bellamy hadn't been bored in decades. But, lately, keeping his hands occupied was also the best way to keep his mind distracted. Annelyse suspected that this was the real reason behind his sudden burst of cleanliness.

"Can I help with anything?" she asked, leaving her shoes on the mat beside the front door.

"You could make us a snack," he replied, much to her amazement. "I think I might be able to eat something."

Annelyse was relieved to hear that her father had an appetite, and she was determined to take advantage of it.

"Instead of a snack, how about an early dinner," she suggested, as she tiptoed across the newly mopped floor to wash her hands in the kitchen sink. "I'm hungry, too."

"No breakfast this morning?" her father asked. "I thought you'd taken the last of that loaf of bread."

"Um, I did, but I didn't end up eating it," she replied, sticking to the truth. "It was a little too hard for me, but the birds didn't mind."

Lighting the stove, she placed a frying pan on the burner and began melting some butter. As she added garlic, a squeeze of lemon juice, and a pinch of salt and pepper, her thoughts wandered over the conversation she'd had with the young man on the beach. She needed to find a way to casually bring up the topic of the poet with her father. Too much enthusiasm might set off warning bells in his head. He was very protective of his daughter, and recent events only increased his vigilance over her.

Peeling some shrimp that she'd found in the larder she tossed them into the pan one by one until they blushed a rosy pink. Meanwhile, Mr. Bellamy put away the last of the cleaning supplies and washed up.

"What can I do?" he asked, with red, swollen eyes.

Cleaning wasn't all her father had been busy doing that morning, Annelyse noted.

"Make a salad?" she suggested.

"Mm hm," he agreed without emotion, as he began collecting the lettuce and cherry tomatoes he'd picked from the garden a few days earlier.

"Where'd you go this morning?" he asked, slicing some radishes.

"Down to Ruhner's Beach. The water's warming up fast. I think it's gonna be a hot summer."

Annelyse considered herself an excellent small talker, almost as good as she was at conjuring-up a sincere *thank you* when necessary. But her father knew her all too well. Her small talk almost always concealed her real purpose.

"What is it?" he asked, drying his knife, and slipping it back into the wooden block.

"What's what?" Annelyse parried.

"It. The It you're not talking about."

Her father's suspicions were now confirmed. Of course, he trusted Annelyse completely. He trusted her to be sneaky, stubborn, and hot headed, most of all. But he also trusted her to set him up carefully whenever she felt like she needed to tread lightly, much like she was doing right now. To her credit, Annelyse knew her father was onto her. She was astute enough to realize that this was the moment to come clean.

"I met someone… down at the beach," she began. Then, with a flip of her spatula, she added, "That's all."

Apparently, when cornered, the wild Annelyse abandons its grip on reality. Instead, this crafty creature defends itself by dropping the subject and retreating as if nothing ever happened. Clearly, she'd forgotten what the poet had said to her. She still thought things "worked that way."

"That's all?" her father said, halting her retreat.

"That's *plenty*. I want to hear all about this *someone*."

Mr. Bellamy set the salad bowl down with a bump! for effect; grabbed two place settings; and prepared the table for their early dinner, all without taking his eyes off his daughter. He was not about to let her wriggle her way out of giving a full account.

"Yes, sir," she said, snapping to attention. She got the point.

Annelyse began her more detailed explanation, in earnest, "There was a young man on the beach. I'd never seen him before. At first I thought he was homeless…"

At the mention of the word "man," Mr. Bellamy dropped the fork he'd been holding, sending it clanging sharply into a cup he'd just set down. Regaining his composure and recovering the fork, he placed it on top of its napkin to the left of his plate. He motioned toward Annelyse's seat, saying, "Sit down. Tell me more."

The first thing that crossed her mind was to answer, "What's to tell?" But Annelyse had learned long ago not to push her luck with her father. The bump! of the salad bowl and the terse emphasis on the first syllable of her name were the only two warnings she'd receive. She knew enough to take them. Where the safety of his daughter was concerned, Edward Bellamy had very little patience.

"Well, he was strange, but not creepy. He just *talked* strange, mostly."

"How so?" Mr. Bellamy asked, passing the salad bowl to Annelyse.

"Like, the first thing he said to me was, 'There you are,' as if he'd been waiting for me… which he said he was. He just made no sense most of the time. But he sure did seem to know a lot about us."

"Us?" Mr. Bellamy passed the dish of shrimp across the table. "What did he know about us?"

"He said he was a friend of mom's," she hesitated long enough to gauge her father's reaction, "And less so, yours."

"He's right about that," her father snapped.

"Then you *do* know him!" Annelyse was so happy to learn that her father knew the man that she didn't notice his sour reaction.

"I did, yes," he confirmed. "A long time ago. But I have no interest in knowing him anymore."

Annelyse sensed the change in her father. Moments before, he'd been terse with her, until he'd guessed the identity of the young man. Now, no longer worried for her safety, the whole event seemed to irritate him. She had no idea why.

All the way home from Ruhner's Beach, she'd been overflowing with questions she wanted to ask her father, certain that he'd be as curious about the stranger as she was. Most of all, she wanted to ask him about the Woolems. If her mother knew about the mysterious creatures, surely, her father would, too.

But his attitude wasn't just mild irritation, it was disdain. He didn't like the poet, for some reason. In fact, he seemed to despise the young man. That would make it very difficult for Annelyse to get any answers out of her father. He obviously didn't want to talk about it. Still, having inherited more than her share of stubbornness from her father, she had no intention of giving up just yet.

His eyes fixed straight ahead, Mr. Bellamy sat across the table from Annelyse, eating and stewing in silence. Attacking each tomato and radish with a quick stab of his fork, his whole demeanor was that of profound displeasure. Annelyse searched for a way through his defenses.

"He seemed nice," she said, testing the frontline.

"He usually does," her father shot back, each word dripping with sarcasm.

"He had good things to say about mom."

"Any fool would."

"And, actually," Annelyse reached into the front pocket of her pants, "he gave me this."

Producing the two sheets of parchment, she unfolded them and handed the poem to her father. Mr. Bellamy paused, as if frightened to lay a finger on the poet's gift. His eyes broke loose from the paper in his daughter's hand and came to rest on her face, instead. He appeared to be looking for some sign of reassurance.

"What is it?" he asked, glancing down at the paper.

"It's a poem," Annelyse replied, then quickly added, "About mom."

Mr. Bellamy's eyes widened into deep wells of fear. Withdrawing his hand, he examined his daughter's face with apprehension.

"It's ok. Really." Annelyse offered it to him a second time, "Please, read it."

With hesitation, he relented. Taking the poem in his hands, Mr. Bellamy began to read in silence.

> *Where Woolems wandered, west of Wehrle,*
> *and ambled airy Averlune,*
> *there lived a lovely little girl*
> *with hair of golden June.*
>
> *She swam the Sault Sea, sun and smile,*
> *while blossom-breezes briskly blew*
> *the Inns of Inidyllique Isle*
> *and glens of Goughlin Grugh.*
>
> *Fair flowers of the Fäerie Fields*
> *she plaited into petalled pearls.*
> *Her youth and yearning yet would yield*
> *a crown for golden curls.*
>
> *And dancing sweet while dolphins dream*
> *in undulating undertow,*

she jumped and jimbled by the stream
where fern and fennel grow.

For, as a minstrel maiden, mild
who told the Tale of Trinket Trove,
she chirped and cheeped, the chatter-child,
through Cor McCrumblin Cove.

Her voice it vaulted down the vale
like kitebirds over Killoughee,
but faint and quiet, over quail
that slept beside the sea.

For rippling ran her rhymes like rain:
a zillion zigzag, zipping words
'xplored 'xcitedly, 'xclaimed
to squirrels and hummingbirds.

Far north of Narrow Nook there run
the horses of the Hyland herds.
And ere the evening ebb is done,
and ere the morning's stirred,

she'd often, out on Orchard Knoll,
in hazel heather's golden grain
enfold, embracing every foal,
her face in flowing mane.

And where the Woolems wander, wild
and where the western winds did blow
there walked this wise and wistful child
who made fair wonders grow.

With great care, Mr. Bellamy set the poem down on
the table, staring at it awhile.

"It's her," he said, tears gathering in his eyes. "It's

your mother."

"The poet said he knew her '*always.*' His poem made me believe it was true."

"Yes, it's true," her father confirmed.

"But there's more," Annelyse added. "Look."

Picking up the parchment, she turned over the second page revealing the rough map drawn on the back. Handing it back to her father, Mr. Bellamy examined it closely.

"I know this place," he said, as recognition dawned on his face. "Those two islands, there. Those are the Sibling Stones in the mouth of the Miralette. I'm sure of it."

Tracing the shoreline with his finger, he followed it north.

"This map extends all the way to the Far Reaches. That's odd. Very few ever travel that far north. I've heard stories," he continued, almost in a whisper, "about the dangerous waters around the Windermere Islands, there. Northwest of King's Bay. And of some great spike jutting up out of the sea, or some such nonsense. Fishermen go out of their way to avoid that area. Why on earth would he give you a map of the far northlands?"

Annelyse reached across the table and rested her index finger below the inscription scrawled across the page. Her father had been so focused on the drawing that he'd overlooked what was written to the left of the map.

Mr. Bellamy read the note aloud, "'Maps can't guide you to a decision, only your heart can. But this one might start you on your way toward discovery.'"

Resting his hands on the edge of the table, he looked with confusion at Annelyse.

"On your way toward discovery? What's he mean?"

"I'm not sure," she began, "But it has something to do with…"

Annelyse stopped herself. She felt as if her father

would surely think she'd lost her mind. She hadn't had time to prepare him for talk of mythical creatures and all. Annelyse feared that it would sound like just so much nonsense to her sensible father. It sure had to her. Still, she had little choice but to continue. But she didn't have much hope of receiving a favorable hearing.

"The inscription next to the map has something to do with… uh… Woolems."

Annelyse waited, watching her father's reaction, expecting him to laugh it off as a childish fantasy or the ravings of a mad vagrant. But he just sat there with a stone face, betraying nothing at all of what he was thinking. Maybe his silence was an invitation for her to continue. She decided to assume that it was.

"I asked him about the Woolems from his poem and he said they were the same creatures in Mom's story about Ruhner's…"

"That drifter is just a crazy fool," her father burst in. "He doesn't know fact from fiction. Why would he even bring up such things? None of it makes any sense…"

"That's what *he* said," Annelyse shot back. "That's *exactly* what he said."

"What?"

"He said that the truest things make the least amount of sense."

"Well, that proves he's a fool," her father said with a chuckle, satisfied he'd made his point.

"But he's right," Annelyse countered. "I *know* he's right."

During her walk back from the beach, Annelyse's brain had been wrestling with all that the young man had said to her. She racked her brain, trying to think of things that might fit the category. Important things, true things that don't seem to make any sense. The more she thought about it, the more she started to understand.

Her hard, practical side had been angry when her

mother had pulled herself out of bed and walked all the way down to the chopping stump only a few days before she'd died. Annelyse didn't see any point in it. She thought it was insane for her mother to go looking for more suffering. Wasn't her pain bad enough already? Why make it any worse by getting up and staggering around the meadow?

But the tender heart at the center of Annelyse's fortress of sass and sarcasm would forever cherish the memory of her mother's final act of love. It was just like Silloah to ignore her own pain in order to show affection for her daughter. If suffering made no sense, Annelyse concluded, then love made even less.

"The poet was right," she insisted. "Just because something doesn't make much sense doesn't mean it's not true. I didn't know it before," she said, half to herself and half to her father, "But I know it now. And that's not all."

Edward was silent, and Annelyse wasn't sure if she was getting through to him or not. But it mattered more to her that she simply be allowed to speak her mind, whether it was well-received by her father or not; whether he wanted to hear it or not.

"The poet said something else, something that makes me think I know why he gave me the map. He said, 'The only things worth writing about are things that are real, even if they're better written about in fiction.' I think he meant Mom's story, the story of Ruhner's Beach, the story of the Woolems. I asked him straight out if Woolems were real…"

"And what did he say?" Mr. Bellamy insisted, ready to catch the poet out.

"He said 'that's for each of us to decide.'"

Edward Bellamy relaxed his posture, almost as if he were a little disappointed in the poet's reply. He'd expected something else, something he could have used to convict the young man of some sort of crime. But it didn't come.

Edward now retreated, in order to regroup.

Taking advantage of her father's silence, Annelyse finally made the point she'd been wanting to make since leaving Ruhner's Beach.

"If each of us has to figure out what we believe, then I intend to decide for myself," she said, sounding more formidably like her mother than Mr. Bellamy could remember her sounding before.

"Mom knew about the Woolems, I'm sure of it. She made up her mind. I want to, also. And I mean to."

"I won't let that lunatic put mad ideas in your head the way he did…"

Mr. Bellamy stopped himself short, took a deep breath, then exhaled slowly. He looked like a deflated balloon, like a man who had fought this same battle before and was loath to do so again.

"Annelyse, searching for Woolems is a fool's errand," he continued, fatigued by having to make his case.

"But the map," she said, taking the paper from her father's hands and presenting it as evidence. "I think the poet gave it to me to help us find…"

"Nothing. That map shows only hundreds of miles of open wilderness. Nowhere does it say where to find Woolems or anything else, for that matter."

"But Mom wouldn't have just ignored something like this. She would have followed the map. She would have gone in search of answers. You can't tell me any different. I know it!"

Edward Bellamy said nothing. He knew the truth. He knew that Annelyse was right. His wife knew about the mysterious Woolems. She would have traveled as far as the Miralette and much farther, just for the adventure. He knew it, and he couldn't, in all honesty, tell Annelyse otherwise. As much as he wanted to deter his daughter, he would not lie to her.

"She believed, Daddy. She knew. And I need to

know, too. I need to know the truth."

Mr. Bellamy looked at Annelyse, with dark circles ringing his tired eyes and worry lines etched deep into his forehead. Whispering through his grief, he said, "You're right. Your mother knew and believed many things. Too many. And look where it got her. Look where it got us. This curiosity is nothing but trouble."

Annelyse stared back at her father, feeling as if all meaning had been cut from her heart. Hope itself had just been trampled upon; but it wasn't the hope of learning the truth about the Woolems. It was the hope that she held out for her father that had just been gutted.

Since losing his wife, he had lost his faith in everything except the hardest realities of life. He'd been abandoned by everything he'd ever put stock in, and he had no use for it any longer. If it didn't help him feed and care for his beloved daughter, then it was only a cruel distraction or worse, a damnable lie. Life was too short and difficult for such things as belief and hope, Woolems and adventures, he thought.

Annelyse now mourned her father's loss of faith as much as she mourned her mother's death. Looking into his eyes, Annelyse saw bottomless pits of sadness. The foundations upon which he had built his life had crumbled, and now the entire structure lay in a heap. The idea of rebuilding was senseless; the reasons from which he had always drawn strength no longer existed. Silloah had been the one person whose approval he'd craved. Hers had been the only opinion that ever mattered. She had been the means and the purpose by which and for whom he had lived.

Until her conversation with the poet, Annelyse had felt exactly the same way. But it occurred to her that she'd seen something within the young man that reminded her of her mother. The same spark of kind, hopeful optimism had burned within the soul of Silloah Bellamy, and now the poet had ignited it in Annelyse's heart, too.

As much as she loved her father, she was not about to let him extinguish the tiny ember that now glowed inside of her. Too much depended upon the possibility of fanning it into flame. She was convinced that this spark would light her way to discovering whether the Woolems were real or not, and she would touch some hidden part of her mother in the process, too.

"I never told you what she said to me," Annelyse began, feeling her confidence grow taller. "I never told you what she said the last time she crowned me."

With a quiver in her voice, Annelyse continued, "She said, 'Do not let the events to come kill what is most precious inside of you.'"

Annelyse met her father's gaze with fearlessness, "I guess she should have told you the same thing, too."

She waited for a response, fully expecting to be sent to her room for disrespect. But Edward Bellamy was not the kind of man who defended his rights when he knew he was in the wrong. He was an honest man, above all else. For his daughter to speak the truth was not disrespect, no matter how difficult it was for him to hear it from her lips.

So much had changed in the past few days. His family was in tatters, his life was in disarray. Struggling to regain any scrap of normality he could find, Edward Bellamy tried desperately to preserve what little had been left to him. But now the child had assumed the role of parent, and the parent felt very much like a frightened child. Unable to sort through the wreckage of emotion and find a rational response, he did the only thing he could do.

Edward Bellamy stood up, put his dishes in the sink, and walked out the front door. There was no drama involved, no slamming of the door behind him. This was not a weak protest or an immature tantrum. He just needed to be alone with his own thoughts. Rather than say the wrong thing, he chose to safely say nothing at all.

Annelyse put her head down on her folded arms and stained the kitchen table wet with her tears. She'd failed to break through her father's unexplained dislike of the poet. She had failed to appeal to whatever remained of his faith in the things he and his wife had once held dear. Instead, Annelyse glimpsed only the darkness of despair through the open gashes in her father's wounded heart. She tried to communicate her resolve to find whatever answers could be found about the Woolems and the questions surrounding her mother. She tried to move him out of his hopeless grief and into the hopefulness of action. But, in the end, she was met by silence and fear.

Without her father's permission and help, she *would* never and *could* never explore whatever mysteries the poet's map might hold. Without her father, she could never begin to discover her mother's hidden secrets. Annelyse felt as if she were losing her mother all over again. But, this time, she was desperate to hold on. She would not let her mother slip through her fingers again. She *wanted* to learn the truth about the Woolems, but she *needed* to know the truth about her mother and what she had believed.

Pulling herself up from the table, she ran into her parent's bedroom. On the floor at the foot of the bed there sat her mother's cedar hope chest. Annelyse took the quilt that lay atop the chest and tossed it on the bed. Opening the lid, she began digging through the contents of the chest.

Old dresses worn on various occasions were tightly folded and stacked together on one side. Drawings and finger paintings made by a young Annelyse were preserved with care beneath her baby blanket. A single, golden curl, tied with a red ribbon and wrapped in tissue paper, was kept as a memento of Annelyse's first haircut. There were candles and wine glasses; simple jewelry of no greater value than that which sentiment assigned; pressed flowers; tarnished trinkets; and a child's silver spoon – the moments and memories of a life lived to the fullest and cut short before its time.

Buried at the bottom of the cedar chest, Annelyse found what she'd been looking for, a small, wooden box, simple and unremarkable. A few years earlier, her mother had shared with her the contents of this box. These were Silloah's most prized possessions, and Annelyse needed to hold them in her hands once more. If these items possessed any clarity or wisdom, then Annelyse desperately needed to feel their weight and employ their help.

When Annelyse was a bit younger, Mr. Bellamy would often sail his fishing boat south of Inidyllique Isle into the narrows of Cor McCrumblin Cove. There, in the small bays and tiny inlets of the islands, he'd fish for days on end. His nights would be spent sleeping beneath a purple sky of undimmed starlight. The next morning, he'd rise with the sun to continue his work, until every inch of the boat's little hold was crammed full of fish. It was during these times that mother and daughter would speak of things more easily discussed in the absence of men.

One night, after the dishes had been washed and put away, Silloah called Annelyse to the master bedroom. Spreading the thick quilt on the floor at the foot of her bed, Silloah invited her daughter to sit with her and relive the memories stored within her hope chest.

Candles that had not been lighted in many years lent their orange glow to the room, as the scent of beeswax wafted through Annelyse's mind like incense. Removing some old dresses from the chest, Silloah draped them over Annelyse until she looked like a queen adorned in flowing robes. With every piece of her mother's jewelry dangling from her neck, wrists, and ears, Annelyse sat with rapt attention. Once the scene had been set, Silloah proceeded to paint a picture of wonder and meaning, using only the gentle sweetness of her words.

Every treasured item had its story; every event held significance. Like links in an endless chain, every twist and turn in the lives of those who'd come before had led Silloah and her daughter to that very moment. No one person constituted the entirety of their story. Everyone was contingent upon those whose lives preceded their own. There was beauty in the continuity of heritage, even if not every narrative was a noble one, and Silloah impressed this upon her daughter. By understanding the stories in which her parents had played a part, Annelyse came to know herself better.

Removing the small wooden box from the depths of the chest, Silloah set it down in her lap with great care.

"I keep in this box those things which my heart would enclose if only it could," she said with a smile reminiscent of young love. "When we were courting, your father wrote me a letter every single day. I have them all still."

A bundle of faded parchment, tied with a twist of yarn, chronicled the story of how her parents had met and fallen in love. What took hold of Annelyse's eye, however, was a heart-shaped locket which hung upon a slender chain of gold.

"Your father gave this to me, during a time of separation early on in our relationship. Forced for a while to remain apart, your father entrusted his heart to me for safekeeping." Silloah smiled and raised the locket to her lips. "It remained around my neck until the day we were married. Only then, when his *own* heart was back where it belonged and we were together, did I place this golden heart in my hope chest."

Annelyse reached into the little box and pulled out a curious thing: an iron key, ordinary in every way, and fitting no lock Annelyse had ever encountered. She held it in her hands, feeling the cold smoothness of its design; smelling its tarnished scent on her fingers; and wondering at its meaning.

"What does this key go to?" Annelyse asked her

mother.

Silloah took the key in her own hands, and with sadness in her voice, she answered, "This key unlocks injustice and injury, my child. For keys can imprison and they can also set free. This one has only ever imprisoned… so far."

Returning the key to its place at the bottom of the box, Silloah turned to her daughter, saying, "One day, you'll know more of such things. When you're old enough and able to do what I no longer can, then it will all be revealed. Until then, I will keep it here with everything else that is precious to me."

Annelyse never forgot the quiet contentment of that evening spent among her mother's treasures. She never forgot the mysterious key, or the romance enclosed in the heart-shaped locket. It was for that locket that she now searched. Her father had entrusted it to her mother in a moment of separation, ensuring she'd never forget his love for her and the promise of their future together. Now, in *this* time of separation, Annelyse needed her father to remember so much that had become too painful for him to recall. Perhaps the locket would help remind him.

Beneath the stack of love letters, Annelyse found what she'd been looking for, and something else that she'd almost forgotten existed. Picking up the ancient iron key, she held it in her hand with the same wonder as when she'd first discovered it with her mother. The words Silloah had spoken returned to her daughter's memory, "One day you'll know more of such things."

"Such things as strange poets and their poems, weird maps, and mysterious Woolems?" Annelyse thought to herself. "The time has come for answers," she whispered aloud, "And this key is just one of a whole lot of questions."

Annelyse slipped the key into her pocket, then took the heart-shaped locket and laid it on the floor beside her.

Carefully placing the wooden box back into the cedar chest, she returned the candles, drawings, and old dresses to their rightful places.

She then noticed something new, something she'd overlooked before. A long, thin, pencil box was tucked down between the side of the cedar chest and the stack of dresses. Annelyse didn't remember her mother ever showing this to her. In fact, she was quite certain that she never had.

Opening the tin box, Annelyse expected to find a set of drawing pencils or calligraphy pens. What she did find had not even crossed her mind. Wrapped in a sheet of tissue paper, dozens of solitary daisies had been preserved with great care. Annelyse realized that these were the flowers her mother had held back from Annelyse's daisy chain crowns. These were the flowers her mother had placed in her own hair. Silloah Bellamy had kept every one of them, more precious to her than gold, as a remembrance of a mother's love for her daughter.

Reaching back into her pocket, Annelyse removed the single daisy she'd found on the boulder down at Ruhner's Beach that morning. She felt that it would make an acceptable payment for the locket and key until she could return them later.

With careful reverence, Annelyse placed the daisy inside the pencil box. Returning the tin to its place, she shut the lid and draped the quilt over the top of the cedar chest. She then put the locket in her pocket and left her parent's bedroom, closing the door behind her.

Dusk hung grey and eerie in the cool air, as the sun began to dip below the crest of the western hills. It was going on 5:30 pm and the early onset of winter evening had not yet been replaced by the lengthening days of spring. It was beginning to look like Mr. Bellamy might not make it home before dark.

Annelyse knew precisely where her father had gone

when he'd left the house a few hours earlier. There was only one place he'd choose to be. Lightview Overlook was where he and Silloah often went to be alone. It was there that they had met, so many years before. It was there that they shared their first kiss, one snowy winter's evening. And it was to Lightview Overlook that they always took their daughter to stargaze. Annelyse now headed toward the narrow point of land with her mother's gold locket in her pocket, determined to try one last time to get through to her father.

Taking the path that split off to the left toward Watcher's Island, Annelyse ran as fast as her feet would carry her. She wanted to reach her father before he left Lightview Overlook, a place filled with memories of her mother. Annelyse knew she'd need all the help she could get, and there was no better help to have than that of her mother.

Rounding a bend in the footpath, she caught sight of her father seated on the ground staring out in the direction of Lower Perigoh Light. Annelyse slowed her pace and approached with care. She didn't want to startle him. The moment he heard her footsteps, Mr. Bellamy wiped his eyes, and turned to face his daughter.

"Hi," she said, pausing a few feet away.

Mr. Bellamy stood to greet her, "Everything alright?"

"I think it can be," she replied, reaching into her pocket. "If only we remember."

Handing the heart-shaped locket to her father, Annelyse took one step back to give him space. More than anything, she wanted him to feel like he was alone with his wife in their favorite place. She wanted her father to see the image of his wife's face reflected in the gold of her locket and hear her voice echoing up from the sea. Maybe then he'd recall everything they'd believed and why it had once made sense to him.

Mr. Bellamy took his wife's locket in his hands and immediately began weeping. Covering his face, he dropped to his knees and released a tidal wave of emotion. Annelyse sat on the ground in front of her father, holding his hand in her own.

"'Do not let the events to come kill what is most precious inside of you,'" she whispered, repeating her mother's words. "As long as we remember what's important, then nothing can kill what's most precious. You gave mom this heart so she wouldn't forget your love. Maybe now she's giving it back, so you won't forget hers."

Mr. Bellamy wrapped his arms around his daughter, and through his tears he confessed, "I once believed as your mother did. I once believed in never-ending things, undying things, even mysteries. But she took all of that with her and left nothing behind."

"She left you this," Annelyse said, grasping the hand in which her father now held the heart-shaped locket.

"And she left me you," he said, looking at his daughter and seeing so much of his wife in her character.

"Then it's up to us to follow her back to all that was precious… all the things that made little sense but were the truest of all. All the things she believed in, and that we once did, too. You know she'd want us to. You know she *wants* us to."

Her father nodded slowly. "'Maps can't guide you to a decision… But this one might start you on your way toward discovery,'" he thought aloud, remembering the inscription scrawled across the poet's map.

"Then let's be on our way," Annelyse replied, rising to her feet.

Taking her hand, Mr. Bellamy said, with resignation, "Very well, then. On our way."

Changing Grief's Landscape

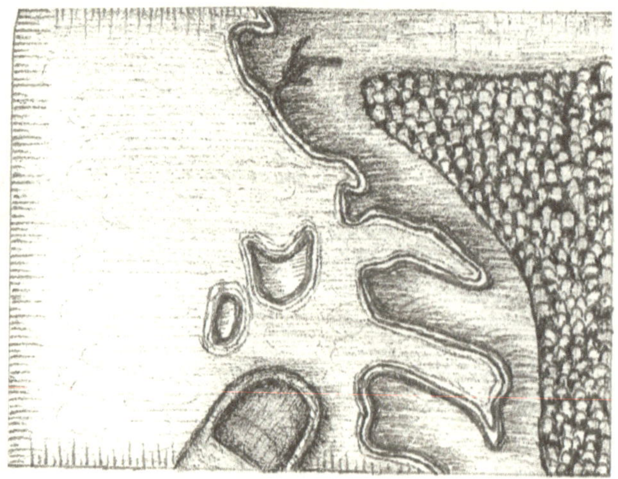

By the time Annelyse and her father returned home from Lightview Overlook, the sun had set beneath the western horizon. In the dark pockets of the meadow, fireflies flickered among the leaves, while tree frogs croaked their rubbery songs in the gathering dew. The moment the sun released its hold on the sky, every living thing was reminded that the days belonged to springtime, but the nights still clung to winter.

While Mr. Bellamy arranged some kindling in the hearth to light a fire large enough to chase the chill from the air, Annelyse hung a kettle over the flames to boil water for their evening tea. The cold, damp sea breeze off Lightview Overlook had invaded their bones; they both needed a warm mug to wrap their hands around.

Annelyse sat down beside the fireplace. Drawing a small table up between her chair and his own, Mr. Bellamy lit a beeswax candle for more light. He then collected the pages of parchment from the kitchen table, laid them out flat beneath the dancing flame, and took his seat beside his daughter.

Handing Annelyse the first page of the poem, he turned the second sheet over and began examining the map.

"Maybe if you read the poem aloud, while I look-over the map, something will begin to make sense. The two go together, we just need to figure out how."

Annelyse agreed. There had to be more to the map than she could see. Perhaps the poem would shed some light on it all.

"'*Where Woolems wandered, west of Wehrle, and ambled airy Averlune...*'" she began, as her father followed along on the map, his finger gliding over every place the poem mentioned.

"This hints at what your mom said about the slave traders of Ruhner's Beach. They were supposed to have kidnapped the Woolems from the lands west of Wehrle… from Averlune and the Fäerie Fields. So far the poem's accurate."

Annelyse continued reading, until she came to, "'*And dancing, sweet, while dolphins dream...*'"

"Windy Point," her father interjected. "There are always dolphins to be found there. They like the brackish waters of the estuary. I've even seen them as far upriver as Pebble Ford. So, either place would fit."

She read on, stopping a moment later with a look of confusion on her face. "What does *jimbled* mean?"

"I don't think it's a word," her father confessed. "He must have made it up. Poets *are* odd creatures."

Annelyse read the entire line, "'*She jumped and jimbled' by the stream where fern and fennel grow.*"

"He must mean the Maidenhair," Mr. Bellamy

guessed. "It runs opposite the Fenneleen, until it loses itself among the trees of the Quibble Woods. There's rumored to be some sort of fern forest somewhere in those cursed woods, though I've never been. It looks like the poem *and* the map are leading us from here to Pebble Ford and up the Maidenhair."

Mr. Bellamy drew an X on the mouth of the Maidenhair River where it meets the Perigoh Fair, while Annelyse kept reading, "'*For, as a minstrel maiden, mild, who tells the Tale of Trinket Trove...*'" She stopped, looking up at her father. "What's Trinket Trove?"

Mr. Bellamy stood, walked over to the hearth, and retrieved the kettle from the fire. Dropping a metal brewing basket into each teacup, he filled them both with hot water, then replaced the kettle. Turning the handle of Annelyse's cup toward her, he sat back down in his chair beside the fireplace.

Edward Bellamy drew a moment of thought from the silence all around, then addressed his daughter's question.

"Trinket Trove is the common name of a place once called Ware Woolem."

"So, it's a real place?" Annelyse asked, having never heard of it before.

"Yes, or it was, anyway. I'm not sure anyone knows much about it nowadays. All I know is that it was in Western Hyland, somewhere between the Quibble Woods and the fishing village of Kwell."

"The poem says that Mom '*told the Tale of Trinket Trove.*'"

"Yes, she sang it often, just like her story of Ruhner's Beach."

"Do you remember it?" Annelyse was hopeful that her father had been paying attention to his wife's story.

"It's in there somewhere," he said, motioning toward his forehead.

"Please, tell me."

"I'll try. But I can't promise I'll get it right."

Taking a sip of tea, Mr. Bellamy rested the cup on his knee, searching through the drawers of his memory for the *Tale of Trinket Trove*. After a moment's thought, he started to speak.

> *"Between the woods of unrest and*
> *the calm of silent Kwell,*
> *a people lived, in ancient times,*
> *where, now, no people dwell.*
>
> *"Their reverence for the gentle beast*
> *of Averlune's Greenfields*
> *compelled them to adorn their town*
> *with sculptures, signs, and seals.*
>
> *"But in the Silent Forest, deep,*
> *where fear and scruples die,*
> *some townsfolk sought a better way,*
> *and bravely questioned, "Why?"*
>
> *"So, gath'ring up the Woolem ware*
> *they'd treasured from their youth,*
> *the people of Ware Woolem dared,*
> *instead, to honor truth.*
>
> *"They carried all their trinkets down*
> *beside the Elmwood Grove,*
> *and, yielding all to crushing depths,*
> *they buried Trinket Trove."*

Mr. Bellamy emptied his teacup then, putting it down on the table between them, looked to Annelyse for her reaction.

"I'm pretty sure that's how it went, though your

mother would have set it to song."

"So, the people of the town buried their statues and pictures of Woolems? I thought they liked the Woolems. And what happened to the town?"

"They did like Woolems; they loved them, in fact. But it seems that they took their love a bit too far and it became an obsession. According to the Tale, they went overboard with all the Woolem stuff, Woolem 'signs and seals.' And all the trinkets seemed to crowd out the truth of what the Woolems *were*, what the Woolems *meant*. They lost the forest for the trees, you might say. They lost the truth in the trinkets. So, they just woke up one day and decided to get rid of it all, to begin again. Where the Trove is buried, no one knows, though there have been some who tried to find out. And now you know as much as I do. I'm afraid I can't tell you any more."

"Just another Mom Mystery, then, huh?" she responded, with unvarnished annoyance. "We'll just add it to the list. Infuriating woman."

Mr. Bellamy smiled at his daughter's sassiness, then moved to change the subject. "Where'd we leave off?" he asked, pointing at the poem Annelyse still held in her hand.

With a grunt and a shake of her head, she continued her reading, "It says, '*Her voice, it vaulted down the vale like kitebirds over Killoughee, but faint and quiet, over quail that slept beside the sea.*'"

Mr. Bellamy rested his hand on Annelyse's arm, stopping her at that point in the poem. Tracing the map with his index finger, he was clearly looking for something.

"Quail," he said. "Beside the sea… right… here."

Jabbing his finger down like an arrow finding its mark, Mr. Bellamy pointed to a long, thin peninsula just east of Upper Perigoh Light. These were the coastal regions of Northern Perigoh Bay, specifically Narrow Nook, War'near, and Catshead Island.

"Those narrow beaches overflow with quail. The

sea oats and saltwater grasses make excellent nesting grounds. This is the only place I know of where quail sleep '*beside the sea.*' And, unlike Killoughee, it's along the route he's leading us on.*"*

The next few lines of the poem, written on the front of the second page, spoke of Narrow Nook, Orchard Knoll, and the horses of upper Hyland. The picture was coming into focus for Mr. Bellamy. The map and the poem were lining up.

"He's clearly taking us up the coast as far north as Orchard Knoll. But I think he wants us to go quite a bit farther."

"Why do you think that?" Annelyse asked, overjoyed to see her father getting wrapped up in the riddle of the map.

"Because the poet not only says the Woolems are real, he says they're still alive, too. And he knows where they are."

"What? Where?"

Annelyse had tried to get that very point out of the young man during their conversation on Ruhner's Beach. When she asked if the Woolems were real, the best answer she received was, "I decided long ago, and now I know the truth of it." His answer had added frustration to her irritation, and now her father was claiming that the poet had, in fact, answered her question after all.

"Where does he say all that?" she demanded, feeling that old, familiar annoyance creeping up on her.

"Right here," her father said, pointing to the first line of the last stanza. "'And *where the Woolems wander, wild…*' Wander. Not wander*ed*. He makes a point of writing it in the present tense."

"Maybe it's a mistake," Annelyse countered. "It's only two letters."

Mr. Bellamy took the other page from her hands and showed her the very first line of the poem, "Look. The only time he uses the past tense is when he talks about the time when the Woolems *used to* live in Averlune. But here, he uses the present tense. He must have meant to. He might be crazy, but he does know his way around a poem."

"Then it's true. It's all true. Mom's story, the poem, even the Woolems. They're real. And the map… the map *will* 'start us on our way,' like the poet said. It already has! Now we know that we *can* find them!"

"If the poet can be believed," Mr. Bellamy cut in with sobering words designed to keep Annelyse's feet on the ground.

"You still don't trust him, do you?" Annelyse wanted very much for her father to change his opinion of the young man.

Mr. Bellamy laid the map on the table, then rubbed his tired forehead.

"It's not that I just don't trust him, Leesy. It's that he's dangerous, irresponsible. He stirs things up that are better left alone. He's a meddler, and I don't care for him one bit."

Annelyse felt as if she'd suffered a setback and that her father might change his mind about helping her with her quest. Again, it wasn't just her desire to better understand her mother, or to search for these Woolems that had begun to mean so much to her. It was her hope of bringing her father out of the darkness of his grief back into the light. She was afraid that this hope was beginning to slip through her fingers.

"Then… why follow the map? Why go looking for the Woolems with me?"

"It's not about the poet, or his map, or the blasted Woolems." Mr. Bellamy took Annelyse's hand in his, "It's about you. Even if it's all nonsense, you're the truest thing I know… you and your mother. I would follow you anywhere, just to be with you… and for the chance to touch her heart one more time."

"I can't stay here," Annelyse whispered. "No matter where I look, I can't find *her* anymore. All I find are shadows of her, places she *used to* be. I can't stay here, not until Mom is here, too. Not until I can bring back some piece of her, some piece of her that I never had before, and so haven't already lost. I have to get out of this house and find what it was that made it home."

"I know. I feel the same way. So, let's go. Not for the adventure. Not to find mysteries, but just to find your mother. There are things she knew that I want to know, too. Knowing them, we can know her better. We can touch her again. I don't know how, but we have to try. Remember, we have a map, and that's not nothing."

Mr. Bellamy smiled, and his smile bore the weight of grief and lost hopes, shattered lives, and broken expectations. It was a fading smile and, if its light was allowed to go out altogether, it might never shine again.

Straightening herself in her chair, Annelyse put on her best business face, and with stony determination, asked, "So, where do we start?"

Mr. Bellamy smoothed out the map on the table between them.

"We need a goal," he said, surveying the area represented in the upper right-hand corner of the map. "And since the first place outside of Averlune that the poem mentions is the horse country north of the Knoll, perhaps that's as good a goal as any. If we hope to have any chance of learning anything about the Woolems, then following your mother's route through the poem is our best bet."

"What's the quickest way to get to Orchard Knoll?" Annelyse asked, looking over her father's shoulder at the map.

"I'm afraid there is no quick way to get there from here. The waters north of Perigoh Bay are too dangerous for our little fishing skiff. I wouldn't even trust it to navigate the eddies of the estuary between Windy Point and the Fenneleen. And there is no direct inland waterway, either. Our safest route is overland, and that means crossing the Perigoh Fair at Pebble Ford, then heading northwest from there."

Annelyse knew the region of upper Averlune well. She knew that the only way to reach Pebble Ford from the peninsula was by crossing the Fenneleen Stream. This was no small feat. The icy waters of the Fenneleen would sooner drown a man than provide safe passage through its rapids. Reaching Orchard Knoll might be the goal but surviving the frigid Fenneleen was their first major challenge. Everything depended upon their success on the banks of this swift and deadly stream.

"But the Fenneleen," she objected, sensing the danger involved in their quest.

Her father looked up from the map, "It's all about knowing where to put your feet."

Folding the poem, Mr. Bellamy set it aside and drew his chair closer to Annelyse's.

"I don't question your resolve, Leesy. I just want to be sure you understand what we're up against. The plan is to follow the poem and the map over Pebble Ford all the way to Orchard Knoll and beyond. While I know the lands between here and the ford, I've never been so far as the Miralette River. Everything I've heard about the Quibble Woods, the Silent Forest, and the Far Reaches is not very encouraging. What I'm trying to say is, what I know of our journey is bad enough, what I don't know may be too much altogether. There's no guarantee that the Woolems still exist, much less, that we'll be lucky enough to find them. Are you ready to make this journey, even if it ends in failure?"

"I need to know, Daddy. I need to find out what Mom knew. The only way I could fail is if I *didn't* try."

Speaking slowly and with emphasis, Mr. Bellamy

held his daughter's attention firmly in the grip of each word, "It will be dangerous… and we may lose more than we find. But if you understand this, and you're still determined to go, then it's settled."

"What more could we lose? We've lost too much already."

"Each other, child," Mr. Bellamy said, with gravity. "We could lose each other."

The coals in the fireplace throbbed beneath a blanket of grey ash. It was nearly 9 pm, and the cold night air was beginning to creep in under doors and through cracks between the logs of the cabin walls. On the table between Annelyse and her father, the candle had burned down and spread itself into a flat wafer of wax. The toppled wick was all but extinguished, when Mr. Bellamy stood and handed the poem back to his daughter.

"This is yours. You should hang on to it and be sure to bring it along. Pack only what you'll want to carry on your back for the next month or so. We'll leave at first light, and plan to make camp on the other side of the Fenneleen before nightfall, tomorrow. I need to go speak with Elmer Ganley about taking care of the farm while we're away. With all those little Ganleys to feed, he'll be glad for the extra eggs and vegetables. Don't wait up for me."

"Daddy," Annelyse whispered, unsure of how to say what was in her heart, "thank you for… well, I thought for sure you wouldn't… just… thank you."

"Thank me if we make it home again," he replied, with not nearly as much humor in his tone as Annelyse would have liked to hear. "Get some sleep. This will be the last night you sleep in a bed for quite some time. Enjoy it. Goodnight, Leesy."

Mr. Bellamy grabbed a jacket from the coat pegs in the entryway, pulled the door closed behind him, and headed down the lane toward Elmer Ganley's homestead.

The Ganley's were always happy to look after their neighbors' farms, in a pinch. The extra eggs, milk, and produce were a welcome boost to their own overtaxed pantry.

Elmer and his wife, Adelaide, had eleven children, which was always a sore subject for Adelaide who had an acute dislike of odd numbers. She felt that, if only they'd had twins somewhere along the way, that would have evened-up the tally quite nicely with only half the effort.

Nowhere was the shortage more annoyingly obvious than at the dinner table. No matter how she tried to space them out and stagger their seating, there was no getting past the fact that six children on one side of the table and five on the other was an afront to symmetry.

Still, the Ganleys were kind and amiable neighbors who never asked questions and were always happy to help. In fact, this was precisely the answer Mr. Bellamy received when he arrived, unannounced and at an impolite hour, and asked his neighbors to take care of his pigs, chickens, and garden for a month or more. No questions were asked.

Instead, Elmer Ganley said, with a look of relief on his careworn face, "Happy to help."

It would have been more accurate, had he said, "Happy *for the* help," since feeding a family of thirteen people (eleven kids plus two parents) was a formidable task. For Elmer's part, he always wished they'd had one fewer child, though, depending on the moment, he was hard-pressed to say exactly which one. He felt that thirteen was an unlucky number to end on, and a family of twelve just sounded that much easier to feed.

With a handshake and a, "Thanks, Elmer," Edward Bellamy walked the mile or so back up the lane to his own little homestead by the sea. Upon entering the handsome log cabin he'd built with his own hands, he found his daughter packed, saddled with her knapsack, and ready to go.

"What are you doing up still?"

"Can't sleep," came her matter-of-fact reply.

"How hard did you try? Looks like you spent the last hour packing everything you own. What d'you have in that knapsack of yours?

From the front, Annelyse looked much like an oyster on a half shell. From the side, she looked more like a snail. Either way, if her lumpy backpack had legs it could have much more easily carried Annelyse than she looked able to carry it.

"Just the essentials," she said, adjusting the shoulder straps.

"Nothing changes your idea of *essentials* faster than a cross-country hike with forty pounds on your back. Anyway, I'm not willing to give up my last night in a bed. I'll pack my *essentials* in three minutes and be asleep in five. 'Night, Lumpy."

Mr. Bellamy kissed his daughter on the head, then turned and headed to his bedroom. The moment his hand touched the doorknob, Annelyse spoke up.

"Daddy?"

Mr. Bellamy paused and turned around, "Aye?"

"Are we crazy to do this?"

"Stay up all night?" her father asked, his exhaustion deepening the lines in his forehead, "Without a doubt."

"This trip, I mean. Are we crazy to think we'll actually find anything?"

"We'll find something. We just don't know *what*, yet. Besides, it was your idea, so if anyone's crazy…"

Annelyse was too tired for even mild humor. She was beginning to have real doubts about the whole trip.

"It's just that… well, I don't really know… I'm starting to think…"

"You're tired. This is no more than fear of the unknown darkening a sleepy brain. Take off the turtle pack, put on your PJs, and get some sleep. Never make decisions when you're exhausted, especially when the decision has already been made. Goodnight, then."

With a nod, Mr. Bellamy went off to bed. Annelyse sloughed the backpack off her shoulders, set it carefully on top of the kitchen table, and ascended the ladder to her loft. Within moments of hitting her pillow, she was fast asleep.

In the corner beneath her bed sat a heap of navy blue and white strips of fabric. In her pocket, an old iron key lay alongside two pages of parchment. She didn't dare forget to bring the poem and its hand-drawn map. But, just as essential, was the key she'd taken from her mother's hope chest.

She didn't yet know why she felt so compelled to bring it along on their journey to find the Woolems. But in a world of mystery, explanations and full understanding are rare. Annelyse was resolved to follow her gut instincts, the poem, and the map wherever they might lead her. Bringing the key along was just another hunch.

Between the torn shreds of dress beneath her bed and the uncertain quest she and her father were about to embark upon, Annelyse now sat at a crossroads. Her life stretched out in ruins behind her, a teetering tower of unanswered questions. Before her lay unknown dangers and unsure outcomes. But we only ever move forward; turning back is never really possible. If she hoped to learn anything more about her mother, if she hoped to discover the truth about the Woolems, forward was the only direction available to her.

The excitement of unraveling the poem had led Annelyse to believe that answers could be found; her mother could be revealed; and even the Woolems might be discovered. But, as she'd sat at the kitchen table that evening waiting for her father to come home, a thought had occurred to Annelyse, maybe the journey itself was enough. Maybe all she needed was to go wandering, and reaching her goal wasn't as important as she'd thought. At least wandering would bring her some relief from the countless constant reminders of an empty home. She'd walk a thousand miles to escape the ceaseless attacks of the grief snipers.

Now, as she slept away the remaining hours before leaving home for the wide wilderness, her restless mind was at peace for the first time in months. This peace would be quickly lost, though, with the rising of the sun. In the waking exhaustion of self-questioning, she would find herself once more trying to reconcile everything she'd ever taken for granted with all the events of the last few months.

But, for now, her greatest enemy – her all-too-active mind– was asleep, and her heart was free to drift among her dreams of what Woolems might look like, and where, at last, they might be found.

As Annelyse and her father spent their last night sleeping in beds, miles away a young man sat beneath an alder tree in a grove beside the banks of the Fenneleen Stream. In his backpack, a leather-bound journal held musings and snippets of various poems finished and unfinished. As he dozed in drowsy contentment, he whispered softly to himself, "I went where I knew you'd be," then drifted off to sleep.

Overcoming Fear with Wonder

Lower Perigoh Light towered over the waters off the peninsula, winking its warning through the early morning mist. Opening her eyes, Annelyse heard her father cooking breakfast in the kitchen below. For a moment, she was seized by the fear that she was reliving the morning of her mother's funeral. Every detail was the same.

Then it occurred to her. Fearing she was reliving something was proof that it had already been lived. Once lived, it was most unlikely that a thing could be lived a second time. And so, it was a very silly thought, indeed. It wasn't often that her painfully practical mind brought her much comfort, but this morning was one of those rare moments. She was already fully dressed and (over-)packed, so getting ready wouldn't take her long at all. She decided to spend the time she'd saved by preparing the night before the best way she knew how, in bed. Rolling over, she buried her face in her pillow, cradling it in her arms.

Every morning for the past several weeks, a mockingbird had visited the pear tree outside Annelyse's window, long before sunrise. The visitor would spend the better half of an hour performing its long list of impersonations, on random shuffle mode, at the top of its powerful lungs. Annelyse was convinced that the mockingbird's sole purpose was to interrupt her sleep with its untimely racket.

Flipping her pillow over on top of her head, Annelyse pulled it down around her ears and growled at the culprit in the pear tree. Undeterred, the mockingbird continued its mockery. Exasperated, Annelyse opened her window in a huff and hissed as loudly as she could. But the bird took no notice, turning up the volume instead.

Desperate to enjoy the few moments she had left before being forced to leave her bed for who-knows-how-long, Annelyse reached down and grabbed one of her hiking boots from the floor. Swinging it up over her head, she sent it sailing through the window and into the pear tree outside. The poor mockingbird was caught off guard and only narrowly escaped being clocked on the head, a fate that would have surely affected its ability to impersonate much of anything ever again.

Though successful in scaring away her uninvited guest, Annelyse's boot failed to return to earth. Instead, it remained stuck in the tree a good eight feet above the ground.

"Ugh!" she grunted, slamming her window shut with a shock that rattled the glass. "Great."

Adrenaline pumping and annoyance levels on the rise, Annelyse gave up on sleep and got up, prematurely ending her last morning in bed. Brushing her teeth and washing her face, she tied her hair in a ponytail; made her bed; and left her room both neat and tidy, exactly the way she wanted to find it upon her return. Beneath her restlessness, a part of her was still looking forward to coming home.

A few moments later, Annelyse descended the ladder carrying her one remaining hiking boot in her hand.

"Breakfast is… where's your other boot?" her father asked, setting his daughter's plate on the kitchen table.

"In the pear tree," she said, taking her seat.

"I won't ask," Mr. Bellamy replied, joining her. "Let's eat up. It's trail food from here on, I'm afraid."

Mr. Bellamy had cooked everything he'd found in the larder that morning, intending to leave no food behind to go to waste. As a result, Annelyse discovered an eclectic assortment on her plate. Five eggs; six strips of bacon; half a chicken breast; three slices of tomato; a dollop of butterscotch pudding; and two shrimp, leftover from the evening before, overflowed onto her placemat.

Her father's plate was even more unappetizingly varied. Still, they both knew that this meal constituted a feast compared to the days and weeks ahead. So, no one complained, as they found new ways of pairing pudding and shrimp together to make them go down and stay down.

"Our best bet is to head southeast toward the mountain," Mr. Bellamy said, between bites of boiled fish and breakfast sausage.

Annelyse was surprised. She'd figured they'd cut east across the peninsula toward the mouth of the Fenneleen where it meets the Perigoh Fair. Traveling south in the direction of Mt. Averly didn't make sense to her.

"Wouldn't it be faster to follow the river?"

"It would… right up until we got there." Mr. Bellamy washed his last shrimp down with what remained of the tomato juice. "The time we'd save by heading due east would be lost when we tried crossing the Fenneleen at its mouth. Even if that were possible."

"Where do we cross, then?"

"Well, normally, you'd ford a river at its widest point. It's shallow where it's wide, and deep where it's narrow. Most folks try to cross with as few wet steps as possible. But, since narrow means deep, those few steps could be their last. The Fenneleen is different, though. Even at its widest, it's still deadly deep – and fast. So, we need a different solution. The mountain will give us that."

Finishing his breakfast, Mr. Bellamy got up from the table and began stuffing an old burlap sack with apples, potatoes, smoked sausages, dried fish, and beef jerky. Everything that had been left in their larder after their mismatched meal now ended up in the bag.

"I'll take the canteens down to the well and fill 'em, if you clean up here."

Annelyse forced the last forkful of eggs down, followed by the rest of her milk, then began collecting plates and cups. By the time she'd washed, dried, and put away the dishes, her father had returned with the canteens. All was now ready, except for one small detail.

"I found this on my way back up the hill," Mr. Bellamy said, handing Annelyse a solitary hiking boot. "It looks a lot like your other one. I figured they might be a pair."

Annelyse's face flushed red, as she took the boot from her father.

"Thanks. I was wondering where it went," she grimaced, shamefaced and repentant.

"I'm sure you were."

Loading themselves down with backpacks and supplies, sacks and canteens, Annelyse and her father paused a moment before walking outside. All of a sudden, the little cabin seemed to be more inviting and homier than it had been just moments before. After all, it was the only home Annelyse had ever known. She was now quite reluctant to trade it for the open spaces of the wild unknown.

Everywhere her eyes came to rest, Annelyse was reminded of a moment in time. There were the teeth marks on the edge of the kitchen table where she'd learned as a child that it's fun to bite things, but impossible to hide bite marks from your parents. There was the crack in the floor tile where her mother had dropped a jar of pickles when she'd realized she'd pickled a black beetle along with them.

The pencil marks on the kitchen doorframe, measuring out each milestone of Annelyse's growth for the last 14 years, were written in her mother's own hand. She remembered straining up onto her tiptoes, trying to gain just one more inch, until her mother pushed her back down on her heels.

Then she saw something that brought a lump to her throat. In a rocking chair Mr. Bellamy had made for his wife, there sat a cushion which bore the imprint of every hour Silloah had spent sitting by the fire. In her mind's eye, Annelyse saw herself as a child seated on her mother's lap, listening to stories of ages long past, while her mother tussled her hair. Upon that cushion sat a lifetime of happiness, but nothing more than memories ever again.

Blinking her eyes, the vision disappeared. In its place, an unseen swarm, like spores on the stagnant air, took aim at her grieving heart. The unlikely image of her mother's chair cushion had been all the cover the grief snipers required from which to launch their attack.

But before the tears had time to pool in her eyes, Annelyse remembered why it was that she so desperately wanted to leave that house. There were questions that needed answering. There were stories that needed to be proven true or false. She was ready, beyond any hesitation, to be on her way.

Without a word, Annelyse walked out the front door. She didn't look back. She didn't even wait for her father but headed straight down the path that led to the road. Behind her, Mr. Bellamy closed the door, turned the key in its lock, then rested one hand on the lintel, pausing a moment before turning his back on the little log cabin by the sea. There were tears in his eyes, as he walked away. Foiled by Annelyse, the grief snipers had found their mark in the heart of her father.

Reaching the end of the path where it met the lane, Mr. Bellamy buried his sadness, put a smile in his voice, and called ahead to Annelyse, "Don't wait for me! I'm only the guy carrying all your food."

Halting dead in her tracks, Annelyse turned, with a false look of alarm on her face, "Whew! I'm glad I didn't lose *you*! Need some help?"

"How would you fit anything else inside that overstuffed turkey of yours? Anyway, I think the food's safer with me, thanks."

"Suit yourself," Annelyse replied, with hidden relief. She was certain she wouldn't be able to carry another ounce on her already drooping shoulders.

Rounding a curve in the lane just past the Ganley farm, the trees began to thin out. Unbroken fields of alfalfa rolled away to the south, like an expanse of green, rippling waves. Off to the east, the sun had just roused itself from another night's sleep, painting Mt. Averly's snowcap in pastel pinks and baby blues.

The mountain appeared much closer than it really was, a testament to its height as compared to the low profile of the surrounding pastureland. But, at a little over 22 miles away, it would take nearly 10 hours for Annelyse and her father to reach the northern foot of the mountain. They would then have to contend with the swift waters of the

Fenneleen before setting up camp for the night. Theirs was a mostly straight, flat route through the meadows of upper Averlune, and that fact would hopefully give speed to their journey.

At first, Mr. Bellamy led from the front, with Annelyse following in silence a few feet behind. But once Mt. Averly was clearly in view, Annelyse needed no guide except the mountain itself. Walking next to her father now, she was better positioned to engage him in conversation. She had a confession to make.

"What did Mr. Ganley say?" Annelyse inquired, testing the waters.

This was a strange question, since Annelyse could assume with certainty that Mr. Ganley had agreed to watch over the Bellamy farm in their absence, otherwise they would not have left. Mr. Bellamy sensed that his daughter was up to something. He decided to have some fun with her.

"Mr. Ganley said he was tired of people pushing their produce on him and he wouldn't stand for it any longer."

Mr. Bellamy watched Annelyse's reaction out of the corner of his eye, suspecting that she was using her silly question as an ice breaker and really had no interest in his answer.

"That's nice," she said, her mind already occupied with her next question. "I always liked Mr. Ganley. Mrs. Ganley was always a bit bothered by numbers, I thought. Always trying to find ways to add or subtract *one*… kinda odd, really."

"Not with that many kids, it isn't," Mr. Bellamy pointed out, with a chuckle. "But Adelaide Ganley has no love for *odd* numbers, true enough."

Annelyse was still ignoring her father pretty thoroughly. "That Esther, though. I never knew *what* to make of her. She used to pull my ponytail, then run off and tell her mother that I pulled hers! I'm sure Mrs. Ganley thinks I'm a perfect monster."

"I'm sure Mrs. Ganley thinks nothing of the sort," Mr. Bellamy replied, knowing he was still being ignored. He was well aware of the fact that his daughter preferred the sound of her own voice to that of anyone else's.

"Daddy?"

"Here it comes," Mr. Bellamy thought to himself, then aloud he replied, "What is it Leesy?"

"I did something."

"What sort of thing did you do?"

"I took something."

"Oh? What's that?" Mr. Bellamy was a patient man. One had to be, with Annelyse around.

"This," she said, pulling the iron key from her pocket. "I found it in Mom's hope chest."

"You found it?" Her father asked, knowing full well there was more to Annelyse's story.

"Well, she showed it to me. And then yesterday, I went into the chest and took it."

"What's it go to? I've never seen it before." Mr. Bellamy eyed the big, iron key.

"You've never seen it?"

"No. It fits no lock I know of. As far as I'm concerned, you can have it."

Annelyse's curiosity was piqued. How was it possible that her father had no knowledge of the key's existence? He was acquainted with everything in that hope chest; had this one item been overlooked? Annelyse was sure that her mother must have kept the key for a reason. It must have had some purpose, some significance. Annelyse tucked it back into the safety of her pocket alongside the poem, map, and all her other unanswered questions.

"I thought we might need it," she said to her father. "So, I brought it along."

Annelyse felt the weakness of her words. She knew

how ridiculous they sounded.

"What we really need is a bridge," Edward proposed, looking ahead to all the challenges they would face. "You wouldn't happen to have one of *those* in your pocket, would you?"

Annelyse made no answer. She was lost in thought. Walking alongside her father, she thought only of the key in her pocket. She felt silly, stupid, even, "Who brings a key on a camping trip?" How many doors did she really expect to find in the fields and forests along their route? Despite every objection her brain could conceive, her heart was assured. The key was essential. Intuition rarely gives its reasons, but then, its track record often speaks for itself.

As the path they'd been following intersected with another, Mr. Bellamy paused a moment to consider which one to take. Footpaths in upper Averlune shift like sandbars in the sea, as farmers alternate between cultivating and letting their fields lie dormant. Livestock react accordingly, following different grazing patterns depending upon which fields were left fallow. In the process, new paths are created, and old ones soon grow-over. So, it wasn't surprising that Mr. Bellamy was wrestling with which to follow.

"Are we lost already?" Annelyse said, in her usual saucy manner.

"I'm afraid so," came her father's confirmation.

"Really?" Annelyse hadn't expected that.

"If we're going to make it to Mt. Averly and cross the Fenneleen before nightfall, we need to make the right choice here and now. Otherwise, we could waste hours on the wrong path. Wait here."

Mr. Bellamy walked on ahead for several minutes, until he was able to see around a bend in the path they'd been on. Returning to where Annelyse stood waiting, he seemed to be more confident of their route.

"I think we want to follow the new road. It slopes

upward and more southerly. Unless I'm mistaken, the path we were on curves down to the west toward Averly Point. This is the way to go. I'm certain of it. Come on."

The moment the decision was made, and Mr. Bellamy started walking, Annelyse took one step then froze in place, stricken with fear.

"Daddy," she whispered, failing to get her father's attention. She repeated herself, this time, louder.

"Daddy!"

Mr. Bellamy turned to look over his shoulder, "What is it, Leesy?"

Annelyse's face blanched white as mist, as she struggled to answer her father.

"There," she said, trembling, "Behind that tree."

Mr. Bellamy moved to position himself between his daughter and whatever it was lurking in the shadows. He made no quick movements, but remained silent as thought, until he could determine exactly what it was that had frightened Annelyse. Wrapping both hands tightly around the walking stick he'd been carrying, Edward Bellamy was ready for anything.

From behind a red maple tree, a slow, slinking movement disturbed the tall grass. An area of more than six feet in length now shook with each breath the concealed creature took. A flash of brown fur revealed enough of the animal to make Annelyse draw herself up close to her father. Resting both hands against his back, she peered over his shoulder with terror.

Without warning, one of the tufts of grass disguising the beast disappeared, as if cut off at the base and swallowed whole by the earth. A long, sloping back of short, chestnut fur was now clearly visible, framed by what remained of the undergrowth.

Mr. Bellamy loosened his grip on the walking stick.

"Squat down," he said over his left shoulder.

"What?"

"Squat. Down."

"Shouldn't we run?!"

"There's no outrunning this foe," Mr. Bellamy said, with a hint of something comical in his eyes. "It's better just to get down low and hold one arm out."

"Hold an arm out?!"

"Like this," he said, kneeling and extending his right hand in the direction of the mysterious creature.

Annelyse wasn't sure what to make of her father's behavior. She'd seen the tuft of grass disappear. She knew that any animal capable of extinguishing a wide swathe of meadow like that was clearly dangerous.

Squirming to fit herself behind her squatting father, Annelyse complained with a whine, "Daddy, stand up…"

"Leesy, calm yourself," he chuckled, unable to hide the humor of the situation any longer. "It's only a Leporidae."

"A *leopard*?!"

"No, child," Mr. Bellamy laughed, "A Leporidae. Notoriously vicious and deadly to vegetables of every kind."

"A Leporidae?" she repeated, still confused, but beginning to fear that maybe she was acting foolishly.

"Yes," her father said, picking up a handful of grass and holding it out toward the half-concealed creature. "A bunny."

"But it's huge!"

Poking through the tall grass, a large pink nose twitched with curiosity in the direction of Mr. Bellamy's outstretched hand. A moment later, one ear followed by a second pushed their way through the thick undergrowth. Before long, the largest rabbit either Annelyse or her father had ever seen stood in the clearing, merrily munching on the succulent weeds in Mr. Bellamy's hand.

"Careful, Daddy," Annelyse cautioned, still overwhelmed by the rabbit's enormous size.

"She's an herbivore, Leesy. It's unlikely she'll bite my arm off. Look how beautiful she is."

Mr. Bellamy reached out his left hand and rested it on the rabbit's back. At first, the spot where he touched the bunny quivered. But as he stroked the soft fur, the rabbit soon ignored his attentions altogether. She was far more interested in eating.

"Come pet her."

Annelyse walked around her father's right side and carefully began petting the rabbit's back. She could feel the warmth of the great creature and wanted very much to wrap her arms around its neck and bury her face in its brown fur.

"It's so enormous, I could ride on its back!"

At the suggestion of being ridden, the bunny stopped chewing and looked Annelyse dead in the eyes. With a slow and deliberate shake of its head - back and forth, back and forth - it appeared to be responding to Annelyse's impertinent suggestion.

"Oh, well, I didn't mean… that is, I'd never…"

Content that it had made itself clear, the rabbit returned to its chewing.

"Did you see that?" Mr. Bellamy said. "It's almost as if she understood what you were saying. I could've sworn, she… No, that's nonsense." Changing the subject, he continued, "We should get moving if we hope to make it to Mt. Averly by nightfall."

Reluctant to say goodbye to the remarkable rabbit, Annelyse took advantage of this once-in-a-lifetime, chance meeting to give it a big hug. The bunny didn't mind one bit. But, as they started down the new path they had chosen earlier, the rabbit suddenly took three giant, thundering hops and landed in front of them, blocking their way in no uncertain terms.

"Go on, then," Mr. Bellamy said, "Move aside."

The rabbit didn't budge an inch but sat there grooming itself in the middle of the footpath.

"Maybe she doesn't want us to go this way," Annelyse suggested.

"What does a rabbit care which way we go?" her father countered. "Even one so big as this."

Mr. Bellamy approached the bunny, intending to walk around behind her, but she simply repositioned herself in his way. Trying a different tactic, Mr. Bellamy now attempted to walk in front of the rabbit but was met with the same result. Try as they might, the remarkable, obstinate bunny would not let them take their chosen path.

"We'll waste more time arguing with this stubborn creature than we would just cutting across fields for a while. The thick grass'll slow us down, but as long as we keep the mountain in view, we can't go far wrong."

Doffing his hat to the tenacious rabbit, Mr. Bellamy led the way off the footpath and into the tall grass of the surrounding fields. Annelyse decided to press her luck and steal one more hug before leaving the bunny for good. Pausing a moment from its fastidious grooming routine, the rabbit accepted the uninvited hug with patience, then returned to the task at hand.

Watching Annelyse and her father recede into the distance, the rabbit waited until they were swallowed up by the green landscape and well out of sight, before hopping down the path it had been blocking. A few yards away, it arrived at its destination, the largest rabbit den Annelyse could have ever hoped to see - had she been allowed to, that is. The path Mr. Bellamy had chosen was no path at all, but an approach to her home, made and guarded by the mother rabbit.

Inside the den, three unusually large baby bunnies lay sleeping in fluffy contentment. Pushing her way through the opening, the mother lay down beside her children, and pressed her soft belly against them for warmth. As she did, one of the three babies stirred in his sleep. Caressing his forehead with her cheek, the remarkably large mother rabbit whispered, "There now, sleep, little one."

CHAPTER SEVEN

Struggling Over Obstacles

Annelyse and her father had been wading through hip-high grass for hours, when they finally happened upon another footpath. This time, there was no doubt about where it led, being marked by an arrow which read, "Mt. Averly –> 10 miles."

"I wonder if this is Middlelune," Mr. Bellamy said, scrutinizing the landmarks. "It's been years since I've walked these paths, but I recall a north-south road the locals called Middlelune Lane. My guess is we're standing on it now. If so, then it's a straight shot to Mt. Averly from here. We should be able to make it by 4:00 pm, if we put a good foot beneath us.”

"4:30,” Annelyse haggled, “It’s noon, now. Back home, that means lunch.”

"Make it 4:10,” her father settled, “We’ll take a *short* break and dig out something to eat on the road. I don’t wanna waste more than ten minutes and risk having to make camp in the dark.”

Annelyse never considered eating to be a waste of time. Furthermore, she was in no hurry to dip her feet in the icy Fenneleen. She was quite happy to enjoy a moment’s rest, if she were allowed – which didn’t appear likely.

Choosing a soft, sunny spot, Annelyse plopped down on her bottom, then laid back among the wildflowers. The spring sun warmed her face and glistened in the gold of her hair, while the perfume of a thousand different nectars tickled her freckled nose with delight.

Closing her eyes, Annelyse was attuned to the sound of a squadron of bees busy at work nearby. She felt as if she were sinking into a great, green pillow of nature’s wonders. If she’d been able, she would have pulled the meadow up around her shoulders like a downy comforter and dozed the lazy day away.

Removing her hiking boots with some difficulty, she freed her feet from their socks and wiggled her toes in the cool breeze. Annelyse was in her element and anyone who knew her knew she could stay there for hours.

"Don’t get too comfortable, Leesy Marie. We won’t be here long.”

Despite his use of her middle name, Annelyse decided to take her chances and “get too comfortable,” as her father had put it. Every second without those hiking boots on her feet was worth the trouble of having to lace them back up again.

Overhead, a herd of fluffy clouds meandered through the sky, sparking the question in her mind about what Woolems might look like. Did their name indicate a sheep-like animal, some sort of variation on square bails of wool with spindly legs? Or were they smaller, like plump, curious cotton balls? With her hands behind her head, Annelyse closed her eyes and lost herself in her pleasant daydream.

After a few minutes, Mr. Bellamy brought a canteen, an apple, and a couple slices of beef jerky to his daughter. "Drink up. We'll refill on the mountain. This'll tide us over until we make camp. Up you go!"

And with that, Annelyse's short break was over, her boots were laced up, and the first of many walking-meals commenced. She loved beef jerky. She could eat barrels of it without every craving anything more than its sweet, salty tang. But apples always made her feel hungrier after eating one than she'd felt before taking a bite. She never quite knew why that was. So, Annelyse decided to stow the apple in her backpack and concentrate on the much more satisfying jerky.

As they drew closer to Mt. Averly, the wildflower meadows gradually thinned out into a sporadic carpet of greens and browns. Fewer and fewer trees now punctuated the landscape, as the grass dispersed itself in patches of sparse stubble. The ground was now heavily strewn with stray stones of various sizes, like oversized chicken scratch scattered in a barnyard.

Much to Annelyse's puzzlement, there wasn't a hill or rise in sight. One might have expected Mt. Averly to mount its heights on the backs of foothills, but the path Annelyse and Edward were on was as flat and level as one could hope for on a cross-country trek. However, one new feature did begin to make an appearance.

Portions of Mt. Averly's western and northwestern feet lie just below sea level. Centuries of erosion have laid bare the living bones of the mountain, and the endless ebbs and flows of tidewater have forged numerous inroads around its base. As a result, saltwater marshes appear with high tide, and with low tide, they become treacherous quicksand. It was the scent of these swamplands that Annelyse now sensed.

"Are you sure we didn't take a wrong turn?" she asked from behind.

"That's Averly in front of us," her father replied, assuring her they were still on course.

"But I smell the ocean."

"What you smell are her fingers wrapped around the feet of the mountain. Very soon, we'll need to mind our step, or run the risk of being seized from below."

And Annelyse thought the giant bunny behind the maple tree was frightening. She'd been dreading the Fenneleen, but now, the quicksand lurking in the marshland around Mt. Averly made crossing the deadly stream look tame in comparison.

It was nearly 3:00 pm, and they'd been walking nonstop since 6:00 that morning. Annelyse decided not to count the 10-minute break she'd had around noon, since some of those minutes were spent removing her hiking boots and even more of those minutes were spent putting them back on again (it's always faster removing than putting on, for some reason).

The remaining few minutes - though wonderfully pleasant - spent lying in the grass did not constitute much of a break from walking, and only a brief break from fiddling with her boots. All of this added up to a full 9 hours of walking, in Annelyse's assessment.

The landscape in which they'd been traveling had changed dramatically within the span of one hour. Fields and meadows receded like floodwaters in the direction of the northern horizon, leaving rocky moonscapes in their wake. Cattails and reeds began popping up unexpectedly, as the land fell away into muddy ditches and moist depressions.

Everywhere she looked, Annelyse was surprised to find boulders covered with moss on top and sea barnacles on the bottom. Like the mountain itself, these fractures of stone lived half on land and half in the sea. Nature itself was in turmoil, struggling with an identity crisis on a vast scale. On the one hand, tidal basins and narrow waterways slithered through the increasingly sloppy landscape. On the other hand, even the ubiquitous residue of salt could not deter wildflowers from taking root in every crack and crevice they could find. The drama played out on every side, as the shadow of Mt. Averly now lay itself at the feet of the cautious travelers.

"Stay right behind me," Mr. Bellamy instructed. "Put your feet only in my footprints… unless I go under. In that case, well… don't."

Annelyse was not amused.

On heightened awareness now, she scrupulously followed her father's instructions. Not only was she careful to walk in his footsteps, but she also kept a watchful eye on where he chose to put his feet. She was anxious for them both to avoid the grip of the quicksand.

Tiptoeing their way through the muck of the salt plains, their pace slowed to a crawl. All around them lay reminders of the deadly greed of the mire. Skeletons of birds who had landed only to examine a crab or scoop up a sand flea, now stood silent and motionless, one leg trapped in the thick muck. Like driftwood, fish bones littered the divots where saltwater had been trapped by the receding tide. In the long hours before the rising tide returned to carry them home, a thirsty sun had drained away the fishes' hopes of survival.

At one point, Edward's right boot slipped and started to sink into the gurgling mud. Seeing her father lose his balance and succumb to the suction of the quicksand, Annelyse grabbed his arm, pulling with all her might. In a moment of quick action, Edward used the walking stick he'd been carrying to brace himself against a stone and extract his foot before the rest of him followed.

Annelyse looked at the ground beneath her feet with deep distrust and mounting fatigue. The ever-present danger seemed to add weight to the burdens on their backs, as if their packs had been stuffed with stones. Even their legs were limp, lifeless sandbags, just another load for them to carry.

With all their powers of concentration trained on the task at hand, not a word was spoken. Not a sound was made. With the mountain approaching, they were cautious to avoid faltering so close to their goal. Annelyse imagined that her last sight as she sunk into the viscous darkness would be that of nearby Mt. Averly, and how humiliating a failure that would be.

Every step was taken with great deliberation, as the minutes grew heavy, and the spinning of the earth ground to a halt. It was not unlike threading their way through a minefield; any step could be disastrous. Neither Annelyse nor her father looked up, so intent were they on the perils at their feet, as they spent the better part of an hour holding their breath and trekking their way through this somber swampland.

But, with terror still throbbing in their ears, they now began to see that the ground was gradually growing firmer, and the small, fallen stones were swelling to boulders. The realization began to dawn on them that they were finally coming out of the danger. After an eternity of sweat-drenched concentration, they had reached the northern face of Mt. Averly.

Mt. Averly was mind-bogglingly beautiful and made no sense whatsoever. The mountain looked as if it had slipped from a hole in a giant's back pocket. Landing with a plop!, it took up its new residence on the shore, while the giant continued on his way - one stone poorer, though no worse off for the loss. Even the sea marveled at this wonder, wreathing itself around the feet of the mountain to get a better view of its unparalleled originality.

Annelyse had only ever seen Mt. Averly from afar, a constant, gleaming companion on the southern horizon. She had no concept of its immense size, until she stood in the glowering chill of its shadow. It was like standing in front of a wall that supported the sky itself. The whole world ended where the mountain began, and hidden among its slopes and cliffs, there was only grey mystery.

There were no foothills tumbling down the plains. There was no mountain range for trackers to follow. In fact, there were no signs or warnings of a nearby peak at all. Instead, at one moment, Annelyse's feet rested upon spongy marshland. The next moment, her toes bumped up against jagged boulders vaulting skyward. There was nothing in between sea level flatness and the windy peak, except the promise of a deadly fall from a dizzying rockface.

From where Annelyse and her father now stood at the foot of the mountain, a sound could be heard like that of wind-driven rain on a windowpane. Around to their left, billowing high above the craggy cliffs, a cloud of mist hung in the chilly afternoon air.

"There," Mr. Bellamy said, pointing in the direction of the cloud and the glistening rocks below it. "That's our destination. Up we go."

Mounting the grey stone, he began guiding Annelyse over chasms and around outcroppings, at times crawling, at times leaping from foothold to ledge. As they went, the sound of falling water grew louder, becoming the roar of a tumbling cataract. It was now clear to Annelyse that the cloud they were following was the moist breath of the waterfall itself.

The mountain exacted its toll for passage in each scrape, bump and bruise it leveled against knees and elbows. Stubbed toes and jammed fingers measured out every inch of ground between the salt marsh below and the winding heights above. Annelyse harbored a suspicion that the mountain was intentionally placing boulders in their path, just to test their patience and resolve - and she wasn't far wrong. Mt. Averly does not willingly endure the feet of strangers on its slopes.

Having clambered across much of the north face for well over 30-minutes, they finally turned a corner and found themselves on the northeastern slope of the mountain. There in front of them were the headwaters of the Fenneleen Stream. Tumbling in three stages, at a height of over 850 feet, Fenneleen Falls was a sight to behold, and one that few people ever see.

"This is it," Mr. Bellamy called over the thundering noise of plummeting water. "This is where we cross the Fenneleen."

Annelyse's face contorted into a grotesque gasp of horror. How could *this* be a safer place to ford the river than downstream where at least it was horizontal and wouldn't crush them from above? Surely, her father wasn't serious.

"Are you kidding?" she yelled, both to be heard above the falls and to adequately communicate her terror.

"Why else would I have brought us here? The whole point was to ford the river at its source and avoid the deadly current. There is no safer way to cross than this."

"Isn't *this* a deadly current?! How on earth do we cross *that* thing?!"

"We don't," her father said with a knowing smirk. "We go under it."

For the first time in her life, Annelyse was doubting her father's sanity. She'd much rather get her feet wet wading through a river than get pummeled to death trying to go *under* a waterfall. This was insane. But, whether by habit or out of desperation, she found herself following her father straight into the madness.

Lowering himself down through a gap in the rocks, Mr. Bellamy led Annelyse to a deep gash in the face of the mountain. Peering into the opening, she saw what appeared to have been one enormous slab of stone, before some mighty force caused it to split in two. Over time, or in one great cataclysmic crash, the two halves were thrust apart, coming to rest less than shoulder's-width from one another. The result was a narrow corridor of slanted rock. Annelyse was sure that if she tried to walk between them, the two halves would slip back into place, squishing her flat, and yet, in they went.

"It's called Devil's Kitchen," her father said, stepping into the chasm. "Although I don't know why."

"Charming," came the typically sarcastic response of a thoroughly apprehensive Annelyse. She had no time to say anything more, as her father motioned for her to follow.

The ground upon which they now walked was flat and level, though barely wide enough to plant two feet side-by-side. Mr. Bellamy's shoulders were much too broad to fit between the steeply slanted walls, and so he was forced to walk sideways and hunched over down the long gap. Even Annelyse was unable to stand erect and had to shuffle along at an angle.

Running down the high walls of grey stone, mist from the nearby waterfall condensed and maintained the floor in a constant state of muddiness. The huge slabs on either side leaned inward so steeply that they appeared to be pinched together at the top. The overall effect was more like walking between two stone skyscrapers - built inches apart - than squeezing through a wound in the mountain's thick skin.

Adding to their discomfort, occasionally, loose stones rained down on Annelyse and Edward from thirty or forty feet above their heads. Like buckshot from a hunter's gun, the shrapnel stung Annelyse's bare skin and set her nerves on edge. In a place formed by the movement of rock, shifting stones were worrisome, to say the least.

The passage now grew increasingly tight, becoming darker and danker with each step, until apprehension itself seemed to press in upon them. Annelyse was quite certain that she'd suffocate if they didn't get out quickly.

"Look," Mr. Bellamy said, pointing toward the far end. "Almost there, Leesy."

The wall of white noise trampled the air and thumped against Annelyse's eardrums like mallets on the head of a drum. She felt as if the incessant sound was coating the inside of her ears with cotton. Even her thoughts were drowned in an ocean of garbled noise. It was quickly becoming unbearable.

The closer they drew to the end of the thin valley of stone the more mist there was hanging in the air. Soon, their hair, clothing and faces were all covered in a fine gauze of tiny droplets. Licking her lips, Annelyse refreshed her growing thirst, as she tried to work out what her father had in mind next.

"Is the waterfall blocking the exit?" she asked.

"Not blocking it, no. You'll see."

The stone slabs began to open up, widening as they neared the end of the passage, while the slanted rockface ran heavy with sheets of glossy moisture. Through the opening in front of her, Annelyse could make out endless, frothing curtains of water slapping the smooth stone floor and ricocheting upward with undiminished force.

"Take hold of my arm," her father shouted over the roar of the waterfall. "And test your footing before putting your weight on it. The floor'll be slick, but it shouldn't be too slippery. We'll take it slow. Ready?"

"We're walking *through* that?" Annelyse yelled in a panic.

"Trust me, Leesy. All will be well."

Resigned to the fact that she had no other choice but to follow her father into the plunging wall of death,

Annelyse grabbed hold of his arm with both hands. Mr. Bellamy took the first step outside the safety of the passageway. To Annelyse's surprise and great relief, he was not swept over the edge or consumed by the torrent of water. In fact, he wasn't even wet.

Following closely, she now saw that they were standing behind the waterfall, and the ledge upon which they were walking extended all the way around to the other side of the stream. Mr. Bellamy had led them to a place where they could ford the treacherous Fenneleen by walking under it and circumventing it altogether.

Shuffling along behind her father, Annelyse couldn't resist reaching out her arm and poking one finger through the wall of thundering water. Any more than one finger and she would have been yanked into the current and lost forever.

Since the frigid stream originates just below Mt. Averly's snowcap it has very little time to warm up before reaching the place where Annelyse's finger now tickled its underbelly. Barely above freezing, the bitter-cold water sent chills up her arm, down her spine, and into her tailbone. Her finger burned with throbbing fire long after recovering it from the biting falls. But the sensation of running her finger through the awesome force of the mighty Fenneleen was exhilarating. She felt the anger in its icy heart and laughed to herself at the unexpected way in which her father had outsmarted such a cunning stream as this.

In a matter of only a few minutes, they'd crossed the full width of the falls and reached the opposite side. Looking back over the path they'd just taken Annelyse could see that it was really a perfect arrangement. The rockface curved inward away from the wall of water, while the falls bowed outward, widening the distance between traveler and danger. It could not have been a better design.

The thought then occurred to Annelyse that she'd

never heard of Devil's Kitchen or Fenneleen Falls before today. It struck her as odd. Being such an ideal way to ford the deadly stream, why wasn't it more widely known? She decided to ask her father.

"Because of what comes next," was his ominous reply. "If all anyone had to do was shimmy through Devil's Kitchen and walk behind the falls, it'd be marked with a great red X on every map. But there's still one more challenge before we're home free."

Annelyse's heart sank like a lead weight in her chest. Any *challenge* challenging enough to keep this ideal ford off the map had to be most unpleasant. Her curiosity recoiled into a trembling collection of jitters. "What could be worse than a claustrophobic chasm and a narrow walk behind a fierce waterfall?" she thought.

The ledge now curved around to the right, leaving the falls behind as it descended a gentle slope. Puddles of mist pooled in cracks and depressions, like shards of broken mirror on stone pavement. Trickling down a series of crevices in the rockface, a cold, clean spring of fresh water provided the perfect place for Annelyse and her father to refill their canteens.

Unscrewing the top from his canteen, Mr. Bellamy suggested, "You might wanna take your poncho out while we're stopped. You'll have use for it soon."

"Is there another waterfall?" Annelyse asked, opening her backpack.

"No, just a short passage through the mountain. Still, you'll be glad for the extra cover."

Locating her rain cover, Annelyse repacked her bag and slung it onto her back. Draping the heavy, poncho over her shoulders, she looked much like a circus tent. She was beyond tired, and the strain of everything they'd had to navigate was beginning to catch up with her. This was already the most hiking she'd ever done in one day, and the weight of her backpack was becoming too much for her aching shoulders to carry. The soreness in her legs had hardened to concrete, and every step felt heavier than it should. Annelyse was desperate for soft ground and gentle surroundings where she might spread herself out in comfort.

But the landscape all around her was perilous and unfriendly. The hardness of the stone was designed only to bruise flesh and break bones; there was nothing soft or comfortable about any of it. She was ready to get off that mountain and feel the spring of spongy earth beneath her feet again. Rapidly approaching the end of her patience with slippery rocks, treacherous falls, and dark chasms, Annelyse could see why having to navigate "one more challenge" might keep people from taking the Fenneleen Pass. But she couldn't imagine what lay in store next.

The ledge they'd been walking along since crossing the waterfall had gradually been lost among the boulders and loose stones in their way. They were back in the rocky thickets of the mountainside, where no defined footpaths could be found except those carved out by the meandering rain. Half the time, she and her father were forced to crawl on all fours, so uneven was their route.

Rounding a corner, Annelyse looked up and suddenly saw the dark opening of a cave looming in front of them. Their unexpected arrival startled what Annelyse assumed was a bird that had been hiding just inside the entrance. She had to duck to avoid being hit in the head by the panicked creature.

"Ugh! What kind of bird was *that*?!" she yelled, swatting wildly in the air above her head.

Mr. Bellamy's eyebrows arched, as he swallowed hard in a moment of sympathy. He didn't have the heart to answer her question.

"Pull your hood up over your head, Leesy… and down over your face, too. I'll guide you through the cave, but you'll need to hold onto me."

"Pull my hood over my face?" she clarified, reluctance beginning to stiffen inside of her. "Won't I need to see?"

"Not if you hold on tight," Mr. Bellamy replied, turning to face the entrance, "Stay with me, now." Then, under his breath, he added, "The less you see, the better."

Stepping into the thick blackness of the cramped cave, Annelyse was immediately overcome by the weight of the shadows inside. Behind her, the mountain breeze was cool and unfettered. Inside, the humid air oozed idleness. Whereas, Devil's Kitchen had merely been a long, open valley of stone, they were now enveloped in the rank bowels of the earth. The further in they went, the more vehemently light itself refused to follow, for it was altogether unpleasant inside the cave.

But there was something else. An odor. No, a stench rising up from the floor burned itself into Annelyse's brain. The stagnant reek caused her gorge to rise and brought tears to her eyes. Then, she heard something drawing near, something that filled her with horror.

At first, Annelyse thought it was the sound of the wind rushing through the tunnel. But the rigid air lay motionless all around. She strained her ears in the void, as the noise grew steadily louder. It now sounded less like a hurricane and far more like the frantic beating of a million wings. Bouncing off the rounded ceiling and the narrow walls around her, Annelyse could hardly tell from which direction the sound was coming. She crouched down, hoping to avoid being seen by whatever it was that now approached.

"Don't sit down," her father commanded. "That's not mud on the floor. Stay on your feet, no matter what."

"What's that noise?!" she screamed, forcing herself to stand up.

"Just keep your hood on tight and stay close."

Mr. Bellamy was practically dragging his daughter

by the arm, desperate to find the outlet as quickly as possible. By now the pursuing noise had found them in the dark and was swirling around like a frantic tornado.

Annelyse felt something smack her on the back of the head, then again, on her left shoulder. Reaching up to pull her hood down over her face, she felt another one graze her bare hand. Whatever it was, it felt stiff and wiry, like the giant limbs of an overgrown grasshopper. But Annelyse was certain there was also something dreadfully sharp about it, sharp and pointed like a dagger. A scream escaped her lips, as the pack of whatever-they-were began striking every inch of Annelyse's tense and terrified body.

She grabbed onto the back of her father's shirt, determined that the repeated blows on her exposed hand would not succeed in dislodging her grip. Annelyse could tell from her father's position that he must have been shielding his face with one arm. His back was bent, and his head was down. He was trying to present the smallest possible target. Still, the pummeling continued, inside a tsunami of deafening sound and pitch blackness.

At one point, Annelyse ran head-on into her father who had failed to detect an oncoming curve in the tunnel walls. Struggling to regain their path, with his free arm held straight out in front of him he felt his way along the edge of the corridor as best he could in the darkness. Once he'd found the safe center of the passageway again, Mr. Bellamy quickened their pace.

Through a tiny crack in the wall up ahead, the faint glow of evening could now be seen, pale, but hopeful. Sensing the light, Annelyse peeked one eye out from beneath her hood. All around her, a swarm of what appeared to be a million oversized, flying insects filled the cave with incessant commotion. She and her father were caught in the dead center of the cloud of chaos. It was clear, they would have to push their way through it all if they were to escape the cavern.

With the exit coming into view, they ran as fast as panic could drive them. Annelyse kept one hand on the front lip of her hood, pulling it down over her face, occasionally shooting an eye out in front of her. With the other hand, she held fast to her father's shirt, her knuckles white with fear. All the while, the endless battering continued.

In a flash of searing agony, Annelyse felt a sharp pain on the back of her bare wrist. Screaming out in torment, she struck at it repeatedly with her other hand, until whatever-it-was let go of her hand and fell to the ground at Annelyse's feet. Immediately, weakness invaded her body, and she felt as if she would faint. Holding her left hand close to her body, she staggered forward, trying to keep up with her father. The exit was now only a few feet away, and the evening sky illuminated their goal. The fire of hope was kindled, and it was the only warmth her reeling body could feel.

"The second we get out, find cover!" Mr. Bellamy yelled, panting hard from up ahead. "Just get down, as soon as you can!"

As Annelyse and her father leapt out of the gaping mouth of the cave, landing among an outcropping of boulders, the foul hole belched a brown cloud of gargantuan mosquitos over their heads. The horrible whine of buzzing wings bruised the night air in an endless parade of blood-thirsty demons. Stirred to a frenzy, the enormous mosquitos were countless in number and unequalled in madness. Like a flood of putrid water, the swarm gushed past the horrified Annelyse who huddled herself against the cold ground. Minutes passed, until at last, the colony fled down the mountainside and out into their nightly hunting grounds. For the first time in what felt like ages, the air fell silent.

"It's alright now, Leesy. They're gone."

But Annelyse was so completely traumatized that

she was reluctant to remove her hood. She was afraid to expose herself to the crashing bodies of the hideous insects again. The throbbing in her left hand extended up her entire arm, in an undeniable reminder of what she had just endured, and she trembled in pain. Feeling the blood drain from her face, Annelyse lay her head on her forearm.

Again, her father reassured her. "It's ok. We made it."

Taking a deep breath to calm her growing dizziness, she poked her head out from under her rain poncho like a shell-shocked turtle. Still shaking in a daze of confusion, she closed her hands in a fist around the gravel beneath her. When, at last, Annelyse was able to coax her eyes open, she was surprised by a sight so beautiful it could scarcely be real.

The northeastern reaches of the Fäerie Fields in all their vibrant shades of green stretched out before them, running down to the banks of the Fenneleen like a playful herd of ponies. Striations of lights and darks swayed among the tall grass, beckoning the dismayed travelers into the arms of the meadow. At the distant edge of the northern horizon, Annelyse could just make out the glistening strand of the Perigoh Fair shining beneath the rays of the sun.

Only a few yards downhill from where they had weathered the storm-cloud of mosquitos, Mt. Averly wore a wide and flowing apron. The prairielands, vaulting up from the south, did so with such ardor that they spread themselves like a bib beneath the mountain's chin. With no more chasms or caves to contend with, Annelyse and her father could now set their feet upon soft ground once again.

"Are you ok?" Mr. Bellamy asked, knowing full well that no one could endure the throbbing hurricane of Culicidan Cave unscathed.

Annelyse just stared into thin air with vacant eyes, shaking her head and cradling her left arm like a newborn. In shock and overwhelmed, she was unable to speak. With growing concern, Mr. Bellamy brushed himself off and walked over to take a look for himself.

"Are you hurt?" he asked, gently pulling her hood back.

Annelyse just shook her head again - or rather, she hadn't stopped shaking it since her father's first question. Clearly, she hadn't comprehended what he was asking, or she would have shown him the bite on her left wrist.

"Let me look at you," he said, carefully standing her up by the shoulders. "Is it just the one bite?" he asked, finally noticing her hand.

Annelyse nodded, her limbs quivering.

"Good. One is bad enough. More than one can be deadly."

Drawing her near, Mr. Bellamy wrapped both arms around his daughter and hugged her until some assurance of security returned to her mind.

"That...that... was..."

"I know, Leesy," he said, rubbing her back. "But there was no other way. At least the worst of it is behind us. Let me tend to your wrist, before the itching begins."

Removing a small box from his backpack, Mr. Bellamy located a bottle of salve.

"This will sting a bit on the puncture, but only for a moment."

Pouring a few drops onto the red, inflamed welt disfiguring much of Annelyse's left wrist, Mr. Bellamy rubbed the ointment into her skin. At first, she grimaced with pain, but soon the angry sting abated, and the swelling lessened.

"If it starts to itch, don't give in to the urge. Rub it gently, but never scratch it. We'll apply more medicine before bedtime."

"What... what was on the floor?" Annelyse asked, afraid of her father's reply. "In the cave. What was it on the floor?"

Mr. Bellamy stowed the first-aid kit in his backpack, then turned to answer his daughter's question.

"Filth, mud, rainwater…" he paused a moment, "And wrigglers."

"Wrigglers?"

"Newly hatched mosquitos. Millions of them. Still unable to fly, they look like worms, but most of them are bigger than… well, bigger than you want to imagine. Nasty, vicious creatures, full of bloodlust," Hoisting his backpack over his shoulders, Mr. Bellamy went on, "I'm not sure I blame 'em, really."

"The mosquitos?" Annelyse asked.

"Well, them, yes, I suppose. But I meant the folks who'd rather not step foot inside that blasted cave. They'd rather test their luck with the Fenneleen. But our chances of crossing the river downstream would have been too slim for success."

Wiping the perspiration from his forehead, Mr. Bellamy checked the sun's position in the sky. "We should set up camp. We could both use a hot meal and a good night's sleep. I know the perfect place, and it's very close by."

Somehow, even with an echoing stomach, the thought of food just didn't appeal to the bug-battered and bitten Annelyse. All she wanted was her old, familiar bed and four insect-proof walls around her.

They'd been away from home for only 12 hours and were barely out of upper Averlune, but Annelyse was already regretting ever having left. Losing her mother and everything that had made them a family was bad enough. Why did she have to go and give up the little comfort she had left? Was the chance of finding the Woolems worth the trouble? Was it worth risking her life for? In this moment of overwhelming fatigue, she just didn't know for sure, but she had the horrible feeling that they'd made a big mistake.

Mr. Bellamy sensed his daughter's mood and

decided that the best thing to do was to distract her with activity. It was nearly 6:00 pm and they needed to make camp before daylight was entirely spent. Taking Annelyse's backpack, he slung it over his own shoulder, then led the way down the broad, sloping lawn. Barely able to hold one clear thought in her mind, Annelyse staggered-on behind her father like a zombie, still cradling her left arm close to her body.

Every few feet, a jagged boulder sprouted up from among the daisies and dandelions, a bothersome reminder of the stone giant still lurking behind them. In the lengthening shadows cast by a slowly setting sun, the mountain appeared more ominous than before. Cloaked in featureless darkness, it looked like a single, sharp fang set within a receding gumline. Perhaps, it was merely the memory of their perilous passage which disfigured the mountain's visage. But, either way, they were glad to leave its grey severity behind.

The eastern side of Mt. Averly was very different from the northern and northwestern approaches. With no salt marsh or quicksand to navigate, the eastern slope of the mountain joined so seamlessly and effortlessly with the Fäerie Fields that it was difficult to say where one ended and the other began. Very soon, the boulders along their path – which had tumbled from the face of the mountain – began to disappear, and even the litter of stones lost itself amid the wildflowers of the meadow.

Where the incline of the mountainside gave way to the vast flatness of the fields, a small grove of alder trees grew. Sheltered from the sea breezes and northerly winds by the mountain itself, Alders Idle was a popular stop-over point for those traveling from Killoughee in the south to Pebble Ford on the Perigoh. It was here that Mr. Bellamy intended to make camp and spend their first night in the wild.

The sun was hidden behind the grey giant when, at

last, they arrived beneath the first alder tree. The grove was comprised of fifteen or twenty trees and formed a fat line pointing southeast away from the foot of Mt. Averly. The ground beneath the canopy of leafy branches was a thick carpet of grass. At the center of the grove, there was a small opening in the trees, ideal for the open-air-chimney of a campfire.

"You go ahead and roll out our sleeping bags. I'll get a fire started," her father said. "We'll wanna sleep close to the fire, both for warmth and protection."

"Protection?" Annelyse was almost too exhausted to ask, but not quite. "Protection from what?"

"You never know in the wild," he replied, gathering some fallen branches from beneath an old tree.

Annelyse didn't really want to know. In fact, she was sorry she'd asked. Her wrist had begun itching so intensely, she could barely keep from tearing at it with her nails. She'd had enough of the wild for one day.

Within a few minutes, Mr. Bellamy had a small fire burning in a pit he'd found scratched out of the ground. From the look of things, this place had seen many campfires in its long past. The collection of fallen branches, the existing fire pit, even a scattering of partially burned logs all spoke to the fact that this was one of the few groupings of trees between Mt. Averly and the Rindle Mire. If a traveler needed a roof of branches over his head for the night, Alders Idle was his best bet.

Dropping two potatoes into a bed of coals he'd prepared, Mr. Bellamy removed an iron skillet from his bag. After heating it on top of three flat stones he'd arranged in the flames, he produced some linked sausages from the larder-sack and began frying them in the skillet. The smell convinced Annelyse's rumbling stomach that dinner *was* a good idea after all.

"I'm afraid it won't be as interesting as breakfast was," Mr. Bellamy said, with a tired grin on his face, "But it's good, hardy food and it'll draw the sleep to our eyes."

Annelyse wasn't sure her eyes needed any help falling asleep, but she was eager to have a full stomach again. Right now, she was impatient for food, rest, and more ointment on her itching wrist.

"Your mother would've loved 'em," he said, rolling the sausages over with a fork.

"What?"

"Those mosquitos. She loved bugs. She used to call mosquitos *swamp angels*. Pretty name for such an ugly creature." Mr. Bellamy chuckled to himself. "That was her way, though. Nothing was ugly to her."

Annelyse thought for a moment. Her father was right. It hadn't occurred to her until he'd said it, but it was true. Her mother would've actually *enjoyed* the trek through Culicidan Cave. It sounded strange to say it, but she wouldn't have wanted to leave. Annelyse could picture her mother with a little torch in her hand introducing herself to each individual mosquito. She would have given every one of them a name, too.

"I can hear her laughing at the top of her lungs, surrounded by a barrage of ballistic bugs! She absolutely loves…" Mr. Bellamy stopped himself, caught between a pleasant thought and the sudden, awful realization that it was something that could never again be true. Hidden behind a pleasant memory, grief had taken aim like an expert marksman and found its target at the center of Edward Bellamy's heart.

Annelyse wasn't sure how to help her father find his way out of his awkward moment. She was beginning to learn that it's often best simply to allow the grief snipers and waves of dredged-up sadness to run their course. When the source of pain is inside yourself, there's nowhere to hide. Silence settled-in between father and daughter and they were, once again, alone in their shared grief.

"The potatoes should be ready soon," Mr. Bellamy

said, unable to find any better way of breaking the silence. "Let me put some more salve on that bite, while we wait."

Embers from the fire flitted up through the opening in the trees and out into the starry night. As she ate her dinner, Annelyse watched them escape and mused on how a soul must follow the same path when someone dies. Maybe stars are just holes punched in the black, crepe paper sky, holes made by souls speeding along their way to eternity. She wondered which hole had been made by her mother.

Annelyse and her father held their own thoughts close, eating without conversation, both too exhausted for such things. They'd accomplished their goal for this first day's hike. Under any other circumstances, they'd be feeling understandably proud of themselves. But tonight, their one desire was for sleep.

Finishing their dinner, they rinsed off the skillet and plates with water from their canteens, then stowed everything back in their knapsacks. Mr. Bellamy put another log on the fire, pulled his sleeping bag up around his neck, and stretched his body out to its full length.

Annelyse laid down, with the top of her head near that of her father, completing the semicircle of sleeping bags around the campfire. She felt safer with her head close to his. Feet were expendable, heads were essential.

"Sleep well, Leesy," he whispered.

Annelyse hesitated. Then, with deep thoughtfulness, she said, "I think she *still* loves bugs." Closing her eyes, she fell fast asleep.

CHAPTER EIGHT

The Courage to Look Deeper

Annelyse knelt on the floor at the head of the bed, opposite her father. Searching his eyes for the slightest hint of hope, she could find only empty heartbreak. As she returned to studying her mother's features, Annelyse saw such stillness as she could never have comprehended. Life had been extinguished, and she wondered exactly what that meant.

How had her mother been alive one moment and

then, a fraction of a heartbeat later, simply *was* no more? What had changed? What had broken or slipped out of place inside of her? How was it possible that something which had always been taken for granted had now proven to be so fleeting, so fragile?

They'd been kneeling beside that bed for several minutes - maybe hours, who could say? - watching as the labored pulse of her mother's heart slowed. All the while, they harbored an unspoken hope that, as long as her heart continued to throb, the situation might improve. But then – with nothing like a last long sigh or shudder to signal the end of life - Silloah Bellamy simply stopped… and her daughter's world crumbled to ash and took flight.

Now, as Annelyse lay dreaming beside the campfire under the stars, everything her brain recalled was just as it had happened. Everything except for one horrible detail. In this latest nightmare, Annelyse saw her mother turn to face her. Then, without opening her eyes, she scolded Annelyse, saying, "You let it happen. I warned you, but you let it happen, anyway. And now you're dead inside. More dead than I am to the waking world."

With a scream, Annelyse awoke abruptly from her dream. Unable to move a muscle, she scanned her surroundings for specters in the night. Finding only fear crouching low in the shadows, cold perspiration pooled in the creases of her neck.

"Leesy, are you alright?!"

Mr. Bellamy had been awakened by his daughter's jarring shriek. Having lost the power of speech, Annelyse lay motionless, but for the labored heaving of her chest.

"Leesy? What is it?" her father whispered.

In an instant of sudden release, Annelyse began sobbing. The hideousness of her nightmare was steeped like tea leaves in the stress and fatigue of a long day. The mixture was too bitter to keep inside. Playing on her darkest emotions in the bare vulnerability of night, the grief snipers stirred memory into absurdity, until Annelyse's sadness overflowed its banks.

"What is it, child?" her father asked again, raising himself on his elbows.

"Just a stupid nightmare," she replied, through a flood of tears.

"Do you want to talk about it?"

"No. I don't even wanna think about it. I'm so over it…" Annelyse wiped her eyes with the back of her hand. "I'm so over it all. Why did she have to die?"

Annelyse's question revealed to her father everything he needed to know about her nightmare.

"Why?" she continued. "What sense does any of it make? What's the point? I've had enough. I've just had enough of all the nonsense."

Her father leaned his forehead against Annelyse's brow, cupping his hand on the back of her head.

"I don't want to believe any of it," she said, her tears becoming arid anger. "Everything Mom believed in, what good did it do her? What good is it to her now? You were right. Fairy tales is all it was. Maybe this whole idiotic journey is just to prove that it was all a lie. Nothing but a lie. So I can forget about it and move on."

Mr. Bellamy dropped his head into the palm of his hand. The flickering light of the campfire illuminated his face in shades of orange and shapelessness. The strong contrast between light and shadow made him look old to Annelyse's eyes. Without his wife, Edward was torn between needing someone to talk to and needing to be strong for his daughter. In the face of her raw questioning, unable to restrain his own struggles, Edward Bellamy's grief rose to the surface.

"I know, Leesy. I know, and I wish I had the answers. I wish I knew what to say. For me, it's much simpler. I struggle with one demon above all the others. I cannot believe that I'm a better father than The Father of all things. If I had the power to keep you from harm and I didn't use it, I'd be guilty – and well I should be. Why doesn't the same rule apply to Him, then? No, I don't have the answers, not for any of the questions, and I hate it."

"So, where *do* we find the answers? What can we do?"

The horror of her nightmare had begun to loosen its grip on Annelyse. In its place, only exhausted frustration and endless questioning remained.

"We're doing it," her father replied.

"What, though?"

"All we can. We're doing all that we possibly can to find the answers, Leesy. But it might not be enough."

Mr. Bellamy kissed his daughter on the forehead, then laid back down with his face toward the fire. Annelyse paused, still resting on her elbows, still staring into the flames. No thoughts stirred within her; she would not allow them to. Thoughts too often become questions, and questions brought her no peace. Annelyse was beginning to suspect that thinking was overrated. There were far more riddles in the world than a lifetime of puzzling could solve.

The warmth of the fire caressing her face and the hypnotic pulsing of the embers soon lulled Annelyse's mind and slowed the blinking of her eyelids. She was ready to lay down her head again. The restless fatigue had quieted, the distractions had faded. There would be no more nightmares tonight. Her brain had learned its lesson and would not make the same mistake twice.

While Annelyse drifted back to sleep, her father lay awake watching each individual coal dim and then close its eyes to sleep. He wondered about Annelyse's nightmare. Without a doubt, it centered around her mother's death.

Everything his daughter had said echoed his own questioning. He knew that he'd lost his faith in too much. But it wasn't even true to say that he'd lost his faith. He hadn't lost anything that he hadn't been willing to part with, except his wife. And now, he was angry, shattered. But it wasn't as if something unheard of had happened to Silloah. People die every day. It wasn't even that her death had been exceptionally tragic or that she'd died too young. These were not the circumstances under which he had surrendered so much.

Edward Bellamy had lost his faith in the people who wanted to feel engaged and helpful but who never truly drew near to his family's pain. He'd lost his faith in systems that had promised to provide comfort and support, but, in the end, only increased his family's burden. Finally, he'd lost his faith in every reason for joy and hope he and his wife had ever clung to - not because joy had been an illusion, but because hope had proven to be too elusive. Hope must eventually be fulfilled, or else it rings false and empty in the end.

Still, here he was on a journey of hope. They'd set out to find proof of all that Silloah had believed in, especially the mythical Woolems. Beneath his protective shell of cynical disbelief, Edward Bellamy felt something stirring within himself. And it sprung from the realization that what he'd told Annelyse earlier was true.

"We're doing all that we possibly can," he'd said, when asked how they could find the answers they so craved. Amid the darkness of doubt, the only way they could fail to see the light of truth was by choosing to curl up and do nothing at all. The only way they'd stumble in the dark was if they chose to keep their eyes closed.

Taking the first step out their front door that morning was "doing all that they possibly could." Risking danger and failure with an openness to discovering whatever they might was "doing all that they possibly could." Having the courage to embark on a journey of hope when they had no real hope of success was "doing all that they possibly could."

What Edward Bellamy now felt stirring within him

was a fragile new hope to replace the shattered ones. Or maybe what he experienced was the nascent renewal of old hopes. It was a gift, and he recognized it as such, immediately. Like one, small daisy on a barren boulder, it was unremarkable and easily missed. But it bore all the markings of his wife's own doing. Like the dying embers of his campfire, he would have to fan this new hope into flame. He would need to nurture it, for fragile things are easily lost.

Turning his gaze heavenward, Mr. Bellamy laid back and stared up at the stars. He was reminded of nights spent at Lightview Overlook, and how he and his wife would spin yarns for their daughter of how the constellations got their names.

His eyes were drawn to the constellation Capreolina, the deer, and to the red star at its heart - the Silloah star. The far distant flame flickered in the void of space, as if throbbing in the graceful doe's breast. This was the star for which Silloah Bellamy had been named at her birth, and it looked down over her broken family tonight.

Fixing his eyes on the heart of Capreolina, Edward whispered up to the heavens, "Lead the way, my sweet queen of Averlune."

His mind experienced a moment of peace, and, beneath the beating heart of the Silloah star, Edward Bellamy drifted off to sleep.

Moon and planets, stars and galaxies turned overhead like clockwork gears, ordered with precision from the moment they were set in motion. As the world spun upon its cockeyed corkscrew, the sun slowly started to rise on the eastern horizon.

Down below, the northern meadows of the Fäerie Fields caught the first rays of sunlight in the tips of their slender, green fingers. A blaze of sunrise spread like fire across the eager landscape. Inside the grove of alder trees, Mr. Bellamy had just awakened and was busy stoking the campfire for their morning tea.

"Good morning," he said to a very groggy Annelyse. "How'd you sleep?"

Stretching and yawning like a bear fresh from hibernation, Annelyse made some vaguely positive reply.

"Good, you can fill this with water for us. Thanks."

Mr. Bellamy handed Annelyse a tea kettle, adding, "But don't fall in, or else surviving all those monstrous mosquitos will have been for nothing."

Annelyse squeezed off a fake smile in the direction of her father, then took the tea kettle from his hands and headed back toward the mountain and the banks of the Fenneleen.

As they'd discovered during their earlier adventure, high atop Mt. Averly the icy stream plunges in three stages spanning over 850 feet in height. The stage behind which Annelyse and her father had cleverly snuck was the third and final of the three. Below that, where the water stops falling and before it begins its frenzied flow to the Perigoh, it rests a moment in a basin of splintered stone and boulders.

Depending upon the amount of water in the pool, it can present either a placid or a perturbed face. For this reason, it has earned a reputation for being devilishly mercurial. From the stillness of the pool, after recovering from its traumatic descent, the stream rages on for miles in a furious freeway of rapids and whitewater, until it is arrested by the gentle flow of the mighty Perigoh.

Every rock along the Fenneleen's path is a sharp and slippery needle, offering no toehold and no sure footing. There are no shallows in which to wade anywhere along its course since the bed of the stream is V-shaped and of an ever-increasing depth. No one in their right mind would attempt to skip across the roiling rapids on the backs of its jagged boulders. One misstep, and you'd either wind up impaled upon a stony spike or else the frozen deep would swallow you whole.

No, the entire length of the stream - between the basin in the south and the Perigoh Fair in the north - is practically unfordable. Only here in the pool at the base of the falls could anyone hope to cross over the Fenneleen on foot. For the basin is constructed of large, flat slabs of stone, beaten smooth by the thundering water.

Indeed, there is an excellent path of level rocks leading straight through the heart of the pool all of which are wide enough for man and beast to pass without care. But the pathway is not reliable since it is only visible when the flow of the falls is at its lowest. After a few days of heavy rains, or in the early spring when runoff from snowmelt is at its peak, the smooth stone pathway is entirely hidden beneath the churning waters. Such was the case today when Annelyse first arrived at the Weeping Pool of Fenneleen Falls.

The air was chilly, held captive by rock walls on three sides. It was so cold, in fact, that Annelyse was surprised to see that the mist from the falls didn't turn to snow and blanket the surrounding area in white.

Behind her, the meadow stretched back toward Alders Idle where Annelyse and her father had spent the night. The sun had just shown its sleepy face above the treetops, casting rainbows in the mist before her. The close-up view of Fenneleen Falls bathed in the gold of an Averlune sunrise was breathtaking, to be sure. But, even separated from the dangerous waterfall by a wide basin, Annelyse still felt it was far too close for comfort.

Choosing a place just around the corner of a stone outcropping and out of sight of the falls, she knelt down on the banks of the pool. The water was layered in striations of various hues. At the top, the less frigid layer was crystal clear and held aloft by much denser water below. Beneath that, a colder layer of translucent blue extended almost beyond the eye's reach. Further below, where the

Fenneleen keeps its darkest secrets, great blocks of ice formed, shifted, and reformed as the temperature of the pool fluctuated. Their lumbering, white bodies, in contrast to the violet of the deep water, were clearly visible. It was these submerged icebergs that now held Annelyse's attention.

They were lifeless giants, and many of them suggested shapes that could easily be mistaken for large animals. From where Annelyse knelt peering deep into the pool, it looked as if an army of elephants had long ago fallen in and were instantaneously coated in thick, white ice. There they lay, as a warning to careless elephants everywhere. It was a silly idea, but Annelyse thought it would make a fitting story for a place called the Weeping Pool.

Scooping-up a kettleful of water, she closed the lid before standing to return to camp. As she turned to go, out of the corner of one eye, Annelyse saw something move. Deep beneath the surface of the water, an iceberg rolled in the unseen current. As it did, Annelyse thought she spied something trapped inside the heart of the great ice block. Before she could focus her eyes on the curious sight, the berg heaved over and was lost in the depths.

For a moment, though, it seemed like her elephant theory might not be so crazy after all. But everything had happened so fast, she just couldn't be sure of what she'd seen. Chuckling despite herself, Annelyse shook her head and started back down the meadow toward the alder grove. Lack of sleep was playing tricks on her eyes. If every sleep was to be like the previous night's, she was quite sure she'd be raving mad by the time they made it home.

Inhaling the fragrance of the wildflowers jostled by her footsteps, she imagined she was walking the paths behind her little cabin by the sea. For the few minutes it took to cross the meadow and reach the grove, she almost forgot about the quicksand, chasm, mosquitos, and cave of the previous day; so sweet was the scenery all around her.

Approaching the first alder tree on the edge of the Idle, Annelyse noticed something out of place. A white daisy had been pressed into a crack in the tree's bark and stood out against the dull brown of the trunk. As she drew closer, Annelyse saw that the daisy was not alone. A fragment of folded parchment was wrapped around the flower's stem, holding it snuggly in place.

Even before freeing them both from the tree bark, Annelyse had a suspicion about how they came to be there. Putting the tea kettle down on the ground, she removed the note-wrapped daisy, and opened the parchment. Inside, she found these words, written in a familiar hand.

> *Deep myst'ries in the Weeping Pool,*
> *too few can say what's there.*
> *But one who knows is easily found*
> *along the Maidenhair.*

"It's him," Annelyse exclaimed aloud. "He's been here!"

Clumsily tucking the message into her pocket along with the daisy, she picked up the tea kettle and ran back toward the campsite at the center of the alder grove. Dodging branches in her way, she burst into the clearing, startling her father in the process.

"Whoa, child! What's the matter? Something wrong?"

"Nothing's wrong. I… well, I went to the pool, and I thought I saw… but it couldn't have been. So, then I found, stuck in the tree bark, it's him. It has to be him! Look!"

Mr. Bellamy's eyes spun in their sockets, as he tried to make sense of the flood of words flowing from his overexcited daughter. When he saw Annelyse produce the note from her pocket, his cautious curiosity was piqued. He was also more than a little relieved. At least he would be able to read the note at his own pace, rather than trying to sort through an early morning explosion of bubbling Annelyse.

Taking the square of parchment, Edward opened it with interest, and began to read the note to himself.

> *Deep myst'ries in the Weeping Pool,*
> *too few can say what's there.*
> *But one who knows is easily found*
> *along the Maidenhair.*

Annelyse watched her father's face closely. She was still apprehensive about raising the topic of the Poet of Perigoh with him. She knew that her father didn't care for the young man, though she still couldn't understand exactly why. She maintained hope of changing his opinion and maybe this latest encounter would help.

"Where'd you say you found this?" Mr. Bellamy asked.

"It was stuck in a tree at the edge of the grove."

"It couldn't have been there long. The last rain was only three nights ago, and this parchment is as good as new."

"Well, that means…"

"That means the poet left it there either yesterday or the day before," Mr. Bellamy interrupted, reasoning it all out.

"Or early this morning," Annelyse suggested, catching her father off guard. It hadn't occurred to him that the poet might be only a couple of hours away from where they now stood.

"But how would he have known we'd be here?" Annelyse asked.

"Who's to say the note was left for us?" her father countered.

"Well, I…" Annelyse hadn't thought of that. "I guess I just assumed…"

Mr. Bellamy reassured his daughter, "And it was a

safe assumption, knowing him. But what *mysteries in the pool* is he talking about?"

Annelyse began to shuffle her feet, averting her eyes from her father.

"Why am I not surprised?" he asked, although it sounded more like an announcement than a question.

"Surprised about what?" she said, not yet knowing the best way to bring up what she'd seen in the Weeping Pool.

"You obviously have some idea of what he's talking about. So, let's hear it."

Mr. Bellamy took the tea kettle from Annelyse and placed it over the fire. Handing her a plate with a few sausages and a hunk of stale bread on it, he sat down on a stump and awaited her answer.

"Well, that's just it," she began, as she tore off a piece of bread and dipped it in the grease from the sausage. "It's only an idea. The fact is, I'm not sure what I saw… or even if I saw anything at all."

Popping the morsel of bread in her mouth, she continued speaking, chewing at the same time.

"I had just filled the tea kettle and was about to come back to camp when I saw an iceberg deep down in the water. It was rolling so slow it hardly seemed to move. But then, as it sort of bellied-over and started sinking, I thought I saw…"

She felt foolish for what she was about to say and was reluctant to continue her thought. But, deciding it was best to say it quickly and just be done with it, she blurted it out anyway, "I thought I saw the face of a creature in the ice."

"A creature?" Mr. Bellamy clarified. "What? An animal?"

"Well, yes, but also… no."

"Which is it, Leesy?"

"It was like an animal, only… well, different."

"That helps," Mr. Bellamy said, with a hint of sarcasm. "How was it different?"

"It looked like it… ugh, this is going to sound stupid."

"Just say it, no matter how it sounds. It's alright." Mr. Bellamy waited on Annelyse's choice of words.

"It looked like it had… something to tell me."

"Why? Did it have its hand up?"

"Dad!"

"I'm sorry, I'm sorry. I'm just trying to understand."

"Well, it feels more like you're making fun. I told you, I'm not sure what I saw. But it looked like it was trying to get my attention or something. Then, the moment it caught my eye, it rolled over and sank into the dark water."

"And now, this," Mr. Bellamy said, with a thoughtful look on his face, fingering the parchment in his hands.

"I think he left it for us. Somehow, he knew what I saw… or what I was going to see… or whatever. Does he want us to find this person who lives '*along the Maidenhair*'? How do we know *who* it is?"

Folding the note and handing it back to Annelyse, Mr. Bellamy took a bite of his food. "That's easy," he said, between chews, "No one lives along that river. Some say the woods around it are haunted. So, whoever he means, either he isn't real or he's a ghost. Either way, I reckon we have an equally impossible chance of finding him."

"But he wouldn't lie about it and then go to all the trouble of making sure we find his note. There *must* be someone living in those woods, and he must know something about whatever it was I saw in the pool."

"I'd planned on following the north shore of the Perigoh, after we cross Pebble Ford. That would have taken us through only a thin sliver of those haunted woods. But if you want to follow the Maidenhair, it'll lead us straight through the deepest parts of that cursed forest. And you'll only have your poet friend to thank for *that*."

"We have no choice," Annelyse replied, making the decision for them both. "We need to follow the Maidenhair and find this person."

"You put an awful lot of trust in that crazy poet."

"Dad…"

"Fine," her father conceded. "But we still have some country to cross and a river to ford before we reach the Quibble Woods. Best get to it."

"How far do we have to walk today?"

Mr. Bellamy wrinkled his face, hoping to smooth out what was sure to be an unpopular answer.

"Same as yesterday, I'm afraid. But the good news is, it's all downhill along well-worn paths."

Annelyse was only mildly consoled by her father's "good news." She thought, for sure, the Perigoh was much closer than a 12-hour hike. After all, she could see it from the northeastern slope of Mt. Averly.

"If we were heading right for the Perigoh, we'd go almost due north and reach it in under 6 hours," her father said, reading her befuddled thoughts. "But it's not the river we're aiming for, it's the ford. And that's much more easterly than northerly. We can cut the corner, and it will only take us 12 hours. Or we can head north to the river then follow its shoreline east to the ford. That would take the better part of 16 hours. It's up to you, Leesy."

It was really no choice at all. Compared to a 16-hour hike, 12 hours of downhill walking was much more appealing. The decision was an easy one. But then it hit her. Even if they set out for the ford right away, they wouldn't reach it before 9:00 pm that night. They'd be far too late to cross to the other side of the river let alone make camp before nightfall. It looked like they'd be spending one more night on the south side of the Perigoh River.

"I'd rather take the direct route instead of a 16-hour detour," she said to her father, who was busy washing up after breakfast. "But where will we spend the night?"

"If we get going, we just might be able to sleep beneath a roof tonight. I seem to recall a place not far from the ford - if it's still there. But we have no time to waste. Help me pack up."

The idea of spending the night under the cover of a roof soon took root in Annelyse's fertile imagination. The thought then grew to include a lavish dinner, two soft beds, a stack of pillows, clouds of fluffy blankets, and a proper breakfast the next morning. That was all the motivation she needed to pack quickly, sling her backpack over her shoulders, and be ready long before her father had finished lacing his boots.

"That's the spirit," he said, joining her with walking stick in hand. "Lead the way!"

"Which way?" she objected.

"We really can't go too far wrong," Mr. Bellamy replied, pointing straight ahead. "We make for the river, and then…" swinging his arm toward the east like a weathervane in the breeze, "…we just head a bit more to the right."

"Gotcha!" she said, and Annelyse was off, leading the way toward Pebble Ford astride the Perigoh Fair.

She'd never been on this side of the Fenneleen before, so every step was a first step in a new direction, carrying her farther and farther from home. But, rather than homesickness, Annelyse felt a sense of excitement stirring inside of her. She and her mother had explored every detail of upper Averlune and the peninsula upon which they lived. But she knew that her mother had traveled farther than that, and now Annelyse was walking where her mother had once walked without her – perhaps, where she'd walked even without her husband by her side.

The farther north they traveled, the less familiar

Edward Bellamy was with the lay of the land. He knew
Averlune well, but he'd always avoided the Quibble Woods
whenever possible. He was a coastal creature, accustomed
to the vast openness of the sea. Forests were little more
than crowded and contorted mazes, in his mind. The whole
idea of willingly choosing to enter the haunted woods filled
him with grave apprehension. Very soon, his apprehension
would be confirmed.

Those Who Understand

Their hike through the northeast region of the Fäerie Fields couldn't have been more different than the previous day's journey. Whereas, yesterday, Mr. Bellamy had taken the lead and driven them at a steady pace, today he took his time, enjoying what felt to Annelyse like a leisurely stroll through the meadows.

The landscape through which they now moved was a welcome contrast to the treacherous salt marshes at the northern foot of Mt. Averly. Between Alders Idle and Pebble Ford, there was nothing but 12 miles of gently sloping fields, all rolling gracefully down to the southern banks of the mighty Perigoh Fair. At no point along their path did the river hide itself from view. It was a constant and steadily growing ribbon of silver on the horizon. The breeze was soft on their faces; the sun sat delicately on their shoulders; and on either side, birds sang in the thickets lining the road. The day promised to be pleasant in every regard.

Annelyse soon found herself enjoying the walk, when earlier she'd felt only dread at the prospect of another long trek. But, when her mind was free to wander the countryside (instead of agonizing over every step through dangerous terrain), she discovered that cross-country hiking suited her quite nicely. Her overactive mind was kept occupied by the constantly changing scenery. Her tender heart took an interest in every creature she encountered (except for unnaturally large mosquitos). And her curiosity found plenty of things to discover and ponder, everywhere she looked.

As with prairielands the world over, there are very few trees to be found among the tall grass and wildflowers of the Fäerie Fields. In fact, east of Alders Idle, there isn't a single tree over three feet tall, until one encounters the weeping willows in the valley of the Rindle Mire. Which is why, when Annelyse and her father happened upon something inexplicable only a few hours into their journey to the ford both were totally perplexed.

"What's that," Annelyse asked, noticing a dark object on the horizon, "Is it another mountain?"

"If it is, it's awfully lonely," her father replied, certain that there were no mountains between Mt. Averly and the Perigoh. "Whatever it is, it appears to be in our way."

As they drew nearer, the nondescript blob took the shape of a rectangle. A few yards closer, and dark hues sharpened to green as blurred shadows became branches. It was now undeniably and mystifyingly clear that, in the middle of the treeless grasslands, five, tall evergreen trees had somehow made their home.

Mr. Bellamy was hard pressed to explain the existence of a group of trees he'd never seen before; trees that appeared to be older than he was, by the height of them; trees located in a place he'd visited many times in the past.

"This is odd," he said, in a textbook example of understatement. Then, rubbing his chin as he sized up the mysterious discovery, Mr. Bellamy inquired of the trees, "Where'd *you* come from?"

"I thought there were no trees on the prairie," Annelyse objected.

"There aren't," her father affirmed, while examining the forty-foot-tall cypress trees standing as conspicuous as they pleased right in front of him.

Annelyse just motioned with both hands in the direction of the misplaced evergreens, as if to ask, "What do you call *these,* then?" but she resisted the urge to say it out loud, which was always good advice - and advice she seldom chose to follow.

As far as Mr. Bellamy could tell, the trees *were* there. That was the first question that needed answering. Moving down the list of questions, he now decided that they were, in fact, *real* trees in all the ways that trees are expected to be real. Second question, also, answered to his satisfaction.

However, when he arrived at question number three (which centered around precisely *how* such trees might sprout up to a height of forty feet in the space of only a year or two since he had last passed that way), he was stumped.

As a result, his suspicions were greatly aroused. There was something strange at work here.

"What are you looking for?" Annelyse asked, as her father actively scrutinized every twig, branch, and limb.

"Something out of place," he replied, his full attention absorbed by the oddity.

"You mean *more* out of place than five evergreens in the middle of a prairie?"

Annelyse made fewer and fewer attempts to curb her sarcasm, but her father took no notice. He was too engrossed in the subject at hand.

Each tree in the line was full and fat, and planted so close to the next one, that the five together formed a single, dense wall of evergreen. Standing on one side of the trees, Mr. Bellamy was unable to detect any daylight filtering through from the opposite side. Indeed, he could not see through the crowded branches at all, even so far as the interior tree trunk. The walls were quite as solid as if they'd been made of stone.

"Wait a minute," Mr. Bellamy said, as he was bending over to push aside a branch, "What's this?"

There, in the front of the first tree on the left, hidden among a tangle of branches, Mr. Bellamy found the most unusual thing. A doorknob, protruding from the wall of green leaves, sat above a keyhole and, indeed, proved to be far *more out of place than five evergreens in the middle of a prairie.*

Mr. Bellamy wrapped his hand around the doorknob. With disbelief, he began turning it, until the knob came up against a hard stop. The tree's door was locked. Wiggling the handle, he thought that it might have simply rusted sluggish beneath the raw elements. But when wiggling failed to produce a result, he began applying more brute strength to the challenge.

Although hard at work on the problem of the locked door, he was obviously failing to appreciate just how strange it was to be attempting to open a door in the side of an evergreen tree in the middle of a prairie. It was not unlike Edward Bellamy to become so focused on a problem that he lost sight of the greater absurdity. He was a man of singular focus.

"That key," he said, in a moment of realization, "You brought that iron key with you, right?"

Reaching into her pocket, Annelyse produced the key she'd taken from her mother's cedar chest. Handing it to her father, she mused, "What are the chances!?"

Mr. Bellamy inserted the key into the keyhole beneath the doorknob. Holding his breath, he rubbed his hands together before turning it in the lock.

"Zero," he replied to Annelyse's question. "No chance at all. It doesn't work."

"It was worth a try," Annelyse whispered, visibly disappointed, though she didn't really know why she should be. In a way, she was glad the key didn't fit. If it had, it would have been a bit too weird for comfort. Solutions are rarely found without effort. Things that come too easily should be viewed with suspicion.

Remembering her manners, Annelyse thought it best to take a different approach.

"Maybe we should knock."

"Knock?" her father asked, "On what?"

"The tree, I guess."

"I'm not sure there's much here to knock on, but I'll try."

Pushing against the wall of branches, Mr. Bellamy's hands sunk in up to his elbows, but still, he could find nothing solid upon which to knock. Having very little experience with such things, he decided he had no choice but to knock on the soft branches that formed the door.

Making a fist, he rapped hard against the front of the tree, sending shivers along the floppy limbs as he did. As expected, his knocking made no sound above the vigorous rustling of feathery evergreen leaves. Turning to gauge his daughter's reaction, Mr. Bellamy felt rather silly for having just knocked on a tree. But Annelyse motioned for him to try again and, feelings of silliness notwithstanding, her father obliged.

This time, the result was altogether different. From within the clump of evergreens, Annelyse and her father heard an indistinct, muffled noise. They couldn't be sure, but it didn't seem like the sort of thing you'd expect to hear coming from a tree. They decided that another knock on the door might be in order.

"Coming, I said!" was the reply - this time, loud and clear - from inside the group of trees.

A split-second later, the door swung open, nearly knocking Mr. Bellamy off his feet. In the doorway, there stood a stout, little man wearing a look of intense annoyance on his red face.

"What is it?!" the round, ruddy man asked, clearly eager to get back to whatever he'd been doing.

"It's a treehouse," Mr. Bellamy said, answering the mystery of what lay behind the door rather than the man's question.

"What? Well, of course it is," the stranger replied, "What did you think it was?"

"A bunch of trees," Annelyse answered, since her father was too distracted, trying to get a look inside, to answer for himself.

"Oh, well, yes. Astute observation, my dear. I suppose one might make that mistake."

The man was as wide as he was tall, and if that suggests an enormously large figure, allow me to correct your mistaken assumption right away. He stood barely four feet off the ground and, since every feature appeared to have been made of lumpy dumpling dough, the overall effect was that of a very small, very round, very plushy little character.

He was dressed in green overalls, which bulged at the waistline as if he'd swallowed a watermelon. On his feet, he wore two mismatched boots. One was brown with yellow laces, the other was grey with blue laces. Annelyse couldn't be certain (and was unwilling to inspect the situation any closer, for fear of giving offense), but both boots appeared to belong to the left foot. She wondered to herself if he often walked in circles, since wearing two left boots must surely cause him to drift leftward a bit. She caught herself just in time to prevent a chuckle from escaping her clenched lips.

"Was there something that you needed, or may I go *bake* to my *backing*?"

Having used up her last ounce of self-control on *not* chuckling aloud at his boots, Annelyse had no reserves left to meet this new challenge. As a result, out came the question both she and her father were thinking, "Don't you mean, *back* to your *baking*?"

"That's what I said, child. Bake to my backing. Do you take me for a fool? Prepopsterous!"

Annelyse bit her lip and glanced over at her father who was doing the exact same thing. It wasn't polite to correct someone she'd just met (especially in his own tree), and Annelyse knew this quite well. As a result, she was reluctant to fix his mispronunciation of *preposterous*. Even Annelyse's sass had its limits.

"I really must bake my tread out of the oven. If you're coming in, then now would be the time."

Spinning around in the doorway, the little man scurried off surprisingly fast for someone with such short, stout legs. The door was open, and the invitation had been extended, so Mr. Bellamy led the way. There was no chance he was going to miss out on an opportunity to inspect this wonder more closely. Annelyse followed, closing the door behind her, and marveling at the unlikelihood of it all.

Born of sunbeams winding their way around branches at the ceiling's peak, the light inside the treehouse was a soothing shade of jade green. Far from being dark and gloomy, the whole interior swam in undulating luminance, like sunshine caught up in shifting ocean tides.

The four walls of the treehouse were made of tight-knit branches of every width and size and were very nearly impenetrable. But, as the group of trees narrowed at the top, there were gaps in the branches large enough to let air and sunlight in while still keeping the rain out. It was an ingenious design in every regard.

Annelyse and her father could see that the five great evergreens formed one open space that the man had partitioned into rooms to suit his needs. He even had a second-story loft, the floor of which was made by branches that had been allowed to grow from one side all the way over to the opposite wall. From what they could tell, this was where the man's bedroom was located. It reminded Annelyse of her own bedroom loft back home.

The scent of pine mixed with that of freshly baked bread made this strange little house the most intensely pleasant place Annelyse had ever smelled. From where she stood, Annelyse could see the man hard at work in his kitchen. He'd obviously been busy all morning, as he already had four loaves cooling on a rack beside his oven. Having removed two more, he arranged them with the others, with a look of satisfaction on his face.

Calling to his guests from the kitchen, he said, "You never told me."

"What is it we didn't tell you?" Mr. Bellamy asked.

"Exactly," came the man's peculiar reply.

"I'm sorry?" Mr. Bellamy said, not quite following the conversation.

"All is forgiven! Come, join me for a lute lanch."

Mr. Bellamy just looked at Annelyse and shrugged his shoulders. At the very least, "all was forgiven," whatever that might include. So, Mr. Bellamy decided not to concern himself with it any further.

The man placed a loaf of fresh bread in the center of his square wooden table, along with some sliced ham and a block of yellow cheese. Motioning for Annelyse and her father to be seated, he returned to the kitchen to fetch a jug of water and three cups.

"Sit wherever you like," he called from the other room. "Just not in my chair, please. And beware, there's a broken leg among 'em. I'd hate to see anyone tumb a takele."

Now, Annelyse and her father faced a dilemma. There were four chairs around the table. One of them belonged to their host, and apparently, one had a broken leg. Mr. Bellamy began rocking each chair back and forth, trying to identify the one with the shaky leg and improve their chances of making the right seating decisions. Discovering the wobbly seat, he eliminated it from contention.

At the same time, Annelyse examined each of the four chairs, trying to determine which one might be the man's favorite. She noticed that only one chair had a cushion on the seat and decided this must surely be his.

Feeling confident in their selections, Annelyse and her father sat down just as the lumpy, little man returned from the kitchen.

"Right, then," he began, "You sit there, and you sit over there."

Annelyse and Mr. Bellamy quickly hopped up and changed chairs, following their host's directions, with Annelyse ending up in the chair that had the cushion and Mr. Bellamy ending up in the chair Annelyse had been sitting in. The little man chose the chair with the broken leg, carefully lowering himself onto the seat so as not to upset its delicate balance.

"That's it. Much better. Everyone comfortable now?

Good. I do love this chair," he said, not noticing the surprised look on his guest's faces. "I always sit in it. Maybe that's why it has a loken breg. Hm. Oh well. Now, who's hungry?"

The little man dug right in, slicing the bread, piling on the ham, nibbling on the cheese as if he hadn't eaten in days. He seemed quite content to forego any conversation and focus exclusively on his lunch. Annelyse and her father weren't sure precisely what the table etiquette was when dining in a stand of evergreen trees, so they decided to follow their host's lead and dig right in, too.

The bread was light and fluffy and still warm enough on the inside to soften the cheese. The ham was tender and juicy, and even the water seemed to be blessed with a hint of pine like a thirst-quenching zest of citrus. No matter how much she loved beef jerky, Annelyse was very grateful for the change of menu. And, of course, any meal taken while seated instead of hiking was a luxury.

Soon enough, as hunger subsided and curiosity grew, Annelyse and her father started to get antsy for answers to all the questions piling up inside their heads. Conversation would have to be made, no matter what Evergreen Etiquette might say.

Mr. Bellamy started the introductions. "My name's Edward Bellamy, and this is my daughter Annelyse. It's nice to meet you, Mister…?"

With his mouth stuffed full of food, the little man mumbled something in reply. Neither Annelyse nor her father had the foggiest notion of what he'd said, so Mr. Bellamy decided to give it a second try.

"I'm not familiar with your last name," he said, fishing for information, "Would you spell it for me?"

The man wiped his mouth with the back of his hand, took another bite of bread, then responded much the same way as before. Not a single syllable was intelligible. The Bellamys were now two questions into their conversation and none the wiser.

Annelyse put her cup down on the table with a bit too much emphasis for her father's comfort. He knew all too well what that meant. Catching Annelyse's eye, he glared a warning at her, but it was already too late.

"Would you please *not* talk with your mouth full," she said, looking their host directly in the eye. "It's rude and we can't understand a word you're saying."

Mr. Bellamy tried to head off the impending disaster by kicking his daughter under the table before she had a chance to continue her tirade any further. Unfortunately, he missed her leg entirely, and the toe of his right foot landed squarely against the broken leg of their host's chair. With a crack! followed by a snap! the wobbly leg collapsed, the chair pitched sideways, and the little man tumbled to the floor, landing hard on his lumpy dumpling backside.

Jumping up from his chair, Mr. Bellamy grabbed hold of the man's arm and struggled to help him back onto his feet. Annelyse just stayed put, shaking her head, and enjoying another slice of the delicious bread.

"I'm so sorry. I didn't mean…"

"Happens all the time," the little man assured them, "In fact, yust jesterday, I was eating my breakfast, when without warning the leg just… bam!"

The whole time he was talking, the unsuspecting stranger busied himself with piecing together the various fragments of leg and balancing them under the seat of his chair. Satisfied that he'd reconstructed a trustworthy support, he once again lowered himself down onto his favorite seat and continued eating. He had no clue that he'd been felled by Edward's misplaced kick, and Annelyse giggled with wicked delight at her father's unlucky miss… or rather, his lucky *near* miss.

Mr. Bellamy knew he'd dodged a bullet. He wanted very much just to enjoy a nice, quiet meal seated on a chair at a proper table. But the moment he returned to his ham and cheese sandwich Annelyse started up again. At the sound of her voice, he dropped his forehead into the palm of his right hand, a tired and defeated man.

"Before you take another bite, would you be so kind as to tell us your name?" she asked. "Thank you."

Mr. Bellamy was afraid to look up and see what the man's reaction to his daughter's impertinent request might be. Instead, he held his breath and quickly finished eating, in the event that they had just overstayed their welcome and would need to make an early departure.

The man took a drink of water, put his cup down on the table, and wiped his mouth dry with his sleeve

"Of course, my dear."

Mr. Bellamy breathed a sigh of relief.

"My name is Albert. Albert Prume. Helcome to my wome," he said, with a slight bow and a flourish.

"It's a most unusual home, sir," Annelyse continued. Having secured his attention, she was determined to hold onto it until she got some more answers. "How long have you lived here?"

"Here? Oh, about 47 hours."

"Hours?" she asked, certain she'd misunderstood his response.

"No, you're right. It's been about 47 and a half, now. I arrived closer to soon on Naturday."

"You did all this work in two days?"

"What work is that, my dear?"

"You moved all your furniture in, made the loft, set up your kitchen and…?"

"In only two days?" he interrupted. "Prepopsterous! No, indeed. No, no, no, indeed! It took me years to make this hovely louse my home."

"But you said you've only lived here for 47 ½ hours."

"Closer to 47 hours and 32 minutes, now," the

lumpy little man corrected her.

"Right. Yes. But I don't understand." Annelyse was beginning to lose her patience.

"Understand what, child?"

"How long have you lived in this treehouse?" She was almost shouting, by now. Edward began bouncing his leg under the table, channeling his growing anxiety into the floor beneath his foot.

The man paused, counted on his fingers a moment, then answered, "Seven years, nine months, thirteen days, and, well, it gets cloudy after that."

"Then this whole thing, the five evergreen trees, all of this is where you live?" Mr. Bellamy asked, beginning to comprehend.

"It is!" came the reply.

"And you just moved your whole house to this part of the Fäerie Fields last Saturday?"

"Soonish on Naturday. Right you are, my good man!"

"And where were you before Natur… I mean, Saturday?" Annelyse chimed in.

"In the Quibble Woods," the little man replied, with a hint of something not unlike dread in his voice. "But I had to get out."

Then, in a whisper, he continued, "It was much too crowded in that wretched forest. And the noise…" He stopped cold, a shudder running up his spine.

Mr. Bellamy perked up at the mention of the Quibble Woods. "What noise do you mean?" he asked.

"The trees. The nonsense. The endless garbling of misused words. Stripped my nerves raw. I had to get out of there."

Changing his tone from cautious whispering to boisterous excitement, he added, "It's nuch micer here! Wouldn't you agree? Let me refill your cups for you!"

It was clear to Mr. Bellamy, by the rapid change of

subject, that their host did not want to talk about the Quibble Woods. Still, it was not only Edward's curiosity that had been riled, but his apprehension, too. He'd heard plenty of rumors about the haunted woods to know that it was best to avoid them altogether. Now, with what Albert Prume had said about the trees - some sort of noise, garbled words, and raw nerves - Mr. Bellamy was beginning to think that maybe he should exercise his fatherly authority and forbid Annelyse to lead them there at all.

"One more question," Annelyse said, while Albert refilled her cup with water. "How?"

"How, my dear? How what? I'm afraid I don't follow."

"How did you move your whole treehouse from the Quibble Woods, over the Perigoh River, and all the way down here… in two days?!"

"47 hours and 37 minutes, to be precise," Albert interjected.

"Right. Yes. But how?"

"Well, sprictly steaking, I didn't."

"You didn't move here?" Annelyse wanted to reach down Albert's chubby throat and pull a straight and proper answer out. It would've been a most welcome change.

"Not at all! That would be…"

"Preposterous," Annelyse interjected, finishing his sentence for him.

"Precisely! Prepopsterous! No, my dear, I didn't do the moving. The trees did, of course!"

"Of course," she said, with more sarcasm than was, *strictly speaking,* entirely appropriate.

"Ah, right. Ok, then. I can see how there might be some confusion on the topic. Allow me to show you what I mean."

Walking over to the third tree in the line, Albert located a small, wooden handle affixed to a metal arm that was bolted to the main trunk. A set of concentric dials, each bearing a series of numbers, ringed the bolt which secured the metal arm to the tree.

Turning one dial after another with great precision, Albert found the numbers he was looking for, then took hold of the handle and cranked it around in a circle five or six times. Immediately, the entire house of five, forty-foot-tall evergreen trees began moving.

The motion was not the least bit jerky or mechanical. Instead, the whole treehouse seemed to glide forward like a boat through glassy waters. The only sound that could be heard was that of a gentle breeze wafting through the leaves and branches outside.

There was no telling how fast they were traveling. In fact, there was barely any sense of movement at all. It was as smooth and pleasant a mode of transportation as one might hope to experience over land. But, if there had been *some confusion on the topic* before they started moving, there was even more confusion now.

"Are we…? But *how* are we…?" Annelyse was speechless, which, as her father can attest to, is not a common occurrence.

"How, you ask? Well, we're tietopping… toetipping… tiptoeing! That's it! We're tiptoeing! Isn't it grand?!"

"On the tips of whose toes?" Annelyse demanded, the pitch of her voice increasing with her general state of alarm.

"The trees', of course!"

"The trees? The trees have toes?!"

"Look."

Albert got up and cleared away the fallen evergreen needles near where Annelyse was seated, revealing that the floor upon which they'd been standing was not earthen after all. Just as the floor of the loft above their heads was composed of interlocking branches, the entire floor of the treehouse was formed in the exact same way.

Kneeling down, Albert began prying the woven limbs apart as if breaking up a riot of snakes. As he untangled the knotted branches, daylight began flooding in from the hole in the dining room floor, illuminating the childlike, doughy face of Albert Prume. There was wonderment in his eyes, as he smiled up at Annelyse and her father.

"See?"

Looking down through the hole in the floor into the space between the bottom of the treehouse and the bare earth, everything Albert had said began to make sense. Rather than digging into the soil, the roots of the five trees were scurrying along like a million multi-legged crabs. As they tiptoed with great haste over the meadow, their slender, tapered limbs were a worm's nest of perpetual motion.

"Keep watching," Albert instructed, as he returned to the handle and numbered dials.

Giving the arm five or six turns in the opposite direction, Albert brought all motion to a gentle halt. Down below the floor of branches, the chaotic mesh of roots stopped their tiptoeing and slowly began wriggling their way into the soft earth again.

"Hurrah! Isn't it grand?!"

Mr. Bellamy and Annelyse looked at each other with mouths agape. Staring down through the hole in the floor, they were both beyond dumbfounded.

"These trees are the one good thing to come out of that accursed forest - five good things, to be precise. They'd had enough, too. So, we struck up a partnership, you might say. A butually meneficial arrangement."

"What arrangement is that?" Mr. Bellamy asked, trying to wrap his head around it all.

"They get to visit new places, and I get a nice place to live! We usually only ever stay-put for a day or two before we're off again. I don't call it my Tree RV for nothing. RV stands for *roaming vehicle,* don't ya know? They're a restless lot, to be sure. So much to see and so tittle lime in the day."

Albert began rearranging the branches, repairing the hole in his floor, as he spoke. In no time, he had it all woven together tight as new.

"It's really the perfect home," he said, spreading some feather-shaped leaves and loose needles back over the bare spot on his floor.

"I'm rarely ever bothered by visitors. Of course, those who do drop in tend to go about spreading word of Prume's Wile to everyone they meet. But thankfully, most people are reluctant to believe stories of mobile treehouses and the like. In fact, now that I think of it, it's been years since I had a caller. The last one was… well… I forget. It's been a tong lime, for sure."

Sitting back down in his favorite chair, Albert cast an inquisitive eye over his two visitors. He had some questions of his own.

"You never told me," he began, in his usual vague manner.

"We never told you what, exactly?" Mr. Bellamy asked, feeling that they probably did owe their generous host some answers.

"Anything, really. Besides your names, that is. Where are you from? What were you doing at my door? Where are you going to next? How long have you been traveling? And, most of all, what do you think of my grand treehouse? That should get us started. You may now answer."

Albert sat back in his chair, carefully maintaining his balance so as to avoid falling again. Folding his arms, he waited patiently for Mr. Bellamy to respond.

"Well, where do I start?"

"By answering my first question," Albert directed.

"Right," Mr. Bellamy cleared his throat, then took it

from the top. "We live on the peninsula, just west of the town of Averlune. We left home yesterday morning…"

"Surely, you didn't ford the Fenneleen by foot," Albert said, interrupting Edward midsentence.

"No. We took the path behind the falls."

"Is that so? My, my. Very wise of you," Albert said, nodding slowly. "And bery vrave, too. Go on, don't let me interrupt you."

"We spent the night in Alders Idle. Then…"

"Of course, you did. No better place between the mount and the Rindle. Continue."

Edward struggled to locate his lost train of thought.

"Um… uh, oh yes… It was then that we spotted your home. It just seemed so out of place, we had to take a closer look."

"And so, you have. A much closer look. Keep going. Tell me more."

"We're on our way to Pebble Ford, and then… into the Quibble Woods."

At the mention of the haunted forest, a look of alarm shot across Albert's startled face.

"Why on *earth* would you go there? What possible business could you… no, no, no. That dimply won't… that simply don't… that's a terrible idea!"

"We really don't have much choice," Annelyse said, her own sense of uneasiness beginning to grow.

"My dear child, there are any number of places you might choose to go! You certainly do have a choice!"

"But the poet said…"

"That's him!" Albert exclaimed, startling both Annelyse and her father with his excitement.

"You know the poet?" Annelyse asked.

"Not well, no," Albert replied, scratching his head. "But *he* was my last visitor. I just remembered. Nice chap. A bit odd, but good company. It has been a tong lime, though. A very tong lime, indeed."

"Well, the poet told us to look for someone who lives *along the Maidenhair*. Someone who might know what it was that I saw in the…"

Annelyse stopped short of mentioning the Weeping Pool. She wasn't sure if it was a good idea to give away too much information. Better to keep some things secret, perhaps. Fortunately, Albert seemed to be distracted by the mention of *someone who lives along the Maidenhair*.

"Someone… along the Maidenhair… why would the poet… no, no, no, my child, you mustn't go into that forest. You simply mustn't, and that is all."

"There isn't much chance of us reaching the haunted forest today, at any rate," said Mr. Bellamy. "We'd never make it to the ford before sundown, let alone to the forest."

He was relieved to be able to put off any decision about entering the Quibble Woods for a little bit longer.

"Nonsense," Albert replied, sensing a challenge. "We could be at the ford in only a mew finutes."

"A few minutes? The ford is a good ten miles from here."

"My dear Bister Mellamy, my trees could cover that distance in half an hour or less. Less, for my money. Time me!"

Without another word, Albert ran over to the center tree, spun the dials to the correct heading, then gave the hand crank a few good turns. The treehouse responded in its usual prompt and steady fashion, and they were off.

Noticing the look of wonder in Annelyse's eyes, Albert smiled, reached one hand up, and took hold of a bulbous wooden handle dangling from a cord above his head. Pulling on the handle, he watched his guests' faces, as all the branches surrounding them opened to let in the afternoon sun and cool, spring breeze. The limbs of the five evergreen trees were like louvered blinds and, now that they were open, Annelyse and her father could clearly see just how fast they were traveling.

Daisies, daffodils, and buttercups flew by in a blur of whites, greens, and yellows. Birds pulled themselves up short, pausing a moment to regain their bearings. The sudden sense of immense speed created by their own flight and the rapidly approaching group of evergreens was disorienting to the bewildered birds. Stretching out behind the traveling trees, a wake of bent grass and befuddled wildlife was all the evidence a traveler might receive of the passing of Prume's Wile.

Below the living floor of tangled branches, an armada of tree roots tiptoed over the prairie at twenty miles per hour, faster than the speed of a bicycle. Each toe was careful to avoid bruising either petal or blade, for all living things were kin to the trees.

Inside, Albert invited his guests to make themselves comfortable and enjoy the ride, while he anxiously watched the wall clock tick off the minutes. He loved a good challenge, especially when it meant proving that his treehouse was truly grand in every way. There was one challenge, however, none of them had anticipated and it lay just up ahead.

Letting Go

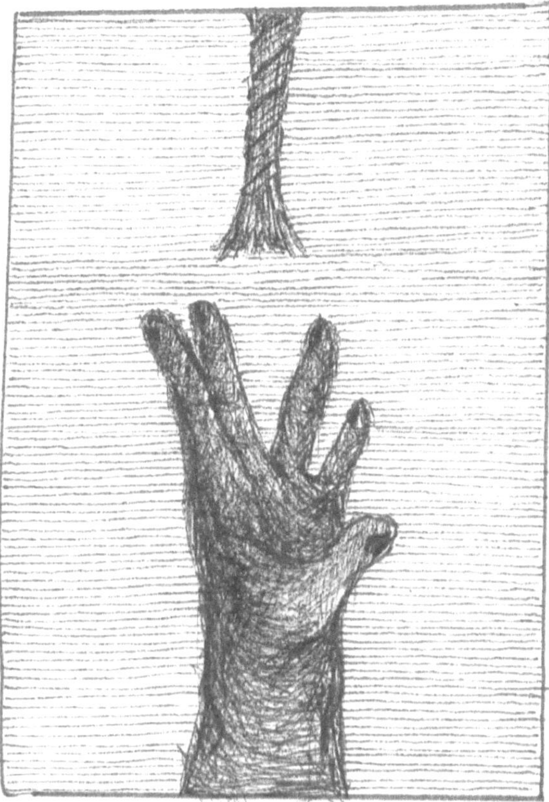

Through the gaps in the branches, Annelyse watched the silver strand of the Perigoh Fair take on all the characteristics of a mighty river. Its restless shoulders, shimmering in the sunlight, carried snowmelt from as far away as the Luna Mountains northeast of Mydland Dells. Raindrops that had once glistened like emeralds upon a million waxy leaves in the Forest of Silhouette, now trickled and slithered their way southward until they were swallowed in the insatiable brown of the river. Everything was in motion. Everything had purpose, and the Perigoh ran as deep as time itself.

White seagulls flew leaderless and chaotic above the fish-rich waters, the noise of their endless chatter growing louder by the minute. To the road-weary Bellamys, the familiar sound was a comforting reminder of their little cabin by the sea.

They were now surrounded by water on three sides. Directly in front of them, fewer than three miles away, the Perigoh Fair barred their passage north. To their left, Buckhorn Creek splintered off from the main flow of the river, heading inland half the distance back toward Mt. Averly.

On their right, a great circular basin bulged southward, as the Perigoh struggled and clawed its way to the sea through the rocky soil. The basin was called Luckless Pond, though in reality, it was neither. The local fishermen coined the name as a way of deterring those who didn't know any better from fishing there. Truth be told, Luckless Pond was one of the best fishing holes along the central Perigoh, and just one of many fishermen's secrets preserved by tall tales.

As the Tree RV approached Buckhorn Creek, something caught Albert's eye. The tributary had overflowed its banks and turned much of the surrounding floodplain into a marshy mess of massive puddles. More concerning, the Buckhorn was running high and wild, foaming at the mouth like a rabid animal. If this was any indication of the state of the Perigoh, then even Pebble Ford might prove to be too dangerous to cross.

"I don't like the looks of *that*," Albert said, pointing

to the swollen creek. "I had hoped that the recent rain had reached the bay, by now. But it appears to be timing its take."

Annelyse looked at her father, trying to read the severity of the situation in his eyes.

"We may have to camp on this side of the river for one more night, after all," he said, rubbing the stiffness from his neck with one hand.

"It would be a soggy sleep, for sure," Albert said. "The whole plain is flooded for miles around."

"Maybe we should turn back, just until we reach dry land," Edward replied, thinking it best to err on the side of caution.

"Nonsense. These trees don't mind getting their toes wet. We're sot nunk, yet!"

Albert returned to the command console. Locating what looked like a handle from an old fashioned well, he began pumping it with all his might. Annelyse scanned the room for a spigot, fully expecting to see a gush of brown water spurt out of the floor. Instead, through the open branches, she noticed the world outside appear to sink steadily into the waterlogged earth. The traveling treehouse was growing taller with every pump of the handle. The ground was much farther below them now.

"That'll put us up above the wet," Albert said, wiping the sweat from his brow.

Thanks to Albert's efforts, the stand of five, forty-foot-tall trees now stood an extra four feet taller. Instead of dragging their skirts of green-feather leaves through the mud, they now wore them just above the knee where they were sure to stay dry. Marshland and mud puddles, no matter how deep, posed very little problem for Albert Prume's Tree RV.

The speed at which they'd been traveling had not been diminished in the slightest by the wet terrain. On the contrary, the tree roots seemed to take hold and slide through the mud with greater ease. Annelyse couldn't be sure, but she got the feeling that these exceptional evergreens enjoyed traveling just as much as Albert did. Indeed, it was a *butually meneficial…* or rather, a *mutually beneficial* arrangement.

Their destination was now in sight, marked by the only sign they'd seen since the previous day. Much to Albert's delight, they'd arrived at Pebble Ford in only twenty-seven minutes and fourteen seconds. It was a new land speed record for trees, and the driver of these victorious evergreens beamed with pride like a paunchy lightbulb.

But the victory was short lived.

Pebble Ford was a narrow point in the Perigoh River where the enormous flow of water was eased upstream by Luckless Pond and downstream by Buckhorn Creek. In the middle of the river, Pebble Island stood fast against the flood, forcing the Perigoh to straddle the rocky spit of land.

Here, the banks on either side were much higher than at most places along the river. This allowed for the construction of a rope bridge which was strung from both shores. The bridge spanned the water and was secured to a solitary oak tree on Pebble Island in the middle of the stream. Travelers were able to safely ford the river by means of the rope bridge, provided they didn't mind a fair amount of bouncing and swaying. Pebble Ford was not for the fainthearted.

West of Mount Silhouette and the Woods of Westerwerhle, there was no other way to cross the Perigoh. Aside from the occasional kindly fisherman, the nearest reliable ferryboats were over 60 miles away near Oxbridge. West of Pebble Ford, the river was too wild to endure anyone but skilled seamen.

Under normal circumstances, Pebble Ford was the best and fastest way to cross the wide water. But today, circumstances were anything but normal.

An unusually early spring had caught winter off guard and ill-prepared. This would have been enough, in and of itself, to overwhelm the rivers. But the winter months had seen more snowfall than most folks could recall in years. Now, with a warm spring sun bearing down on it, the snowpack held captive by the mountains of Wehrle and East Hyland flowed freely at last.

At first, the snowflakes began to curl, curving inward, crumbling beneath the weight of their own delicacy. Lace unraveled, becoming frozen droplets; droplets drooped, settling into a heavy slush; and underneath it all, a thin layer of wet snow was pressed into slick sheets of ice.

Sweating beneath the sun, the slippery mixture lost its footing and slid downhill in a thousand tiny rills, weaving their way between the sharp boulders of the mountainside. Once the snowmelt reached the Greater and Lesser Forktongue rivers, it lost track of itself, joining a countless multitude of water droplets bound for the great river.

But the Perigoh is unlike any other waterway in Laprofonde, for it tastes vaguely of sea salt even as far inland as Oxbridge. Almost imperceptible to man or beast, the drops of water that had once been innocent snowflakes soon felt the sting of the brackish water.

But when Annelyse, Edward and Albert arrived at the ford, the waters of the Perigoh Fair were as fresh and sweet as the Wee Runnel of northern Hyland. The mountains had combined their frigid flow with the recent rains, and every river and creek in central Laprofonde was overrun.

"The ford," Mr. Bellamy said, pointing to the river.

"I can't see it," Annelyse complained, straining her neck to see.

Where Pebble Island should have stood, a churning

gurgle of foaming rapids now swirled around a drop of land barely large enough to give root to the oak tree growing at its center. Where the rope bridge had once spanned the river, now only the frayed and tattered threads of torn knots remained. Even the wooden posts on either shore, which had anchored the bridge to dry land, leaned like drunkards in the waterlogged ground. It was only a matter of time before they fell over and were swept out to sea by the flood waters.

"That clinches it," Mr. Bellamy said, with an ironic chuckle. "We've got no choice but to head back. We can't make camp in a swamp!"

"You can't go back," came Albert's unexpected reply. "There's no back to go to. Never is. There's only ever now and here. There and then are gone already! So, the question is, do you still mean to cross that river or don't you?"

"We did, but…"

"Nut bothing!" Albert interrupted, excitement causing his tongue to slip yet again. "You can't let a setback change your plans. If you mean to go forward, then going backward won't get you where you're headed. All it can do is lead you farther away."

Mr. Bellamy had no idea how to respond to Albert's self-evident logic. It was true enough, but with no way to ford the river what else could they do but turn back and find someplace safe to make camp? Just as he was about to reiterate the wisdom of abandoning their plan, Mr. Bellamy was cut short.

"Right then," Albert said, rubbing his hands together. "Here we go."

The stout little man approached the control console as if he were searching for his favorite pastry in a bakery window. It was clear that he delighted in driving his grand invention. He stood there a moment, poring over a panel of knobs and switches, looking for something in particular.

"Ah!" he exclaimed, resting his finger on what looked like a red rubber ball protruding from the panel. "Haven't needed to use this button in quite some time," he said from over his shoulder.

Leaning in, he took hold of the old-fashioned well handle and started pumping until the Tree RV had grown to three times its previous height. He then set the navigation dials to the desired heading and turned the hand crank about a quarter of a turn. The treehouse began tiptoeing down the riverbank with great care, like a child approaching a chilly swimming hole.

Annelyse and Mr. Bellamy watched the scene unfold, holding their breath all the while. An apprehensive part of them was certain that they'd all be rolled under the whitewater and drowned. Another more adventurous part of them still couldn't believe they were really inside a walking treehouse! It was all a bit too much to take in.

Annelyse couldn't decide which was more fascinating to watch, their descent into the path of the mighty Perigoh, or the feverish activity of Albert Prume as he piloted his most unusual vehicle. Her eyes kept darting back and forth between the two spectacles.

Just as the RV reached the water's edge, Albert leaned over and gave the big red button a push. Without a sound, all the branches comprising the walls and ceiling of the mobile treehouse began to open like a flower in the morning sun. Spreading out and laying down flat, the dense branches formed a raft which bore the whole treehouse up on the waters of the Perigoh River.

Beneath the floor of woven wood upon which Annelyse, Edward, and Albert now stood, the roots of the five evergreens paddled their feet like expert swimmers. Prume's Wile was now a boat riding the waves of the largest river in Laprofonde.

At first, the tree-boat barely bobbed in the gentle current running along the riverbank. But, as they entered the central stream whipping its way around the southern shore of Pebble Island, the raft began to heave – and Annelyse very nearly did, too.

The sensation of riding the floodwaters on a raft of evergreen branches was much like being carried along on the backs of a herd of stampeding cattle. At any given moment, they found themselves moving in multiple directions at once. Jetting forward toward the north shore, they were propelled by the paddling feet of the tree roots. All the while, the water rolling beneath them lurched and jerked the little raft skyward.

At times, the water seemed to drop out from under the raft, causing them to freefall through the air. The elusive whitewater would then take them by surprise, smacking the bottom of their raft and compressing Annelyse's spine like a spring. With cruel delight, the relentless current pushed them downstream closer and closer to the boulders that foamed below the surface.

Still at the controls, Albert reached over and took hold of a wheel attached to the center console. Spinning it to the right, the whole floor of the treehouse pitched in the same direction, as if bracing itself against the onrush of boulders. Foreseeing the inevitable, Albert grabbed onto the nearest branch and wrapped it around his waist like a safety rope.

"Hold on tight, friends! Here come the rocks!"

Mr. Bellamy wrapped one arm around Annelyse and the other around the main trunk of the first tree in the line. Annelyse followed her father's example and wrapped her leg around the trunk, too. With her head spinning amid the endless motion, her stomach felt as fluid as the river they rode. Adrenaline coursed through her veins, as the pain of panic throbbed behind her eyes.

The impact of the raft as it struck the boulders broadside sent everyone tumbling to the floor. Albert and Edward were quick to get back on their feet and secure themselves to the trunks again. At the same time, Mr. Bellamy helped Annelyse stand and steady herself against the tree. They had far more control on their feet than they had on their hands and knees. Tossing their weight from one leg to the other, they held their own against the mercurial motions of the river.

Albert turned the wheel back toward the left, trying his best to level the floor, but it was of little use. The heaving waters slammed into the right side of the raft, driving it further up onto the boulders at a 45-degree angle. Before anyone could react, all four dining room chairs slid down the sloped floor and into the river. The table would have followed, had it not been for a wave that lifted the raft off the boulders and returned the floor to a more or less horizontal state.

By now, everyone and everything aboard the boat of evergreen trees was soaking wet. The loaves of freshly baked bread were now five mushy blobs on the soggy countertop. The block of cheese had lost its natural shape and color, and the three drinking cups and pitcher were overflowing with river water. The whole place was a washed-out mess.

"Halfway there!" Albert yelled, over the chaos.

Off to their right, a much smaller Pebble Island was only a few feet away and fairing much better in the raging river than they were. Around its shrunken shoreline, foaming rapids marked-out where the island ended, and the river began.

With her face pressed up against the tree, Annelyse was so cold that she was having a hard time holding onto the trunk. Her fingers were purple and numb, and she could barely feel the bark beneath them. She wanted desperately to fling herself off the floating nightmare and onto the solid soil of the island. There, she'd live out her days, quite happy never to cross that blasted river again.

As the raft sailed past the lonesome outpost in the

middle of the stream, they could see that the waters north of Pebble Island presented a different situation. As with most things, it was a trade-off, though. Narrower and wilder waters lay to the south of the island; calmer but wider waters to the north. Annelyse wasn't sure which was better. She'd almost have preferred to face a few more minutes of whitewater madness just to be done with it sooner. But she quickly realized that appearances could be dangerously deceptive. The calmer waters concealed a new, more deadly threat.

Despite the powerful current (or maybe because of it), there were fewer obstacles in their way. That much was a relief. As a result, the paddling feet of the tree roots were able to maintain their heading more easily - even picking up speed as they went. Convinced that all the perils were now behind them, Annelyse relaxed her grip on the tree trunk and dropped to her knees, exhausted from the exertion. The moment she did, Albert called to her with alarm in his voice.

"On your feet, child! We're not out of the watery woods yet!"

There in their path, at the edge of a calm patch of water, a whirlpool was boring a deep, black hole in the surface of the river. Twice the width of the raft, the ravenous vortex threatened to swallow them all without the least scruple.

As the calm current approached the hole in the river it increased in speed. Held fast in its tumultuous grip, the whitewater whipped around the rim of the gigantic centrifuge, relinquishing debris it had picked up on its way through the northern forests.

Clinging to the sides of the liquid tornado, the river spun around and around - faster, and faster - a dizzying dervish of nausea and confusion. Like a cyclone out of control, the grey water spat and sputtered, until at last, the river was cast back out of the whirlpool to continue along its westward course to the sea.

Annelyse saw flotsam and jetsam disappear over the edge of the gaping hole, and she wondered where it all went. Driftwood and branches, wood planks and tattered rope were all herded into the mouth of the whirlpool then swallowed deep down into the abyss. It occurred to her that not even their raft of evergreens would prove too large for the river to consume. Hot blood rose to the surface of her skin, thawing Annelyse's frozen fingers as she tightened her grip around the trunk of the tree.

Standing at the console, Albert Prume was busy fighting the persistent pull of swirling waters. He had no desire to be tossed into the hands of fate like an old cork. Tangled in the parade of discarded tree limbs and river refuse, he struggled to break free before it was too late.

Cranking the wheel to the right, Albert turned the raft away from the whirlpool and into the onrushing current, to no avail. The force of the floodwaters barreled down on them without mercy, thrusting them back in the direction of danger.

If they were to have any chance of making it to the opposite shore, they had to position themselves just right. Too far to the left, and they'd end up in the belly of the vortex. Too far to the right, and they'd founder on the boulders surrounding Pebble Island.

But the relentless flow made it nearly impossible to claw their way upstream away from the whirlpool. And it was entirely impossible to hold their position. Try as they might, between the swimming tree roots and the skillful maneuvering of Albert's efforts, whatever gains they made were quickly erased by the mighty river.

Expending all their energy in an effort to avoid certain death, the raft was caught in an upstream-downstream struggle. No progress was being made in crossing the last hundred yards or so of water that separated them from the shore. It was just a matter of time before the push of the current handed them over to the pull of the whirlpool. They needed a change of strategy, and time was running out.

Albert had one more trick up his sleeve; but it was risky, and the stakes were already high. Assessing their situation one last time, he decided that it would undoubtedly be much riskier *not* to give this longshot a try. The decision was made, and Albert swung into action.

On the face of the control panel, protected by a clear, plastic cover, a single key waited in its keyhole. Flipping the cover up, Albert took hold of the key, then turned to give instructions to Annelyse and Edward.

"Keep your feet close to the trunk and mold on with all your hight."

Pausing only long enough to see that his order had been carried out, Albert braced himself against the command center and gave the key a decisive turn.

With no more than a split second of hesitation, the shape of the entire raft began to change. Like a deflated balloon stretched from both ends, the broad central floor upon which they were standing started to narrow and lengthen. Within moments, both sides of the raft were only inches from Annelyse's feet. The whole Tree RV was now barely wider than the five trunks rising up from its middle.

Instead of a square comprised of interlacing branches, the raft had been transformed into an enormous arrow. Every branch was elongated and aligned stern to bow. Stretching and reaching northward with every inch of branch and twig available to them, the root-propelled craft pierced the heart of the river like a needle.

"No matter what happens," Albert yelled, "Do lot noosen your grip!"

On the upstream side of the raft, the river leapt over the edge and swamped the feet of everyone on deck. Nonetheless, their captain directed them to lean to the right - into the rushing waters - to avoid being capsized.

Desperate to keep the bow of the boat above water, Albert began kicking and shoving everything he could move (of what little had not already been washed overboard) toward the stern of the raft. As the weight shifted to the back, the nose rose ever so slightly, and their speed increased. But their enemy now lay within grasping distance of the raft.

Only a dozen or so yards from the northern shore, they were now even with the whirlpool. As the river fell headlong over the lip of the black hole, the overburdened back of the boat began lagging downstream. They were losing their fight against both the suction of the great vortex and the cruel current of the river, and everyone knew it.

"Leesy," her father said, wrapping his arms around Annelyse. "I love you!"

Looking up, Annelyse saw a veil of desperation darkening her father's face. It was a shadow of bitter helplessness, and Edward Bellamy resented living in a world in which love was not enough to defeat suffering. Powerless to rescue his wife from death, he was now doomed to watch his daughter die in the cold floodwaters. His love seemed powerless to save her life. Faced with an all-too-familiar situation, the same brand of anger he'd felt toward the evil that had claimed his wife raged inside of him once more.

"I won't let it happen again!" he yelled. "I will *not*!"

Running to the front of the raft, Edward grabbed hold of a length of rope that had been used as a clothesline. Before anyone could react, he tied one end of the rope around the trunk of the fifth tree and the other end around his waist, then dove into the icy waters off the bow.

"Daddy!" Annelyse screamed, as she watched her father disappear beneath the waves.

"Oh my," Albert fretted. "Oh my, oh my."

A moment later, Edward Bellamy emerged from the depths, swimming with every drop of livid determination in his body. Trailing behind him, the clothesline billowed out and sagged downstream, limp and lifeless in the inexorable current.

Albert's head tilted at a thoughtful angle, as he watched the clothesline bob in the waves.

"Look, child," he said, pointing to the rope. "Catch it warefully."

Annelyse huddled against the tree trunk, squinting her eyes against the stinging spray of water on the wind. It was then that she saw what held Albert's attention rivetted.

The bulge in the rope tied between the bow of the boat and her father's waist had begun to shallow. The sideways U-shape became a semicircle and then a glorious, marvelous, wonderful straight line. Edward Bellamy was holding steady against the current; he was making progress; he was nearing the north shore of the Perigoh Fair.

Albert started throwing everything he could find overboard, in an effort to lighten Edward's burden. The dining room table, a large oak chest, even the armoire his father had made with his own hands, nothing was too precious when a friend's life was at stake.

The clothesline was now quite taut, as Edward reached the first few boulders lining the shore. But the moment he stopped swimming and began dragging himself up onto the rocks, the floodwaters took their revenge. Without any forward momentum, the raft quickly started drifting downstream again, pulling Edward back into the powerful current. Struggling to hold onto the boulder, he arched his back against the deadweight of the raft. But he could not hang on much longer.

Albert ran over to the control panel, grabbed hold of the key, and turned it one more click to the right. Around the keyhole, a dial engraved in successive green, yellow, and red markings now showed the key's position - squarely in the red zone.

Albert motioned for Annelyse to join him in the

bow, as the raft stretched itself out to its full length, no more than one tree limb's width across. They were balanced upon the wet and wobbly, rounded back of one branch, and grasping, with every finger of frayed hope for the shoreline.

The few second's-worth of slack that the raft's change in shape had afforded him was just enough for Edward to climb up out of the water and onto the banks of the river. Once on dry land, he wound the clothesline around a nearby tree, and began pulling as hard as his aching muscles would allow. Little by little, one tug at a time, the distance between the raft and the safety of the shore lessened, until only two or three feet separated them.

"Forgive me, my dear," Albert said, as he picked Annelyse up and threw her across the watery gap and onto the riverbank. Landing hard on the soft, wet ground, she was dazed by her sudden and unexpected departure from the boat.

With a holler that sounded more like a cry of adventure than fear, Albert Prume took a running start and leapt from the front of the elongated raft. Tucking himself into the shape of a doughy fritter, he landed on the shore and rolled to his feet in one graceful motion.

"I can't hold it much longer," Edward yelled, as the rope began to slip from his grip.

Checking on Annelyse, Albert then ran over to Edward's side, rested one hand on the man's shoulder, and with great peace in his voice, said, "Let it go, my friend."

"What? No! Your home…"

"Let it go. You've done enough."

"But, the whirlpool. It'll be lost," Edward countered, the rope shifting in his wet hands.

"Nothing good is ever truly lost," Albert replied, then took the rope from Edward and relinquished it to the river.

As they stood there, dripping, and shivering on the

shore, Annelyse, Edward, and Albert watched the treehouse-turned-life-raft drift downstream; circle the rim of the whirlpool; then tip stern-over-bow and plunge deep into the heart of the river.

"Your beautiful home," Mr. Bellamy said, exhausted and trembling. "I'm so sorry."

Albert wiped a tear from his tired, red eyes and whispered to himself, "Aye, and wasn't it grand?"

Sifting Through the Wreckage

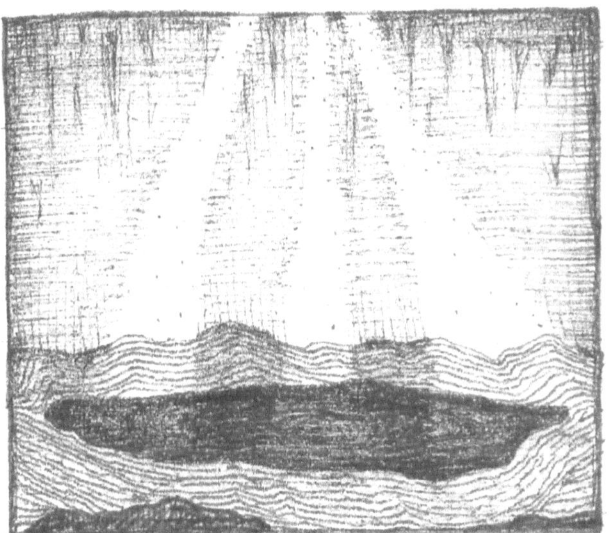

Fording the Perigoh had taken them the better part of the afternoon. Worn thin in body and mind, the three battered mariners flopped down in the grass and rested, unable to walk another yard.

Their heads were awash in the embers of burned-out adrenaline. And each one of them was beyond the ability to make sense of all that had happened. It was just a blur of whitewater and heartbreak. If she'd had the energy, Annelyse would have wept for the loss of such a wonderful and unique home as Albert's. Instead, she mourned in the silence of her thoughts.

Despite what he'd said about good things never

truly being lost, Annelyse couldn't help but feel the emptiness of Albert's words. In the space of a week, she'd lost her mother, her sense of family, and so much in which she had always believed. Now she'd witnessed Albert's magnificent treehouse being swallowed by the fearsome Perigoh Fair. In Annelyse's opinion, there was nothing fair about any of it.

Nearby, Edward Bellamy lay on his back, still trying to catch his breath and feeling like every cell in his body had burst from exertion. In a moment of frustration and anger, he'd channeled his ire into unexpected strength. But the moment was gone, and with it all his energy. He'd left everything he had to give in the river, and the river had washed it all out to sea.

A few feet away, sitting cross-legged on the shore, Albert Prume was unusually quiet. Annelyse could only guess what turmoil must have been simmering inside his heart. He was homeless now, but it was much more than that. He'd lost all his belongings; his five best friends; and their wonderful, wandering way of life. It would have been truer to say that Albert Prume was now an orphan, much the way Annelyse felt.

She couldn't for the life of her understand how he was able to just sit there. Had it been her, she would have been raging in tears against the injustice of it all as she had done only a few nights before after burying her mother. But there he sat beside the river where everything he'd ever known and loved now lay buried. Surely, it was too much for one man to bear.

Upending all of her assumptions, Albert hopped to his feet, startling Annelyse in the process. Clapping his hands together, the indomitably positive, frumpy, little man looked his companions in the eye and said, "I'm certain, by now, it's been long enough. Let's be off!"

Unsure as to precisely what he meant, Edward and Annelyse pulled themselves up in a pitiful show of support.

They were reluctant to ask questions, sensitive to what they assumed was a fragile state of melancholy in their guide. Besides, wherever they were off to, it couldn't be any worse than where they'd just come from. They were willing to follow Albert, for lack of any better plan.

The direction he chose to lead them in was a complete surprise. They'd made clear, earlier in the day, that their intention had been to press on into the Quibble Woods after fording the river. But Albert was now heading northeast across the Lesser Mydland Dells instead of northwest toward the haunted forest.

Edward may have been too tired and sympathetic to Albert's grief to ask any questions, but Annelyse was unwilling to walk a single stride farther than she had to. Never one to let anything stand in the way of a good objection, she didn't hesitate to speak up.

"Why are we going the wrong way?" she asked, stopping dead in her tracks, hands on her hips. "The Quibble Woods are over there."

"Against my jetter budgment, we *are* going to the haunted forest, my dear. Or rather, you are. We're just taking a bound-a-rot… a wound-adroit… a roundabout way!"

"Roundabout?" Annelyse protested, hands still firmly on her hips, nostrils flaring. "If we go this way, we'd have to circle the whole globe before coming back around-about again!"

"There are more ways to get from here to there, young lady, than one might expect."

"And faster ways, too!" Annelyse added, rolling her eyes.

"Priorities, child! Speed is rarely more important than purpose. There's something I need to collect, and it's this way, not that."

Mr. Bellamy steered clear of this argument. He was still exhausted and a bit shell-shocked from his experience in the river. Guilt over having been unable to save Albert's treehouse weighed heavy on his mind. More than anything, he simply wanted to disappear for a while, but remaining silent was the best he could manage.

"Fine," came the inevitable spirited response from the 14-year-old. "But let's see if we can combine speed *and* purpose, ok?"

Albert ignored her rudeness and continued trudging along, with the other two in tow. Every step Annelyse took in the opposite direction of the Quibble Woods irritated her more than was reasonable. She was tired, hungry, sore, and emotionally raw. She neither knew nor cared where they'd be spending the night. She just wanted to get there and stay there long enough to eat, sleep, and set her mind aright. It had been less than 20 minutes since they'd left the shore, but fatigue has a way of multiplying everything unpleasant. If wherever-they-were-heading ended up being too much farther, she was seriously considering mutiny.

Barely had the traitorous thought crossed her mind when Albert announced that they'd arrived at their destination. The roundabout detour had proven much shorter than Annelyse had expected. Their destination, however, would prove far more dreadful than she imagined.

The forests of the Lesser Mydland Dells were bounded by the Perigoh to the south and the River Wehrle to the east. To their west, the wide-open pasturelands ran undeterred to the Quibble Woods, and as far north as Hyland and the Sillough Run.

This was scenic country, where verdant fields leapt into rolling hills in the blink of an eye. All along the northeastern horizon, snowcapped mountains formed an impenetrable wall of grey stone behind which the sun emerged every morning. Down below, herds of wild horses from the Mydland Dells and beyond ran free among the tall grass.

It was said that the thriving herds had descended

from horses that had made their way to shore from the many shipwrecks entombed beneath the waves of King's Bay. Migrating inland, the docile creatures passed through the northern reaches of the Quibble Woods and found happiness thriving in the vast open spaces of Hyland.

Along the north shore of the Perigoh, not far from Pebble Ford, the woods of Westerwerhle sweep seaward, coming to a point at the grotto of the Echoing Caverns. Locals avoid this place, for fear of the many terrors described in legends that have grown up around it over the centuries.

The mysterious caverns are said to extend deep into watery darkness, allowing all manner of foul things to enter our world from otherworldly realms. Less mythical, however, is the fact that the caverns are prone to unexpected flooding and have a well-earned reputation for drowning anyone foolish enough to think he might explore their secrets.

Rather than a series of enormous caves, the caverns are hollowed-out sections of a vast underground system of rivers. Though much of their length lay hidden beneath the earth, portions of the subterranean waterways find their way above ground in the form of, among others, the Maidenhair River of the Quibble Woods and the Lesser Grumpkin further north.

Perhaps, the best example of these shy rivers is the Rindle Mire. The Rindle flows above ground, then disappears for miles at a time before poking its head out of the stony earth to continue along its way. Like some sort of liquid mole, up and down, in and out of the ground it flows - one single, though visually fragmented stream.

At various places along their course, these subterranean rivers encounter obstacles too large to surmount. Often, a river will simply change direction, abandoning its old ways for a new and better path of least resistance. In these cases, the stream leaves behind an empty riverbed above ground and fathomless caverns below. Some such holes dry-up, over time. Others gradually fill with rainwater, becoming dreadfully deep and deadly beautiful.

Echoing Caverns was just such a place. Once part of the mighty underground river system, portions of the caverns had long since collapsed into dried-up ruins. Others still act as underground collection basins for debris that the Perigoh Fair is unable to carry. Periods of flood and highwater bring runoff from the Perigoh down through ancient, subterranean tunnels and into the blind terrors of the caverns. Beneath finely sharpened stalactites, amid shifting river junk, danger lurks unseen in the Echoing Caverns. Yet, this is precisely where Annelyse and her father had been led by the unassuming Albert Prume.

They'd arrived at an enormous pond on the westerly point of the forest. The water in the pond sat below the level of the surrounding ground, as if enclosed by the mouth of an invisible crater. There were no boulders, signposts, or guardrails to alert an unsuspecting traveler. One moment, a rambler would be walking along; the next moment, he might be swimming for his life.

The watering hole was perfectly round, big enough to swallow a house in one gulp, and well camouflaged by last autumn's fall of leaves. The only thing that betrayed its depth was the jade and turquoise brilliance of the sunbeams foolish enough to court its cold embrace.

There was a strong smell of dissolved sulfur rising from the clear waters, a fact that supported the local's belief that the pond was the gateway to Hell. In fact, it was the gateway to the subterranean river system and the nearby caverns, in particular. They had arrived at the Cenote of the Echoing Caverns.

"If we wait much longer, we'll have some digging to do," Albert said, turning to his companions. "As it is, I hope to find it near the hop of the teap."

"Find what? What heap?" Annelyse asked, interpreting Albert's odd dialect, and feeling her uneasiness descend into dread.

"Better to show than tell," Albert replied, removing his shoes. "Don't wanna shoes my lose down there," he added, "In a way, that'd be worse than losing my tree house!"

"Down there?" Annelyse exclaimed. "Down where, exactly? We're not going *in* that water, are we? Are we?!"

"Gotta go in to bring it out," came the reply. "If I can just reach the controls..."

At the mention of *controls,* Mr. Bellamy's ears perked up.

"In *there*?" he asked, with more than a little disbelief in his voice. "How did it...?"

"Where else? That's where it all goes. It's gotta go somewhere, doesn't it?"

Annelyse still wasn't following Albert's meaning, though her father seemed to have caught on. As if he had found his second wind, Edward now moved with renewed purpose. Taking off his own shoes, he readied himself to follow Albert and help in any way he could.

Annelyse didn't know what to make of the situation. She'd received no instructions, was aware of no specific plan, and had no clue what all the preparations were for. But she was unwilling to be left out of whatever was about to happen. Throwing her hands up in the air, she shook her head with exasperation, and started removing her boots, as well.

"Now, we must be careful. Oh yes, yes, yes, cary vereful, indeed. And quick, too. There's no time to get used to the cold. Once we get in, we need to get going. But don't take your last breath until *after* you get in, or the cold will drive it out of you before your head's underwater."

"Then we *are* going in that pond! Are you out of your mind?! We'll all drown in there!"

"Maybe so, oh yes, oh yes, maybe so, child. But not if we're quick. The nood gews is that you'll be able to see clearly down there. Just follow me and we'll soon be out of the water."

"*Out* of the water? But we're going *into* the water! Why go *in* at all if the point is to get *out* soon?! This is crazy!"

"Gotta go in to get out. No other way, nope, no other way."

Annelyse could not believe what she was hearing. The deep, shaded waters of the Cenote must have been barely 50 degrees. At that temperature, their muscles would stiffen, and they'd be helpless to swim their way out again. This was suicide, plain and simple.

"Remember, stay close, move fast, and don't draw your last breath until *after* you feel the first shock of cold. We'll head down and wind the fay out fast as you can say Prume's Wile! In we go!"

Stuffing their shoes in a knapsack, Albert then slung it across his back, and plunged head-first into the cold, shimmering waters of the Cenote. Mr. Bellamy motioned for Annelyse to go next. He was determined to bring up the rear and keep an eye on his daughter. Annelyse gave one last hopeless shake of her head, then jumped into the water with a screech to wake the dead. Without hesitation, Mr. Bellamy walked a few feet forward, then dove in as straight as an arrow.

Once they'd all taken the plunge, Albert's round, ruddy face bobbed to the surface several yards away from where Annelyse and her father were now treading water.

"The tock is clicking, my friends. Deep breaths, now. Follow me!"

With that, Albert Prume dove beneath the surface like a pink-bellied dolphin. Annelyse and Mr. Bellamy gulped great lungs-full of air, then followed the red glow of their guide's chubby cheeks down into the abyss.

Submerged in the frigid water, Annelyse's eyeballs immediately began to ache in their sockets like jagged ice cubes. The skin of her face was stretched and taut, as her body struggled to conserve heat, drawing her closed-tight as a handbag.

As she descended into the crystal waters of the pool, she could feel her lungs constricting like two desperate fists. Her body was frantic to hold onto what little breath remained. Or, absent that, to inhale whatever else it could. Her mind knew better; a lung-full of anything but air would not end well.

Whatever their goal, Annelyse was certain they couldn't possibly reach it in time. The demands of her lungs were becoming quite insistent and holding her breath while exerting herself swimming was like burning a candle at both ends. Time was running out. She'd been in the water only a few seconds and already the situation was becoming dire.

The cenote was not to be trusted. Boulders and branches growing from its depths appeared much closer to the surface in the glassy lens of the water. Shafts of sunlight cast ominous shadows and blinking, luminous sparkles from the limestone walls, as it rippled through the distinct layers of the pool. Were it not for the danger it posed, the lustrous jade waters of the cenote would be enchantingly beautiful. As it was, Annelyse was less than enchanted.

Just then, out of the corner of her eye, she spotted something alarming. Half in shadow and less than an arm's length away, a long, lithe body wrapped itself around a sunken tree limb. Annelyse gasped, catching herself just before letting go of all but the smallest sip of air in her lungs. Kicking her feet with wild terror, she dragged herself through the water with flailing arms.

Daring to glance back over her shoulder, she spotted the blur of something moving toward her. Panic flared as Annelyse screamed through clenched lips. Whatever it was now took hold of her ankle, pulling her backward through the water. Annelyse spun around, twisting her body to meet her captor, and fully expecting to find the snake she'd spied encircling the sunken branch.

Instead, the worried face of her father stared back at her, his hand clutching her ankle. Pointing upward, he took her hand and led toward the sun. Once they'd reached the surface of the water, Mr. Bellamy supported his daughter, while the two of them gasped for air beneath an astonished sky.

"Are you alright, Leesy?" Mr. Bellamy asked, still breathing hard.

The round, snowcapped head of Albert Prume appeared a few feet off, redder than usual, though somewhat less lumpy-looking for the constricting cold.

"You seem to have lotten gost, my friends. We've already been here, I'm afraid."

"Snake," Annelyse said, trying to catch her breath. "There was a snake… on the branch. I thought… I thought it..."

"My dear, there are no snakes in the cenote. That could not have been what you saw."

"It was a vine, Leesy," Mr. Bellamy said, with as much reassurance as he could muster. "I saw it, too."

Annelyse felt embarrassment flush her face red. She was glad for the warmth of it, even if she was mortified for having panicked.

"We must try again, my friends," Albert insisted. "And this time, we must succeed. Come now."

With deep breaths and great reluctance, the three swimmers pierced the heart of the cenote a second time. Keeping close to their guide, Annelyse and her father concentrated on settling into a tranquil pace. If they were to conserve their breath, they needed to avoid sudden bursts of over-exertion. A gentle rhythm of wide breaststrokes and serene paddling was their best bet.

Annelyse locked her eyes on Albert's feet, which helped her stay on course and provided some degree of distraction. She thought about how his feet were undeniably his own. They were composed of ten pudgy, little toes - each one a miniature of Albert himself. The eight larger toes looked just like snowmen made of cookie dough. The two little toes looked like fat, baby dolphins. They were quite youthful, for a man of however-many-years; and were even almost cute, for feet. Annelyse chuckled at the thought of snowmen toes, releasing one tiny air bubble from each nostril as she did.

Up ahead of them, she now saw something peculiar. Sculpted from the wall of the cylindrical cenote, an overhanging ledge appeared. Beneath the ledge, everything was shrouded in darkness. As they drew closer, the shadow cast by the shelf of rock punched a lifeless blackhole in the otherwise translucent water. She couldn't explain it, but Annelyse felt as if boulders, branches, water, and all would be swallowed-up by whatever lay hidden under the ledge. Foreboding crept out of the darkness and into her heart.

Albert reached the edge of the void first. Pausing a moment, he placed one hand on the overhanging rock to steady himself in the water. Looking back at Annelyse and Mr. Bellamy, Albert gave a quick smile and a nod, then turned and ducked beneath the ledge. As Annelyse had feared, Albert was swallowed whole by the inky blackness and disappeared.

Mr. Bellamy swam past Annelyse, arriving at the overhang before her. Inspecting the scene with caution, he could find no reason for fear except the unknown. The decision to follow Albert had been made when they'd all plunged themselves into the icy waters of the cenote a few moments before. There was no going back, no leaving their friend behind. Hesitation only put greater strain on their already burning and oxygen-deprived lungs. All they could do was trust Albert and follow him into blind uncertainty.

Mr. Bellamy took Annelyse's hand, then turned in the direction he'd last seen Albert. Ducking their heads below the leading edge of the rocky overhang, they abandoned everything but loyalty and courage, and swam into the shadows.

The pair of lone swimmers were now engulfed in total darkness. Above, an enormous stone ledge pressed down upon them. Below, unfathomed depths waited with patience to welcome them should they fail to escape. There was nowhere to go but forward, and no way to know where that might lead.

With one hand on the stone ceiling above their heads, Mr. Bellamy guided them as straight as he could. He was already nervous about having lost sight of Albert, he did not want to run the risk of straying to the right or the left. They had no time to lose. If they wanted to reach Albert, they'd need to do so soon, or risk becoming trapped and drowning beneath the great stone slab.

Feeling as if she were on the verge of a panic attack, Annelyse gripped her father's hand in the cramped darkness. She held her eyes closed, trying to imagine herself swimming in the wide-open ocean back home. But fear put her senses on high alert, and keeping her eyes closed only aggravated her claustrophobia.

Annelyse now clutched her father's hand with both of her own. She was beginning to feel lightheaded as if she might blackout at any moment. Mr. Bellamy was now pulling his daughter's half-conscious body through the water, desperate to find safety. The thought of turning back and heading for the surface now presented itself to him. Perhaps that was the most rational course of action. His daughter's situation was becoming critical. He could not risk it much longer.

As these thoughts played out in Edward Bellamy's mind, the black abyss around him mercifully began lightening to grey. Moments later, the brilliant turquoise and jade of the water returned. Despite the shelf of stone above, sunlight had somehow found its way down to them.

Annelyse could now see her father's hand in hers. She could see him swimming along in front of her. New hope paved the way for renewed efforts, and they both began swimming faster in the direction of the light.

Without warning, Mr. Bellamy's hand slipped off the ledge that had formed a rooftop above them. Or rather, the ceiling simply disappeared, abandoning his hand to the open water above. No longer held down in the depths of the cenote, Edward and Annelyse suddenly bobbed upward like two buoys. Passing through a foot or two of water, they suddenly found themselves above the surface, gasping for air, and face-to-face with a very pleased-looking Albert Prume.

"You made it! Well done, well done, indeed. I dever noubted it for a moment! Not a moment, I tell you. Come now, let's pull ourselves out of this wigid frater."

Mr. Bellamy and Annelyse followed Albert up out of the pool and onto a broad, stony beach. Flopping down on their backs, they felt as if their bodies had hardened to lead. Every finger and toe, each arm and leg weighed 1,000 pounds. Their heads throbbed with the pain of having gone too long with too little oxygen, as the burning they'd felt in their lungs now raged in every cell of their bodies.

Opening her eyes for the first time since reaching the shore, Annelyse did a double take, then demanded with a start, "Where's the sky?"

"Outside, where it belongs," came Albert's exhausted reply.

"Then where are *we*?"

"Inside the Echoing Caverns, my dear."

The first thing Annelyse noticed about the Echoing Caverns was that there was no echo. On the contrary, all she could hear was a swirling, whooshing sound like that of a distant hurricane. It wasn't loud - it was more like white noise than the main event – but it was endless and ever-present.

Deciding to test-out the suitability of a name like the Echoing Caverns, Annelyse gathered enough strength to call out, "Hello…"

Rather than the echo of her greeting, no sound returned to her ears except the same old incessant whooshing noise. She tried it again, this time cupping her hands around her mouth.

"Hello! Hello! Hello…"

Still, no echo.

"What *is* that sound?" she asked, turning her aching head, and trying to pinpoint the source of the whooshing.

"It's the cenote," Albert replied. "It calls up to the sky, through the hole we swam in by."

"It drowns out any chance of hearing an echo. This place wasn't named by some fisherman, was it?" Annelyse quipped.

Ever since hearing the lie of Luckless Pond, Annelyse had nothing but distrust for fishermen and the places they name. Surely, the Echo*less* Caverns were just another example of tall-tale-telling fishermen with too much free time on their hands.

"It's called the Echoing Caverns for good reason," Albert replied, sitting up with some difficulty.

"Good reason?" Annelyse said, with a derisive chuckle. "It wouldn't echo in here if it were filled with holes."

"It's not your voice that comes back to you, child. Not in the Echoing Caverns. It's other things. Many things. Lost things."

Annelyse didn't like the way Albert said *lost things*. She was becoming irritated with what she considered to be unnecessarily secretive behavior. She had as much right as anyone to know why they were there, even if she *hadn't* figured it out on her own. She'd risked her life in the cenote, and now she was ready for some explanations.

"Enough!" she said, struggling to her feet and slapping her hands on her tired hips.

"What?" her father asked.

"Will someone *please* tell me *what* we're doing here?"

"Look," Albert said, pointing toward the heart of the caverns. "That's what we're doing here."

About 100 yards to the left of where they now sat, the narrow, rocky beach opened onto a vast cathedral of stone. Sculpted over the course of a million years and counting by the tireless hands of moving water, the enormous room was a perfectly smooth, bowl-shaped basin. In the center of the ceiling, a circular opening let in the sun. Having found its way in, a single shaft of sunlight, dressed in flickering distortions as if filtered by the sea, danced among the dripping stone.

Attached to the ceiling, stalactites tapered down to fine, pinprick points inches from the floor. Everything appeared to be coated in sparkling snowflakes and shimmered in a wedding gown of mineral jewels. The scene was breathtaking in its otherworldly beauty, and the newly-arrived travelers found themselves admiring their surroundings in reverential silence.

Always a victim to her overactive mind, Annelyse worried about how the world above kept from collapsing into such huge underground holes as this. A chill ran up her spine at the thought of the danger they might all be in down there.

Below the domed ceiling, a large subterranean lake filled the room and flowed down darkened tunnels beyond sight. The surface of the water was alive with dancing raindrops, like a million, little, jumping fish tumbling from the ceiling above. But it was the odd feature growing out of the center of the lake that demanded attention.

Directly beneath the hole in the roof of the cavern, a heaped-up skyscraper of junk sat surrounded by water and illuminated by the flickering sunlight from above. Drops of brown water fell in silence through the air and covered the pile in a thick blanket of green algae. Even so, Annelyse was able to distinguish objects from among the myriad slimy shapes. Tree limbs, discarded boots, a rusty sword, even an entire rowboat sat moldering on the damp heap. A human skeleton dressed in the tattered clothes of a fibbing fisherman still clutched one of the rowboat's oars.

As disturbing a sight as this was, it was what happened next that caused Annelyse's jaw to drop. While she and her father had been standing there surveying the scene, Albert had gone on ahead and was now wading into the waters of the lake. Reaching the junk pile, he started scurrying up toward the summit, carefully testing the stability of every board and tree limb he encountered.

For a moment, he was lost to their view, obscured by what appeared to be an entire tree sitting on top of the pile. A few seconds later, the lumpy, white-tufted face of Albert Prume popped up out of the wreckage and called for his companions to join him.

Wading into the underground lake, Annelyse was soon up to her waist in ice-cold water. The thought occurred to her that maybe the time she'd spent in the chilly cenote had toughened her so much that she wouldn't freeze to death now, but she doubted it very much.

The deeper she went, the colder she got. Soon, the shivers running up and down her spine became uncontrollable chattering in her teeth. If she had stopped and stood still, her trembling would certainly have caused a tidal wave in the lake. Rather than getting used to being uncomfortable, Annelyse was just plain annoyed by it all. By the time she reached the junk heap, her lips were purple, and her ire was up.

From where she now stood, Annelyse was unable to

see the top of the pile. In fact, the hoard of discarded junk was so tall and wide that it blocked out the daylight streaming in through the ceiling.

As she followed the heap around to the left, she moved out of the shadowed side and into the relative warmth of sunlight again. Catching sight of her father who had begun climbing up to meet Albert at the summit, Annelyse noticed something fall through the hole at the center of the cavern's roof.

"Look out!" she yelled, in an attempt to alert the others.

At the sound of her warning, Albert instinctively looked up. Mr. Bellamy glanced around, unsure as to which direction the danger might be approaching from. With a loud crack, a piece of driftwood landed on top of the pile, bouncing several times before coming to rest near Edward's feet.

"Where did *that* come from?" Annelyse asked with alarm.

"Same place as the rest of this stuff," Albert replied, without really answering her question. "Come on up!"

Scaling the enormous pile on her hands and knees, Annelyse arrived at the top moments after her father. What greeted their eyes explained exactly why Albert had led them through the cenote and into the Echoing Caverns. Dripping wet and looking completely battered and haggard, five forty-foot-tall evergreen trees lay in the cool, watery sunlight.

"Isn't it grand?!" Albert said with a wide smile.

"But, how…?" Annelyse marveled, standing with her mouth hanging open.

"It's the whirlpool," Edward said, having figured it all out the moment Albert mentioned reaching *the controls* before their icy swim in the cenote. "This is where it all goes, huh?"

Pointing up toward the hole in the ceiling directly

above the pile of discarded objects, Albert confirmed Edward's suspicions, "*That's* the whirlpool, my good man. Everything that gets sucked in there, comes out here. We're relow the biver now; birectly deneath the hole in the Perigoh. No telling who or what might fall through, so best be on the lookout."

Making his way over to his five beloved trees, Albert paused a moment to survey the damage. They were clumped together, drawn out to their full length, and in the same position as when he'd last seen them going over the edge of the whirlpool. Nothing important appeared to be broken, as far as he could tell. They had obviously landed on top of the heap as gently as they could manage.

Albert stepped aboard his tree raft, inspecting every corner, and clearing away debris as he went. Finding the control panel, he collected a few pieces of driftwood and tossed them off to one side. Placing his hand on the key, he took a deep breath then turned it to the left, back into the green portion of the dial.

Slowly, the tangled mess of roots and branches began reassembling itself, as if playing backwards the events of the last few hours. Trunks stood straight again, lining up in a stately row of evergreen columns. Limbs unfolded themselves, shaking their crumpled, feathery leaves dry. Serpentine roots spread out like a million feet of dangling, dripping toes which had spent the day crammed into a pair of last year's shoes.

Little by little, as the Tree RV rebuilt itself around its old friend, Albert was engulfed by his unique and marvelous home, back at the controls, and none the worse for the loss of a few chairs. When the whole process was done, and the trees had once again taken shape, Prume's Wile stood tall and proud atop the junk heap beneath the Perigoh Whirlpool. Though dented and bruised, cracked, snapped, and noticeably light on leaves, it was a grand sight to see, and ready for its next adventure.

CHAPTER TWELVE

Grief Snipers & Uninvited Voices

A small, round window in the side of the Tree RV flung open revealing the sweaty face of Albert Prume.

"Get inside," he called to Annelyse and her father who were still standing on the junk heap a few feet away. Holding a dripping clot of canvas above his head, he added, "And your backpacks survived the whirlpool, you'll be happy to know!"

Eager to experience the warm hominess of the treehouse once again, the Bellamys wasted no time in joining Albert. Though most of his possessions had gone over the brim of the whirlpool along with his home, very few were found atop the pile. Of the few that were found, all but two items were smashed beyond repair.

"Welcome, friends! Do have a seat."

Albert motioned toward a rusty, old, dented pail that had been flipped upside down as a makeshift stool. Beside it sat a familiar friend. Albert's favorite wobble-legged chair had survived the fall and looked as good as ever, which was hardly a compliment. Apparently, there was so little about the chair left to damage that it came through the ordeal unscathed. Annelyse chose the pail, leaving Mr. Bellamy to balance on the three-and-a-half-legged chair.

"Right then," Albert said, addressing the command console.

"We're not going swimming again, are we?" Annelyse asked, disturbed by the prospect of another icy dip in the cenote.

"Don't be prepopsterous, child! There's more than one way to cin a skat… to kat a scin… well, whatever it is, it's a vile phrase. There's more than one way out of the Echoing Caverns. My trees are good at a lot of things, but underdiver watering is not one of them."

Spinning the dials to his desired heading, Albert took hold of the handle and cranked it several times. Though a little off kilter, the treehouse began navigating its way down the steep side of the junk heap as best it could. There was a noticeable hitch in its gait, as it shimmied and shifted over debris in its path. It was clear that the trees were still lightheaded and a bit dazed by their whirl around the whirlpool and subsequent fall. But with every step, they seemed to regain their old confidence.

At the bottom of the mountain of jetsam, the five evergreens hiked up their leafy skirts and tiptoed through the waters of the subterranean lake. Once they'd made it to the shore, the trees picked up their pace, striding along with a renewed sense of purpose.

Aboveground, the travelers had steered east to find the Cenote of the Echoing Caverns on the westernmost point of the forest. Once inside the cenote, they were forced to swim westerly again in the direction of the whirlpool.

Now, they were headed due north beyond the ford to the very borders of the Quibble Woods. There, they would make their way aboveground.

The journey from Pebble Ford to the cenote had taken them less than 30-minutes. Down below, their route was more direct, and in little over 15-minutes they'd reached their destination.

At the southeastern edge of the Haunted Forest, beneath a grove of poplar trees, an outcropping of rock marked the ancient gateway to the region of Hyland. Hygate Ruin was the sole surviving slab, leftover from the western wall that once barred entrance to the Mydland Dells. For centuries, here it lay, toppled-over at a 45-degree angle to the ground. In the shadow of the mighty stone, bushes and weeds grew thick around its base. With each passing year, it became more and more difficult to even locate Hygate Ruin, as the forest encroached eastward.

One hundred feet below the surface, Annelyse, Edward, and Albert now moved through a shaft of sunlight. The light entered the caverns through a chasm at the foot of Hygate Ruin, and, like everything else, became trapped below. Swimming through the air, tiny specks of dust held close to the warmth of the sunbeam. Far from the sounds of dripping water, a blanket of silence now hung heavy around the ears of the travelers.

There was no subterranean lake or river in this part of the Echoing Caverns, only roots from the trees above disappointed to find a great hole where they'd expected lush soil. Dangling overhead, a million clumps of grass and plant tendrils, like the frizzled hair of wizened old heads, lent an eerie feel to the abandoned chamber.

"There's our exit," Albert declared, bringing the Tree RV to a halt just below the rift in the ceiling.

"And where's our ladder?" Annelyse asked with alarm.

Albert Prume never grew tired of showing off all

that his grand treehouse could do. Rather than explain that no ladder would be necessary, he simply swung into action. On the console, beneath a cracked plastic cover, sat the key in its keyhole, the key Albert had turned to make his treehouse take the shape of an arrow. Grabbing hold of it, he turned it toward the left where the dial was marked with numbers instead of colors.

"That ought to be just about right," he said, lining the key up with the number ten on the dial.

As he did, six branches started extending themselves upward, two at either end, two in the middle of the group of evergreens. Like long, thin arms, the branches telescoped out of the top of Prume's Wile, stretching toward the roof of the cavern. Once they'd reached the opening in the ceiling, the smaller branches at the ends of the main limbs latched onto the rim of the chasm like clawing fingers.

Albert then turned the key back to the right until it lined-up with zero again. With slow and steady smoothness of motion, the six long branches began retracting, pulling the Tree RV up toward the ceiling as they did. Moments later, the tops of the five, forty-foot-tall evergreens were even with the opening in the cavern's roof.

Walking over to the pump handle, Albert starting pumping in earnest. Beneath the treehouse, the roots began to spread wide. Grabbing hold of the rim of the chasm, they then hoisted the Tree RV up and out into a soft spring evening beneath a drowsy, purple sky.

As soon as they were all safe and sound on the ground, the clever roots and branches returned to their rightful stations, and Prume's Wile found itself in an all too familiar place.

"Quibble Woods," Mr. Bellamy said, peering through the little round window. "And just in time for nightfall, too."

"The Haunted Woods are no place to spend the

night," Albert said with a shudder. "Or daytime, either, for mat thatter."

Annelyse stuck her head out of the window and gazed at the leading edge of the forest nearby. There was something menacing about the Quibble Woods. It wasn't that the trees looked different from those of any other forest. It wasn't that it was darker or more dense than other woods. Annelyse couldn't be sure, but what made her uneasy was not the appearance of the trees, at all. It was that they seemed irritated, restless, even annoyed. She couldn't tell if it was with her or with each other that the trees took exception, but it was clear that they were not pleased.

As Annelyse stood with her head poking out of the little window, a sudden crack of thunder startled her, and she smacked her head on the window frame. Off to the east, a thunderstorm was approaching, making its way westward toward the open sea.

"That's all the reason I need," Albert exclaimed.

Mr. Bellamy didn't quite follow, "For?"

"Staying put for the night! You'd be wise to join me. My trees have seen detter bays, but at least we'll be dry in here. Let's see what food survived the river."

Albert busied himself searching through the crushed and jumbled pantry for anything that might have escaped the day's turbulent events. Tidying as he went, he was able to cobble together a fine meal of canned kippers, canned kidney beans, and a jar of pickled eggs with a small crack and a slow leak.

A minute or two of sitting in the pouring rain, and Albert's water jug was refilled for drinking. Given the fact that the Tree RV had lost most of its belongings in the river; had been flushed down a giant drain in the middle of the Perigoh; and then spent much of the afternoon atop a subterranean junk heap being pummeled by falling debris, no one was tempted to complain about the food.

As the company enjoyed their dinner, plans for the next day were discussed. It soon became obvious that this was likely to be their last meal together.

Annelyse's mind was far away, as she pushed a pile of kidney beans around her plate with her fork. "*But one who knows is easily found along the Maidenhair,*" she repeated under her breath. "*Easily found...*"

Speaking up, she asked, "How far are we from the Maidenhair?"

"I'd reckon hess than a lour's walk," Albert replied, looking to Mr. Bellamy for confirmation.

"Yes, even less than that, I'd wager."

"And how long is the Maidenhair River?"

"Hard to say, Leesy. None have ever mapped its course, that I know of. But the Quibble Woods are as big as all Averlune from the River Yore to the Perigoh."

"I see," she said, having made a line of kidney beans on her plate to represent the Maidenhair. "Doesn't sound so *easy* to me."

"What's that? Easy?" her father asked.

"To find someone. Along the Maidenhair, I mean. Like the poet's note said."

"It's easy, if you low where to knook," Albert interjected.

"Which we don't," Annelyse replied with dour disappointment.

"*...she jumped and jimbled by the stream where fern and fennel grow,*" Mr. Bellamy added.

"Jimbled? Why, that's not a word at all. Prepopsterous!"

"*...where fern and fennel grow.* That could be a clue," Edward reasoned. "Isn't there supposed to be a field of ferns in the middle of the forest, or some such thing?"

"Wouldn't know about that. I never did have the courage to go that deep into the Haunted Woods. Always try to keep to the fringes, I do. Still think you're crazy for wanting to go in, yourselves. But it's too late for tuch salk. I'm spent, and I'm off to bed."

"We'll be getting an early start, tomorrow." Mr. Bellamy said, glancing over at Albert.

"Then our goodnight is goodbye, as well," the little man replied. "For now," he added. "For now, is all we can ever say."

"Goodbye?!" Annelyse objected. "Just like that?!"

"How would you prefer to part, child?"

"Well, not at all, if you really want to know."

"If we don't part, how can we ever know the joy of meeting again," came Albert's characteristic reply. "And won't it be grand when we do?"

"Yes," Mr. Bellamy said with a smile, nodding his head in agreement. "Yes, it will."

The thought of striking out again without Albert Prume and his cozy, traveling trees filled Annelyse with a mixture of reluctance and foreboding. The world had already proven to be planted thicker with dangers and unpleasant things than she'd envisioned. Albert's Tree RV had brought *home* to the emptiness of the wild prairie, and Annelyse wanted to hold on to it with every ounce of homesickness that now flooded her heart.

"I'd offer you breakfast, but I'm afraid this meagre meal was all I could coax out of my poggy santry."

"We'll eat on the road," Edward said, remembering the beef jerky. "Thank you, just the same."

"What will you do?" Annelyse asked Albert, the reality of their imminent departure settling in.

"Clean up, for one. Then stock the lantry and fill the parder. And it looks as if I have some bake to bread. The last batch didn't turn out the way I'd hoped."

Mr. Bellamy rose to his feet and took their host by his plump, little hand.

"We owe you our lives," he said, in a half-whisper.

"And I owe you mine. You're one progidious…

pridogious… uh, fine swimmer, sir."

Walking over to Annelyse, Albert bowed with some ceremony, saying, "Until we meet again."

Annelyse threw her arms around Albert's pudgy girth and squeezed so hard his head turned red.

"Thank you," she whispered. "For everything."

After a moment, Albert stepped back, took Annelyse's hand in his, and kissed it. Then the round, ruddy-faced Albert Prume ascended the ladder of tree limbs to his second-story, loft bedroom, and left the Bellamys feeling alone and utterly inadequate to the task before them.

They stood there in the living room, looking up at the ladder, as the events of the past 24 hours washed over them. The full weight of their journey now rested on their shoulders alone. And it was a heavy burden, indeed.

"About tomorrow," Mr. Bellamy slowly began, "As much as I hate to say it, I think we should head straight up the Maidenhair into the heart of the forest. If there is someone *to be found along* the river, we'll need to pick it up at its mouth. We wouldn't wanna risk missing them."

"How far are we from the river's mouth?" Annelyse was dreading the answer.

"Half an hour, at most," came the encouraging reply. "Even though the Perigoh is due south of here, it meets the Maidenhair directly west. The Perigoh slants northward as it heads to the sea, we're just as close to the mouth of the Maiden as we are to the ford."

"Why such an early start, then?"

"We'll need to collect whatever food we can find along the way. We lost too much to the river. That'll slow us down. The earlier we get going, the better."

Outside, the thunderstorm raged against the branches of the treehouse. Lightning stamped the night sky, and the tortured wind wept a mournful moan. A few feet away, the Quibble Woods cast-up a wall of trees which ran unbroken all the way from the Perigoh in the south to the

Lazy Grumpkin in the north. It was in and among these trees that suspicion and fear took root.

From where Annelyse and her father now sat, a faint sound could be heard, a trick of the mind, perhaps. Beneath the battering rain, behind the growling thunder, a hint of bickering rustled among the trees of the forest. Like a crowd in disagreement or a mob of mumbling grumblers, the strange sound originated in the canopy of leaves and limbs high above the ground. Mr. Bellamy was the first to notice it. Falling silent, midsentence, he trained his ear on the darkness.

"Listen," he whispered. "Do you hear that?"

"Is someone out there?" Annelyse asked, holding her breath.

Mr. Bellamy shook his head, "I wouldn't have believed it, but… maybe it's true what Albert said about the trees." Turning, with a look of disbelief on his face, he added, "You still want to go in there?"

Annelyse made no reply. What could she say? What choice did she have? They'd set out on this journey to find what they could about the Woolems. It was, "*go forward* or *go home*," even if moving forward meant moving deeper into danger. She was afraid. But with each passing moment, she was increasingly unwilling to give ear to her fears. She would simply ignore them.

"I'm going to bed," Annelyse said with determined purpose.

"Good idea."

"Early, then?"

"First light, Leesy. We'll need every drop of daylight, tomorrow."

"Right. Goodnight, Daddy."

Annelyse chose a spot on the floor as far away from the front door as she could. Even the seam around the door to Albert's Tree RV was too much open space for comfort. The further away from the woods outside, the safer she felt.

Fluffing her backpack into a passable pillow, she lay down against the wall on a bed of evergreen leaves. Despite the endless chatter of the trees and the sudden clashes of thunder, Annelyse was soon fast asleep.

Mr. Bellamy sat on the floor not far from his daughter. Leaning up against the wall, he was lost in thought. His mind was tired and every muscle in his body ached. Still, sleep alluded him. He was uneasy, and he didn't quite know why.

The further he and Annelyse ventured away from home, the more he felt like a rowboat tethered to shore being slowly let out to sea. At some point, he was sure, the rope would drop free of its mooring, and they'd find themselves adrift in the deep unknown. Here, on the edge of the Haunted Woods, the rope was already beginning to slip from its post.

There was a time when he was part of a team drawing on each other's strengths and strengthening each other's weaknesses. But since his wife died, he'd been all too willing to abdicate his position and allow his daughter to steer their course. He'd lost his confidence; he'd lost his reason for everything. Now, on the doorstep of the Quibble Woods, he was beginning to wonder if maybe he'd given up too much. Perhaps it was time to take back the rudder once again and steer their rowboat away from danger.

Then something occurred to him, something his wife had said to him not long before she'd died. It was a clear, starry night at Lightview Overlook. Silloah lay beside him on the grass. Hand-in-hand, they looked up at the stars. As if reading her husband's thoughts, Silloah broke the silence.

"It can't be *saved,* you know."

"What can't?"

"Life," she replied. "You can't *save* it for later. You can't store it away like rain in a barrel."

Edward lay still on the cool grass, listening, while

his wife continued.

"Life is for living. If it isn't lived, it's lost."

Edward raised Silloah's hand to his lips, kissing it in the darkness.

"The past is for remembering. The present is for living. The future…" she paused, "The future is an illusion, my love. What do we know of such mysteries? We can only live in the now, there is no other way."

Now, as he leaned against the wall of Prume's Wile, Edward Bellamy heard his wife's voice in his thoughts, "Life is for living."

If he steered Annelyse away from the Haunted Forest, they could avoid danger for a while. But they might also never learn the truth about the Woolems, and that would certainly not be *living*. It would only be *existing*. You can exist anywhere, he thought. It requires no effort. But you can only live here and now, and that, only by choice and determination. They must have the courage to search for the truth, and more courage, still, to accept it. Truth is the most dangerous of things.

Leaning over, Edward Bellamy blew out the solitary candle restraining the darkness. Laying down, he made up his mind. He would not choose merely *existing* over truly *living* ever again. He would choose life. He would not extinguish it like a candle in the dark. In the morning, they would enter the Haunted Forest, come what may.

The hours passed, carrying the storm with them, until the pale light of morning softened all shadows. Annelyse was the first to awaken, an unusual occurrence under any circumstances. She knew how exhausted her father was, so she quietly prepared their things herself. When the backpacks were all in order, she tiptoed over and laid her hand on her father's shoulder.

"Daddy? Daddy, it's time."

"Hm, mornin', Leesy. Did I sleep too long?"

"No, there was no reason for you to wake up.

Everything's ready"

"It is?" he asked, raising himself to a sitting position. "Thank you, baby. Time for me to pull my weight, then, huh?"

Stretching his long limbs, Mr. Bellamy roused himself and gathered-up his belongings. Without a sound, Annelyse and her father tidied the living room, slung their backpacks over their shoulders, and stepped outside the treehouse into the cold, damp morning air.

Upstairs in his bedroom loft, Albert Prume snored in blissful sleep. A long day spent fixing-up his home lay ahead of him. But, thanks to the tiptoes of his houseguests, he would not awaken for several more hours.

Leaving Hygate Ruin, Mr. Bellamy led them almost due west through a few straggling trees on the edge of the Quibble Woods. Their goal was the mouth of the Maidenhair where it joins the Perigoh Fair. If they were going to search the length of the river for the mysterious person mentioned in the poet's message, they'd need to start at one end and work their way toward the other, to avoid the possibility of missing anyone.

The thunderstorm had left the ground spongy and littered with puddles. There was little point in trying to avoid the mud, since every step brought them closer to the wetland estuary. Even if it hadn't rained the night before, they'd still encounter muddy ground sooner or later.

Ducking through a small stand of trees, they spied the mouth of the Maidenhair River sprawling out before them. Unlike the maritime estuary where the Perigoh meets the sea, this was the gentle convergence of a tiny rivulet with the floodwaters of the mighty Perigoh. It was as peaceful as the reunion of two old friends.

"Daddy, look!" Annelyse stood on the shore motioning in the direction of the water.

There before her, not a dozen feet away, a pod of dolphins played in the brackish waters of the Perigoh.

Among them, four babies leapt and rolled in the lapping waves, their white bellies glistening in the newborn sun.

"And dancing sweet while dolphins dream in undulating undertow... I'd say we were on the right path," Mr. Bellamy said, smiling at the graceful creatures.

"They're beautiful. Such sweet faces."

"Yes, now you know why ancient sailors thought they were mermaids."

Mr. Bellamy stepped down off the shore and into the muck left behind by low tide. Opening a sack that he'd been carrying in his backpack, he started collecting clams and mussels - at least those that the birds hadn't gotten to yet.

"These will make a fine supper, though they won't keep much longer than dinnertime."

While her father filled his bag, Annelyse watched the dolphins play. They looked like they were attached to a giant, half-submerged wheel turning in the water. Jumping up from below then diving beneath the surface again, they rolled along down the shore. Every few minutes, they'd disappear for longer than expected, only to reappear further upstream. They seemed to delight in putting on their show for Annelyse.

"That's about all we'd likely eat," Mr. Bellamy said, closing the bag and stowing it in his backpack. "Let's be on our way."

Saddened to have to leave them so soon, Annelyse whispered in the direction of the dolphins, "Thank you, sweet friends," then turned and walked back up the shore. Before entering the trees, she glanced over her shoulder in time to see one last parting leap. With that, the pod continued their fishing expedition eastward.

The tree line ventured down almost as far as the water's edge, so that very soon Annelyse and her father found themselves standing under the eaves of the forest.

Even with the sun rising at their backs, they could only see a few feet into the westering woods.

The forest's floor was carpeted in leaves of various kinds and colors, all matted down by the previous night's rain. There was no undergrowth, as far as Annelyse could see. In fact, it appeared as if their path through the Quibble Woods would be an easy one, without brambles or bushes, branches or debris to contend with.

An altogether different picture presented itself once they'd left the open spaces of the Mydland Dells. Stepping foot inside the forest, they saw that there were, indeed, very few obstacles lying on the forest floor. Instead, every tree was planted in such a way as to make walking in a straight line maddeningly impossible. There appeared to be no random chance of nature involved in the scattering of fallen acorns and seeds. Rather, the trees intentionally positioned themselves so that every single one of them had to be sidestepped, walked around, or outmaneuvered in one way or another.

Determined to press on without hesitation, Mr. Bellamy took up the lead. From the outset, they were required to weave their way back and forth, side-to-side, and around each elm, beach, maple, and poplar in their path. Much like maneuvering through the salt marshes at the foot of Mt. Averly, this would require all their attention.

Outside the canopy of trees, the sun had freed itself from behind the distant mountains. It was going to be a pleasant day. Inside the forest, the air was stagnant and heavy with moisture. The morning's chill still clung to every leaf and limb and soaked into Annelyse's joints. Only the squirrels and birds paid tribute to the pleasant day dawning beyond the wood. Within the borders of the Haunted Forest, each day was much the same as the last.

The constant back and forth motion of their meandering path began to take its toll on Annelyse and Edward alike. A growing difficulty in focusing on the ever-changing landscape caused a nagging ache behind their eyes. Dizziness followed and, with it, the gathering clouds of confusion which only made their task more tiresome.

The morning dragged on in silent boredom, with only the myriad, different tree trunks to challenge the monotony. Inward and onward the travelers trekked, following the wandering course of the Maidenhair deeper into the forest. Compelled to take the most round-about route possible, the forest was determined to make them walk farther than the distance required.

Forcing her mind to engage its surroundings or risk giving-in to boredom and lethargy, Annelyse started to notice an odd pattern among the trees. Every so often, growing on the banks of the river, they encountered a large tree with a cinnamon-red trunk vaulting up toward the sky. By its side without fail, grew a short, scrawny tree with jagged leaves. Wherever one was found, the other was close at hand. Never was there one without its partner.

The bark of the red giant was composed of loose fish scales of fragile parchment. From its trunk, a fragrance like that of herbs and incense wafted through the thick, forest air. Annelyse found the scent quite soothing.

Drawing close to examine the smaller of the two trees, she noticed that the leaves were a dark, waxy green. Every tooth lining the leaf's edge was as sharp as a thorn. There was no pleasant fragrance, only a clear oil which coated the broad, shiny face of each leaf. Annelyse rubbed the oil on what was left of her enormous mosquito bite, but it didn't appear to have any medicinal properties. She wondered if the oil might at least be useful for cooking.

The unlikely pairing of trees was strange, and Annelyse passed the hours challenging herself to find one without the other. In the space of a four-hour hike, she counted 42 pairs of the red giant with its scrawny, saw-toothed friend, but not one single incidence of an orphaned partner. Always together and never far from the river, water lilies floated within sight of the two trees. Gazing up from their seat upon the surface of the water, the lilies adorned the light-brown locks of the Maidenhair and lent their perfume to the forest breeze.

Around midday, the travelers arrived at a clearing in the forest. Here, the Maidenhair took a hard turn eastward before continuing north. For the first time since they'd picked up its path, the river offered several shallow opportunities to easily cross over to the opposite shore. The shallows also offered another benefit, fish.

Mr. Bellamy suggested they stop a while and do some fishing. Whatever they caught, he would clean, pack in salt, and add to their stores. It was the perfect opportunity to do some grocery shopping.

Annelyse loved to fish. Everything about it appealed to her. From the strategic choice of homemade lures to the nuances of casting and reeling, it all made her feel like a *made member* of her father's fishing club. She'd built on his years of knowledge and experience to develop her own unique techniques. Of these, her favorite was what her father referred to as the Whiz Plunk.

Untying her two-piece, bamboo rod from the side of her backpack, Annelyse attached the reel and selected her fail-proof, cuddlefly lure. She then walked down to the river's edge and surveyed the territory, spying-out the most likely hiding place for the biggest fish.

Eyeing a deep pool just behind a boulder, she raised her rod behind her right ear. With a flick of her wrist, Annelyse sent her cuddlefly sailing through the air. The reel made a satisfying whizzing sound as it released a length of fishing line in a smooth, unbroken motion.

The moment it reached its mark, Annelyse snapped her wrist back, stopping the lure midair and dropping it in the deep pool with an equally satisfying plunk. Once the cuddlefly came to rest on the surface of the water, Annelyse began gently reeling it back. The lure skirted along, tantalizing all the hungry fish below. Once it had returned to shore, Annelyse repeated the Whiz Plunk process all over again. It never varied, and it never failed.

Almost as soon as her lure broke the surface of the water, Annelyse started reeling in fish after fish. The first few, her father quickly cleaned and sauteed for their lunch. After that, it was all he could do to keep up with the cleaning, salting, and packing of as many fish as Annelyse could deliver. When all was said and done, she'd caught twelve fish and one unlucky crawdaddy that had grabbed hold of her line and found itself reeled to shore.

In the space of an hour, thanks to Annelyse's Whiz Plunk technique, they'd enjoyed a delicious lunch and restocked their supplies. The twelve fish (and one crawdaddy) would last them for days. Since they no longer needed to hunt or gather along the way, they could now travel at a faster pace, too.

With all the fishing work behind them, they washed their hands and faces in the cool Maidenhair, then laid down to rest a while in the sunshine.

"Leesy," Mr. Bellamy whispered. "Did you feel that?"

Annelyse lay still in the grass, listening. She had, indeed, felt something. Motionless, she strained her senses to pick it up again.

"There," he said, keeping his voice low, "There it was."

"What was *that*?"

A dull thud shook the blades of grass all around them, sending ripples from the shoreline out into the middle of the river. Nearby, a cloud of birds rose up out of a thicket and took to flight. Even the animals were on high alert.

Whatever it was, it sounded as if it was approaching from the east. The thuds became more frequent, the sound of snapping twigs and branches, more alarming. Fearing the worst, Mr. Bellamy was not about to let whatever-it-was trap them with the river at their back. It was time to cross over, get out of the clearing, and hide among the trees on the other side. From a position of safety, they could then determine what the source of the thuds might be.

Grabbing their backpacks, Annelyse and Mr. Bellamy plunged into the shallow part of the river. The cold water and hot adrenaline proved to be effective motivators, even without the thuds closing in behind them. Running hard against the resistance of the sluggish water, they pushed their way toward the opposite shore.

At its deepest point, the river lapped at Annelyse's chin like an overeager puppy. The occasional, misplaced wave swamped her ears, leaving pockets of water in their wake. She could hear nothing but the gurgle of the river and the throbbing of her own heart.

Both Annelyse and her father were now forced to hold their backpacks over their heads to avoid drenching them in the river. This made keeping their balance in the wall of shifting water even more difficult. Mr. Bellamy's only thoughts were for his daughter's safety and saving all the fish they'd worked so hard to catch and preserve. He needed no other encouragement to find the safest route to the other side.

The moment he was within range, Mr. Bellamy threw his backpack onto the shore, then turned and took Annelyse's pack from her hands. Once he'd tossed the baggage on ahead, Mr. Bellamy clasped his daughter's arm and steadied her until she'd made it out of the deep, central channel of the river. With her knees above water and her boots on hard-packed sand, Annelyse powered her way out of the Maidenhair and into the trees beyond.

Safely concealed among the leaves, Mr. Bellamy paused long enough for them both to catch their breath, and to observe the opposite bank for whatever-it-was that had been doing all the thudding.

Despite the distance and the river between them, each regularly occurring thud still shook the ground upon which the Bellamys now stood. Whatever-it-was, it was enormous. Mr. Bellamy concluded that it was best to put more distance between them and the thudding.

"Let's go," he said with insistence.

Annelyse was in total agreement.

Turning due north, they began weaving their way through the obstacle course of trees as fast as they could manage. It was going on 4 o'clock in the afternoon, and they only had a couple of hours of sunlight left – even fewer, among the dark shadows of the forest. They needed to outrun their thudding pursuer quickly if they hoped to find somewhere safe to pass the night.

Far behind them, they could hear muffled thuds punctuated by the sound of splashing water. The creature was fording the river. A few more thuds, through what Edward guessed was the small clearing in which they had just been, and all the thudding came to an abrupt halt.

Edward and Annelyse ran a few more yards, then slowed to a stop. They both stood motionless, listening, eyes locked on each other's face. They were dripping wet, shivering with cold. They needed a warm fire and a place to dry their clothes, or the night would be very long and miserable.

A moment more and Annelyse cautiously shook her head, eyebrows raised. There was no sound of their pursuer.

"Maybe it gave up," she suggested.

"Or maybe it's too big to maneuver around these trees. Either way," Edward decided, "A bit farther wouldn't hurt."

Without another word, Mr. Bellamy began leading Annelyse deeper into the forest. As they went, the Maidenhair curved back toward their right, meeting the travelers again on their northbound route.

Edward found himself wishing they might stumble upon a boat. Even though it would be a tiring row upstream, they'd almost certainly be able to outrun any pursuer, especially one whose path led through the uncooperative trees. He trusted the Maidenhair far more than he did the Haunted Woods.

Off to the left, Mr. Bellamy spotted an enormous tree root climbing up the face of an overhanging hillside. The space beneath the overhang formed a vast, cave-like room. Feeling that they'd put enough forest between them and the clearing, he decided that this might be an excellent place to pass the night in safety.

Signaling with one hand, Mr. Bellamy paused to listen for a moment, "I think we're free of it… for now, anyhow. Let's make camp and boil those clams."

The forest floor beneath the overhang was dry, even after the previous night's thunderstorms, and the elaborate mesh of tree roots extended the earthen roof by a good four feet. The result was a space almost the size of the Bellamy's living room back home, and nearly as sheltered from the elements. It was the perfect location in which to store their gear, lay out their sleeping bags, and get a good night's sleep.

Mr. Bellamy built a small fire near the wide entrance and handed Annelyse a pot to fill with water from the river. Her father busied himself with the bag of clams he'd collected earlier that morning. By the time Annelyse returned, the fire was ready. Mr. Bellamy set the pot atop some stones he'd arranged in the fire.

"Let's find some more dry wood while we wait on the water to boil. I wanna keep the fire going all night."

"Will it be cold tonight?" Annelyse asked, suspecting there was more to her father's plan.

"Yes, but a campfire is just the thing to keep away any unwanted visitors."

As they gathered up some dry limbs, Annelyse

became aware of a growing feeling of discomfort. What had begun as mild itchiness, was now a raging rash spreading over both hands and up her arms. The tips of her fingers were bright red and speckled with tiny bumps. Every time she touched something the bumps would pop, releasing a few drops of clear liquid. Wherever the droplets encountered bare skin, her skin became inflamed and new bumps formed. It looked and felt much like poison ivy, but with one notable exception, everywhere the rash appeared, a complete loss of feeling accompanied it.

Halfway back to the campsite, Annelyse suddenly dropped the pile of sticks she'd been carrying. Though she'd been clutching the branches in both hands, she could no longer feel what she was carrying. Her hands were completely numb and had become sluggish. All she could feel was the incessant itch and the intense heat in her skin. Her lower arms had also fallen asleep and tingled with a million tiny pinpricks; the paralysis was spreading up her arms.

"Need some help, clumsy?" her father asked, picking up everything Annelyse had dropped, one branch at a time. Then he saw her hands.

"What is that?"

"It itches so bad."

"Let me see."

Mr. Bellamy took Annelyse's arm in his hands, careful to avoid touching her bare skin. The look on his face was grave.

"I can barely feel my fingers or my hands anymore. Just the itching."

"Did you touch anything that could've caused this? Think hard."

Annelyse then remembered the saw-toothed, oily leaves on the scrawny tree. The fingers she'd used to rub the oil on her arm were the first to become enflamed. That tree had to be the culprit.

She'd never seen this particular tree before, she didn't know its name or its dangers. She'd simply been curious, and now Annelyse was certain that her curiosity had caused the mysterious rash. A terrible thought then crossed her mind. Earlier, she had wondered if the oil might be useful for cooking. If Annelyse had given that a try… well, she shuddered at the thought of what might have happened.

"There," she said, pointing in the direction of a pair of trees growing together a few yards off. "The small one."

Mr. Bellamy turned to see but did not recognize the species. Noticing the jagged leaves, he whispered to himself, "*A menacing form is a warning to all.*"

Removing his outer shirt, he wrapped it around Annelyse's shoulders, pulled the sleeves all the way down, and buttoned the cuffs closed.

"Try not to scratch it, Leesy. And don't touch anything else if it can be helped. We need to keep it covered while it runs its course."

"How long will *that* take?"

"I don't know, baby. Longer if you can't leave it alone. You must try."

Mr. Bellamy's face paled ashen with worry. If only he knew what this mysterious tree was and what its antidote might be. This was not the terror he'd expected to find in the Haunted Woods, but it was just as bad.

It wasn't the rash that had him beside himself with fear; it was the numbness and loss of feeling in her limbs. If her growing paralysis spread to her heart, his own would break beyond repair. He needed to find a cure and find it quickly.

Beneath the sleeves of her father's shirt, Annelyse's arms burned like fire in a hornet's nest. Her skin was feverish to the touch; and deeper, her muscles were becoming increasingly weak. Try as she might, she could not keep from rubbing the sleeve against her itchy arm. As she did, the blisters burst and soaked through the fabric and onto her hands.

Without knowing it, she was spreading the rash to every patch of bare skin from her fingertips to her face. Soon, she would be completely covered in flaming blisters and utterly unable to move.

Worse Comes to Worst

Mr. Bellamy made Annelyse comfortable beneath the shelter of the overhanging hillside. He was determined to prepare a good meal for her, something to help keep up her strength. He would then address her rash and take a closer look at the saw-toothed tree while she ate. Edward knew enough about poisonous plants to know how to fight the rash. What he didn't know was how to combat the creeping paralysis. Maybe the tree itself would give him a clue.

Leaving Annelyse with a plate of boiled clams, a cup of broth, and some bread, Edward took an empty bowl and headed down to the Maidenhair in search of a solution. On the shore of the river, he found what he was looking for.

The Maidenhair receives its name from the long tufts of blondish-brown grass lining its bed. As the gentle stream flows south to the Perigoh, the submerged tussocks point downstream, gliding side to side in the current. Along its banks, yellow clay and chalky, white boulders bleed their sandstone and gypsum into the otherwise clear waters. Sweeping up the milky dust, the slow-flowing river shimmers and sways like the golden hair of a maiden fair.

Along the banks of the river, Mr. Bellamy knelt and scooped hands-full of clay into the bowl he'd brought for that purpose. Returning in haste to the campsite, he carefully removed the outer shirt he'd used to cover Annelyse's arms. The skin of her hands, forearms, and shoulders was rubbed raw and oozed a clear liquid from a thousand tiny pustules. The shirt was soaked through and so no longer safe to handle. Using a stick, Edward picked it up and tossed it onto the fire.

Taking a glob of white mud in his fingers, he covered Annelyse's hands, wrists, and arms in a thick coat of plaster. He was careful to avoid touching her bare skin with his own, as he worked away transforming his daughter into the likeness of a statue.

At first, the fine grit of the clay stung in Annelyse's open wounds. Then, the soothing cool started working its way into the burn raging within her muscles and bones. The weeping blisters slowly began to dry, as her skin drew tight beneath the stiffening mud. The itch subsided, the fire abated, and the combination of relief and a full stomach allowed sleep to take hold. Annelyse dosed off, while her body fought hard to repair itself.

Relieved to find her sleeping, Mr. Bellamy pulled a blanket up over his daughter, threw a few logs on the campfire, then took advantage of Annelyse's slumber to go examine the saw-toothed culprit.

In the half-light of the forest evening, Edward Bellamy stood before the foe that threatened his daughter. He saw no purpose in the tree. Such wretched poison made the leaves inedible; the scrawny trunk and limbs added nothing to the forest canopy and provided no shade. The tree did not enhance the beauty or harmony of the woods in any way. On the contrary, it was quite obscenely out of place.

From what Edward could see, the little tree was dangerous in its deception. It was simply a parasite, feeding off the world around it, giving nothing in return. What was worse, it kept its secrets to itself, and offered no hint as to a possible antidote. Despite his close examination, Edward would receive no help from this enemy.

Returning to the campsite, Mr. Bellamy checked on Annelyse. She was sleeping peacefully, her arms encrusted in white mud, her cheeks slightly swollen. When she woke again, Edward noted, he would need to apply the muddy mixture to the new blisters appearing on her face. For now, the best he could do was to keep her warm and safe. The morning might bring a brighter outlook, or it might bring with it greater cares. Either way, the night was upon them and nothing more could be done.

Stoking the fire one last time, Edward Bellamy stretched himself out on the ground. The entrance to the small enclosure in which Annelyse now slept was barred by the campfire on one side and Edward's body on the other. If any intruder was brazen enough to approach the flames, it would have to contend with her father before getting to Annelyse. For now, the mounting exhaustion in his body and heart at last took hold, and Edward fell asleep.

In the shadows and hidden places of the night, sylvan creatures awoke. Tree frogs and crickets, wood owls and racoons all lent their voices to the nightly chorus. Bats left the sanctuary of their caves and ventured out into the forest in search of bugs. A few were lucky to happen upon some giant, cave mosquito and return with full bellies to an early sleep. Others would have to work harder to satisfy their hunger.

Black bears wandered eastward from the caverns of Shatter Lake, plundering beehives and berry brambles as they went. Every so often, the sound of a fox's cry - like the shriek of an old woman - cut the night and sent shivers up the spines of rodents and fowl alike. The wilds of the world are ever in motion.

At some point during the small hours of the night, Annelyse awoke with a start. She struggled to open her half-swollen eyes and search the darkness all around her. Shapes and shadows cast by the flickering fire danced upon the screen of trees encircling the campsite. But it wasn't these that alarmed Annelyse the most. It was the voices; the same she and her father had heard before.

Bickering voices hung in the trees. Heated arguments composed of unmistakable anger but without a single intelligible word wrapped every branch in thick turmoil. Annelyse strained her ears to comprehend, but she could discern no language except that of hard-wooded quibbling. The ceaseless noise engulfed the forest, as it radiated from the canopy of leaves above her head and the army of trees stretching out in every direction around her.

Annelyse was frozen with fear, unable to open her mouth or make a sound of warning to rouse her father from sleep. She tried to lift her arm, hoping she might shake him awake. But, either from terror or her creeping paralysis, she could not move a finger. Instead, she lay there in the dark, surrounded by a thousand voices, and helpless to raise the alarm.

Panic stirred within her, and with one great effort of movement, Annelyse shot her leg out, kicking her father in the hip. Jumping to his feet even before opening his eyes, Mr. Bellamy was dazed but ready for a fight.

"What is it?!" he yelled, snatching his walking stick

from the ground.

"Listen," Annelyse whispered, her eyes wide with fear.

As the fog of sleep lifted and awareness dawned, Edward became conscious of the voices in the trees. Swirling in a quarrelsome cyclone, the bickering grew louder and more contentious by the minute.

Unintelligible to Annelyse, the *un*-words spoken by the trees seemed to cut Edward Bellamy to the heart. Somehow, they held meaning for him alone, though he could not explain how or why. Dropping the walking stick, he shielded his ears with his hands, his brow contorting with raw emotion.

By now, the arguing voices had become so loud that they drowned out every other sound in the forest. Unable to lift her hands to cover her ears, Annelyse buried her shoulders first in one ear then in the other, alternating as best she could and trying to gain relief from the overwhelming ruckus. Edward ran over behind his daughter and fell to his knees. Holding his hands against his own ears, he extended his elbows from behind Annelyse's head and cupped them against her ears. Closing their eyes, the frightened travelers lost all hope for a peaceful passage through the Haunted Woods.

When every sight and sound had ceased to exist except for that of the quibbling trees, a new sensation now crept into their awareness. The familiar feel of a gut-wrenching thud stopped the trees midargument and rendered the forest speechless. It was as if every creature was holding its breath, dreading the approach of whatever-it-was. Annelyse and her father followed suit. A moment later, a second thud brought awful confirmation, followed by the sounds of countless creatures scurrying for cover. It was coming.

Mr. Bellamy leapt to his feet and began heaping wood on the campfire to build a wall of flame between his incapacitated daughter and whatever-it-was that drew near. There was no time to flee. Even if there had been, it was unlikely that Edward would be able to outrun danger while carrying Annelyse on his back. They'd have to take their chances and make a stand where they were.

Pulling a stick from the fire, Edward held the flaming brand in one hand and his heavy walking stick in the other. He positioned himself in the gap between the fire and the entrance to where Annelyse lay. Casting his eyes deep into the darkness beyond the campfire, Edward waited and watched as the thuds approached.

Behind him, Annelyse struggled to a seated position, wriggling herself up by pushing her back against the hillside. Above her head, the ground bowed outward, supported by the overhanging mesh of tree roots. The thought occurred to her that this ideal shelter might now become a trap in which to catch her and her father. Without a rear exit, the only way out would be through the gap in which Mr. Bellamy now stood, but that would mean walking right into the teeth of whatever-it-was that had been pursuing them. She had long since lost the use of her arms. Standing up would require help. Soon, even walking would be impossible. Without assistance, she would be defenseless against the intentions of their foe.

Edward did not have long to wait before the pursuer's thuds came to a dreadful halt a scant few yards in front of them. Staring back at him through the dark, two, large, glassy eyes shone in the light of the campfire. Edward adjusted his grip on the flaming branch and walking stick, ready to employ them both in defense of his almost entirely paralyzed daughter. Unwilling to provoke the intruder, Mr. Bellamy stood motionless, his fear hardening to resolute courage. Still, the creature made no move.

"What do you want with us?!" Edward yelled.

The creature remained silent.

"Leave us alone!"

Edward Bellamy took one step closer to uncertainty and danger, increasing the distance between the battle to come and his helpless daughter behind him. Holding up his left arm, he cast the light from the flaming branch out toward where the creature was standing. He was desperate to assess his foe.

In the shadows before him, Edward now detected movement, as if the pursuer were preparing to pounce. Planting his feet firmly at shoulder-width, he readied his weapons in his hands. Before he could draw another breath, the creature leapt from the darkness, knocking the torch out of Edward's left hand, and sending him toppling to the ground. He rolled over onto his hands and knees, struggling to rise and face his attacker again, to no avail. Much to Edward Bellamy's horror, the pursuer had vaulted past him and was now standing over Annelyse. Clearly, she had been the target all along.

"No!" her father screamed, trying to deflect attention away from his daughter.

The enormous shape took no notice of Edward but steadied its attention on the girl. Springing to his feet, Edward grabbed his walking stick and ran toward the creature with all the ferocity of a mother bear whose cub was in danger.

Before he could land a blow across the huge back of the beast, it turned and, with one broad foot, kicked Edward clear across to the other side of the campfire and into the scraggily pine trees. Landing in a heap, his head swam in a sea of sweat and trickling blood. The red stream, oozing from a cut in Edward's forehead, dripped down into his eyes, obscuring his vision.

As he tried to scramble to his feet, Edward discovered that his walking stick had snapped in two probably under the weight of his own body. There, on the far side of the raging campfire, Edward was weaponless, dizzy, and unable to clearly see either the enemy or his daughter.

Seizing the advantage, the ominous, black shape scooped-up Annelyse in its arms, then turned and disappeared into the silence of the night.

"No!" Edward cried, grasping the incorporeal air, pitiful and powerless. "My child…"

Wiping the blood from his eyes, he cast himself with wild abandon into the thicket of trees and brambles through which his daughter had disappeared. The tangle of undergrowth wound its way around his legs, stifling his efforts and dragging the weakened Edward to the ground. It was no use. The forest set its will against him, and Edward Bellamy was quickly defeated. Paralyzed by pain and desperation, his strength seeped into the cold, hard earth beneath him, as he sunk to the ground. His whole world had been stolen away, and with her, his reason for living. All was futility, all was meaninglessness, and now, nothing at all mattered anymore. Seeing Edward laid so low, the grief snipers now moved in to finish him off.

"Annelyse!" he whispered, through his wounded despair. But the only reply was a slow, gradual return of murmuring from the wooden throats of the surrounding trees. The quibbling had begun again.

Edward floundered among the grasping undergrowth and, at last, struggled to his feet. Stumbling over obstacles in his path, his face was lashed and torn by branches crouching among the shadows. The further he ran from the campfire, the more the night engulfed him until, running headlong into the trunk of a tree, Edward Bellamy collapsed under the weight of his own body. He couldn't even see so much as the tree that had felled him in the pitch-black emptiness of night; how could he ever hope to find all that he'd lost?

Leaning his bleeding forehead against the trunk of the tree, he wept without restraint. Alternating without distinction between old and new grief, bitterness poured in upon bitterness, and Edward Bellamy finally surrendered and sank into the dregs of hopelessness. Pursuit would have to wait for the light of day but, by then, his daughter could be miles away. The forest and everything in it seemed to conspire together against Edward's efforts. In his heart, he cursed the Quibble Woods and his own complacence in allowing them to journey so deep into danger.

Somewhere amid the malice of the haunted forest, Annelyse lay limp and unconscious in the arms of her abductor. Moving at great speed away from her father, she was carried against her will into dire uncertainty. When morning arrived, it would bring little comfort.

Wisdom is Always Gentle

Edward's awareness dawned with the cold, reluctant sunrise. He was soaked through with the morning's dewfall and shivered in the pale shadows of the forest. The gash in his forehead had crusted-over with caked-on blood and matted hair. Thoughtlessly brushing his bangs to one side, the motion of his hand reopened the wound and blood flowed anew - an unwelcome reminder of all he'd endured the night before. He was weak and hungry, and the empty hollow of his heart was draining away what little strength remained. Despair quickly made its home in his thoughts.

Over and over again, Edward relived the moment when his daughter had been taken from him. He saw the dark shape standing over her. He heard the snap of branches yielding to the creature as it disappeared into the forest. He could hear his own voice cry out then fall silent in despondent agony. Now, in the tangible absence of his daughter and the drab hostility of the morning, the air itself echoed with anguish.

In his heart, panic and fatigue wrestled with one another. He was desperate to set out in search of Annelyse, but his injuries made forming a clear thought almost impossible. He needed to address the wound in his forehead if he was to regain some degree of clarity.

Pulling himself to his feet, Edward reeled with dizziness. The forest floor appeared to wobble on the shoulders of a gigantic gyroscope, pitching this way and that, but always away from where Edward set his feet. His eyes refused to focus, as he scanned the surrounding area in search of his bearings. Spying the burned-out pit that had once been their campfire, he made his way from tree to tree toward it, steadying himself as he went. Operating entirely in survival mode, he was intent on finding the first aid kit and taking stock of what remained of their provisions.

Where his daughter had lain helpless, Edward now saw four, broad footprints in the soft earth. At the leading edge of each print, claw marks scored the soil. The tracks were unlike any he'd ever seen before. Whatever it was, the creature was enormous, and its powerful feet were big enough for a grown man to stand inside a single footprint. A chill ran up Edward's spine.

Beside the firepit, Edward found both backpacks undisturbed. At first, he was relieved to discover their provisions intact. Then, the realization dawned on him that Annelyse was in the arms of the enemy and all her food and water had been left behind. Panic surged within him, emboldened by his own weakness and the intense pain in his wounded forehead.

Struggling to one knee and opening his own pack,

Edward located the first aid kit, and began tending to the cut on his forehead. Cleaning the wound was an excruciating experience. Not only did the antiseptic sting as he dabbed it on, but the dried blood and matted hair proved to be very stubborn and had to be picked apart by hand. By the time he'd freed the gash from a tangle of blood, hair, and debris, Edward's forehead was throbbing with pain, and his vertigo threatened to topple him again.

Tying a bandage around his head with difficulty, Edward stowed the first aid kit, then turned his attention to food. Luckily, he still had plenty of fish to eat - enough, in fact, to last him for a week or more. Selecting a lump of hard bread and a handful of salted fish, he reclined against a tree stump and fortified his flagging strength. As he ate, he formulated a search and rescue plan.

The creature was fast, by virtue of the fact that one of its strides equaled several of his own; but its size should make it easy enough to track, Edward reasoned. Broken tree limbs and large footprints in the dew-soaked ground would be readily visible. Tracking was not the problem.

The problem was that Edward could only see well enough to pursue his foe during daylight hours. The creature appeared to be able to travel in darkness as well as light. This meant that every morning, after Edward had been forced to pause for the night, his quarry would be at least twice as far away as it had been the previous evening. In all likelihood, it was covering more ground and traveling much faster than Edward could ever hope to pursue. He'd never be able to overtake the creature, let alone keep up.

Then there was the problem of what to do if he should find them. The attacker had effortlessly kicked him clean across the campsite. It was bigger, stronger, and faster than Edward. There would be no defeating it in battle unless Edward could hope to outwit the creature. Complicating everything was the fact that the enemy had Annelyse in its grip. She was in danger and any attempt to free her might end badly. There seemed to be no viable solution. Edward resolved to focus on simply locating them first. He'd worry about how to free his daughter, if ever it came to that, later.

Breakfast had worked wonders in the battered body of Edward Bellamy. The throbbing in his head had ceased, and his dizziness now settled down into a dull thickness of mind. It was such an improvement that Edward gathered their belongings, slung them on his back, and – wobbly but determined – decided to set off in haste in search of the creature that had stolen his daughter.

As he'd hoped, his foe had, indeed, left a clear trail of snapped twigs and soft impressions for Edward to follow. What started off as tentative steps soon quickened to a jog, as he sped along the path marked out for him by the retreating creature.

The sun arced through the clear blue sky, casting shafts of light through the canopy of leaves above Edward's head. As the morning progressed, the grass shed its layer of dew and stood upright in the warmth of the sun. What had been crushed by the feet of the enemy now regained its original shape, making it more difficult for Edward to spot footprints in the earth. As Edward slowed his pace and sharpened his attention, the trees began to grow thin, leaving more space through which the creature had been able to wind its way without leaving a trace. Edward knew he was losing the trail.

Appearing on his right, the Maidenhair shown like tarnished brass among the receding tree line. Edward decided it was best to stick to the western shore of the river, as much as the terrain would allow. If the creature had somehow forded the river, surely it would have left its telltale footprints in the soft mud on the banks. If it had not, then the river would act like a guardrail ushering Edward along what was likely the same path his enemy had been forced to follow.

Thirty-minutes or so after first striking out from the campsite, the forest became little more than a straggling dispersal of solitary trees. The rooftop of branches and leaves now opened onto a cloudless sky, and Edward Bellamy discovered himself stepping foot into a most unexpected place.

At the center of the Quibble Woods where the trees yield to nature's whims, the Forest of Ferns extends outward in a circular clearing two miles in diameter. Sheltered by the surrounding woods, the ferns grow to an exceptional height. From the perspective of an owl in flight, the odd feature looked like an ocean of green-lobed, leafy waves swaying in the spring breeze. To Edward Bellamy, the ferns looked far less poetic and more like a densely planted, spiteful obstacle. There would be no way around it, only through.

Pushing his way into the thick crowd of ferns, Edward found himself in a stifling stillness of snarled vines. The enormous fronds wrapped themselves around one another, like squirming children desperate to cling to their parent's limbs. Each breast-high plant clung to the hand of its neighbor, as if one of many in a barricade of protesters dead set upon opposing any who tried to pass their way. The broad leaves presenting their wide, green faces, resisted Edward with all the stubbornness in their stems. The very width of his torso only added to his difficulties, providing more surface area against which the flat-faced fronds could push. Only his head remained above the fray.

Seeing no alternative, Edward suddenly dropped to his hands and knees and began making his way through the entangled trunks like a four-legged creature of the forest. He now discovered that the stagnant air brooding under the ceiling of ferns was quite intolerable. Shielded from the refreshing breeze by the overpopulation of stems and leaves, the temperature just beneath the surface was nudged ever higher like a pressure cooker. The overall effect was much like crawling through a maritime forest under the crushing depths of a tropical sea.

By now, Edward's clothing was soaked through with perspiration and the wound in his forehead stung in the stream of sweat running down his brow. Dehydration set his head throbbing again, only compounding his growing misery.

After an hour or more of crawling, Edward found himself slowly approaching the far side of the fern forest. He could see the shimmer of sunlight reflected off the surface of a nearby pond. To the left, he spotted a small house standing alone at the edge of the clearing. Painted in the colors of the forest, its hunter green walls and dark brown roof were easily overlooked. The one, solitary feature to stand out, however, was its red door. Like a holly berry among green leaves, the conspicuous door appeared right at home.

Desperate to reacquire the trail of his foe or learn any news of Annelyse's whereabouts, Edward resolved to seek help from whomever might live in the little cabin. He had no other option if he hoped to get back on track.

As he drew near the house, Edward could make out a shape carved into the face of the front door. A cat with its tail wrapped around its shoulders and, in its two front paws, it was holding knitting needles. Encircling the right-hand needle, the end of the tail became the yarn with which the cat was knitting. What was stranger still, however, was that the product being knitted was the cat itself. She was knitting herself into being, using her own tail as the yarn. Edward cocked his head to one side, trying to decide which it was that came first, the knitting cat or the cat being knitted.

A single, thready vapor rose from the brick chimney above the log cabin. Blue against a whitewashed sky, it resembled the tail of the cat, and held its shape in the breathless afternoon. Approaching the front steps, Edward could smell the woodsmoke and it brought a comforting sense of home to his overburdened heart.

From inside the house, a faint voice was heard, as sweet as moonlight. It was the voice of a woman, and she was singing. The words of her song came clearly through the closed door; and, for the second time since arriving at the little house on the edge of the Forest of Ferns, Edward's spirits were lifted. The voice seemed so familiar that, for a moment, he almost believed it was the voice of his wife he heard singing.

> *I hear the language of the trees*
> *Wooden echoes of creaking words*
> *Leafily lilting on a blossom breeze*
> *I hear the language of the trees*
>
> *I've heard the secrets of the wood*
> *Sung to me from the beaks of birds*
> *I'd gladly share them, if only I could*
> *I've heard the secrets of the wood*
>
> *I've seen where shades and shadows dance*
> *To rhythmic chords of fifths and thirds*
> *Exquisitely staged, leaving naught to chance*
> *I've seen where shades and shadows dance*
>
> *In Fäerie Fields and Killoughee*
> *Far north of the wild Goughlin Grugh*
> *From the Perigoh to the Great Sault Sea*
> *They all whisper their rhymes to you*
> *They all whisper their rhymes to you*

The sound of singing faded, as the door opened of its own accord, and Edward felt himself compelled to enter.

In the entryway, there sat a small bench in the back of which was carved the familiar figure of the self-knitting cat. Perhaps this was some sort of coat of arms or family crest. It was a curious emblem, to be sure, and Edward wondered at its meaning.

On the wall above the bench there hung a shelf with four wooden pegs. From three of the pegs, a pair of long, tapered candles dangled by a shared wick. From the fourth peg, there hung a bag filled with woolen mittens, scarves, and hats. There must have been enough knit goods in that bag to accessorize half a dozen chilly children.

On a tall, narrow table beside the bench there sat a vase overflowing with eucalyptus branches, the scent of which was refreshing to body and soul. A circular stand, placed beside the nearby coat rack, held a collection of mismatched and varied umbrellas. From the inviting hospitality of the entryway, there was a feeling that this home stood ready to welcome guests and provide for their needs whatever they might be. Everything had a place, and everything was happily in its place. Whoever the owner was, she was fastidious, without a doubt.

The walls, floor, and ceiling of the entryway and adjoining hall were made of richly lacquered wood. The warm color added to the feeling of hominess, and the scent of growing things made the house feel one with the surrounding forest. This was a place in harmony with nature. Peace and calm sat upon the lintel of every doorway, welcoming the weary and comforting the troubled. Edward felt that this was a place of hope, though he'd be hard pressed to say exactly why.

Almost inaudibly, Edward heard a voice call to him from the next room.

"Please come in," it said with a kindness that was right at home in the little cottage.

Following the invitation, Edward rounded the corner, walked down a short hallway, and entered the living room.

As he did so, he was greeted by the flicker of a

woodfire crackling in a fireplace made of river stone. Above it, a row of lighted candles surrounded by evergreen branches ran along the mantle. Aside from the flames, there was no other light to illuminate the room, and the sun had not yet found its way to the westward-facing windows.

On the chimney above the mantle there hung an old map, framed, and faded with time. At first glance, Edward saw that it depicted the Quibble Woods and the region between there and the sea. But it was marked with countless notations and points of interest that he had never seen on a map before. Edward had no knowledge of the existence of such places as Stumphole Hollow, Willow Bend, or Squirrel Thicket. A suspicion now entered his mind. Perhaps, even the world he thought he knew was largely foreign to him. There was more hidden in plain sight than the light of day revealed.

As his eyes adjusted to the dim firelight, Edward Bellamy now saw the shadowed shape of a woman seated in a rocking chair beside the fireplace. In her hands, she held two knitting needles which were casually at work fashioning the beginnings of a blanket. When Edward entered the room, the woman looked up from her knitting and smiled.

There was an ageless quality about her. Perhaps it was the wisdom in her eyes that made her seem older than her years. Or maybe it was her youthful smile that made her appear younger. In that first moment (and ever after), Edward Bellamy was unable to say which of her qualities prevailed: wisdom or youthfulness. All he knew, right then and there, was that he liked the woman. Any understanding deeper than that would unfold with time.

Beyond this description, it would be difficult to paint a picture of the woman called Halla. All who had the privilege of meeting her would agree that, looking at her, the first thing you saw was her heart. It was a force of kindness, a flash of beauty, a vision of serenity. She was adept at giving others her full attention, so that, when she was listening, you felt like you were the most important person in the world. Her spirit shone through every pore and the glow made it impossible to see anything else.

Placing her knitting in a wicker basket beside her rocking chair, the woman set aside the blanket covering her lap and stood to greet her guest.

"Mr. Bellamy," she said, with a slight bow, "My name is Halla. Welcome to my home."

The woman did not wait for a reply but turned, picked up a poker from a black, metal bucket beside the hearth, and began to stoke the fire.

"Thank you," Edward replied, not noticing that she'd called him by name. "But I'm in some haste," he continued with obvious anxiety.

"Yes," Halla interrupted, "I'm aware of your errand."

"My daughter has been taken," Edward cut in, again, without hearing what his host had said. "A creature, last night… she's been taken, she's in grave danger."

Halla replaced the poker in the bucket, then turned and, patting Edward on the hand, sat back down in her fireside rocking chair.

"Mr. Bellamy," she said with emphasis, "I know of your errand."

"You do?" Edward replied, finally taking notice.

"Yes," Halla continued. "And I know…"

"But, how…"

"That's a question without purpose," she said, unwilling to entertain such useless distractions. "And I know of the poison of Pólcrit, too," Halla continued. "You must soon address the wounds on her skin, before irreparable harm is done."

Edward was utterly confounded. Who was this woman who knew so much? Who was this Pólcrit? And how did Halla know Edward's name? He was filled with questioning, but his anxiety to reacquire the creature's tracks and locate Annelyse had sharpened his focus and pricked the rawness of his urgency.

"Do you know where my daughter is?" he asked, the faintest hope rising in his heart.

"I know where she isn't, and that can be just as useful. You must now prepare for when she is found."

Hanging above the flames in the fireplace, a cast iron tea kettle began to whistle. Rising again from her chair, Halla opened a small, wooden box on her mantle and took out what appeared to be fragments of tree bark.

Opening the lid with a potholder, she dropped all three scraps of bark into the tea kettle. The moment she did, the entire house was filled with a pleasant aroma the likes of which Edward was unable to identify. Sitting herself down again, she looked directly into Edward's eyes.

"Do you know of Pólcrit and Kalósyi?" she asked.

"No. Those names are strange to me," Mr. Bellamy said with growing impatience.

Sitting back in her chair, she began to rock, staring into the fire as she did.

"They are opponents. Enemies. Trees which grow only in the Quibble Woods." She paused a moment, then whispered, "Doomed to linger in each other's company for all time."

"The great red tree?" Edward inquired, piecing it together.

"Yes, that is Kalósyi. And the jagged-leafed tree is Pólcrit. There is a story about them, an ancient story. It explains much. And we have some time now."

Halla turned her head back toward the fire. There was a distance in her eyes, as if trying to remember events from long ago. After a moment of silence broken only by the creaking of her rocking chair, she began to speak.

"Pólcrit was a cruel and hateful man. His strength and skill in battle made him arrogant, and he delighted in tormenting others – both people and animals. He had no respect for those weaker than himself, and even less for what was right.

"Kalósyi was quite different from his older brother. Kind and upright toward all, Kalósyi knew that true strength lay in restraint, mercy, compassion. He, too, was a powerful warrior, but he wielded his sword only in defense, whereas Pólcrit wielded his in anger.

"Both brothers bore a secret love for the graceful maiden, Niktyah. She was as modest as a water lily, and more kindhearted than a dove. Though her own heart belonged to Kalósyi, she knew nothing of the other's love for her.

"One day, the wicked Pólcrit approached Niktyah and confessed his desire for her. His treacherous heart was filled with selfishness and a will to possess. His was but a dim perversion of love. For love's true desire is for the good of the beloved, and love's only wish is to set others free. Without a concern for her freedom or a care for her happiness, Pólcrit demanded that Niktyah bind herself to him forever. If she would not agree willingly, he would persuade her by force.

"In desperation, she fled, and sought the protection of the noble Kalósyi. Pledging to defend her, Kalósyi professed his love for the maiden, who declared her own hidden devotion to him. The two lovers vowed to marry before the next full moon, but it was not to be.

"For, when Pólcrit learned of their love, he gathered together the most noxious plants from the dark places of the forest, brewing them into a poison of deadly intent. One night, while his brother lay sleeping, he spread the vile mixture on Kalósyi's bare skin. By morning, Kalósyi was covered in a rash of oozing blisters, unable to move, unable to defend himself from harm.

"Returning to his stricken brother, Pólcrit mocked him in his helplessness. He bragged of having poisoned

Kalósyi and swore on his sword that he would not rest until he found Niktyah and took her for his own. Raising his blade, Pólcrit then savagely slew his own brother in cold blood, burying the body along the banks of the Maidenhair.

"When news of her soulmate's murder reached her ears, Niktyah set out alone in search of Kalósyi's grave. Unknown to her, somewhere in the Quibble Woods, the enraged Pólcrit was already hunting the forlorn maiden.

"Following the river as it crept through the forest, Niktyah soon discovered what she'd been looking for: a cairn of rocks, and at its top, a single stone etched with the words, '*Here, Weakness Lies Defeated.*' Overwhelmed by the loss of her love and devastated by the taunting words of the epitaph, Niktyah wept in bitter despair, until heartbreak took her life, and the river carefully claimed her body.

"Pólcrit wandered the woods in vile hatred, intent upon finding Niktyah. His jealousy and tangled mind drove him to madness, and his madness consumed all reason. Days became months, and still his hunt continued.

"But a warped mind always turns inward upon itself, and, in the abyss of self-loathing, it is lost to the waking world forever. Such was the fate of Pólcrit. Little by little, sanity abandoned him, until there was nothing left but a withered and pitiable beast. As his frenzied grip on life weakened, Pólcrit faded into legend and then into myth.

"Now, the tortured spirit of Pólcrit lives imprisoned within the venomous tree that bears his name. Punished for his crimes, his true nature gives no shade to the traveler and adds no beauty to the forest. Day and night, Pólcrit oozes only contagion, a reminder to all who pass that evil can lurk even in the shadow of goodness.

"Always within reach, though, the Kalósyi tree offers the antidote to its brother's venom. Defeated in life, Kalósyi is triumphant in death, and towers victorious above the ragged, little Pólcrit tree. This is why, behind my home, beneath the Pólcrit tree that grows there, I set a remembrance plaque inscribed with the words, '*Here, Wickedness Lies Defeated.*' For love always triumphs, whether in time or in eternity.

"And, never far away, upon the clean waters of the Maidenhair, a delicate water lily gazes lovingly up at the red tree in heartbreak. Beneath the water, Niktyah's light-brown maidenly locks still sway in the passing current, her innocence and beauty ever serving to prick the wicked heart of the saw-toothed Pólcrit. Only now does his guilt yield to remorse. But for Pólcrit, it is too late. Only love is its own reward; hatred knows only vengeance. Indeed, all three – the pure maiden, her brave lover, and his evil murderer - are eternally bound together, and their tragic story plays out for all ages.

"And now you know, Mr. Bellamy," Halla said, as she rocked beside the fireplace.

Edward hesitated, not wanting to sound childish, "You tell it like it really happened. Surely, it's not true."

Halla turned and looked him in the eyes, "Anyone can see the face, but few there are who know the heart of a matter. As someone I know is fond of saying, '*The truth is for you to decide.*'"

Edward stopped cold. He knew those words, those vague, frustrating, irritating words. They were the words of the poet, spoken to Annelyse on the beach. In the blink of an eye, it all came clear. Halla and the poet knew one another. Of course, they had to.

Edward sat forward in his seat.

"The poet," he said, scrutinizing Halla's reaction.

"The same," came Halla's confession.

"But…"

"All things work together," Halla assured him. "There is no coincidence, only coordination," she smiled.

"Then you're the person we were meant to find," Edward surmised. "The person mentioned in his note."

"What note is this?" Halla asked, a look of wry

curiosity twinkling in her eyes.

Edward pulled the scrap of paper from his daughter's backpack and handed it to the woman.

"*Deep myst'ries in the Weeping Pool; too few can say what's there. But one who knows is easily found along the Maidenhair,*" Halla read aloud. "I see," she said, handing the note back. "Then you've looked into the Weeping Pool."

"Yes," Edward began. "Or rather, Annelyse did."

"He said you might. He was sure you'd see."

"How would he have known what we'd see?" Edward demanded, the old disdain for the poet rising in his chest.

"You'd have to ask him that question, Mr. Bellamy."

Edward was beginning to think that answers were scarce north of the Perigoh.

"Was he right?" Edward asked, referencing the poet's note.

"Yes, my friend. He was right. I know what lies hidden in the icy waters of the Weeping Pool. For I have seen it, too. It was long ago, though little has changed since then."

"Then she really *did* see something beneath the water," Edward said, as the realization leapt into his mind that Annelyse hadn't imagined what had happened beside the pool at the foot of Mt. Averly.

"Doubt your senses if you will. But never doubt your heart. For the head knows, but the heart understands." Halla replied.

"But what was it she saw? And why was it there?"

"What your daughter saw was one of many like itself... one of many that perished in the waters of the Weeping Pool. For the pool was named for tragedy, the same tragedy that befell many just like the poor creature who is still entombed there."

"Why is it there?"

"It was driven there against its will," Halla sighed, "by evil men intent upon enslaving the innocent."

"The pirates. From my wife's story." Edward said, skepticism giving way to cautious belief.

"Your wife would not lie, would she?"

"Well, no. But I thought it was…"

"Just a fairytale?"

"Yes," Edward replied, with a hint of shame, "Just a fairytale."

"It *was* a fairytale," Halla continued. "A fairytale that came true."

Edward glossed over Halla's words.

"But do the Woolems still exist."

"They do," Halla affirmed, each word steeped in sadness. "But they have suffered. They suffer still."

Edward Bellamy sat on the couch opposite Halla, staring into the fireplace. The full weight of Halla's assurance that the Woolems still lived, and the stress of the last twelve hours now settled onto his shoulders. All of a sudden, he was exhausted. But he dared not rest a moment longer. Somewhere out there, Annelyse was alone with whatever it was that had taken her. She had no food, no water, and – thanks to the poison of the Pólcrit tree - she was unable to move or defend herself. Edward's restlessness began again in earnest.

Halla sensed his growing impatience. Dropping her hands in her lap, she looked Edward in the eye.

"The day is long spent," she whispered. "The sun will set soon."

"But I…"

"My friend, the night demands patience. Nothing can be accomplished without the aid of the sun. And I still have more to give you."

Edward knew Halla was right. There was nothing more to be done that day. Even if he did leave, he'd be forced to make camp before long. His head was splitting again, and the pain blurred his vision. If he hoped to continue the search in the morning, he'd need to restore his strength with a good night's sleep. Reason must reign in his fear, for a time.

As he came to terms with this second forced delay, Halla's story about Pólcrit and Kalósyi wove its way through his thoughts. Unlike the poet, who seemed capable only of speaking in riddles, Halla spoke as if from experience and memory. Her calm and soothing kindness was a testimony to the believability of her words. There is nothing that compels belief quite so powerfully as force of character, and Halla's character was a force for goodness.

Edward trusted her, and at last he felt all the bitterness in his heart begin to soften. The bitterness he harbored toward the poet, the bitterness he'd had to swallow over being unable to pursue his daughter until morning, it all began to subside. In its place, Edward now discovered a growing openness. He wanted to follow Halla's every word, he needed to hear more.

"Please," he whispered, "tell me about the Woolems."

CHAPTER FIFTEEN

Seeing Beyond the Self

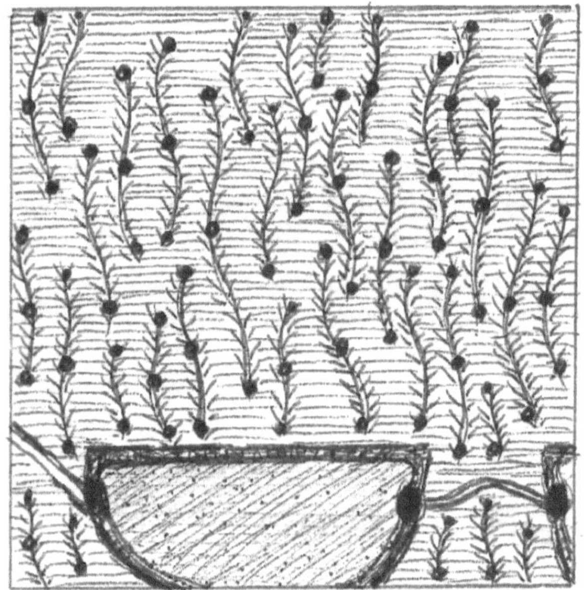

With a gentle nod, Halla picked up her knitting and began to speak. The rhythmic clicking of her knitting needles, the way she paused to push the stitches together, and the slow rocking of her chair were all mesmerizing. Edward watched and listened, taking it all in and letting it ease his troubled mind, while golden flames danced in the hearth.

Halla began, "When the pirates carried their captives across the Great Sault Sea to the Isles of Wanton, many Woolems were lost along the way. Perhaps, they were the lucky ones. For those who survived the crossing were soon auctioned-off into slavery. Herds were dispersed, families torn apart, and the gentle giants of the Greenfields were scattered to the four corners of the world.

"Enslaved and abused, the Woolems were forced into cruel labor. Shouldering heavy burdens, pulling tremendous loads, even submitting themselves to the indignity of carrying a rider on their backs, the Woolems passed their days in hopeless toil and their nights in tearful despair. Their great size and strength were dwarfed only by the sweet nature of their docile hearts, and so they made no effort to free themselves. But there were others, strangers, friends who did try to free them. And their efforts paid off.

"A group was formed for the sole purpose of rescuing the Woolems. A group called, simply, *The Ransom*. Men and women, young and old, even other animals joined together in secret to track down each and every Woolem who'd been sold into oppression. Far and wide they traveled, always alone or in pairs, in order to avoid the attention of pirates and slaveholders alike. Their work of mercy was fraught with mortal dangers, and some there were who paid the price of a Woolem's freedom with their own lives.

"The Woolems were secreted away by members of *The Ransom,* under the cover of darkness, when their masters were asleep. The rescuers would silently unshackle and lead the Woolems to safety before the morning light revealed their absence. By the time their owners had realized what had happened, the Woolems were well on their way to freedom.

"Once they'd been rescued, the vulnerable Woolems could not be returned to their homes in the Fäerie Fields of Averlune. Instead, they had to be hidden away from the wicked designs of others, or risk being captured all over again. And so, a new home was found; a home well beyond the reach of those who would do them harm; a home shrouded in mystery and shielded by myth; a home that could be protected by the vigilance of those few who knew of its existence."

Halla paused a moment, her head and shoulders sagging beneath some unseen burden. Then, with a deep sigh that sounded as if it had originated in the secret storehouse of her soul, she continued her story.

"It took years to find and free each Woolem – years of suffering. But the work succeeded in the end, as all labors of love do. Not one Woolem was left behind to languish in slavery far away from home. All who survived captivity were returned to a life of security.

"Still, the victory was bittersweet. For there was one slave owner who, in stealth, had learned of the location of the Woolems' secret sanctuary. And this one unfortunate revelation threatened to undo the work of the rescuers and endanger the life of each and every Woolem.

"Among the members of *The Ransom*, there were two young rescuers. The younger of the two, a 10-year-old boy, had heard of the Woolems' plight and convinced his 15-year-old sister to join in the search. The boy was impulsive and easily excited, and his persuasive words had appealed to the adventurous nature of his older sister, much to their peril.

"From their home in Upper Averlune, the pair made daily excursions into the surrounding countryside looking for captive Woolems. They were resolved to aid in the work of *The Ransom* any way they could. If there were Woolems enslaved nearby, these two young adventurers were determined to find them and return them to freedom.

"One day, they happened upon the homestead of a man named Gióstou Póthou. Gióstou lived just south of the village of Averlune, not far from Ruhner's Beach. He was a loner and outcast among the inhabitants of the peninsula, for Gióstou was a hunter. The people of that area were peaceful and solicitous for the well-being of all the creatures of the Greenfields. The recent disappearance of the Woolems had made them that much more protective of the animals of the prairie, and as a result, Gióstou was looked upon with suspicion.

"Indeed, there was something suspicious about the activities that took place inside the hunter's barn. Without the benefit of flowing water to turn a water wheel, the sounds of a large mechanical band saw could be heard coming from within at all hours of the day and night. It appeared that Gióstou had discovered some unknown source of power. That discovery allowed him to drive the tools he used to make quick work of the bones and sinews of the poor creatures he'd felled by weapon or trap. The productivity of his butchery was increased by some unexplained, devious asset.

"That day, outside Gióstou's barn, the young girl and her little brother hid in the tall grass waiting for him to leave on his daily rounds spent checking his traps. From down among the brown stalks, they watched as a pair of stained, leather boots tramped off toward the wetlands east of Ruhner's Beach. Once the trapper was safely out of sight, the two would-be-rescuers made their way out of the overgrown meadow, down a deeply rutted path, and into the clearing that encircled an enormous, weatherworn barn.

"Hanging from the barn door, a chain, knotted around both handles and secured by a large padlock, rusted in the salty breeze. In any of the four walls of the great barn, there was nothing but this solitary entrance – no windows and no other door. With only the mystery of the mechanical noise, and a sense of foreboding, the young adventurers could not know what else might lay inside.

Scanning the building for another way in, the boy spied a large drainpipe exiting the western wall of the stone foundation. Above the pipe, a sign hung, inscribed with only one word: WARNING. There was no grate spanning the opening of the wide, terra cotta pipe. Only a horrific odor, emanating from the shadows within, reiterated the sign's message."

Halla laid her hands in her lap, "To this very day, I cannot say which would have been better, treating that wretched pipe as a locked door or using it the way they did."

Her eyelids fell like evening, and for a moment the warmth of her heart was hidden from view. The room grew dark, and the fireplace became a drafty hole of cold, pitiful fire. Edward sat on the couch, waiting. But he wasn't sure what it was that he awaited with greater eagerness, the break of sunlight on the eastern horizon, or the dawn of Halla's kind and confident eyes.

Removing her tiny, half-rimmed glasses, Halla rubbed the fatigue from her face before returning to her story.

"Despite the hideous odor and oozing unknown, the young boy started squirming his way up the drainpipe and into the perils of the old barn. Too big to follow, his sister kept watch outside, sending insistent whispers into the mouth of the pipe, urging him to be cautious.

"From inside the pipe, the sins of one man dripped and sloughed their way into the outside world. Originating from behind the ragged walls of the hunter's barn, what flowed down that drain had no rightful place under the light of a chaste sky. It was vile and hateful in every regard, to spill the blood of innocence in the shadows of shame. But, into this wickedness, the young boy now crawled, dragging himself like a slug up the long, curved walls of the drainpipe.

"When he finally reached the other end, everything became clear. The filth through which he had just sloshed; the lock on the front door of the barn; the mechanized noise emanating from within; and the ominous sense of foreboding and danger he and his sister had experienced on the outside, it all made sense in the blink of his young eye.

"Animal hides, stretched like drumheads, dried in the musty air. On the floor beneath the band saw's table, things too hideous for description lay dripping in the shadows. Flies gorged themselves on the discarded spoils of the hunter's excesses. The scene was more than anyone should be compelled to witness, and the boy gasped aloud.

"Dwarfing all else by its sheer immensity and chained to a wooden post in the middle of the room, there stood the largest creature the boy had ever set eyes upon. Around the post, a deep groove was worn in the earthen floor of the barn. It was obvious that the animal had been forced to walk in endless, tiresome circles, driving the mechanism that powered the hunter's merciless blades.

"The young rescuer stood staring at the creature. It was enormous, at least as big as an elephant, and covered in black ringlets of fur. The deep, glassy eyes shone forth unfathomed intelligence. The face was drawn with exhaustion, but from somewhere inside, a nobility of spirit shone with unexpected strength. Sadness sat heavy on the animal's brow, but there was in its face no malice. Wisdom and kindness often abide in harmony.

"The boy was struck to the heart with a mixture of pity and awe. He was sure that he was standing in the presence of a Woolem, though he'd never seen one in person before. Only his sister had, long ago. He'd only ever seen the scribblings she'd made as a child. But there was no doubt in his mind about what it was that stood before him.

"On a twisted nail in the wall beside the door, there hung a ring of iron keys. Moving quickly, the boy seized the keys, found the one that fit the manacles around the Woolem's feet and neck, and freed the poor beast. Without a word, he motioned for the Woolem to stay put, while the boy slid back down the drainpipe and out into the sinless air of springtime.

"Explaining all that he'd seen to his waiting sister, he located the key that would unlock the padlock securing the front door of the barn. Flinging both doors wide open, the two young rescuers now stood face to face with a unique creature, indeed.

"Willem Woolem was the oldest and wisest of the Woolems of Averlune. His memory was the longest, his understanding the deepest. Where Willem went, the herd of Woolems followed. Because of his age, he had not been targeted by the kidnapping pirates. Instead, he'd been left behind to witness the dwindling of his herd and experience the heartbreak of helplessness.

"Although of little interest to the marauding pirates, Willem was easy prey for the unscrupulous Gióstou Póthou. The hunter saw his chance to entrap the old Woolem and force him into a life of endless circling, tracing his steps to power the saw that made quick work of his fellow creatures. It was too much for Willem to bear, and his spirit soon sank into a consuming sadness. Until the doors of the barn flew open, and the light of the sun once again fell across his sagging shoulders.

"The two children led Willem out of the barn and into the countryside northwest of the hunter's homestead. They were desperate to put as many miles as they could between the old Woolem and his captor. The greater the distance, the more their sense of safety grew. Willem's strength returned with each step, until, with deep humility, the noble creature invited his new friends to sit astride his back. He would carry them, at greater speed, to the one haven he knew.

"Traversing the prairie of Upper Averlune, bounding the mighty Perigoh Fair, the ancient Woolem wound his way through the trees of the Quibble Woods, following the same path that led you, Edward Bellamy, through the Forest of Ferns to this very cabin."

Halla stopped a moment, allowing Edward's mind time to catch up and understand what it was she had just said. There was something significant about the fact that he had been following the same path that the two young rescuers and the ancient Woolem had taken. As of yet, Edward could not guess what that might be.

However, an unexpected certainty had taken root in the wordless rooms of his heart. He knew the two youths in Halla's story. He was sure of it, no matter how little he wanted to admit to the fact. He had heard bits of this story before from one of its two protagonists.

The storyteller continued, "For time out of mind, the kind and generous Woolems of Averlune would collect skeins of their cast-off wool and bring them to me to be knit into scarves and mittens, hats, and sweaters for the creatures of the north. It's true, the animals of the winterlands owe much to the warmth of their more southerly friends, for Woolem wool provides as much protection from winter's cold as it does from the summer rains."

Edward reached a hand over and caressed the yarn in the basket at Halla's feet, the yarn from which she was knitting her blanket.

"This?" he asked, fingering the soft wool.

"Yes, my friend. This is Woolem wool."

"And your coat of arms," Edward asked, changing the subject, "The self-knitting cat. What does it mean?"

Halla laughed to herself, with a laugh like that of a child delighting in her first finger painting.

"We take the best and finest of all that we find around us, Edward Bellamy. We spin it together, fashion it anew, and give it again as a gift to those we meet. In so doing, we constantly remake our lives into a work of art for the benefit of others and the betterment of ourselves. Like the clever cat on my coat or arms, we are always knitting our own tale, always creating, always becoming. And we must ever be on guard against unraveling. It's always easier to maintain than it is to start over again."

Halla's words slipped easily into the widening gap between Edward's indignant grief over the loss of his wife and his increasing desire to, once more, believe all that he'd cast aside. Like the healing blade of a surgeon's scalpel, what she had said about being on guard against unraveling now lay at the root of the cancer inside of him. He had forgotten so much, and he had rejected the rest. In its place, Edward Bellamy had adopted a small, self-pitying outlook on life.

He now realized that this pettiness had replaced the code by which he had been taught to live by those he'd loved and admired: burden no one, leave all better than you found them, spread goodness with reckless abandon, make your life a work of art. He now readily surrendered his grief, his sorrow, and his jaded cynicism. Hanging his head, silent tears now glistened in the orange glow of the fireplace, as Halla proceeded with knitting her tale.

"When the travelers arrived at my door, I took them in. But if I was going to help Willem, I needed the assistance of others. So, I conferred with the creatures who had long been the beneficiaries of the kindness of the Woolems. Speaking with the squirrels, the hedgehogs, the otters, and other inhabitants of the northlands, a new home was chosen for the Woolems far away from Averlune and the wickedness of men. We resolved to bring all the rescued Woolems to the Forgotten Meadows. Those who had rescued them, the creatures of the northlands, and even I – in my small way - would maintain a constant vigilance to keep their new home secret and safe for all time."

"With gratitude, the ancient Woolem offered his thanks. With awe, the brother and sister accepted it and pledged themselves to keep the secret of the Forgotten Meadows in their hearts. Safe passage was given, not only for Willem, but for every Woolem rescued by the efforts of *The Ransom*. Hidden in the land of their newfound freedom, the Woolems flourished in peace for a time."

Edward interrupted, "For a time?"

"Peace is a fragile flower, Mr. Bellamy, and so

easily spoiled by those who grow nothing but turmoil in their hearts. Even the most innocent of acts has unintended consequences. The price of love is vulnerability, a risk worth the taking."

Smoothing the blanket covering her lap, Halla continued her knitting. "And so it was that, a few years later, the two young rescuers – now 13 and 18 years old - wanting only to sit in the company of their old friend, snuck back into the Forgotten Meadows. But they had been seen. And, what's worse, they had been followed. For it was not only the friends of the Woolems who had maintained their vigil. One enemy had, as well.

"Once there, the cunning foe hid in the shadows, watching, unseen by the unsuspecting Woolems. He was searching for his target, one Woolem among the rest. Unleashing the hatred in his heart, this wolf among Woolems made his move."

"Alone on a hillside, Willem stood eating clover beneath a willow tree. Just over the brow of the hill, the villainous hunter approached with shackles in hand. The moment Willem dropped his head to take another mouthful, he was clapped in irons. With a manacle fixed to his hindleg, a chain was secured to the trunk of the tree.

"Turning the iron key in the lock, Willem's captor spoke these words to the helpless Woolem, 'Although all your witless friends are now free, I will crush their hearts in a prison of my own making. You will die shackled to this tree, old Woolem, for this chain cannot be cut and I take the only key with me when I go. May yours be a long life and may many a cold wind strip this hillside bare.'

"Vanishing as suddenly as he'd appeared, Gióstou Póthou took the key and departed, never to return. He'd worked his revenge on those who'd freed his slave. He'd struck a blow in the tender hearts of the most innocent of all creatures. The chains and shackles were hardened by some wicked will. They would yield to neither force nor flame. With no key to defeat the lock and no way to sever that which bound him, Willem would surely die from exposure on that hillside.

"When his fellow Woolems found him, a great cry went up through all the land. Desperate to free their revered leader, some of the younger Woolems even proposed pushing the ancient willow tree down, but Willem would not permit them.

"'We should not trade one life for another,' he said. 'Especially one so innocent as a tree.'

"When the brother and sister realized that they'd been followed to Willem's great misfortune, they were heartsick. Running to the old Woolem's side, they tried to free him, but to no avail. They vowed, then and there, to set right their unintended misdeed and bring freedom to Willem, restoring happiness to the Woolems who loved him. Efforts were made to keep this vow, but without success.

"Until this very day," Halla said, a change coming over her like the first breath of spring, "their vow has gone unfulfilled. Indeed, until now, it appeared as if there was no more hope left for the Woolems. Yes, until now…"

With a soft smile, she added, "And that is all I have to share, my friend. All, except for this…"

Halla laid aside her knitting, stood, and walked across the room to where a small, wooden box sat upon a shelf. Taking it down, she brought it over to where she'd been sitting. Without a word, Halla handed the box to Edward, then sat back in her rocking chair beside the fire.

"What is it?" Edward asked.

"Open and see. All will become clear."

Given his experience lately, Edward seriously doubted that *all would become clear*. Still, his heart swelled with expectation as he took Halla's gift in his hands.

The box was made of dark-stained cherry wood and lined with red velvet. There were no carvings, no self-knitting cat crests, no markings at all. There was only a brass clasp and two tarnished hinges securing the top. Opening the lid, Edward moved slowly and with great care, as if whatever was within might escape in an instant. Inside, he found one single item wrapped in white tissue paper. Edward removed the small parcel, then closed the box and set it beside him on the couch. Gingerly, he unfolded the paper.

There, in his hands, Edward held a small painting. It appeared to have been the work of a child, for it was possessed of more character than artistic skill. The image on the canvas was that of a large animal not entirely unlike a giant, fluffy sheep. Above its head, the sky was painted in thick, blue brushstrokes. All around it, the creature was surrounded by a sea of green paint speckled with white and yellow dots. Even in its primitive rendering, Edward was sure he was looking at the depiction of a Woolem standing among the flowers of the Fäerie Fields.

Halla, who had been watching with great interest, now broke the silence. "And look at the back, too. We must always look at a thing from all sides," she said, nodding in hearty agreement with her own words of wisdom.

Edward turned the little painting over, revealing the scribbled name of the artist.

"Silloah Uhl," he read aloud, with a look of stunned confusion on his face. "How did you come by this?" he asked, turning to Halla in amazement.

Halla began rocking gently, staring into the fire. "It was given to me," she replied.

"But by whom?"

"A friend of ours, though less so of yours," she said, with a twinkle in her eye.

Edward understood. Of course, the poet would have kept this little memento of his sister's own making. Edward's suspicion that he knew the two young rescuers was confirmed. In fact, Silloah had been acquainted with

Woolems at an even earlier age, as was evident from the little painting. It would have been easy for her little brother to convince her to help find and free the captive creatures. She loved them of old. But now Edward Bellamy wondered why he'd never heard all the details of Willem's story from his wife's own lips. Why had he never been told of these efforts to fulfill their vow to free the old Woolem?

"Uhl," Edward whispered, caressing the signature on the back of the painting with his fingers, "That was her maiden name."

"It was left with me for safekeeping, until I might give it to you," Halla said.

"But why?" Edward asked, trying to wrap his head around this latest mystery.

Halla looked at the man and smiled, "Because, along with the key and the task, it now belongs to your daughter, my dear."

CHAPTER SIXTEEN

Never Truly Alone

Edward reached into Annelyse's backpack and pulled out the iron key she'd taken from her mother's hope chest. She didn't really know why she'd brought it along. It just seemed like it wanted to go with her. Now, as her father held it in his hand, Edward was overwhelmed with panic. The events of the night before came rushing in to flood his mind and heart with fear for his little girl. Halla noticed the wave of emotion which now threatened to sweep her guest over the abyss and back into the dark waters of despair.

"You will find her," Halla whispered through the firelight. "And you will tell her all you have learned. Now that you have the map, the poem, the key, your wife's little painting, and the truth of all that happened, you have what you need to find your own way... and soon you will have

Annelyse, too."

Edward could hold back the torrent of emotion no longer. Burying his face in his hands, he wept at the thought of his daughter alone with some creature in the Haunted Woods.

"Forgive me," Edward said through his sobs, "I must be more exhausted than I thought." Wiping his eyes with embarrassment, he looked at Halla and struggled to master his quivering voice, "What am I expected to do with these things? I don't understand."

"Remember the story I told you. Remember Willem in chains."

"This?" Edward looked at the key in his hand with wonder. "This is *the* key? The key to Willem's lock? But how did she find it? Why did she never tell me?"

"Because you did not want to know," Halla replied with an edge to her voice sharp enough to lay waste to the forest. "She did not hide the details of these events from you. You shut them out. All you could see was her brother stirring up what you thought were dangerous dreams of adventures in the mind of your wife. You drove him away, thinking it would protect her. But all it did was stifle an opportunity for you to know her better… and deny her the redemption she so desired. She'd found the key. Together, she and her brother were ready to bring it back to the Forgotten Meadow and free Willem, but you would not permit the young poet from speaking with his sister. And so, here it remains."

Edward's eyes were opened for the first time in many years. Halla was right. He had made it clear to Silloah's younger brother that he was not welcome. He saw the young man as an irresponsible adventurer and dreamer. Edward didn't want him anywhere near his wife or daughter, even going so far as to force the young poet to watch his sister's funeral from the cover of the trees, on the outskirts of a loss he should have been allowed to mourn freely. His final tribute to his older sister was a flight of birds he'd sent mounting to the sky in her memory. This was all that he was permitted.

With compassion, Halla moved to place herself between Edward and his bruised conscience, "What's important is that the key be brought full circle. It was used to bind; it must now be used to set free. Because she was not able to do it herself, your wife has left this task for you and her daughter to complete. You must follow the same path she once took and free Willem at last."

Edward sat in silence as Halla's words soaked into his understanding. He had set out to help his daughter find the truth about the Woolems. In his own mind, he'd hoped to prove that these things had all been myths, fantasies, even lies. He wanted to kill anything that remained of his old beliefs, his wife's beliefs. They were a part of Silloah and holding them too near was more painful than Edward could bear. An unspoken part of him had wanted to see the spark of faith extinguished from his daughter's heart, too. That way, he would not be alone in his own faithlessness.

Now the burden of finding and freeing the old Woolem had been thrust upon him. His disbelief and disdain were no longer relevant. All that remained was a task his wife was entrusting to him and their daughter. What choice did he have but to accept? Indeed, he wanted to accept with all his heart, and find his own redemption along the way.

Edward pulled out his brother-in-law's poem and began examining the map on the back. "The Forgotten Meadows," he whispered, "beyond the Miralette."

"Yes. Beyond the Miralette, across the Fishbones, through the Silent Forest and over the Borderland Hills… where myth and Woolems live. That is your destination. But there's more." Lowering her voice to a hushed whisper, she continued, "There is great danger just north of the Miralette. Traps and pitfalls, enemies of different kinds will plague your path. That region is planted thick with peril. But you need not face it alone. This path has been trodden before, and even those who traveled it before had company."

Edward stared at the map in his hands. He knew only the rumors that surrounded that part of the world. Now, Halla was confirming that those rumors were true, and that the way to the Woolems lay among the legendary terrors of the northlands.

While Edward sat in stunned thought, Halla got up from her rocking chair and stepped into the entryway. When she returned, she was carrying the large bag stuffed full of knit goods that had been hanging on the peg by the front door - things made with the wool of the Woolems, and by the hands of Halla herself.

"You must do something for me along your way. Something that will once again rally the beneficiaries of the Woolems' kindness to our cause. Those who helped long ago still have a role to play. Yes, yes, it is as it should be."

"Um, yes, of course," Mr. Bellamy replied, becoming somewhat lost in Halla's seemingly disjointed thoughts. "I'll do whatever you ask."

"Very good. At the southern tip of Shatter Lake," she began, sounding somewhat businesslike, "there is a small cabin behind which grows a large, knotty beech tree. This is the home of Isaiah Weaver and his family. Please give him this," she said, handing Edward the bag. "He will know what to do with it. Yes, all will be as it should be."

"I will," Mr. Bellamy replied, somewhat curious about Halla's repeated, cryptic words. She seemed to be resolved and focused, as if moving from watchfulness into long-awaited action; while Edward's mind was still stuck in cautious apprehension.

"Thank you, dear friend. Now, you should rest a while. You have had precious little sleep and tomorrow you'll face another long journey."

Before saying goodnight, Edward paused and carefully ventured to ask one final question of his host.

"Please," he began, "What did your song mean?"

"Which song is that, Mr. Bellamy?"

"The one I heard through the front door when I arrived. The one about the *language of the trees.*"

Halla brushed her long grey hair aside and began to sing. Her voice was like a wandering breeze on a warm summer's day, touching everything with softness, leaving nothing unchanged.

> *"I hear the language of the trees*
> *Wooden echoes of creaking words*
> *Leafily lilting on a blossom breeze*
> *I hear the language of the trees"*

"Yes, that's it," Edward spoke. "What does it mean? Can you… can you hear the bickering, too?"

"It isn't all of the trees who bicker, dear friend," Halla assured him with a smile. "Some trees soothe. They speak words of comfort and memory. They hush the troubled soul. Shhh… listen outwardly, and you too will hear the language of the trees."

"Then which trees do I hear arguing? In the forest at night. The clamoring voices."

"You hear the wrestling words of your own grief, Mr. Bellamy, echoed back to you by the bitterwort trees. They attune themselves to grief, fear, anxiety, and they hurl it around amid the canopy of leaves and limbs. Whatever is brought to the Quibble Woods, the bitterworts use to drive the bearer mad. Your grief was fresh when you arrived, and so the quibblers spoke it back to you as poignant as it was when first you carried it in."

Edward knew what Halla was referring to, for he had heard the bickering words. He knew what they were saying. When he and Annelyse had first arrived at the edge of the forest with Albert Prume, Edward had clearly heard words when the others had only heard garbled voices.

"I thought I was going mad," he said, not entirely convinced that he wasn't. "But I also thought… well, that I understood what was being said."

"These are but another guise of the grief snipers, Mr. Bellamy. They stir up what settles in your heart and mind, until you are unable to see more than a few steps in front of you. They thrive on turmoil, and they set you against yourself. The bickering you heard was within your own mind. But I hear only… shhhh," she whispered, raising one finger to her lips, "the sweet language of the trees."

Halla smiled again, and her smile was a promise that all would, indeed, be as it should be. Hers was the voice of reason in the midst of a quibbling wood.

"You must learn to let go," she continued. "Not of your wife or the good things you think you've lost, but of the need to make sense of it all. Some things make no sense, they simply are. Death, most of all. Grief is not rational, it is emotional, and no amount of reasoning and arguing within yourself can buffet any sense out of it. You cannot find a quick and easy path through. No, dear friend. Instead, you must allow grief to flow unhindered through you."

A lump rose in Edward's throat, as he recalled the words his wife had spoken to Annelyse after her last crowning.

"'*Do not let these events kill what is most precious inside of you,*'" Edward said aloud. Then, pausing, he confessed, "But… I did. I let it happen… I *helped* it happen inside my daughter, too."

"They are still there. Hidden behind the storms of emotion, drowned beneath the squabbling voices, they lay sleeping. Pick them up, hold them close once more, and grief will find its way out."

Halla turned, blew out the candles on the mantle, then slowly disappeared up the stairs. Edward sat down on the couch and pulled a blanket up over his chest. A lone tear escaped his control and made its way over the curve of his cheek, resting for a time on the edge of his chin before falling onto the blanket. He was tired, tired of so very much, and he just wanted to rest his head on his wife's shoulder and cry until every ounce of bitterness was wrung from his heart.

Laying his head down on a pillow, his mind went numb, and all thoughts settled like so much dust on a windowsill. The warmth of the fireplace soon weighed heavy upon him, and sleep carried him away.

The night wore on in slow, steady slumber, until the crackling pop of a log in the hearth startled Edward from his sleep. The room was dark, but for the fireplace, and no light could be seen through the windows. Edward had no idea if it was midnight or early morning, or how long he'd been asleep. All he knew was that, for the first time in days, he felt like himself.

Lifting his body off the couch without a sound, Edward walked to the entryway, turned the knob on the front door and slipped outside.

The moon was low in the northwestern sky, and the dew lay heavy on the grass. All around him, Edward could hear the sounds of the forest. Shapes and shadows cast by the trees veiled the lobed leaves of the Forest of Ferns. In the silence of the early morning, there was a serenity, a beauty he did not expect to find in the Haunted Forest. He forgot all his prejudice and breathed deep the dewy air.

Like a shaft of sunlight cutting through the morning mist, the realization that all was not right roused him from this gentle moment. His daughter was missing, and Edward Bellamy was determined that before the sun set on this day, he would find her. Nothing, not wounded foreheads or dizzying weakness, would stand between him and his quest. It was time.

Running back to the house, Edward grabbed his

things and the bag of knit goods he'd promised Halla he would deliver, then turned to leave. From beside the fireplace where - he could have sworn – a moment ago sat only vacancy, Halla looked up from her knitting and spoke in a hushed voice.

"You will find her where she isn't."

Edward was startled by the sudden appearance of the woman framed by the flickering movement of the throbbing coals.

"Where she isn't?"

"We are always found where we aren't," she continued, rocking slowly in her chair. "For we are far more than what we appear. If we only ever looked for the obvious, we'd forever miss the wonderful. You will find Annelyse where you are sure she could not be, where – in your mind – she is not. But, you must open your mind, Mr. Bellamy. Begin with the errand to Isaiah Weaver, this will put you back on the trail of your daughter. And when you find Annelyse, remember the tale I told you of the two trees. Healing is often found where we least expect it. If only we are willing to see."

Edward was dumbstruck and could not begin to make sense of what Halla was saying. Before he could force a question from his lips, the mysterious woman faded into the darkness with the dying coals in the hearth. All that remained was an empty rocking chair by a cold fireplace.

Shaking his head with disbelief, Edward Bellamy stepped out the front door of the empty cabin in the woods and followed the path which led to the great clearing east of Shatter Lake.

A combination of determined purpose and a good night's sleep spurred him on. The morning held an unspoken promise of progress. Hopefulness gave speed to every step and assurance to every decision. Edward felt the earth itself turning beneath his feet. Within half an hour of leaving Halla's cabin, he found himself among dwindling trees once again. He was nearing the edge of the forest.

To the north of where he now stood, the hardwood trees of the Quibble Woods gave way to a vast apple orchard, in the center of which stood the hill called Orchard Knoll. Around the base of the hill, extending outward for miles in every direction, grasslands mixed with fruit trees, both of which were irresistible to the herds of wild ponies living beneath the fringes of the forest.

According to the poem, a young Silloah Bellamy used to visit Orchard Knoll and bury her face in the flowing manes of newborn foals. It's true that the wild horses are so unaccustomed to the presence of people in the grasslands that their natural curiosity overrules their apprehension. Edward no longer harbored any doubts about the veracity of the poem's claims, least of all this one. He could easily see his wife as a young girl befriending the creatures of the northlands.

North of Orchard Knoll, the Lazy Grumpkin wanders, splits, and rejoins its meandering path, spreading itself wide in King's Bay before drifting out to sea. The cold mountain stream is so swollen with rain and snow melt, much of the year, that it has gained a reputation for loitering along its way westward. Like an old man who has seen it all and is in no hurry to see it again, the Grumpkin mumbles and putters as it flows south of Hyland Manor.

But it was directly to the west that Edward now turned. Shatter Lake lies among the grove of elm trees constituting the lesser, western branch of the Quibble Woods. Its irregular coastline is honeycombed with caves and caverns, many of which are occupied by black bears and families of foxes.

The place itself has a long and mysterious history. Some claim that the unfathomed lake is the very same mentioned in the *Tale of Trinket Trove,* or at least some of the myths that grew up around that tale. It's believed that the lake conceals the site of Ware Woolem and that concealed in its unexplored depths the fabled trinkets can be found. As with most myths, it was impossible to prove or disprove. One must decide for oneself.

As Edward approached the elmwood grove, the words of the *Tale of Trinket Trove* echoed in his thoughts.

> *"Between the woods of unrest and*
> *the calm of silent Kwell,*
> *a people lived, in ancient times,*
> *where, now, no people dwell.*
>
> *"Their reverence for the gentle beast*
> *of Averlune's Greenfields*
> *compelled them to adorn their town*
> *with sculptures, signs, and seals.*
>
> *"But in the Silent Forest, deep,*
> *where fear and scruples die,*
> *some townsfolk sought a better way,*
> *and bravely questioned, "Why?"*
>
> *"So, gath'ring up the Woolem ware*
> *they'd treasured from their youth,*
> *the people of Ware Woolem dared,*
> *instead, to honor truth.*
>
> *"They carried all their trinkets down*
> *beside the Elmwood Grove,*
> *and, yielding all to crushing depths,*
> *they buried Trinket Trove."*

"…beside the Elmwood Grove… crushing depths," he thought, and the feeble belief that Halla had fanned into a smoldering spark now began to enlighten the way he saw the world around him. This change inside of himself did not go unnoticed by Edward Bellamy and, somehow, he suddenly felt as if his wife was walking by his side.

Rising from among the elms on the edge of the clearing, Edward spotted a large, knotty beech tree. It was unmistakable, being the only beech in a grove of elm trees; the fact of its knottiness added nothing to its uniqueness. Straining his eyes, Edward searched for the small cabin Halla had told him to expect in front of the beech, but there was none to be seen.

As he approached the place where the cabin should have stood, Edward's hopes sagged. Doubts began to nest themselves in his brain. Had Halla misled him? Had he somehow gotten turned around? Panic at the thought of having wasted time and failed to find the path taken by Annelyse and her abductor now burned inside Edward's heart.

Just then, he caught sight of something strange. At the foot of the beech tree, beneath a large, gnarled portion of knotty trunk, there sat a tiny house made of sticks. The roof of the little cabin was grown over with a thick, green carpet of moss. The walls were a collection of twigs that had evidently been gathered from the forest floor. In the front of the cabin there was a door no bigger than what a mouse might require. And, above the door, there hung a sign which read, "Weaver."

Edward didn't know what to make of this finding. Perhaps it was a letter box, and the home of Isaiah Weaver was somewhere nearby. Maybe it was meant by Halla as a joke (although, she didn't seem to be the joking sort), or (more likely) there was some deeper meaning that she'd meant for Edward to discover. If this proved to be the case, Edward thought to himself, then he would be more than a little irritated. He was in no mood for riddles. He was determined to make good progress in rejoining the trail of his daughter, and he had no time for such distractions.

As he stood there working himself up into a state and staring at the tiny twig house, something wrested him from his mounting irritation. At his feet, the door underneath the sign reading, "Weaver," abruptly swung open. Standing in front of Edward Bellamy, not three inches tall, a fieldmouse dressed in red breeches and black leather boots looked up at him, scratching its chin.

"Hiya doin'? Did ya get lost or somethin'?" the fieldmouse asked, with more than a hint of sarcasm in his voice.

"Pardon?" Edward replied, surprised that either of them was able to speak at all.

"I guess I'll havta," the fieldmouse conceded reluctantly, "But, maybe a heartfelt sorry woulda been better. Still, y'*are* only human."

Edward reached down and pinched his own thigh, certain that he must be hallucinating or, at the very least, daydreaming. He might have had no problem with a fieldmouse wearing breeches and boots, but the fact that it could also speak was hard to overlook. He decided to simply go with it.

"Are you… um, Isaiah Weaver, by any chance?"

The fieldmouse rolled his eyes and shot his right thumb over his shoulder in the direction of the sign hanging above his door.

"Right," Edward said, clearing his throat.

"Well?" Isaiah demanded with a raise of his eyebrows.

Edward found himself at a loss.

"Did ya bring it, or did *that* get lost along the way, too?"

Remembering the bag of knit goods Halla had entrusted to him, Edward swung it down from his shoulder and set it on the ground in front of Isaiah. "You mean this, of course."

"Well, I don't mean a lumpa Roquefort, although that woulda been appreciated, too, come ta think of it."

With the tiniest little huff of annoyance, the fieldmouse began pulling hats, mittens, scarves, socks, and sweaters out of the bag. Separating them into piles according to his own organizational plan, Isaiah mumbled to himself as he went.

"Mittens for Mia. A hat for Kendra. This sweata here for Patricia Aarre, I'm thinkin'. And two pairs of socks for Rikson, big ones, too! Boy's got size fourteens on 'im! Yeah, that should do the trick. Excellent," then, looking up at Edward, he exclaimed with an uncomfortable increase in volume, "Excellent!! Ha!!!"

Putting everything back in the bag, Isaiah's excitement mellowed back into mild grumpiness.

"You'll be wantin' some news, now, won't ya?"

"News?" Edward asked.

"News, news! Word of ya daughter's whereabouts! That kinda news! Try an' keep up, would ya?"

At the mention of Annelyse, Edward's mood shifted.

"Do you know where she is?!"

"Well, I should think so," Isaiah replied with a snort. "I saw…" he continued in a whisper. "I saw what it was that took her. And I know where they're headin'."

"Sir, please tell me everything!"

"Not here," Isaiah said with caution. "Some stuff's betta talked about behind closed doors, know what I mean? You betta come in."

Edward hesitated. Scrutinizing the tiny front door of the little twig cottage, he was certain that the fieldmouse had miscalculated.

"In?"

"Yeah. In. Further in. Outta the clearin'. Into the forest. Outta earshot of anybody who mighta followed ya here, bumblin' and blunderin' as you did, I'm sure."

Catching sight of Edward staring at his front door, Isaiah added, "Oh, no, no, no. Forget about it! I neva ask strangers into my *home*. Come on, den."

Scurrying a few yards back beneath the canopy of

leaves, Isaiah led Edward into the woods behind the lone beech tree. A small, fast-running stream chattered and gurgled over rocks in its path. The sound of rushing water seemed to be what the fieldmouse had been looking for. It wasn't unfriendly eyes but, rather, unfriendly ears he'd been concerned about.

"That's betta," he said, motioning to Edward to draw closer. "Now, pay attention, please. I'm only gonna say this once. More than that, and we'd be invitin' unwanted ears."

Edward dropped to his knees and inclined one ear in the direction of where the fieldmouse was standing.

"Two nights ago," Isaiah began, "a dark figure – huge, just plain huge - come crashin' through the clearin', almost stompin' my cottage to bits. In its arms, I see it's carryin' a girl. I watched the two of 'em, hidden in the branches o'my beech tree, see? With every step, it was pushin' over trees in its path, using nothing but its shoulders. I couldn't believe my eyes! All the while, clutchin' your daughter."

"What was it?" Edward could hardly contain the sense of terror rising in his heart.

Isaiah hesitated, something so out of character for the decisive fieldmouse that it demanded even Edward's attention.

"That's just it," Isaiah said, his whisper falling to little more than a breath, "It makes no sense at all."

"What? What makes no sense?"

"A creature like that ain't been seen around these parts for years, decades, even. Still, I ain't neva heard of no…" he paused, scratching his chin again, "Nah, it's crazy. It couldn'ta been."

"I don't understand," Edward demanded, increasingly wary and impatient for some straight answers. "What sort of creature has my daughter?"

"Before what I saw two nights ago, I woulda said

the very best sorta creature has your daughter. But now, I just don't know no more. These are strange times, if a Woolem goes stealing through the dark o'night carryin' a helpless child. It just don't make no sense, I tell ya."

"A Woolem?" Edward said, with fear and disbelief rising to the surface of his mind.

"Without a doubt, I'm sorry t'say," Isaiah confirmed, sadness punctuating his words. "I wish it weren't true, but I'm certain of it, now. A Woolem took your daughter, Mr. Bellamy. And that means..."

"But why? I thought the Woolems were friendly creatures."

"They are," Isaiah replied. "They were. I don't know no more. After I saw… what I saw, I went to tell Halla. She didn't seem surprised, which only confused me the more. It's a strange world we live in. A strange world, indeed."

Edward dropped his forehead into his hands, "The creatures she set out to find…"

"What's that ya sayin'?" Isaiah asked, straining to hear.

"They took her," Edward replied, too loud for Isaiah's comfort. "The very creatures she hoped to discover. To find out if they really existed. To know what her mother knew…" Edward let out a cry of anger, "They took her! They took her from me!"

Jumping to his feet, Edward spun around and ran back into the clearing, tripping over the bag of knit goods, and scattering scarves, socks, sweaters, and mittens in his wake.

"Wait!" the startled fieldmouse yelled, but Edward was well beyond hearing. "I ain't done yet!" Stomping his foot on the ground, the fieldmouse complained to himself, "Humans. Crazy, impulsive creatures. Ah, rats! There ain't nothing for it, I guess."

And with that, Isaiah Weaver walked back to his

little cottage in front of the beech tree, picked up the knit goods Edward had strewn across the forest floor, and loaded them back into the bag Halla had sent.

Dragging the bag behind himself, he began walking in the direction in which Edward Bellamy, in his angered, had stormed. Isaiah had unfinished business with the "crazy, impulsive" human.

CHAPTER SEVENTEEN

Greeting a Smile with a Smile

Annelyse was unable to move. Her weakened legs now dangled from her body like two knotted lengths of rope. Her lifeless arms, which had been powerless to fend off the creature pursuing her, could no longer support their own weight. Even her scream went limp in her throat, as her captor snatched her up from beside the campfire and vaulted away into the darkness. Carried against her will, she heard her father's voice cry out, then dissolve among the trees behind her.

The incessant itching had disappeared with every other sense of feeling. Though her arms, legs, and face were still covered in weeping blisters, she was neither compelled nor able to scratch at them.

Whether from the tight grip of her increasing

paralysis or that of the creature in whose hands her fate now rested, Annelyse quickly lost consciousness. By the time she awoke, the sun was just peeking over the horizon, heralding the start of a new day. But what day of the week it was, she could not tell.

Flopping and bobbing along, she felt like a ragdoll being carried under the arm of some overgrown child. Hanging unnaturally against the creature's flank, and bent in the middle with her right side facing the ground, she was certain she'd snap in two at the waist.

But it was just as well. Had she been flung across the back of the great beast she would surely have fallen off. Annelyse lacked the strength to grasp its fur, let alone hold onto its body with her limbs.

But was it fur? Not really, she thought. Not quite fur. Even less so, hair. It was too dense to be either. Unable to move her head, her vantage point was terribly limited. Still, she caught glances as she was able, and formed a mental image of the creature who was carrying her.

Its thick, black covering was soft to the touch and possessed the slightest hint of oil, not unlike lamb's wool. The arm that held Annelyse against the creature's body was obviously one of its legs. The gait at which they were proceeding seemed stilted, as if the animal was more accustomed to making its way on all fours.

Apart from the abrupt way in which the creature had snatched her up, Annelyse did not sense any hostility. She was held firmly, but there was no cruelty in her captor's grip. If anything, it seemed concerned with keeping her from falling or being jostled too roughly. There was a gentleness to this giant.

The creature did not say a word, and Annelyse wasn't sure if it was unable to speak or simply chose not to. Nonetheless, she sensed an intelligence behind the kindness of its care for her. Cruelty often conceals ignorance, and there was neither at work here.

An endless parade of tree limbs sped past her, as they made their way through the dense forest. Her thoughts swam in a sea of fear, each step taking her farther away from her father, and deeper into loneliness than she had ever known. Where were they heading, she wondered with ever-increasing concern? How could her father possibly find her or hope to keep up when each stride of her giant captor was equal to five of his own? She needed to know what was going on.

Never one to shy away from striking up a conversation, Annelyse took a deep breath then commenced her interrogation.

"Where are you taking me?" she demanded, her voice sounding thinner and less commanding than she would have wanted.

The creature made no answer. Thinking, perhaps, it had not heard her faint voice, Annelyse tried again.

"Where are we going?" she asked, louder this time.

The creature turned its ear toward Annelyse's face. Clearly, it had heard her question this time. Annelyse now waited for any sign of understanding or, better yet, an answer.

A low rumble, like the leading edge of thunder making its way across the summer sky, awakened deep inside the creature. It was not a growl or a grunt, but a soft, earthy sound, like tree limbs yielding beneath a bending breeze. Annelyse could feel it from her place pressed up against her captor's enormous, wooly side. The rumble rolled until it reached the creature's voice box. What Annelyse heard next was a sound not heard by human ears for many years.

"We go home," came the lumbering, thoughtful reply.

"But my father…" Annelyse began.

With a deep roll, the creature continued, "He can't help. Only you. Only the daughter."

"Help? Help with what?"

"Home. Only you."

Annelyse began to suspect they were not talking about the same home, "But whose home are you taking me to?" she demanded.

"Woolems' home," the gentle giant said, "We go to Woolems' home. Secret. Only you. Only the daughter."

Annelyse's face turned to stone, as she let the creature's words sink in.

"Woolems' home," it had said. "Then, they *are* real," she thought to herself. "The Woolems *are* real. They truly exist, and we're going to see them."

But why? Why her? What help could she give? And who was this creature who had, apparently, been sent to retrieve her? She was determined to get some answers. She would begin by gaining the creature's trust.

"What's your name?" Annelyse asked softly.

In a voice that sounded like a wave gathering on the open ocean, the gentle giant sighed, "Willemina…"

"I'm Annelyse. Pleased to make your acquaintance."

"Pleasure," the creature rumbled.

"Do you live nearby?"

There was no reply.

"Do you live in the woods?"

Still nothing.

"I'm from Averlune," Annelyse said in a show of good faith.

At the mention of the name Averlune, the creature stopped cold in its tracks.

"What is it?" Annelyse inquired, thinking that her captor had heard something concerning from the surrounding woods.

"Av-er-lu-ne," Willemina repeated, savoring each syllable.

"Yes. Have you ever been?"

A tremor now spread throughout the body of the creature. A deep trembling seized its limbs. Without warning, it began to cry, as if all the sadness of the southern wastelands had invaded its tender heart.

"What is it?" Annelyse asked. "Did I say something wrong?"

"Averlune," Willemina said slowly between sobs, "Averlune…"

"I'm sorry," Annelyse assured the creature, though she didn't know exactly why she should be sorry. "Did something happen there?"

"Home," Willemina replied, regaining her composure, "Home. Secret. Only you. Only the daughter. Must go now."

Repositioning her load, Willemina began moving again. Her renewed sense of purpose was evident from the speed at which she was now lumbering. But Annelyse wasn't ready for their conversation to be over.

"Why are you taking me to the Woolems' home?" Annelyse asked as sweetly as she could, politely adding, "If I might know."

"To help," Willemina rumbled.

"To help with what?"

A moment of silence followed Annelyse's question, but then the great creature replied with all the slow profundity of a glacier in flow, "The key."

Something thrilled inside Annelyse's chest, as if she had just glimpsed the missing piece to a puzzle she'd nearly forgotten had existed. It all came back to her. The key she'd felt compelled to take from her mother's hope chest, of course! Somehow, she knew she'd need it. Somehow, she'd been certain it would play a part. She no longer cared much for the whys and hows of such unexpected things. By now, she just wanted to know what to do next.

"The iron key from my mother's hope chest?" she clarified, intentionally erring on the side of specifics.

"The key," Willemina confirmed in her own unexcited way.

A day or more ago, she would have allowed herself to get tangled up in how this strange creature could possibly know a detail like this, but not anymore. Annelyse had come to realize that belief is not about suspending reason as much as it is about suspending ceaseless questioning. Still, there was one problem to be addressed.

"But I don't have the key," she confessed. "Not with me, anyhow. My father has it. Well, he does if he has my backpack."

Willemina ground to a slow halt and stood still, pondering. After a few seconds, she turned around and began walking back in the direction from which they'd come.

"Only the daughter," she said to herself, working through the change of situation. "Now the father, too," she added, much to Annelyse's surprise. "The father, too. Must go now. To help."

And the great Woolem walked on.

Edward Bellamy was running as fast as he could, hands outstretched to ward off the lashing whips of tree limbs in his face. After hearing of his daughter's situation from the fieldmouse, Isaiah Weaver, he'd been seized by a panic that propelled him headlong back into his search. Now, the old throbbing from the wound in his forehead had returned, dulling his vision, and sapping his waning strength.

There had been no sign of tracks or well-worn paths since the morning after Annelyse had been taken by the creature. All Edward had to go on were the words of Halla which seemed to suggest he'd pick up the trail somewhere near Isaiah Weaver's little twig cottage. Her comment about finding Annelyse where he did not expect to find her was proving to be unhelpful in the extreme. There were countless locations where Edward did not expect to find his lost daughter. Was he supposed to search them all?

From the woods behind him, Edward now became aware of a sound that could only be described as something being dragged across the forest floor. An unbroken swooshing sound was accompanied by muttering not unlike the grumbling he'd heard in the trees. Except this was not a quibbling conversation. This was the sound of one voice complaining to itself in no uncertain terms.

"Crazy human," the voice muttered, "Couldn'ta waited to hear what I had t'say, no. Had t'drag me away from home. And for what? *Another* crazy, impulsive human! That's what! I gotta mind t'let the both of yous wander these woods for a month a Mondays!"

Edward came to a full stop. He knew that voice. Spinning around, he saw Isaiah Weaver, the fieldmouse, dragging the bag of knit goods behind him, and looking far from pleased.

"What are you doing here?" Edward demanded, catching his breath.

"Finishin' our conversation," Isaiah replied, dropping the handle of the bag, and propping both hands on his hips. "I'd rather have finished it back at the cottage, but, well, here we are!"

"There's nothing more to say," Edward countered, pulling a canteen from his sack, and taking a drink. "If you don't know where my daughter is, it's up to me to find her myself. I can't be wasting time."

"I don't need t'know where she is. Just where she's going to. And that, I can guess. Which is more than you could 'find out' in a fortnight o'fumbling through this forest!"

"Then tell me and I'll be on my way. I'm in haste."

"Oh yeah, in haste," Isaiah said, with unrestrained sarcasm. "Always in haste."

"Well?" Edward demanded, prodding the fieldmouse along.

"They're headin' for the Forgotten Meadows beyond the Miralette. They gotta be. Ain't nowhere else a Woolem would go, even a crazy one. And so, ya gonna need some help, if ya hope to find your way there without gettin' lost."

"The Forgotten Meadows was my goal all along. Before being forced to take this detour to deliver knit goods, that is. And I suppose you know the way?"

"I mighta been there before, yeah."

"So, you're my guide, then."

"Heck, no!"

"I thought not," Edward snapped back, then turned to leave.

"But this'll help."

The fieldmouse scooped up the handle of the bag and offered it to Edward.

"Knit goods?" Edward asked with disbelief.

"Well, not *all* the knit goods," Isaiah replied. "I kept the stuff Halla made for me, thank ya very much."

"I don't see how a *partial* bag of knit goods is going to be of much help to me."

"Well, it *wouldn't* be much help, now, would it? Not without this," Isaiah said, handing Edward a sheet of paper he'd pulled from the bag.

From the piece of parchment in his hands, Edward read aloud a list of names.

"Kendra: one hat. Patricia: a sweater. Mia: a pair of mittens. Rikson: two pairs of socks. Sandra: one scarf..."

"Yeah, she went an' lost hers somewhere, I hear. Shame, that. A good scarf comes in handy."

"Am I supposed to deliver all of this?" Edward asked with astonishment.

"That's the idea, yeah," the fieldmouse confirmed.

"I don't have time for this, and I *don't* see how it

will help me find my daughter. In fact, it'll only slow me down, like you are right now! I won't waste another minute. She's out there and I have to find her!"

Edward crumpled up the list and threw it on the ground in front of Isaiah.

"STOP! Right! There!" the fieldmouse commanded. "Not anotha move!"

In an instant, Isaiah Weaver appeared much more intimidating than his three-inches-from-the-ground might suggest. And, this time, Edward decided to listen.

Isaiah continued, "I ain't gonna follow you again. Either ya take my advice and heed Halla's request, or you're on your own from here. Yours ain't the only time that's precious, ya know? But without Halla's help, you ain't neva gonna find the Meadow, and good riddance to ya."

Edward stared at Isaiah, mouth agape.

"Halla knows what she's doin'. You gonna need any help these folks on the list can give, and brand new, Halla-made knit goods is just the thing to sweeten the deal, if ya follow."

There was something in the fieldmouse's voice that demanded respect. Something about him that required belief. He had nothing to gain by finding Edward. It was clear that, in truth, Isaiah had made a reluctant sacrifice to go after him, and perhaps Edward should heed his advice. On top of that, Halla's wisdom in sending Edward out loaded down with gifts for those who might help was beginning to make sense.

"Very well," Edward conceded, with a slow thaw loosening his apprehension. "I'll do it. Where do I begin?"

Picking up the crumpled parchment, Isaiah smoothed it against his knee, then handed it back to Edward.

"With the list, of course. And the map… there, on the back. Take it in order and get goin'.""

Edward turned the paper over and examined the map on the back.

"Stumphole Hollow: K. Willow Bend: P. Squirrel Thicket: MRS," he read. "The initial indicates who lives there?"

"Right y'are, Edward Bellamy," Isaiah said, each word steeped in sarcasm.

Edward felt he might deserve that, so he decided to take it in stride, "Of course," he said humbly. "They all live in the woods north of the lake, then. Shatter Lake."

"Yeah. And if y'quick about it, ya might just spend the night there. Good luck, Edward Bellamy. And, hopefully, we will *not* meet again."

The little red breeched, black booted, grumpy fieldmouse gave a flourish with one hand, then scurried off into the undergrowth. In no time, he was hidden from view by the leaves and shadows.

Edward was alone again, this time, with an additional task to perform. And hoping against hope that Halla's words would bring him closer to finding his daughter. He was inclined to trust that they would, even if he could not possibly see how. He had little choice.

The revelation that Annelyse was in the hands of a Woolem simply didn't jibe with what Halla had told him about the creatures. It was troubling to think that something so powerful might go so wrong. Then there was the question of why Halla hadn't told him this fact herself. Why send him on this delivery errand when his daughter might be in grave danger? It was clear that he was being asked to trust, and Edward Bellamy struggled to give in and simply go along with Halla's instructions. Something inside assured him that this was the best course of action.

Edward knew he should be beside himself with worry, but the cloud of anxiety that had descended upon him two nights earlier was now shot through with rays of unexpected sunlight. Halla had not seemed too concerned, neither had Isaiah Weaver. Of the three of them, those were the two who should know. After all, Annelyse was in the hands of a Woolem. From all Edward had heard of the mythical creatures, he should have nothing to fear.

Even in the face of all the dire possibilities surrounding his daughter's situation, his newfound friends were at ease. And so, Edward decided to ignore his own nagging doubts.

Something his wife once said to him now came to mind, "Thinking is overrated. We just need to decide to trust. We can't be right unless we risk being wrong." He was risking so much, but Edward Bellamy had had enough of over-thinking. And there were knit goods to be delivered, after all.

Turning northwest, Edward Bellamy skirted the eastern shore of Shatter Lake. Its amber waters shimmered in the mid-day sun, lapping the smooth stones with all the nonchalance of Annelyse twirling her hair between her fingers. Not fifty yards from where he stood, a mother goose and her five goslings were gliding along the surface of the lake. Raising her head, the goose caught sight of Edward and turned into the tall grass on the bank, driving her children ahead of her, and startling a flock of wood finches in the trees overhead.

On the edge of the forest wall, just below the eaves of overhanging limbs, there stood a small, wooden signpost. Engraved on the arrow which sat atop the post were the words, "Stumphole Hollow." At the foot of the signpost, a path leading into the forest appeared among the disheveled undergrowth. It was onto this path that Edward now turned.

According to the map Isaiah had given him, Kendra's home should be less than two hundred yards down the footpath. Edward hoped that Kendra's house was a bit more obvious than Isaiah Weaver's had been. Just to be sure, he looked carefully before putting a foot down. He didn't want to be a home crasher, in any sense of the phrase.

Fifteen minutes of walking had taken Edward nearly three quarters of a mile into the forest, with no sign of a house or a hollow of any kind. Sitting down on an old tree stump, he examined the map once more. After a few short moments of puzzling over his current location, Edward heard a faint sound.

"Ehcue-ee," came a muffled voice, its words entirely unintelligible. "Ehcue-ee!"

"Who's there?" Edward demanded, somewhat startled.

"Ehn-rah!" was the reply.

"Huh? Where *are* you?" Edward asked, not at all sure in which direction to direct his question.

"Uhn-dah-eer!"

"What?!"

"Uhn-dah-eer!"

"I can't understand you!" Edward exclaimed, as he jumped to his feet in a huff.

"Under here!" the voice repeated, this time loud and clear and bright as bells on a winter's day.

From the hollowed-out stump upon which he'd been sitting, a face appeared, staring up at Edward and wearing a pleasant, furry smile.

"Thank you, kind sir! I was beginning to think we'd never properly meet. I was sure there must be more to you than I was able to see."

"I'm sorry," Edward began, "I had no idea…"

"Quite alright, sir. No damage done. What brings you to Stumphole Hollow, if I might ask?"

The face that emerged from the hollowed-out tree stump was small and thin and came to a fine crease in front, as if it had been forced to sit in a corner too long. On either side of the crease, two, dark, circular eyes looked out at the world with wide wonder. It wasn't until the rest of the creature climbed out of the hole that Edward realized he'd been talking to a squirrel.

"I'm looking for someone named Kendra," he stated.

"Kendra Herron! You're in luck! You've found her! Or rather, backed into her, if you get my meaning."

The grey squirrel with the brown-tipped whiskers squeaked merrily to herself with a laugh that sounded like steam escaping from a leaky pipe.

"Oh, yes. Well, I apologize for that. I didn't know you were in there. If I had, I wouldn't have…"

"Plugged up my stump quite so effectively?" the squirrel joked with a wink.

"That… yes," Edward blushed, trying to regain his composure.

"Now, like I asked," Kendra said, brushing her fur with the two tiniest, smartest, most delicate hands Edward had ever seen, "What brings you to the Hollow?"

Edward began rummaging around in the bag of knit goods he'd been given by Halla, "It appears I have something for you."

"Oh, delightful! Thank you! I love, love, LOVE surprises!"

"Yes, well, it's from Halla, actually. She asked me to deliver it to you, among the other deliveries on her list."

Producing a tiny, knit hat, Edward presented it to the squirrel.

"Lovely," she exclaimed, running her fingers over the weave. "Kind of her to think of me! This will do just fine. Oh, yes, just fine, fine, fine indeed. Halla makes the nicest things!"

Kendra slipped the hat over her head, popping her two tiny ears out of the holes Halla had left in the top for just that purpose. She swiveled her shoulders this way and that, with one hand on her hip and the other behind her head, modeling her new hat for heaven-knows-who. As she did, her grey, puffy tail twitched with joy like a cloud of dandelion fluff in a breezy sky.

"Now, how may I be of service to *you*?" Kendra said, folding her diminutive hands in front of her.

"I'm not quite sure," Edward began. Halla seemed to think that, if Edward made these deliveries for her, somehow it would lead him to Annelyse. But how could a squirrel "be of service"?

"Come, come, come," Kendra said, clapping her hands on each word for emphasis, all the while beaming a bright grin.

"I don't really see how you could…" Edward stopped himself before saying something offensive.

"Just because you don't see how I could, doesn't mean I couldn't possibly," Kendra replied, folding her hands again and smiling with a sweetness rarely seen in grey squirrels. Encouraged by her kindness, Edward decided to simply unburden his mind.

"My daughter… I need to find my daughter. She was kidnapped… by a Woolem…"

"A Woolem?!" Kendra stopped him. "Kidnapped? That's concerning. Yes, yes, yes, very, very, very concerning," she said, shaking her head in vigorous disbelief.

"I'm not sure which way it's taken her, but they could be heading for the Forgotten Meadows. If only I knew their route, I might reach them before they get too far…"

"Right!" Kendra exclaimed, shooting one tiny finger into the air. "Let's have a look about, shall we?!"

Scurrying across the forest floor in a blur of grey and brown, Kendra vaulted up onto the trunk of a sycamore tree. Bouncing and bounding from branch to branch, the nimble squirrel was soon too high among the broad leaves for Edward to see. After a while, the rustling and swaying in the uppermost branches subsided, and a thin, high-pitched voice could be heard calling down from above.

"If it really was a Woolem," Kendra shouted, "The big, big beastie should be easy to spot from up here. Let me see what I can see when I look and see from in the leaves!"

"Brilliant," Edward said to himself. This was precisely the kind of help he needed, sharp eyes and a gifted climber. His spirits rose, buoyed by hope.

"Wait… just… a… minute…" Kendra squeaked then, a moment later, added, "Nope. Nope. Nope. Not a thing. Drat!"

A minute or two of scratching claws against the trunk of the great sycamore, and Kendra was standing in front of Mr. Bellamy, panting.

"I couldn't see 'em," she said without emotion. "That means they're either hiding – which would be no small accomplishment for a big, big Woolem – or they've moved beyond the horizon and out of sight."

Edward was crestfallen. For the past few days since his daughter had been taken from him, he'd experienced nothing but panic, followed by fruitless efforts to help from others, and made unbearable by the sense that he was just wasting precious time. The groundless suspicion that everyone he'd met had been bent on misguiding him, threatened to rear its head. But, instead of giving in, he took a slow, deep breath.

After a moment (and with a sigh that seemed to clear his mind and blow away unhelpful suspicions), Edward responded to this latest setback with calm.

"Which way do *you* think I should go, then?" he asked. "I'm afraid I'm lost."

"When in doubt," Kendra said with a snap of her little fingers, "Stick to the list!"

"The list?"

"You mentioned other deliveries on Halla's list. So, when in doubt…"

"Oh, right. Stick to the list," Edward added.

"Who's next? Tell me, tell me, tell me," Kendra was rubbing her hands together with eager interest.

Edward pulled Halla's list out of his pocket, unfolded it, and began to read it aloud, "Kendra: one hat. Patricia: a sweater. Mia: a pair of mittens. Rikson: two pairs of socks. Sandra: one scarf. And look. On the back," he said, turning the parchment over and showing it to Kendra, "There's a map with initials. See? Stumphole Hollow: K."

"That's me! That's me!" Kendra squeaked.

Edward nodded, then continued, "Willow Bend: P. and Squirrel Thicket: MRS."

"Oh yes, yes, yes. Patricia Aarre. Of course. I know her well. Delightful. Yes, simply delightful. Well, there's your path, then! And away, away, away go those doubts!"

Edward examined the map more closely. Kendra's house (or stump, rather) stood on the eastern side of the forest that rings Shatter Lake. His next delivery would be to Patricia whose home was at the northwestern point of the lake, some two or three miles away, he reckoned.

"What should I look for," Edward asked, "What sort of house does Patricia live in?"

"Oh, no house at all," Kendra said with a matter-of-fact tone. "No, no, no. But she'll find you. Yes, yes. She'll find you, no worries. She's always out and about clicking away. Click, click, clicking away!"

Edward then paused to say something he wished he'd thought to say to Isaiah Weaver. Something that really hadn't occurred to him. "Thank you for your help," he whispered with sincerity. "I'm very grateful to you."

"My pleasure," Kendra replied with a smile, folding her tiny, little, delicate hands in front of her.

Edward turned, then hesitated. There was something he was curious about.

"Kendra *Herron*, you said."

"The same!" came the squirrel's chipper reply.

"But you're a squirrel…"

"Right you are!"

"Not a heron…"

"Not a bit!" Kendra said with a smile. "I find that, if the unfriendlier birds think I'm a bird myself, then they're less likely to take an unwanted interest in me!" She looked very pleased with her reasoning.

"Hawks and eagles and the like, right," Edward said in agreement.

"But a heron *is* a very friendly sort, even if it *is* a bird," Kendra added, always wanting to be friendly whenever possible – which was all the time.

"Very friendly," Edward agreed, then added, "but not as friendly as a squirrel, to be sure."

"Oh yes, most assuredly! Few things are! Well, best be off, then! And remember, when in doubt, stick to the list! Farewell!"

With a bow, Edward took his leave of Kendra the grey squirrel, who stood atop her hollowed-out stump waving goodbye until he was well out of sight. Then, straightening Halla's nice, new knit hat on her head, she said to herself, "This will do just fine. Just fine, indeed. Halla makes the nicest things!"

She then popped back down inside of her Stumphole Hollow, the friendliest squirrel of them all – and that truly is saying a great deal.

CHAPTER EIGHTEEN

Learning to Receive

From Kendra's house, the northeastern shore of Shatter Lake bends almost due east before rounding a curve to the west. As a result, Edward was forced to head in the opposite direction from where he wanted to go, for a good half mile or so. Edward counted an increasing number of daisies growing in the grass along the way. They did not stray far afield but seemed to be carpeting the path he was on; until, without even noticing it, he found himself following the daisies.

As he reached the northern shore of the lake, he was again traveling westward, surrounded by a forest of dense trees. Consulting the map, he determined that Patricia's home should be about 2 miles to the northwest, toward what appeared to be a small, three-pronged river jutting inland from the sea. He was now entering the area just south of the twin islands in the Miralette River known as the Sibling Stones.

As he hiked along, he began to sense something pleasant on the westerly wind. The faint scent of the sea filtered through the trees and alighted in a fine, salty mist on his lips. Suddenly, the thought - or rather feeling - of the little cottage by the sea in Averlune filled him with intense longing. He wanted nothing more than to find his daughter and take her home, never to venture out into the wild, untamed world again. His pace quickened, even as the terrain grew rockier. He was determined to stay alert and pick up some hint of Annelyse's trail. The days that had elapsed since her kidnapping had left him at a disadvantage. It was time to regain the upper hand.

Up ahead, Edward spied an open meadow and a shimmering body of water on the horizon, the three-pronged river he'd seen on the map. Patricia's home should be nearby. He only hoped Kendra was right that Patricia would find *him*, otherwise he'd have no idea where to start looking for her. Edward heightened his awareness, alert to every movement and sign of a stranger's presence.

A small stream, little more than a brook, trickled from a rocky spring near the foot of a great willow tree. Crouching down, Edward paused to refill his canteen and wash his face in the cold, clear waters. As he looked up, he noticed something peculiar. Carefully concealed in a sort of miniature duck blind, a small, prickly animal sat behind a tripod topped with a box camera. The creature was a picture of patience, its hands folded across a quilt draped over its lower half. Without moving any more than was necessary, the animal's large, brown eyes shifted, landing on Edward Bellamy.

Slowly raising a finger to its lips, the creature mouthed a silent, "Shhh…" in Edward's direction.

Edward froze, still crouched beside the stream,

canteen in hand and water dripping from his face. Looking in the direction in which the little photographer's camera was pointed, he saw a deer – maybe 20 feet away – drinking from the same stream from which he'd just filled his canteen. Her lithe body shone like brushed velvet in the midday sun.

Without a sound, the prickly animal hidden in the duck blind squeezed a trigger it was holding in its hand, briefly exposing the film inside its camera. The moment she did, the deer looked up from its drink, turned its head in the direction of the shutter click, then bolted off into the woods.

"Gotcha!" the prickly photographer exclaimed, relaxing in her little chair. "Magnificent!" Then, turning toward Edward, she added, "You may move now, sir. And thank you. I'd been waiting for that shot since dawn."

Edward screwed the top back onto his canteen, wiped his face with his shirt sleeve, then stood to get a better look at the animal behind the box camera.

Busy disassembling her station, the creature had laid aside her multicolored, patchwork quilt. Edward could now see that she was no bigger than a cantaloupe (though he would not make that comparison aloud, for fear of giving offense). Her face was intelligent and inquisitive and came to a point at the end of a long snout. Her nose punctuated the end of her snout like a small, round, black button.

Her active eyes formed the central features of her face, as they darted from subject to subject seemingly without blinking. The most noteworthy characteristic of the creature's appearance, however, was the preponderance of spiny quills covering her small body. Clearly, the nature photographer in her mini duck blind was a most extraordinary hedgehog.

"Since dawn?" Edward began, "I hope the photo was worth a day of waiting."

"If it doesn't turn out to have been, then at least the day of waiting was most pleasant. Yes," she said, unscrewing the camera from its tripod, "Most pleasant, indeed. Ah…"

"Do you take many photos?" Edward said, sitting down on a stump nearby (and checking for squirrels before he did).

"Oh yes. Every time I find something worth photographing. Which is everything, everywhere, everyday! So, yes. I suppose, I do take many photos. There *is* so much to see. If only the camera could see as well as I do," she said wistfully, pausing to consider what she'd just said. "Ah, well…"

Edward had a sneaking suspicion that perhaps he'd found the recipient of his next delivery. Rather than asking her directly, he decided to test his suspicion in a roundabout way.

"I'm looking for Willow Bend," he said, referring to the address marked on the map. "But this stream doesn't appear to bend at the willow tree. Is there another willow nearby?"

"Willow Bend, yes. Yes, this is Willow Bend," the hedgehog said, packing her camera into its box with two, oversized, prodigiously-clawed hands. "It's not the stream that bends, though I can see why some would assume it was. No, not the stream at all, but, rather, the willow herself. Yes, and more so, nowadays. Downright droopy, really. Poor dear. Ah, well…"

"I see," Edward replied, examining the willow tree, and noting that it did, in fact, bend like an inverted horseshoe, dipping its flowing mane in the stream at its feet. Like a young woman washing her hair, the willow's fine, long branches billowed out in the waters of the brook.

"Then, if this is *the* Willow Bend, perhaps, I have something for you," he added, reasonably certain that this must be Patricia Aarre.

Reaching into the bag of knit goods, Edward produced a sweater that appeared to be just the right size, further confirming his suspicion.

"I believe this is yours," he said proudly. "Compliments of Halla."

Taking the sweater in her broad, hedgehog hands, Patricia looked it over with a keen eye, "Yes. Yes, certainly her work. No doubt about that. Only Halla knits with… well, that is to say… ah, well… what I mean is… this does bring back memories. Oh, the adventures we had…"

The hedgehog drifted a moment, lost in thought. A faraway look smoothing the lines from the corners of her eyes, leaving youthful remembrance in its place. There was a fire in her spirit, or rather, her spirited nature flared beyond the grasp of her self-control for an instant. The flash was like the glint of sunlight on the blade of a sword wielded to free the captive. There were stories lurking in this hedgehog's past.

Returning to the present, with a shake of her head to set the past aside, she continued, "Exquisite, simply exquisite work. How *does* she make her stitches so small? Ah, well…"

Suspicions confirmed in every regard, Edward now introduced himself, "Ms. Aarre, my name is Edward Bellamy. It's a pleasure to meet you," he said.

"You may call me Pat," she replied, slipping the sweater on over her head. The moment it was snuggly in place, all at once, every one of the hedgehog's quills jutted out through the weave of the sweater. She looked like a sea urchin dressed in its Sunday best.

"Tea?" she asked, picking up her camera gear. "I'd be grateful if you would grab my chair for me. And thank you."

"I'd be happy to," Edward assured her, "And please, call me Edward." He then happily followed the little hedgehog, her chair – no bigger than what might be at home in a dollhouse – in his hand, toward what he assumed would be her house.

Instead, Pat led Edward to a cave, several yards away from where her duck blind stood. Entering the dark opening, the hedgehog was lost to sight, though her voice could be heard echoing back toward where Edward was waiting.

"I'll just put these things away and put the kettle on," she called. "Won't be but a moment. Do make yourself comfortable."

Edward put Pat's chair down on the ground, then looked around outside the opening of her cave. There were no stumps or boulders big enough to be used for sitting. In fact, the cave itself was barely one-third the size required for Edward to fit inside. Everything within sight was too tiny for anyone but a hedgehog. Plopping down on the ground, Edward made himself comfortable as best he could.

"Tea," Pat announced, as she returned carrying a tray with a tiny tea service. "Nothing like it after a long day spent waiting for serendipity! And serendipitous it was! Ah, well, yes…"

"May I help?" Edward asked, wanting to be polite, but unsure of how he might even hope to pick up one of the miniature teacups without breaking it.

"No, no," Pat replied, setting down the tray directly on the ground in front of her guest, "Allow me." Pouring a dribble of tea from the teapot, she handed Edward a cup which he cradled in both hands just to be safe.

Sitting down in the chair Edward had carried from the duck blind, Pat smoothed back the quills growing atop her head, then picked up her own teacup, careful to extend her pinky as she did.

"So," Pat began, sipping her tea, "Tell me your story, Mr. Bellamy."

"My story?"

"Everyone has a story, sir. Endless wonder is always at hand, I like to say. All we need do is listen, look, and learn. So, what brings you north of Shatter Lake? Let's begin there."

"I was told that delivering Halla's gifts might bring me closer to finding my daughter," Mr. Bellamy said, feeling a bit silly. He was running on faith, and this can sometimes feel like running on nothing at all.

Pat set her teacup down on the saucer in her lap. Looking up at Edward with eyes like gaping sinkholes, her tone changed.

"Your daughter?" she said with care.

"She was taken from me," Edward replied, "A few nights ago."

"Yes," Pat said with a long sigh. "I know she was. And I know what took her. I have proof, though I would not have believed it otherwise. Ah, horrible…"

Without another word, the hedgehog stood and disappeared inside her cave, leaving Edward to contemplate what *horrible* proof she might have and what it meant for his kidnapped daughter.

After a few minutes, Patricia Aarre returned carrying what appeared to be a full-sized sheet of paper in her hands. Edward carefully set his teacup on the tray in front of him, then turned his full attention to the little hedgehog. His heart was tense with apprehension, having spent what felt like an eternity waiting for Pat to return from inside her cave, and with nothing more than the word *horrible* for his comfort.

With a look that spoke volumes etched deeply into her care-worn face, Pat handed Edward Bellamy what it was she had retrieved from inside her cave.

Inspecting it closely, Edward saw that it was a photograph, and he immediately surmised that Pat had taken it herself, concealed within her miniature duck blind. The photo was somewhat underexposed, but clearly depicted a creature of enormous stature. Clutched at its side, the creature carried the limp body of Annelyse Bellamy. There was no evidence at all to suggest that she was alive and well. Indeed, every indication visible from the photo suggested that the opposite was more likely.

A lump rose in Edward's throat, bumped to the surface by a wave of terror, and he began to weep.

"My child… my poor little child…"

Walking over to where Edward Bellamy sat on the ground, Pat Aarre, the photographer-hedgehog of north Shatter Lake, rested her paw on the arm of her inconsolable guest.

"I'm so sorry, Mr. Bellamy. I'm so very sorry."

"I don't understand any of this," he said in despair. "These creatures. These Woolems. I thought they were supposed to be friendly."

"Friendly? No. Not friendly. Wary, yes. Wronged, most certainly. And so, not friendly. No. Not for many years. Still, even though cruelty often breeds vengeance in the wronged, I cannot believe that such a corruption could take place within creatures so kind and docile as Woolems. I just cannot believe it. In truth, I will not."

"But the proof is right here," Edward replied, shaking the photograph in the face of the gentle hedgehog.

"This proves only that she was *taken* by a Woolem… and, more importantly," Patricia said with emphasis, "It shows the *direction* in which they were traveling." Pointing to a swan-shaped boulder on the shore of the stream from which Edward had filled his canteen earlier, she indicated the same boulder in the photo.

"Look," she said, "The swan is behind them. They were heading northwest when I took this photo. There's only one reason to head northwest from Shatter Lake, Mr. Bellamy. They mean to ford the Miralette at Sibling Stones and then pass through the Fishbones into the Silent Forest. The Woolem is taking your daughter to the Forgotten

Meadows by way of the fastest route. An old, familiar route, though one I had not given thought to for many years until you brought Halla's gift to me. Yes, it's a familiar route. And one clearly marked, I'll add. But there's more…"

Edward looked deep into the dark eyes of the hedgehog, searching for hope.

"I took this photo last evening. They have a lead on you, but it isn't so wide that you couldn't catch up. With a little help, you can pick up their trail north of the Miralette, and head them off."

"A little help? North of the Miralette? Halla warned me about the dangers there."

"That's where some experience would come in useful. Halla was right to send you along this path," the hedgehog said with a smile. "Perhaps, she had just the sort of help you might need in mind. Who else did she ask you to visit for her?"

Edward pulled the list from his pocket and handed it to the hedgehog, never once assuming she couldn't read.

"Mia, Rikson, and Sandra," she read aloud. "Ah, yes. Perfect. Yes, perfect, indeed."

"What is?" Edward asked.

"You must follow my instructions carefully," Pat began in earnest. "They will take you directly to Squirrel Thicket where you will find Sandra, Mia, and Rikson. They will know what to do. I'll send word on ahead of you, by airmail. That will ensure they'll be waiting for you when you arrive."

"By airmail?"

"Hawk mail, to be precise."

"Hawk? But aren't hawk's dangerous to hedgehogs?" Edward asked with disbelief.

"These quills aren't just for decoration, Mr. Bellamy. They'd turn any hawk into a pin cushion in short order and make no mistake. Besides," the hedgehog added, folding the list, and handing it back to Edward, "Hawks have huge egos. They just love action photos of themselves diving, swooping, whooshing, and doing all manner of aerial acrobatics. And it's a well-known fact that I'm the best photographer within 100 miles of Shatter Lake. Ah, yes… it *is* true. I'm as safe as I can be from hawks, falcons, and their ilk."

Pulling a pencil from the camera bag leaning against the inside of her cave entrance, Patricia Aarre handed it to Edward and began dictating directions to Squirrel Thicket and the home of Sandra, Mia, and Rikson.

"Head northwest, keeping the three-pronged river on your left the entire time. As soon as you clear the eastern-most prong, take a hard right and travel due west until you come to a swampy patch of land. This is Spillwater Swamp, nasty place.

"Directly north of the swamp, you'll find a wild bramble patch, a tangle of brush and driftwood piled high against the southern shore of the Miralette River. This is Squirrel Thicket. Hidden among the thicket is the home of Sandra, Mia, and Rikson. Like I said, they'll be waiting and well-informed. Ah, yes… yes, indeed."

Darting inside her cave, Pat emerged a few moments later carrying a small bag.

"Take this with you," she said. "It might take some getting used to, but there's nothing better for a vigorous hike through the woods."

"What is it?" Edward asked, peering down into the bag.

"Better to not tell you, perhaps. But I want you to eat every crumb before you reach the water. You'll need the energy, soon thereafter, believe me. Now go!"

"I can't thank you enough," Edward said, gathering his things.

"Thank me when you return to introduce your daughter to me."

"I will. I promise," Edward said, handing the photograph back to the hedgehog.

"Keep it," she insisted. "It's not every photographer who manages to capture a picture of a Woolem, so nobody would believe me, even if I showed them!"

With a courtly bow, Edward slung his pack over his shoulder, took a quick look at his instructions, and turned to face northwest. Armed with a photo, a destination, the promise of help from Sandra, Mia, and Rikson, and a snack bag of heaven-knows-what, his hopes had risen higher than they'd been in days.

He wasted no time but pushed through the tall grass and undergrowth of the meadow and on along a path strewn with ever-increasing numbers of daisies. Thanks to Patricia Aarre, the lovely hedgehog and nature photographer, he was on his way.

The instructions Pat had dictated unfolded exactly as she had said. The glistening, three-pronged river he'd seen before spotting Pat in her miniature duck blind was clearly visible on his left. The closer he got to it, the more readily he could make out the eastward-flowing and southeastward-flowing prongs. Veering off to the west, he was soon between the two upper offshoots of the stubby river.

The ground enclosed within the two arms of the river grew increasingly muddy, as Edward turned northward toward the Miralette. After about an hour's walk, he could see a mountain of loose and brittle tree limbs, brush, and driftwood that had been washed ashore over the course of many years by the Miralette shedding its unwanted debris. This was the great bramble known as Squirrel Thicket, and it was more immense than Edward had anticipated.

The closer he got to the southern shore, the more convoluted the landscape became. Edward found himself weaving in and around sun-bleached branches and vines that seemed determined to ensnare his legs and trip him up. Before long, he was climbing like a mountaineer on all fours, picking a path through the thicket.

The stench from Spillwater Swamp wafted in on the sea breezes blowing up from nearby King's Bay. A cloud of gnats hung black in the stagnant air, droning their monotonous hum. If he could navigate his way through the brambles and reach the southern shore of the river, Edward was certain that the wind tumbling down from Mount Miralette would clear the air.

Overhead, Edward heard the screech of a bird of prey - a hawk, perhaps – as it made its way back toward the forest around Shatter Lake. "Lucky bird," he thought to himself, "What I wouldn't give to retrace my steps homeward, my sweet daughter by my side."

Everything around him was becoming more and more foreign with every step. From the wretched swampland on his left, to the dead forest of driftwood brambles beneath his hands and feet, it was all unnatural and decidedly unfriendly. The idea that Annelyse had been carried along this same wicked path by, what Edward could only deem was a Woolem gone mad, sent shivers down his spine. This was no place for his little girl. And it seemed an unlikely place for the gentle, mythical Woolems, too.

Pushing his way over snapping and cracking limbs, Edward Bellamy was approaching the edge of Squirrel Thicket bordering the waters of the Miralette. He'd made it through without losing his backpack, and this was quite an accomplishment. The thicket had a way of winding its fingers around anything a traveler might be carrying. Unwilling to relinquish what it had taken hold of, the brambles often convinced a sojourner to give up any attempt at reclaiming his belongings. As a result, strewn throughout the forest of driftwood and debris, weather-worn backpacks, coats, and footwear could be seen dangling like ornaments among the branches of a dry, discarded Christmas tree. It was in these clutches of cloth and burlap that the squirrels - from whom the thicket received its name - made their nests.

Stepping foot on solid land for the first time in over half an hour, Edward now stood in the mud of the Miralette's southern bank. The floodplain on either shore was a good twenty-or-so-feet wide. Scattered like holes in a block of Swiss cheese, otter dens and muskrat hollows riddled the high, soft banks. A few feet away, the clear waters of the great alpine river hurled themselves down from snowcapped mountains in the east, as they made their way toward the freedom of the sea.

The river was deep and swift. If the Fenneleen Stream had been permitted to realize its full ambition, it would surely have patterned itself after the Miralette. But, unlike the Fenneleen, the Miralette offered many opportunities to cross its wide flow.

There were four islands braving the central channel: the twin Sibling Stones near the mouth of King's Bay; Pelican Perch, just south of the parallel rivulets known as the Fishbones; and Grumpkin's Wretch, the repellant name for the island lying just east of where the Lazy Grumpkin joins with the waters of the Miralette.

All of these islands offered the possibility of crossing to the other side of the river if one could find his footholds between the riverbank and the islands' shores. None of them were inhabited by anything but river creatures, and so there was no one to give guidance as to where the underwater steppingstones might lie. A traveler was on his own, in that regard. Edward had made it through the obstacles of Squirrel Thicket, only to be halted on the banks of the Miralette. If he chose the wrong course, his demise would relinquish Annelyse to her captor forever.

Opening the snack bag given to him by the kind hedgehog, Edward peered at the contents with skepticism. Inside, small cakes of various shapes and unknown composition looked back at him. He was hungry, ravenous, in fact. And whatever solution might present itself to the challenge of finding his path to the islands and across the river would certainly require a full stomach and a good bit of energy. The cakes appeared to be dense and, therefore, packed with what he needed. Edward decided to give them a try.

The little cakes were moist and spongy, and marbled throughout with splotches of green and brown, like a strange, earth-toned confetti cupcake. Holding one to his nose, Edward inhaled its scent and concluded that it was, in fact, most likely edible – and not just for hedgehogs. Though not sweet or savory-smelling, the cakes weren't entirely repellent.

There was only one thing left to do. Opening his mouth, Edward popped-in a morsel and started chewing. The feel of it on his tongue was like birthday cake, but without all the magical deliciousness that makes birthday cake a treat. There was no sweetness, no chocolate creaminess, nothing pleasant at all. The flavor was altogether difficult to place. It was unlike anything Edward Bellamy had ever chosen to eat before.

There was a hint of earthiness, as the scent had suggested. If you could taste a piece of the summer air after a thunderstorm, or the flesh of a river stone, Edward was certain that they would taste like this. But there was something else to the flavor. The word *flesh* brought it to his mind, and Edward did not want to dwell on it too long. He was terrified that his choice of descriptor was more accurate than was entirely appetizing.

There was a gaminess about these little cakes, but Edward was all too aware of the sorts of *wild game* hedgehogs liked to hunt. Insects and grubs, worms and caterpillars could not have tasted much different than these strange little hedgehog cakes. No, he would not try to place this particular taste. He'd simply down the cakes in one gulp and move on.

Folding the empty bag, he stowed it in his backpack and chased his snack down his throat with a long drink of clean water. Squatting to refill his canteen in the cold flow of the Miralette, Edward suddenly tumbled backwards with a start. A face had been staring up at him from beneath the surface of the water, an intelligent face with eyes wide open and full of understanding for what it was looking at.

Before Edward could struggle to his feet, that same face emerged from the Miralette and scurried up onto the riverbank. Edward experienced a tense moment, as the sleek, brown body of the creature sidled up beside him.

Navigating the Dangers

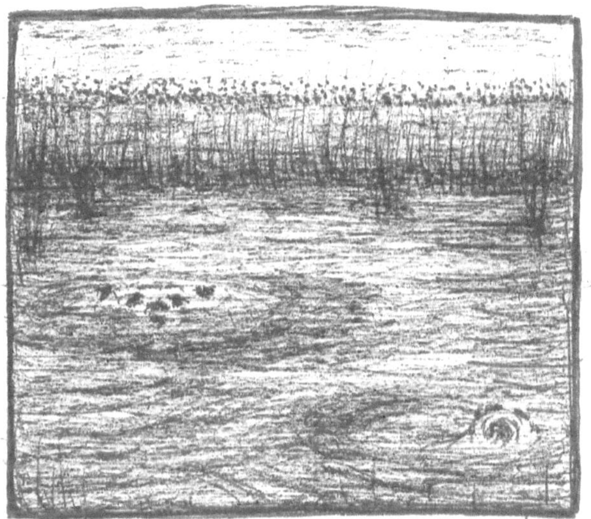

Everything about the animal was commanding. The intelligent face; the athletic build; the long whiskers; and most especially, the formidable claws on each of its four feet were all rather intimidating. Trailing off behind its agile form, a long tail came to a soft point, twitching and flicking with a meaning Edward did not yet grasp.

But it was the face that held him rapt. Edward knew beyond a doubt that the animal understood far more about him than he did about it, and this was unnerving in the extreme. Edward Bellamy was also certain that this was the largest and most majestic river otter he had ever encountered.

"Edward Bellamy?" the otter inquired, with an inquisitive tilt of its head and a sideways glance.

"Yes. And you must be…" Edward stopped cold. Since the otter knew his name, Edward was pretty sure this must be Sandra, Mia, or Rikson. But he had no idea of knowing precisely which one. More alarming, he had no idea if the otter he was talking to was male or female. He didn't want to guess incorrectly and start the relationship off on a sour note. Luckily, the otter took the lead.

"Sandra!" the river otter exclaimed, cutting Edward off midsentence (and saving him from almost certain embarrassment), "But please, call me Sandy!"

"Pleased to meet you," Edward replied. "Then you got Pat's message."

"We did, and we've been waiting for your arrival."

At that moment, two other otters came splashing up toward the riverbank. One, roughly half Sandy's size, swam more like a playful dolphin than an otter. The other, slightly larger than Sandy, lay on its back, paddling along with its big, back feet, displaying very little effort and a great deal of delight.

"Allow me to introduce my children," Sandy said. "This is Mia."

"Hi!" the little otter said, as she leapt out of the water. She looked like a penguin, as she moved seamlessly from swimming, through leaping, and right on into walking.

"And that's Rikson," Sandy continued, motioning toward the paddler still lounging on his back in the water.

With a slight wave of his right hand and a pleasant smile, Rikson tossed a leisurely, "Hello," up toward the shore.

"Now," Sandy said, turning to face Edward, "You need help getting to the islands and then to the other side of the river, don't you?"

"Unfortunately, yes," Edward conceded. "You see,

my daughter…"

Patting his hand with her paw, Sandy looked into Edward's eyes with kind sympathy and assured him, "I know, Mr. Bellamy. No need to relive your pain. Pat's airmail message told me all about it. Let's focus on the challenge at hand. That's the best way we can help Annelyse, now. Ok?"

"Yes," Edward replied, feeling relieved about not having to retell his story, "Thank you."

With one more reassuring pat of her chilly, wet paw on the back of his hand, Sandy turned to call to Rikson, who was still afloat, and to Mia, who was busy practicing her somersaults on the shore.

There was something strong and beautiful about the mother otter. She had an innocence about her which might have been misconstrued by anyone who did not know her well. But, the purity of her heart shone brightly in her eyes, proof that her innocence was but an arrow in the quiver of her strength.

In her tiny eyes, there was a youthfulness, a wonder which embraced the ordinary all around her. She noticed small things. Or rather, she noticed every detail of everything she noticed. Sandra lived and loved in every fraction of every moment. And, into those little fractures of now, she poured herself without reserve.

Edward watched her speak with her children. She gave herself to them like the sun bestows its warmth on the world, causing all good things to blossom and grow. For a moment, Edward saw far more than a river otter, and what he saw, he loved.

The energetic Mia bounded up the riverbank towards Edward, stopping just short of barreling into him. She was alive with electricity, and more than a little curious about the stranger whose imminent arrival had been announced by airmail.

Remembering his errand, Edward bent over and

opened the bag of remaining knit goods, retrieving the gifts Halla had sent for the otters.

"For Mia, a pair of mittens," he said, handing the young otter her present.

"Ooooh, cozy!" she exclaimed, slipping them on over her little, active paws and wiggling them at her mother.

"What do you say?" Sandy prompted her daughter.

"Thanks!" Mia replied, then lost herself in admiring her new mittens.

"For Rikson, two pairs of socks."

The otter looked with skepticism at the socks he'd just been handed. Shooting a doubtful eye in the direction of his mother, she nodded back with confidence. Anything Halla made was sure to fit even the most prodigious of foot sizes. Assured by his mom's optimism, he thanked Edward for the gift and proceeded to try them on, just to be sure. He was not disappointed.

"And for Sandra, one scarf," Edward declared, handing her a beautiful knit scarf with jaunty fringe dangling from both ends.

"Oh, thank you! Mine went missing, recently, and I *have* had need of it." Wrapping the scarf around her neck, she muttered to herself, "I still think it was that Matthew Muskrat, scoundrel that he is…"

"There," Edward said with a sense of accomplishment, "All delivered." Then, turning to Sandy, he added, "Now, about this river…"

Sandy bobbed her head slowly, a look of pensive pondering on her face. She seemed to be sizing up the currents, eddies, and overall behavior of the Miralette as it made its way past where they now stood on the southern bank. Whereas, an unskilled eye might see only the purposeless flow of water, the mother otter sensed deeper realities at work.

The river was a living creature, overflowing with

intention and determination. It was a great problem-solver, meeting obstacles in its path and leaving solutions in its wake. Above all, the Miralette was unstoppable. Never in its history had impediment or ice deterred it from its sole purpose of spreading itself wide in the tumultuous waves of King's Bay. Over her long years of experience, Sandy had reached a profound understanding of the Miralette. There was a oneness about their relationship, and in her wisdom, she had handed on this unique way of seeing and knowing to her children.

"Alright, you two," she said to Mia and Rikson, gathering their attention. Then, motioning with her paw, she gave instructions, "There… and… there."

Like two well-oiled bolts of brown lightning, the young otters were off. Swimming in the direction indicated by his mother, Rikson made his way down stream while Mia swam directly across toward the northern bank.

Twice his sister's size, Rikson moved like an arrow through the strong currents of the river. He was possessed of an easy athleticism that allowed him to swim with effortless efficiency. Barely leaving a wake behind, Rikson paddled his enormous hind feet entirely below the surface of the water, while his front paws moved like the fluid hands of a martial artist or skilled pianist. He was grace and power in motion.

His little sister relied less on fluency and more on her own brand of *perpetual* motion. Kicking her back feet like a boat propeller, she left a whitewater chaos of froth and foam behind her. Mia's specialty was the breaststroke, which suited her quite well since she spent as much time diving below the surface as she did puttering-along the top of it. Still, she motored forward with surprising speed, as she conquered each wave with sheer willpower and a good bit of wild wriggling.

The two young otters reached the locations in the main flow of the river indicated by their mother. Once there, they each began searching. Diving beneath the waves they would, moments later, pop up a few feet away from where they'd been. Over and over, they repeated the drill, zig-zagging their way from shore to shore. There was a process at work, some procedure was being implemented. For the life of him, Edward Bellamy had no idea what he was witnessing.

After several minutes, Rikson called to his mother who'd been watching her children from the southern bank.

"Over here!" he said, bobbing in the water some thirty feet from shore.

As soon as she'd heard her brother's call, Mia zipped over to his location like a paddleboat with a wobbly rudder. There was always a bit more play than purpose in her swimming. She did so love to splash!

"Where?!" she asked, sticking her face in the water repeatedly, as if she were scanning the riverbed below. "Where? I can't see!"

"On my way!" Sandy said from shore, then dove into the river like an Olympic swimmer. Upon reaching the place where Mia and Rikson now floated in the steady current, Sandy disappeared below the surface of the water. A few moments later, the beautiful, brown head of the mother otter appeared smiling above the waves.

"Splendid!" she exclaimed. "Well spotted. This will do just fine."

Swimming a few feet toward the northern bank of the river, she called back to Mia, "Mimi! This is your position."

Bolting over toward the center of the river, she spoke to Rikson, "Right here, I think," she said. With a wink of assurance, Rikson stayed as stationary as if he'd been standing on dry land.

Swimming back to the southern bank where Edward Bellamy had been watching the otters' activity, Sandy at last addressed him.

"Mr. Bellamy," she began, "We can get you across, but you'll need to trust us."

"But, how?" Edward asked, still not clear about what the mother otter had in mind.

"You'll need to walk across," she assured him.

"Walk?! On what? It must be twenty feet deep or more."

"Twenty-seven feet," Sandy corrected him, "In the main channel, at its deepest, that is. But here, you can walk across, while it lasts."

"While what lasts?" Edward asked.

"The sandbar. The one the kids found. The one you will walk on, as long as the river doesn't get wise to our plan and erase our one chance."

"How far below the surface is this sandbar?"

"From this side of the river to the other," Sandy replied, "only five feet. But each minute we spend discussing it, the sandbar gives up a little bit of height to the Miralette. We must be on our way now."

Edward hoisted his packs up high on his shoulders, then looked the mother otter in the eye and said, "Lead the way. I'll follow you."

Wading into the cold water, Sandra felt the sandbar beneath her feet like Braille bumps beneath brilliant fingertips. She read the soft curves and contours of the river bottom, listening with her toes, understanding all it had to tell her, and adjusting her course accordingly. She was a water nymph in her element, and not the subtlest of details escaped her notice.

Edward and his guide moved at a steady pace, eager to make the crossing before their bridge of sand dissolved beneath them. From his vantage point midstream, Edward saw the white-maned herd of raging waters bearing down on him from the east. Bounding headlong toward King's Bay, the river was not deterred by any consideration for someone foolish enough to venture into its path. As the flood reached him, the thoughtless waves curled around Edward's right shoulder, splashing against his chin, spitting anger in his ear, as they tried to drown the intruder.

On his left, a more placid river flattened itself into a drifting sheet of grey slate. The sandbar upon which Edward now walked had sapped the water of its momentum, giving up a little of itself in the process. It was a constant tug of war, a give and take, for nature ever wars against herself.

Edward found the incessant motion all around him disorienting. Losing his footing, at one point, he very nearly stepped off the back of the sandbar and into twenty-foot-deep water. With both his and Annelyse's backpacks strapped to his shoulders, he felt like a top-heavy tree being buffeted by a hurricane. Wobbling like a spinning top leaking momentum, his center of gravity shifted with the sand beneath his feet.

The sandbar led them to the right of the two islands called the Sibling Stones. Shaped like kidney beans, one atop the other, the Stones had once been the footings for a suspension bridge spanning the mouth of the Miralette. But the bridge sagged and crumbled alongside the power and influence of Hyland Manor and, piece by piece, it was delivered into the greedy hands of the river. As fewer and fewer people ventured north of the Miralette, there was never much reason to rebuild. Fears of some unnamed terror, real or imagined, argued the point that it was best to simply allow the Miralette to remain unspanned as a protective barrier for the lands lying to the south.

As Edward and the otters were passing the upper island and approaching the northern bank of the river, a sound like rainwater sizzling in a pan of hot oil could be heard all around them. Turning his head to glance over his shoulder, Edward saw a black wave cresting just above the surface of the water and gaining on them fast. Like splatter from a tipped inkwell, the dark surge tripped and stumbled over itself, unable to get out of its own way. There was a frenzied, reckless sense of malice enveloping the river and all who now made their way to the safety of the opposite shore were in its crosshairs.

"Swim, my children! Swim!" Sandy called to Mia and Rikson. Then, circling rapidly back behind Edward, she yelled above the loud commotion, "You must run now, Mr. Bellamy. Run with all your strength. I'll help you!"

With both front legs extended, Sandy pressed her paws against Edward's shoulder blades and started pushing him through the water almost faster than his legs could keep up. The pressure of the current against his chest, the force of the otter's paws against his back, and the increasing need to keep his chin above the rising tide, made it impossible for Edward to inhale more than the tiniest gulps of air. He felt as if he were using only the upper half inch of each lung, the rest of his body acting merely as ballast against the onrush of water.

Shooting another quick look behind him, Edward could now clearly make out just what sort of black wave it was that was pursuing them. At a distance of fewer than 40 feet, a bedraggled army of thousands of ravenous river rats was swimming and clawing its way toward Edward and the three otters. Like a boiling stew of naked tails and yellow teeth, the soggy rodents were clamoring over one another, using the backs, rumps, and snouts of their fellow rats as toeholds. There was no respect even for their own species, just a vicious, consuming urge to reach their prey and inflict deadly harm.

Rikson's prodigious, paddling feet propelled him through the current and onto the northern bank of the river first. A few seconds later, Mia joined her brother on dry land. But for Edward and his guide, danger was now only an arm's length away.

"Faster, Mr. Bellamy!" Sandy called from behind, slapping one rat after another with her powerful tail. "Dig your toes in and reach hard!"

The rats sunk their grimy teeth into the flailing tail of the brave otter, tearing chunks of fur off and leaving bleeding wounds in their place. Still, Sandy held her ground as the one line of defense between the attackers and the charge she'd been entrusted with.

"A bit farther," she cried to Edward. Then, with a few good kicks of her webbed feet, she cast him up onto the bank and into a mindboggling tangle of driftwood and debris.

Standing like a mountainous burial mound of elephant bones, the northern portion of Squirrel Thicket was much vaster than Edward had anticipated. The thicket through which he had crawled on the southern shore had been bad enough. But Squirrel Thicket north of the Miralette was five times the size and far denser than its southern counterpart.

Comprised of a maddening mess of broken tree limbs, jagged debris, tortured driftwood, and countless bits and bobs of a much less savory nature, Edward could not find an unobstructed line of sight more than a few inches deep anywhere but behind him. Insinuating itself into every available space, the twisted confusion of castaway timber formed a formidable wall through which Sandy now intended to lead him.

Edward had no time to ponder the unique natural wonder in which he now found himself lying, for as soon as she had helped him out of the water, Sandy began ushering him through the convoluted maze of branches on his hands and knees.

"Keep moving, Mr. Bellamy! They're coming!" she called, smacking Edward's legs with her front paws as if he were a carriage horse being driven onward.

Directing her attention to her children, Sandy gave instruction, "Fan out and slow them down any way you can! Be bold, my loves!"

At that, Mia and Rikson moved - one to the left, the other to the right - and circled back behind Sandy and Edward. Flanking the approaching throng of river rats, they enticed many away from the main pursuit. Roughly a third of the rats now pursued each of the three otters.

"There are dangers all around us, Mr. Bellamy," Sandy said. "I will take the lead, but you must stay right behind me. And you must keep up."

Running up the length of a fat tree limb, Sandy executed a record-setting high-jump, vaulted over Edward's head, and landed on the ground in front of him. She was now guiding him through the perils of North Squirrel Thicket from the front, scrutinizing every twist and turn with rapid and flawless judgment.

Crawling along like an otter, himself, over the sharp points and harsh angles of river refuse, Edward scrambled as fast as he could. The palms of his hands now bled a trail of crimson in the sand, and his knees felt as if he was balancing the full weight of his body on nothing but bare bone. Unable to fit into the tiny openings that Sandy could easily have escaped through, Edward was slowing down their progress and making it impossible for them to outrun their pursuers.

River rats swarmed the limbs all around them, nipping at Edward's arms and legs, some even swiping their sharp claws across the exposed skin of his neck and face. Each time he devoted a hand to fending off an attack, he had to sacrifice a moment of forward momentum and speed. If he hoped to keep up with Sandy and try to outrun the rats, he needed to simply endure the constant barrage of biting. Still, there was very little difference between the gnawing rodents and the injuries he received from the surrounding mesh of thorny splinters through which he was forced to drag himself. Inside Squirrel Thicket, injury was unavoidable.

The rats had formed a V-shaped phalanx, the left

and right-side vanguards now running slightly ahead of Sandy and Edward. It became obvious that the villains were not simply pursuing their prey. They were herding them, corralling the three otters and one, dismayed human down dead ends and into violent traps the rats had long since devised and laid.

But Sandy and her children knew these thickets well. Their cleverness was more than a match for the cunning of their enemies. For, crafty as they were, the river rats were also predictable and easily led into the teeth of their own pitfalls.

Squeezing his long, lean body between gaps in the gnarled debris, Rikson's speed allowed him to turn, circle back, and zig zag a dizzying path for his pursuers to follow. Quickly becoming confused in their attempts to not only keep up with their prey but also direct the course of their attack, many of the rats were swallowed by deadfalls, impaled upon spikes of sharpened driftwood, and swallowed by sinkholes of sand. Their blind treachery did not distinguish between friend or foe.

Some rats, forgetting the location of the traps they themselves had set, turned a sharp corner only to end up glued to a wall of woven vines covered in gooey sap. Others, becoming dazed by too many twists and too few landmarks, found themselves freefalling down hundreds of feet of dark caverns, never to feel the earth beneath their feet again. Of the rats pursuing Rikson, those who survived the ordeal would forever rue the day they set their sights on the young otter.

Meanwhile, Mia's sustained bursts of energy and impressive acrobatic feats proved too much for her band of river rats to manage. She was everywhere at once. Now, scurrying along in front of the battalion of rats. Now, popping up beside or behind them. She was a master at maneuvering through the tightest openings and down the narrowest holes. Those rats who were not entangled in nets of discarded fishing line or snagged by the fangs of rusty fishhooks simply gave up trying to catch the wily otter and returned to their slimy mudholes along the banks of the Sibling Stones.

But the rats pursuing Sandy and Edward were more tenacious, and more deadly, by far. Sensing every hidden blade and knife point designed to wound their feet; spotting every ditch filled with quicksand or some other venomous sludge; spying every party of rats lying in wait to ambush them; Sandy led Edward with as much speed as she could coax out of him, further from the river and closer to escaping from the wiles of the thicket. But there was one trap even Sandy could not have foreseen.

Within sight of the three, north-south-running rivulets in the Miralette Valley known as the Fishbones, barely twenty feet from the northern edge of the thicket and the freedom of the open flood plain, Sandy spotted smoke rising from nearby.

"Fire!" she yelled. "They've set fire to the thicket in front of us!"

The remaining army of river rats now concentrated all their efforts on Sandy and Edward, driving them in the direction of the quickly spreading fire near their exit. If the wicked enemy could not catch them, then they'd gleefully push Sandy and Edward into the arms of a fiery death.

Surrounded on three sides by snarling, slavering rats, and running headlong into an insidious blaze, Sandy had one last move up her sleeve, but she was not willing to risk her children's safety. Crying out to them in the language of her own species, she directed them to return together by the safest route to the fireproof haven of the Miralette River. She would rejoin them as soon as she could. Without hesitation, the two young otters disappeared, winding their way back to the cover of cool water.

Sandy now turned her attention to the situation at

hand. They were only a few yards away from the clearing beyond the thicket. Not even the audacious river rats would risk the open sky beyond. The flood plains running along each riverbank were patrolled by birds of prey who'd be more than happy to pick off as many rats as were foolish enough to show their faces. If Sandy could get Edward out of the thicket, he'd be able to cross the plains and enter the Silent Forest unmolested. She'd have to be quick, though.

"Mr. Bellamy, there's your path," she said, pointing in the direction of an opening in the jumbled morass of driftwood. "No matter what, do not slow down, do not turn back. Follow the way marked out for you through the Silent Forest. And hug your daughter from me when you find her." The noble otter smiled, then, before returning to the fight, she commanded once more, "Now go! And Godspeed, Edward Bellamy!"

Despite Sandy's urging, Edward hesitated long enough to see the mother otter cast her dangerous plan in motion. Picking up a branch of flaming driftwood, Sandy began running in one great circle around what remained of the evil river rats. Before long, she had them all surrounded and embroiled in a ring of raging fire. Their attack had come to an end, the brave otter had triumphed. And Edward now had the chance he needed to make his escape.

Bitten, bruised, bloodied, and stunned, Edward pivoted back in the direction of the open flood plains. For the first time since entering Squirrel Thicket, he was able to run undeterred. In no time, he was free of the labyrinth and standing upright once again.

Behind, in the burning thicket, Sandy stood watching, as the fire set by the fiendish river rats spread beyond control. Devoured by their own treachery; reproved by the punishment they themselves had devised; the villains were no more.

But they had left a wound of utter destruction on the land. The dry, brittle driftwood readily caught fire and turned to white ash and toxic fumes in the blink of an eye. Brambles, vines, thorns, and tumbleweed had all been consumed without a trace. River debris, trinkets that had washed ashore, treasures collected by ravens and chipmunks were all melted and disfigured until no longer recognizable.

Every bird's nest; every snagged backpack-turned-squirrel's nest; every badger burrow was now just a smoldering ruin. Squirrel Thicket north of the Miralette was gone. In its place, the airborne embers of a ravenous fire left the scorched earth behind in search of new tinder. The westerly breeze lifted the throbbing sparks onto its shoulders and carried them northeast, over the head of a weary Edward Bellamy, and into the dry wood of the Silent Forest beyond the Miralette.

Faith is a Fragile Footpath

Edward moved with purpose into the clearing between the ruins of North Squirrel Thicket and the Fishbones. He intended to make his way through the gap between the first and second ribs of the skeleton-shaped rivulets. From there, he would enter the Silent Forest just east of the village of Kwell. He was eager to travel unseen, not wanting to draw unfriendly attention to himself in a place where all attention was reputed to be unfriendly.

The open floodplain, north of the Miralette, was a narrow marshland. Winding like veins of lead through a stained-glass window, earthen dikes created small pools of blue and green water in which waterlilies and other aquatic plants grew. Frogs and turtles sat in long queues, sunning themselves on fallen limbs. Pathways - no wider than the

body of a beaver and worn smooth by wet, furry bellies –
leapt up the low banks and ran through the surrounding tall
grass. Tiptoeing angels of downy white and dusty blue
picked minnows from the shallows with needle nosed
beaks. The scenery was a pleasant change from the terrors
of the thicket, and altogether unexpected in this land of
foreboding.

The Miralette gently overflowed her banks
fortnightly, washing out the old and replenishing the
elegant pools afresh. And so, the water held captive in the
little pools was clean and clear. Reflecting the blues of the
shifting sky and the myriad greens of the sunlit grasses,
these stained-glass pools came to be called the Mirrors of
the Miralette for they appeared like shattered fragments of
reflective glass strewn across the landscape.

Just north of here, scarring the wetlands like deep
gouges in the earth, the Fishbones formed a small group of
broken rivulets, not unlike the Rindle Mire east of the
Fäerie Fields of Averlune. But they were different from the
Mirror ponds in that they did not receive their waters from
the Miralette. Instead, from unseen, underground sources,
they welled up in the marshy floodplain before finding their
outlet in King's Bay south of Kwell.

As he made his way out of the plain and into the
space between the first two Fishbones, Edward saw an old,
decrepit rowboat sitting on the shore. Flapping like a gull's
wing in the breeze, a scrap of paper had been pinned to the
side of the boat's blistered hull. Secured in the same
manner, a single daisy hung blushing in the warmth of the
sun.

Edward's reaction to seeing what had certainly been
left behind for his benefit by his wife's brother was not at
all what he'd expected. Having had time to digest all that
Halla had told him about the two, young rescuers, his
opinion of his brother-in-law had started to change.

Instead of an irresponsible, dangerous influence, he

had begun to view the poet as more of an endangered treasure. Aside from Annelyse, the young man was the one remaining piece of Silloah Bellamy left in Laprofonde, and he was in possession of secrets about his late sister which even her husband did not know.

Removing the pin from the weather-gnawed side of the rowboat, Edward held the note and daisy in his hands with care that bordered on reverence. He had begun to wonder if there was more meaning behind these modest, commonplace flowers than he had assumed.

They'd been the flowers used by Silloah to weave circlets for their daughter, but now their frequency along his path gave the suspicion of some greater significance. What did they symbolize, and what might they still have to teach him? Edward twisted the stem between his fingers, pondering awhile.

Placing the daisy in his shirt pocket, Edward now opened the small fragment of parchment and began to read.

> *Where, once, their blessed feet did tread,*
> *this soil was tilled by pain.*
> *But now all wrongs can be set right*
> *along the daisy chain.*

After having followed the poem about the Woolems this far; after having been led to Halla by the parchment left in the tree on the outskirts of Alder's Idle; Edward was inclined to read the words of this latest clue a second time, and more closely. Considering the meaning, he decided that - as Halla had assured him - it was certain that he was walking the same trail taken by the Woolems on their way to the Forgotten Meadows. He was on the right track.

He also determined that many of the animals who had helped him thus far must have played some role in the original rescue mission. They had been members of *The Ransom,* for sure. Halla's gifts of knit goods - fashioned from the wool of Woolems - were a stroke of genius. Isaiah, Kendra, Pat, and the brave river otters must have been reminded by the Woolem's wool of their vows to help and protect the gentle giants, and thereby discovered within themselves a willingness to help Edward along his journey. They knew more than they had let on. They recalled more than they had said. When called upon by Halla's subtle reminders, they had not failed to honor their vows yet again.

And now, Edward was standing at the very door of the Silent Forest, armed with Sandy's instructions to follow the path marked out for him, and this, the poet's latest clue.

Looking around, he noticed a handful of daisies growing among the leaves of the forest floor. Walking beneath the eaves and into the clotted air between the trees, Edward found still more daisies, and more after those.

In fact, an unbroken chain of daisies stretched out in an unobtrusive line well into the Silent Forest from where Edward now stood. There could be no doubt, this was the "path marked out for" him that Sandy had alluded to. This was the Daisy Chain growing from the soil which the Woolems had tilled with their own suffering feet.

Edward only hoped that the Woolem who carried his paralyzed daughter was following this same path. According to what Isaiah and Kendra had said, it was a good bet, and one that Edward was willing place. He'd spent the last few days trying to rediscover the Woolem's tracks. He could not have asked for an easier route to follow, at last.

Folding the note, he tucked it into the same pocket with the daisy. He'd set out, that morning, with the intention of reacquiring Annelyse's trail and gaining the upper hand in his search for his daughter. He now felt that he was on the verge of accomplishing just that. Spurred on by his rising spirits, Edward began running along the daisy-strewn pathway.

Every so often, he caught sight of the red-barked Kalósyi and saw-toothed Pólcrit trees, growing side by side. Without fail, a small pond - complete with water lilies gazing up at the two brothers – could always be found nearby. This reminder of the cause of his daughter's paralysis gave added speed to Edward's feet as they sprinted among the white flowers.

Rounding a turn in the Daisy Chain where it navigated a great boulder in its path, Edward suddenly found himself lying on his back and gasping for air. A long line of viscous drool pooled in the crease of his chin, hanging like a tenuous string of melted cheese from the open mouth of a big, black dog. The beast stood with both of its front paws on Edward's chest, baring its teeth and flaring its nostrils in a threatening snarl.

Edward's lungs, emptied of air by the impact of his back against the hard ground, now gulped with one great heave of his chest. Sensing defiance, the dog barked a warning to remain still. Edward readily complied.

"What've we here, Gyilkos?" a voice called from somewhere nearby.

A pair of stained, leather boots now tramped up behind the enormous dog, stopping near Edward's feet. Towering up from inside his shabby boots, a young man, wearing what could only be described as scraps of fur and cobbled-together animal skins, stood scratching his patchy beard. The dark, grizzled mass atop his head sagged beneath the weight of its own filthiness. Oozing down both cheeks, the slow, greasy flow of hair puddled in a stagnant tuft on the man's chin. Between untidy splotches of beard, the red hide of someone who'd spent too much of too many days laboring beneath the hot sun shone through like a lobster's own blushing backside.

"And who might ye be?" the stranger asked with a misplaced chuckle.

Edward slowly drew a breath of air, "My name is Edward Bellamy. I'm sorry if I startled your…" he labored to take another gulp, "…dog, sir."

"Startle Gyilkos?!" the man exclaimed with a guffaw, "Nonsense! He's the best tracker north o'the thicket. You'd be hard put to catch 'im unawares."

The stranger kicked Edward on the sole of his hiking boot for emphasis then, with a squint in his green eyes, inquired, "What is it you want, little man?"

A chill stole up Edward's spine, beginning in his tailbone and lodging itself like a shard of glass in the back of his neck. The man had shown no interest in calling off his dog, despite Edward's obvious discomfort – or, perhaps, because of it. In fact, the uncouth stranger seemed to take undue delight in Edward's prone predicament. There was a cruelty in the man's whole demeanor, which he took no pains to disguise. Edward thought it prudent to divulge as little as possible.

"I don't want anything, sir. I meant only to pass through the Silent Forest."

"What would an outlier want in the Forest?"

Edward hesitated, searching for a response that would satisfy the question without uncovering the truth.

"A horse," he lied, "I'm tracking a horse. From Hyland, over the river. I thought it ran in here. A beauty, it was."

"A horse?" the man sneered. "What good are they? Can't eat 'em. Ain't got no fat enough."

Edward recoiled at the thought.

"And can't ride 'em through the crowded woods, neither. Worthless things. I'd trap 'n shoot 'em all just to be rid of 'em," he added. "What you mean to do with it, if'n ya catch 'im?"

Edward struggled to take a breath beneath the weight of the immovable hound. His irritation with the stranger for still not having restrained his dog had turned to alarm. This was clearly a man who wielded fear as a weapon. He was a bully, to be sure. But one who commanded the might of a beast with fewer scruples than he himself possessed. Edward chose his words with calculated care.

"Why, ride him southward, of course," he answered. "One less stud to sire a worthless foal," he added, thinking it would appeal to the stranger's coarse mode of thinking.

"Right ya, there!" the man approved, kicking Edward's sole a second time. Reaching for his dog's collar, the man hesitated before pulling him off Edward's chest, "Where'd ya say yer from down south, then?"

Now, much can be said of Edward Bellamy. He was a man who could miss the absurdity of the existence of a stand of five, wandering evergreen trees on the open prairie while embroiled in searching for a doorknob among their branches. It might be said that he went a little too easy on his impetuous and all-too-vocal daughter. But there was never a soul who could, in all honesty, say that Edward Bellamy was devious. Able, in a pinch such as this, to spin a little white lie? Yes. But, capable of prolonged deception and adept at weaving a long, drawn-out untruth? No. And so, without hesitation, he replied, "Averlune." And that was all the man needed to hear.

Withdrawing his hand from the dog's collar, the unsettling stranger drew a blade from a sheath strapped to his thigh and, with an altogether unpleasant tone, he directed Edward to, "Stand yourself up," and "Follow the dog."

With a whistle and a, "Home wit'cha!" the man sent the dog galloping on ahead of them, panting like a nightmare at midnight as it went.

Edward now found himself compelled to jog along behind the very beast that had pinned him so effectively to the forest floor for the better part of a quarter of an hour. Behind him, a stranger who was little more than a beast himself, held a knifepoint between Edward's shoulder blades, spurring him forward with jibs and jabs all the while.

Edward was confused. It seemed as if the man had been willing to let him go, until he'd heard the word Averlune. Nowhere within his muddled thinking could Edward find an explanation for this turn of events. All he could think about was finding Annelyse, and he had no time or patience for such inexplicable detours. He had to find a way to break away from the stranger and his dog. And he needed some answers, too.

"Where are you taking me?" Edward asked.

"Quiet, you," the stranger replied.

"What offense have I committed to be treated like this?" Edward demanded.

Without another word spoken, Edward felt the sharp sting of a steel blade being swiped across the back of his neck. Raising his hand instinctively, he felt the warm flow of his own blood running between his fingers and down into his shirt collar.

"Shut your mouth, I tell ya," the man yelled, "Or next time you'll be pickin' your head up off the ground."

Edward had no doubt that the man meant what he'd said. Despite the mystery of why the situation had changed, there was no question in Edward's mind that he was in mortal danger. His thoughts now turned in desperation to devising a plan of escape. They were still within sight of the Daisy Chain. If only Edward could trip his captor; hit the dog with a tree limb; and then outrun it in its dazed condition; he might be able to rejoin the path that could lead him to his daughter. If only.

But the beast was all legs. His short, sleek hair revealed a lean, muscular physique, and his eyes blazed with ruthless purpose. This animal had been bred for speed and ferocity. Nothing more and nothing less. Even at his fastest, Edward was no match for this animal. He would have to bide his time and look for a better opportunity.

As the man drove him deeper into the Silent Forest, Edward began to notice things hidden among the leaves and dense areas of undergrowth. Spring-triggered, steel-jawed traps of enormous size; stone-weighted nets and intricate rope rigging among the trees; pitfalls of sharpened stakes, big enough to skewer a grown elephant; the forest was boobytrapped with a variety of wickedly ingenious devices. And the man and his dog knew where every one of them lay.

The ominous stranger was a hunter and trapper, that much was clear. But what game he could possibly be hoping to ensnare using traps of this size, Edward could only guess.

Winding their way through the minefield of deadly perils, they soon arrived at a shabby homestead in the woods. The area was comprised of a small shanty, which was apparently the hunter's home, and a much larger – though equally rickety – barn. It was toward the barn that the man now directed his prisoner, while the dog pushed open the door of the house and disappeared inside.

Shoving Edward to the ground, the hunter kicked him in the thigh as a warning not to move. The man then busied himself with a padlock hanging from a chain which secured the great barn door. Opening the door with one arm, he reached down and pulled Edward to his feet, using his other hand.

With unwarranted harshness, the man threw Edward into the darkness of the dilapidated barn, slamming the door shut behind him. Edward could hear the click of the padlock being locked outside, followed by the sound of the man's heavy boots trudging off toward the house. This was his moment of reprieve, and Edward Bellamy intended to use it to assess his predicament.

Edward's eyes were slow to adjust to the blackness enveloping him. The pain in the back of his neck recalled to his mind the injury he'd sustained at the point of the hunter's knife. Lifting his hand, he felt with horror the extreme length of the gaping slit in his flesh. All down the back of his neck and across his shoulders, caked blood stained his skin and shirt.

His mouth was a dry riverbed, and his tongue was swollen with thirst; but his canteen, along with everything else he'd been carrying, had been taken by the hunter. With no provisions and no expectations of receiving any kindness from his captor, Edward Bellamy was quite literally in the dark and running low on hope.

Little by little, as his eyes relaxed, he was able to detect shafts of dust-speckled sunlight breaking through the spaces between the boards in the roof. With every breath of a breeze outside, the dry planks - tenuously held together by rusted nails – relinquished a little more of themselves to the wind. Creaking and choking in the dirty air of the cheerless barn, the rafters splintered beneath the weight of their shame, for the barn had long been used, against its will, for depraved purposes.

In the shadows around him, Edward began to sense a presence. Perhaps it was the faint sound of slow, muffled breathing that first crept into his awareness. Or maybe it was the weight of two eyes straining in Edward's direction through the bleak, musty silence.

Surely, whatever had been there before Edward had been cast inside the barn would have gotten a good look at him before the door was slammed shut behind him. Maybe it held Edward in its gaze, still. Or it could be that the flash of daylight when the door was flung open blinded everything inside. Perhaps anyone else in that room was as completely in the dark as he was. Edward had no way of knowing.

But it was the low, steady sound of sobbing, which he now detected, that Edward found most disquieting. Whatever it was that was concealed in the shadows of the dismal barn, Edward could feel its profound sorrow.

Standing up from the place on the dirt floor where he'd landed, Edward backed himself against the nearest wall. He felt around in the dark for a surface sturdy enough to support his weight, then lowered himself with caution onto what must have been an old box crate.

His now fully adjusted eyes could discern little more than when he'd first opened them. He would have to take a chance and, not only acknowledge to his cellmate that he knew it was there, but address it directly, as well. Edward decided to assume that, since they shared a common enemy, he and his fellow prisoner might have common cause to be friends. One never knows, and Edward needed some slight hope upon which to build.

"What's your name?" he began.

There was no reply from the other side of the room.

"Mine's Edward. Were you captured by the hunter, too?"

Edward felt confident that he already knew the answer to this latest question, but he was desperate to engage his cellmate any way he could.

Still, there was no response.

"Do you live in the Silent Forest?" Edward continued.

The faint sobbing began again, barely audible through the dull, stagnant air.

"I've traveled far, myself," Edward said with a sigh. "Though… not just myself. Not alone." He cleared his throat, struggling to contain his emotion, adding, "Only to end up here…"

Hanging his head, Edward's voice trailed off into desperate introspection. He was talking to himself now, rather than to the taciturn creature on the other side of the barn. Burying his face in his hands, Edward, too, began to weep.

"No more," he whispered to no one at all, "Just… no more."

There was no anger in his voice, no recrimination. He was not searching for anyone to blame for his troubles. Placing blame on others would have removed any possibility of finding a solution for himself. And placing blame on himself would only waste precious energy. He was prone, prostrate, surrendering himself to sorrow, at last. Grief could now have its way with him.

Edward Bellamy had watched helplessly as everyone he ever loved had slipped through his fingers like rain. He was tired of being angry, tired of being bitter, tired of being jaded. In fact, he was tired of being anything and anyone at all.

He'd thrown away his faith in everything he'd held dear, even doubting the fact of Silloah's love for him. He'd vented his anger against the young poet. He'd bargained with his daughter, agreeing to accompany her on this journey, all the while hoping she'd arrive at the same dreary conclusions he himself had espoused. He didn't want to be alone in his darkness. Not like he was now.

But, in the peaceful wisdom of Halla's words, he'd rediscovered hope, and begun opening himself to his old ways of thinking. He accepted with gratitude the help of others like Isaiah, Kendra, Pat, and the brave river otters. In the warm rays of Halla's heart, his own heart had begun to thaw.

But now, after he'd discovered the very path taken by the mysterious Woolem and Annelyse, Edward Bellamy was rendered helpless once more. Everything that he'd regained seemed to be in danger of being lost again. Everything, from the trail of his daughter's kidnapper to the tiny glimmers that had begun to light the darkness inside his own heart, it was all in jeopardy of being snatched away from him.

All his old reactions had been utterly played out: denial, anger, bargaining, depression. None of them had brought him any peace. It was time to simply accept the reality of all that had transpired.

His wife was dead. His daughter had fallen victim to the venom of the saw-toothed tree. She'd been stolen away from him and might very well be dead, herself. He'd failed to save her. If truth be told, Edward Bellamy had failed long before they'd even set out on this journey. He had refused to keep alive that which was *most precious inside of* him and his daughter. This had been his first and greatest failure from which all the rest flowed.

Now, as he sat in this strange, grim place - far away from everything he had ever known, far away from everything he had ever been – in this moment of quiet reflection somewhere in the stillness of the Silent Forest, Edward Bellamy discovered the art of acceptance.

His quest had taken him to places he'd never imagined he would travel, for there is no more-foreign country through which to wander than Grief. But, in the sacred surrender of acceptance, Edward Bellamy had finally come home.

Home. The word, the idea was sweeter on his tongue than honey. The wildflower meadows, the familiar pathways leading down to the sea, Lightview Overlook, the looming profile of Mt. Averly, the unspoiled purity of the Fäerie Fields, all Averlune felt so far from Edward's reach and yet, still so much a part of him.

"Do not let the events to come kill what is most precious inside of you," he recalled. Averlune and all it represented to him was most precious and ever-present inside of him. He refused to let anything kill these treasures ever again. He would defend them from enemies seen and unseen; enemies without and within; those who would pit his own wrestling heart against itself with quibbling words; and those who would conspire to take him prisoner.

He would look beyond himself and see the world with the tiny eyes of the mother otter, and the piercing wisdom of the gentle Halla. And he would never close his eyes – close his heart - in fear or grief again.

Home. Just to taste its sweet name on his lips was the best he could wish for in this moment of solitude. And so, in a whisper, savoring each syllable like the perfume of a three-petaled flower, Edward Bellamy spoke the name of home in this most inhospitable of all places.

"Averlune…" he breathed in the dark. "Averlune… Averlune…"

From across the barn floor, a sound like that of distant thunder on a summer's day echoed back the word, "Av-er-lune…"

The sobbing which Edward had heard earlier now turned to unbridled weeping. Crashing like countless bales of cotton down unfathomed depths, the cries which arose unseen from the shadows moved Edward to pity.

"Av-er-lune…" the cascading voice repeated, "Av-er-lune…"

"Do you know this place, too?" Edward asked with compassion.

"Av-er-lune…" came the mournful reply, "Av-er-lune…"

Edward stood and made his away across the dirt floor, arms outstretched in the dark. He didn't know why, but he felt compelled to draw nearer to the sadness he sensed in his fellow prisoner. He could not remove it, but his presence might help the creature to bear its burden for a while. For love multiplies every kindness and halves every care.

Shuffling in the direction of the sobbing, Edward finally reached its source. With his arms still outstretched, Edward Bellamy now stepped into an embrace he would never forget. Wrapped in his arms, with his face buried deep in its warmth, Edward now held myth and legend in his hands in the person of a Woolem of the Forgotten Meadows, though he did not yet realize it.

The first thing that struck Edward was the immensity of the creature. He could tell from the sound of its weeping that the animal's head towered over his own by several feet. The leg around which his arms were wrapped was as tall as Edward's full height and as big around as his torso. The wool covering its body was subtly fragrant, as if the creature had rolled in a bed of wildflowers.

Though it did not recoil from Edward's embrace, the animal seemed to be shielding one of its legs, as if protecting an injury. Edward became aware of this fact and mistook it as the reason for the creature's tears.

"Are you hurt?" Edward asked.

Falling silent, the enormous animal nodded its head.

"May I help?" Edward continued.

The creature shook its head in slow, sweeping motions, side to side.

"How did this happen?"

With a low rumbling from deep inside, the mysterious prisoner drew a breath and spoke.

"Trap," it said in a doleful voice, "Hunter's jaws."

"That's how he captured you," Edward confirmed.

The creature nodded in agreement.

"Are you able to stand on it?"

"Pain," came the plaintive reply. "Pain."

"Is this why you were crying?" Edward asked with tenderness in his voice.

"No," the creature responded, "Failed. Secret. Only daughter. Now will die. Could not help. Failed."

At the mention of the words, "daughter" and "die," Edward's blood ran cold. Could the creature be talking about Annelyse? The time for circumspection had passed. Feeling all his fears coalesce into wild terror, Edward took hold of the creature's fur, insisting, "Tell me about the daughter!"

The great beast took a step back, as if seized with sudden recognition.

"You," it said, "You, the father. The key. Must help."

In an instant, Edward knew he was standing in the presence of not just a Woolem, but the very same Woolem who had pursued them through the woods. The same Woolem who had kicked him across their campsite. The same deranged Woolem who had kidnapped Annelyse from him. With this realization, all compassion for the injured animal turned to white hot rage.

"Where is she?!" Edward demanded. "What have you done with her?"

Striking Willemina across the face with his fist, Edward yelled, "Tell me!"

The gentle giant of the Greenfields began weeping again, this time moaning and wailing aloud, "Dead," she cried, "Dead. Tried to help. Failed. Now will die."

Edward fell to his knees before the beast who had taken his daughter from him. Crumbling into the dust of the barn floor, he unleashed every demon of hatred, every drop of despair, every ounce of life left in his broken heart.

Grinding his face into the unyielding earth, he cried, "Why?! Why? What sense does it make? My child… my child!"

Gnawing raw gravel between his teeth, Edward Bellamy wanted nothing but to lose himself, swallowed piecemeal by the ravenous earth. His daughter was dead. What else might he lose that could possibly matter to him?

In the moments that passed, Willemina sat in silence, resting her wounded leg, mourning the death of her charge. Edward lay motionless, crumpled like a wad of discarded paper upon which had been scribbled the beginning a story that would never be finished. His life had been systematically dismantled, rendered void of all meaning, and cast aside to make room for the next failed draft.

He no longer cared about what the hunter had in store for him. He no longer cared if he ever saw his home again. How could it be anything more than a gallery of torturous images of a happy past gone forever? He longed only to join those whom he'd lost. He was content to let the hunter do his worst.

As soon as this thought entered his mind, Edward was blinded by a searing flare of sunlight tearing the darkness inside the barn to ragged shreds. The hunter had returned.

"So, you've met, have ya?" the man chuckled.

Willemina cowered in the corner, nursing her leg, while Edward shielded his eyes from the sudden glare of daylight.

"And what about that one there?" the hunter chided, motioning toward the corner in which Willemina was standing. "Do ya know her, too?"

Realizing that the man was not referring to the Woolem, Edward turned to see whom it was he might mean. As his eyes opened to the contrast of a dark corner in a room awash in sunlight, Edward could just make out the lifeless shape of the body of his beloved daughter. She'd been laid with care upon a pile of old flour sacks. In her hands she held a single daisy.

Annelyse's skin was still red with the flame of infection. Her face, disfigured by a constellation of tiny blisters, was swollen and barely recognizable. It was apparent that her body had suffered the full effects of the poison of the saw-toothed tree. Edward had been too late to stop it from running its vicious course. The rampant paralysis had invaded almost every muscle in her body, leaving her unable to grasp, unable to walk, unable to help herself at all.

It was also apparent that the Woolem had not harmed her. Indeed, it was Willemina who had laid her down so gently and placed the daisy in Annelyse's hands. It was Willemina who, despite her own injured leg, had cared for Annelyse and kept her safe. Edward had feared that his daughter's body might have been left in the wild by her captor. But now, he was overwhelmed with emotion at this unexpected chance to say goodbye.

Running to her side, Edward Bellamy threw his arms around his Annelyse's shoulders and wept a rain of desperation down upon her youthful face. From the doorway behind him, the vile hunter laughed with derision, while nearby, the heartsick Woolem turned away in sorrow.

With her cheek pressed up against his own, Edward Bellamy rocked his daughter in one final embrace, one desolate goodbye. In the silence of his anguish, Edward's heart could scarcely trust the words he now heard whispered in his ear.

"Daddy? Is it you?"

Epiphanies

The fires that destroyed Squirrel Thicket north of the Miralette River now smoldered among the ruins left behind. Hungry for fresh fodder, the dying flames sent their embers mounting to the winds. Crossing the open floodplain, they rode the thermals that continually rise from the Mirror ponds and Fishbones until, invisible against the afternoon sky, the seeds of devastation found old wood in which to take new root.

Less than a mile into the Silent Forest, the sparks descended deep into the heart of dry leaves and dead timber, kindling themselves anew. In secret, the flames were winnowed by breezes wandering among the trees.

Known only to the creatures of the forest, deadly danger at last began to spread, driven on by the mercurial wind, without respect for life of any kind.

Like a great, silent cone of ash, sparks rose from the center of the forest, sent as messengers to the four corners of their reach. A slow-motion rain of blazing snowflakes now blanketed the northern sky. Soon, all the woods of the Silent Forest would burn.

In the hunter's barn, less than a mile from the southern border of the forest, Edward held Annelyse in his arms. Her limp body betrayed no signs of life, but for the drowsy flutter of her eyelids and the joy they now revealed. Every muscle in her paralyzed face refused to form itself into anything but an expressionless blank.

She was unable to return her father's embrace, unable to speak above a thin whisper. Her indominable spirit had begun to succumb to the weight of her own all-but-lifeless body. It was little wonder, then, that when Annelyse lost consciousness the compassionate Woolem thought that she was dead. Heartbroken, Willemina had placed Annelyse on the softest surface she could find, putting the most beautiful token any Woolem could imagine into her hands – a daisy from the sacred path they'd been following.

Even now, after her father's arrival had revived her flagging spirits, Annelyse had very little time left before her innocent heart gave way to the poison of the saw-toothed Pólcrit tree. Her situation was grave.

"Enough!" the hunter bellowed from the barn door. "I knew I's right about you Averlune thieves. You weren't chasin' no horse. You was after my property all along. I shoulda slit your neck round front, too!"

"My daughter is sick," Edward yelled, interrupting the man's mindless tirade. "She needs medicine."

"Ain't none of you getting' any healin', 'xcepting that dumb ol' beastie, there," the hunter laughed, "I want *her* nice'n strong. There's work needs doin'."

Reaching for the axe embedded in a stump near the center of the room, the hunter approached the corner in which Edward was cradling his daughter. In the dim light streaming through the half-open door, Edward saw the silhouette of the man's dog guarding the exit behind its master. There was no chance of making a run for it. Edward would need to stand and fight.

"You get yours first, liar," the hunter threatened, swinging the gleaming axe over his shoulder.

Edward carefully laid Annelyse back down on top of the flour sacks, then turned and lunged at the hunter. Scoffing as he raised his foot, the loathsome man kicked Edward squarely in the face with his heavy, leather boot.

At the sight of the bloody nose he'd inflicted, the hunter exploded in vicious laughter, taunting, "Is that the best you got, little man?"

Edward Bellamy now lay flat on his back at the feet of his enemy, with an axe blade poised to split his forehead in two right down the center.

At that moment, Gyilkos, the hunter's dog, who had been standing in the half-opened doorway, suddenly yelped in agony. All eyes now turned in the direction of the beast who was busy biting his own backside and whining like a puppy with a pinched tail.

Through the open door, a cloud of sparks - like a swarm of angry, luminous yellowjackets - blew in on the wind and swirled around the hapless animal, nipping at its wretched hide. The hunter's foul mongrel was now rolling around in the filth of the dirt floor, desperate to soothe the incessant stings of the embers.

Framed in the doorway, the sky outside had hardened to an ominous shade of grey, obscured by a blizzard of ash and thick smoke. The forest beyond was ablaze. Enormous flames raged among the charred skeletal remains of trees. Everywhere one looked, animals of every kind were fleeing the confines of the woods as fast as they could. The whole world had come unhinged and swung freely in the winds of a howling inferno.

The hurricane of embers that had set its sights on Gyilkos, now filled the entire interior of the barn. Licking everything they encountered, the tongues of fire leapt from piles of brittle straw to heaps of greasy rags, setting all ablaze. The wind was drawn in through the draft of the open door, exiting the old barn through gaps in the roof, only to be pulled in through the front door again. Around and around the cyclone spun, feeding the flames, and leaving behind only smoky chaos.

The moment the hunter realized what was happening, he let the axe fall from his hands, grabbed two wooden buckets, and ran to the well in the middle of the compound. Pumping feverishly, he filled the buckets, ran back inside his burning barn, and watched as the water he threw upon the fire evaporated before touching the ground. Even if he had been able to drown the flames that were destroying his barn from within, those consuming the forest outside could not have been stopped. It was time to abandon his belongings and save his own miserable life.

At the sound of Gyilkos's first yelp, when the hunter's attention had been diverted away from splitting his prisoner's head open, Edward had jumped to his feet and swept up his daughter in his arms. This was the chance he'd been waiting for, and he recognized it immediately.

Turning to the Woolem at his side, Edward said, "Follow me!" He then took up the lead position, threading a path for them amid a scene of madness.

The frantic hunter was so preoccupied with trying to save his barn that he'd forgotten all about his three prisoners. Back and forth from the well he ran, never once laying eyes on the escapees. In the commotion, Edward was able to slip right out the front door carrying Annelyse, with a Woolem in tow.

Once outside the barn, Edward snatched up their backpacks from beside the front door of the shack, then headed northwest away from the towering behemoth of flame, and into the fresh breezes blowing off the nearby bay. He was desperate to put some distance between them and the hunter, hoping against hope that the fire would fill the gap behind them and cut off any pursuit.

Willemina's leg, which had been wounded by the hunter's trap, slowed her progress. But even the strides of an injured Woolem are still far greater than that of a man (or a dog, for that matter). They were still able to cover a good distance for the better part of an hour before Edward felt it safe to take a break. There was another urgent matter to be addressed before they could continue their trek.

Laying Annelyse down in a glade of grass on the western edge of the Silent Forest, Edward pondered Halla's parting words to him, *"And when you find Annelyse, remember the tale I told you of the two trees. Healing is often found where we least expect it. If only we are willing to see."*

"The tea," he said to himself, in a moment of remembrance.

Looking up at the Woolem who stood watching at a distance, Edward instructed Willemina, "Keep an eye on her."

Then, letting the words he had just spoken settle into his awareness, he paused.

"Keep an eye on her," he repeated, this time with consideration. "But that's what you were doing, wasn't it?"

Willemina lifted her eyes to meet Edward's.

"Willem in chains," he said.

"Daddy," the gentle Woolem replied.

"You came to find the key… the key that would set your father free. Isn't that so?"

"Help," Willemina said.

"Yes, to help your father."

"Daughter," the Woolem whispered.

"Yes, Willemina, you are a good daughter."

"No," Willemina insisted, "Silloah daughter."

Edward stopped, his eyes slowly widening to let in the full light of understanding. The Woolems knew. They knew that Silloah would come back one day. They knew she would return to free the old Woolem. She must have told them. She must have promised. But… then. Silloah knew when she got sick that she would never be able to keep her promise. And so…

"Silloah said daughter would help. Poet, too," Willemina said with absolute faith.

"Now the father, too," Edward added. "I will help you, Willemina. I will bring the key to free your father. I will keep this promise. Her promise. My daughter and I, both."

Walking over to where the Woolem stood, Edward carefully laid his hand on the place where he'd struck her in anger. Caressing her face, he looked into Willemina's eyes and said, "Forgive me, sweet one. I'm so very sorry."

Willemina's face relaxed in a gradual blossoming of relief and wonder. She'd thought that her mission had failed when Annelyse had "died." She was certain that the enraged Edward would never forgive her for taking his daughter from him. And when he'd struck her across the face, her heart had shattered into countless fragments of bitter failure and despair.

"I understand now," Edward added. "And I'm forever grateful to you for taking care of my daughter, for protecting her from harm."

Edward wrapped his arms around the huge head of the Woolem, burying his face in her fur, whispering, "Dear friend," in her ear.

"Now, I must find the tree that will save her," he said, drawing back in order to see Willemina's face. "Please, watch over her until my return."

With a serene bobbing of her head, Willemina accepted her charge once again.

Without hesitation, Edward ran off into the thickets of the forest to their east, in search of the red-barked Kalósyi tree. Miles away to their southeast, the Silent Forest was a conflagration, leaving only blackened stumps where once a lush, green forest had reigned.

In the path of the relentless fire, red-barked and saw-toothed trees alike were being destroyed, never to grow side-by-side again. Nearby, chaste waterlilies, whose feet now withered in the boiling waters of their little ponds, looked on with concern. This was a tragic new chapter in their epic tale.

Following a depression running along the forest floor, Edward soon came upon a ditch filled with stagnant water. On its surface, waterlilies sat in the shade of the usual accompanying trees. Using a knife he'd taken from his backpack, Edward located the red Kalósyi tree, and pried several strips of bark off into his hand. At last, he had what he needed.

Sprinting back to where he'd left Annelyse under the watchful eye of the Woolem, Edward busied himself with making a fire. Dropping his whole canteen into the coals, he soon had hot water enough for one all-important cup of tea.

The fragrance of the bark steeping in the teacup roused Annelyse from her stupor. She was wide awake for the first time in days, and Edward caught glimpses of his daughter's characteristic curiosity beginning to shine through.

"What's that smell?" she asked at a whisper. "I don't know it."

"The cure we've been hoping for, my child."

Lifting the cup to her lips, Edward poured into her mouth the first drops of nourishment Annelyse had been able to eat or drink in days. At first, she sputtered at the clumsy feel of liquid crossing her lips. Her mouth had grown accustomed to being neglected. But then the warm tea began to yawn and stretch and spread itself wide within Annelyse's tired and atrophied body.

With a start, she felt the muscle of her heart buck with the sudden awareness of a frightened horse. The healing tea flowing within her now rode the surging waves of her lifeblood rushing to every cell in her body.

Before their eyes, Willemina and Edward saw Annelyse's complexion soften and become as supple as a newborn's. The blisters that had so marred her body now disappeared without leaving the slightest sign of scarring. The swelling which had rendered her almost unrecognizable, faded like a swiftly deflating souffle.

And then it happened. For the first time in days, Annelyse was able to raise her arms and wrap them around the neck of her joyful father. Edward returned his daughter's hug, as gingerly as if she'd been made of porcelain. But the strength and vigor of Annelyse's embrace assured her father that she was no longer fragile. Halla's tea had rescued his daughter from the grip of contagion and restored her to herself again.

"I knew you'd find me," Annelyse said, holding her father close.

"And now that I have, I will never lose you again," Edward vowed.

Kissing her father on the cheek, Annelyse lifted herself to a seated position, then pulled herself up onto her own two feet without help. Walking over to where the wide-eyed Woolem watched in amazement, Annelyse threw her arms around Willemina's shoulders. Deeply inhaling the wildflower perfume of the mythical creature she'd set out to discover, the creature who had instead discovered her first, Annelyse marveled at the magic of it all.

"You're a Woolem," she whispered. "I think I knew you were, all along." Looking up at the Woolem's kind face, Annelyse added wistfully, "And you're *really* real. I'm so glad that you are."

Returning to the practical tasks at hand, Mr. Bellamy emptied his backpack on the ground beside the campfire. Taking stock of what was left of their provisions, he sorted everything into piles.

"Nine salted fish, five potatoes, a loaf of stale bread (more like a rock), and enough beef jerky to last us a week." Looking up at Willemina, he inquired, "But what is it that a Woolem eats?"

"Willemina eats grass and growing things. Enough for a lifetime of many Woolems, all around us."

Edward chuckled, "Yes, there is, my friend."

While the three famished travelers enjoyed their evening meal, the late afternoon shadows lengthened, and the western sky ran like a watercolor painting in streaks of pink. Off to the southeast, the horizon from which they'd just journeyed glowed a menacing red. The Silent Forest still burned, and the fire was drawing closer to where Willemina, Annelyse, and Edward had intended to spend the night.

"We can't stay here," Edward said, trying to gauge the distance between their campsite and the leading edge of danger. "We need to get out of these woods and quickly."

"No other way," Willemina insisted. "Must follow Daisy Chain. Must walk in woods."

"The daisies are burning, along with everything else, sweet one. But there's always the coastline."

"Too dangerous," Willemina countered. "Cliffs and drops and windy waves. No, too dangerous."

"There is no more dangerous path than the one we're on, I'm afraid. The coastal road is our only option." Edward assured the Woolem. "And we need to leave now."

The southeastern sky flickered its warning to all in the path of the blaze. Like the throbbing heart of a spiteful dragon, there was a tangible sense that - at any moment, without warning – seething anger might rear back and strike. Cleverly disguised in cloaks of ashen grey, a horde of airborne embers scouted their next line of attack. Nothing flammable was immune from their cruelty.

Stratus clouds, hanging low above the forest to the south, evaporated in the intense heat of the flames, drawing back their curtains to reveal the evening's first twinkle of starlight. The fire-flecked purple of night hung in cold, quiet contrast to the unchecked devastation raging below. The aloof starlight took no notice of the forest's pain.

Swirling around Edward and the others, the breezes blowing in from King's Bay lifted tattered rags of smoke high above the eastern floodplain and off toward Mount Miralette. These same winds slowed the northwestern progress of the flames, but the availability of so much dry wood north of the river made the Silent Forest irresistible to the voracious wildfire. The path of destruction was clearly marked out, it would run the full length and breadth of the old forest. Nothing could thwart its purpose now.

Taking their leave, the travelers made their way from the outskirts of the woods down the rolling banks of the western ridge overlooking King's Bay. The thin, treeless slope of bare earth between the forest and the sea tumbled like a drowsy daydream over chalky cliffs some twenty to thirty feet above the beaches. Centuries of buffeting by salt-winds stripped this narrow no-man's-land and twisted it into a moonscape of precipitous craters, gullies, and sandstone drifts.

The landscape made little effort to remain safely under the feet of any traveler walking its winding paths. But it wasn't just the tendency of the land to drop away without warning that rendered the ridgeline so treacherous. It was the razor-sharp edges of drifted sandbanks hardened by sea salt and the thirsty sun that made landing on anything but one's feet a painfully jagged experience.

This would be Edward's first challenge, choosing a safe route along the steep, unpredictable rockface, and one wide enough for a Woolem to walk. The darkening sky would only make his task more difficult. But, with danger approaching from behind, their only hope was to put themselves in the path of the smoke-free winds blowing in from the bay and squarely on the sands of the fireproof beach.

Choosing a large stick from among those discarded by the trees of the forest, Edward wrapped some scraps of fabric from his knapsack around one end. He then drenched the wad in a liquid he'd taken from his first aid kit. Striking a match against a stone at his feet, Edward lit the makeshift torch, then motioned for the others to follow him. This would be all the light they could count on to guide them off the ridge, and every moment they hesitated only deepened the night's darkness.

Surveying the pitch of the land, Edward moved with caution. In the deepening shadows, every crater appeared bottomless, and every gully was concealed until almost under foot. In places, the ground had been whipped by the wind into a petrified wave like egg whites atop a meringue pie. Willemina's heavy footfalls reduced the crusted shapes to dust, leveling the landscape as she went.

But it was the craters that Annelyse found most annoying. Walking along, her eyes fixed on her father's dimly lit feet, the earth beneath her would suddenly fall. Like the shock of discovering in the dark one last step on a downward staircase, Annelyse felt her spine compress when her foot finally found solid ground.

Edward, on the other hand, dreaded the concealed gullies worst of all. Unable to detect the black gashes in the earth without shining the torchlight directly into them, Edward was on high alert. Inside his hiking boots, each footfall was composed of ten toes stretched like tiny tentacles, fanned out and sensitive to the slightest change in elevation. Every sense and sensor were employed in divining the lay of the land and uncovering any hidden pitfall. Edward almost wished he could crawl along on all fours, at least that way he could deploy twice as many fingers as toes in reading the landscape.

Behind him, Annelyse kept both eyes glued to her father's feet. Behind her, Willemina kept a close watch over Annelyse, so protective was the Woolem of Silloah Bellamy's daughter.

After half an hour of feeling their way along in the gathering darkness, Edward led them to the brink of a short drop. Seven or so feet below, a wide beach waded out in the surf of King's Bay. Holding his roughhewn torch below the lip of the cliff, Edward could see that the landing was cushioned by a bed of soft sand. All they'd need to do would be to leap from the top and trust the beach to catch them with care. He'd be the first one down, as a show of confidence.

Tossing the torch onto the beach below, Edward now had a target to aim for. With a short, running start, he jumped off the ridge, landing with a roll to soften the impact on his knees.

"You're next, Leesy," he called from below.

Before she could even consider how frightened she was at the prospect of leaping into the empty darkness, Annelyse felt the fragrant wool of Willemina brush past her face. The great Woolem had jumped the queue and now landed with a thud beside Edward. Walking back over to the edge of the overhang, Willemina turned and presented herself to Annelyse who had only to wrap her arms around the Woolem's neck. Willemina then sat down on the beach, allowing Annelyse to slide from her back like a raindrop.

The three travelers were now safely on the sand with a barren swathe of ridgeline between them and the approaching forest fires. Caressing their faces, fresh air carried in from the open sea brushed aside the gathering woodsmoke. They were now free to spend the night on the open beach sheltered from harm while, behind them, the Silent Forest burned on.

From where they stood, they could see the yellow eye of Liege Light patrolling the tumultuous waters off to the southwest. Located between the small northern islands and the larger, more westerly Windermere Islands, Liege Light has long stood sentinel at the mouth of King's Bay.

Illuminating sure passage through the boisterous waves that writhe among the rocks, the old light rises nearly 300 feet above sea level. The last manmade structure north of the Miralette, except for the small fishing village of Kwell, Liege Light marks the westernmost point of influence of the kings of Hyland Manor.

It is rumored that the current lighthouse keeper, a man named Baxter Catsworth, is the longest-serving keeper on record. Every evening, for nearly eight decades, ever since the tender age of twelve, Baxter has climbed the 287 steps to the top of the lighthouse. Every morning, he descends only 284 steps, vaulting over the last three to the floor below – a living testament to the benefits of regular exercise and a diet of fresh seafood.

On the beach, Edward busied himself with unrolling sleeping bags. They would opt to forego a campfire, having seen enough of flames and burning wood for one day. Instead, the three weary travelers made themselves comfortable, intent upon a good night's sleep.

Willemina positioned herself between the sea and her companions, providing shelter from the chilly winds. Annelyse snuggled up close to the great Woolem, burying herself as deep as she could in the thick wool of Willemina's side. Edward chose a place beside his daughter where he could easily see the cliff head above. He had been experiencing an increasing sense of foreboding, ever since leaving the cover of the woods. Now, exposed on the open beach with their backs to the bay, he was keenly aware of their vulnerability. He would try to rest, but Edward's uneasiness would make sleep difficult.

Soon after bedding down, the low, guttural breathing of the Woolem soothed both her and Annelyse to sleep. Sitting nearby, Edward watched the southeastern sky pulse with fury. The scent of woodsmoke coated his nostrils and collected in the back of his throat. Even the sea breeze failed to sweep the air clean of smoke and embers. The fire that had been devouring the Silent Forest had finally caught up with them.

Sparks danced like demons on the breeze above their heads. Whirling in wild fits until, between the merciful fingers of the night, their wicked lives were snuffed out and their black hearts turned to soot. Only a few yards away from where Willemina and Annelyse lay sleeping, the woods in which they'd had their dinner were being devoured. Edward could feel the heat of the blaze on his face, even huddled as they were beneath the lip of the cliff.

The sound of crackling timber popped among the flames, as trees succumbed to the fiery assault and toppled to the forest floor. Oaks, alders, and elms who had called the Silent Forest their home from nut and twig now littered the ground like a battalion of fallen soldiers. There was an eeriness to the vast, empty expanse of horizon that now gaped in horror at the place where the crowded forest once stood.

Edward listened with disbelief to the hurricane winds that slithered like serpents around the base of every tree and through the prostrate arms of helpless shrubs. The moment the last morsel of wood had been consumed the winds would die down like gluttons at rest. But for now, the scene was like a blustery night in Hell.

At first just a trickle, a steady stream of woodland creatures scurried down the steep slopes of the ridge and onto the beach. Once their feet took hold of the soft sand, off they ran into the night to seek a life beyond the reach of flames kindled by the treacherous paws of river rats.

As the blaze worked its way westward, a profound silence took up residence in its wake, a silence born of grievous loss and hopelessness. The Silent Forest was aptly named, for it had been a quiet, peaceful, sylvan oasis situated between the lords of Hyland Manor's lust for domination and the volatile sea's turbulent animosity. Now, the silence that descended upon the wreckage of the forest was more like the muffled stillness of a burial shroud. Laprofonde had lost a great treasure at the hands of feckless flames.

In the aftermath of ruin, Edward drifted off to sleep. Far from restful, his dreams were visited by specters of the day's events. In his subconscious, shapes and shadows swayed like sinister reeds in a swamp of growing apprehension. Something was drawing near, something hostile. A warning voice rang out in his drowsy mind. Edward needed to awaken. Danger was upon them.

Opening his eyes in the moonless dark past midnight, Edward saw a familiar silhouette set against the heaving wrath of the red sky. Looking up at the cliff face, where the menacing figure stood looming over him, Edward could almost feel its paws on his chest as he had the first time he'd encountered the hunter's dog.

CHAPTER TWENTY-TWO

Standing at the Precipice

The dog remained motionless, except for the continual slobbering of thick drool dripping from its mouth. At first, Edward wasn't sure if the wretched beast had even noticed him. But when it growled a menacing snarl in his direction, Edward saw absolute recognition in its eyes. The hunter had spoken the truth when he said that his dog was the best tracker north of the thicket. Despite smoke and flame, the vile animal had successfully followed the scent of the three travelers to where they now lay.

The mongrel's sharp bark split the silence like a hunter's axe, startling Annelyse and the Woolem awake. Upon seeing the dog, Willemina drew herself to a standing position and inserted her body between Annelyse and the enemy. There was little she could do to defend the daughter of Silloah Bellamy against an attack, but she would happily give her life trying.

Edward reached for his now extinguished torch. The flame had whittled the end of the heavy stick into a sharp point; it would make an effective weapon if called upon. Standing ready for the possibility of an attack by the hunter's dog, Edward took three steps back away from the cliff face. The moment he did, Gyilkos snarled another warning to remain still. It was clear, the dog had been sent to find and hold the three escapees. That was the only possible explanation for why no attack had come. Reasoning it out, Edward surmised that the nimble tracker had run on ahead of his master. It was only a matter of time before the hunter arrived, too. Something had to be done quickly. In a whisper, Edward gave instructions to Annelyse and Willemina.

"On my signal, head north up the beach with all speed."

Edward reached down and picked up the sleeping bags and backpacks with one hand, still holding the sharpened torch in his other. Gyilkos took one step closer to the edge of the cliff, growling with teeth bared.

Rearing back, Edward hurled the pointed stick with as much force as he could muster. Like a javelin, the torch found its mark, striking the vile dog and sending him reeling backwards in pain. The howl of the beast as it was swallowed by the shadows was like the sound of wickedness being rent in two. The signal had been given. The enemy was in disarray. Now was the moment to make their escape.

Before the spear had left Edward's hand, Willemina picked up Annelyse and plopped her down on her own broad back. Galloping without a thought for her injured leg, Willemina kicked up a cloud of sand as she sprinted up the beach and away from the wounded hound.

Edward followed Willemina and Annelyse, with one eye trained behind him, fully expecting to see the dark form of the hunter's dog leap from the cliff and onto the beach. But no pursuit came. Fearing some deception, Edward called ahead, directing Willemina to keep running.

The eastern sky had begun to drain away the lacquer of night, until a pallid hue revealed the outline of Mount Miralette on the morning horizon. The four-peaked mountain was like the turret of a mighty citadel of stone, guarding the gateway to the Far Reaches.

It is said that the inhospitable lands of the Far Reaches are a maze of frozen riverbeds crisscrossing, doubling back, and luring men to madness at every intersection. No one in Hyland or the surrounding territories had ever traveled beyond the Far Reaches - if there is a beyond.

Some say that the world simply curves back around on itself, over the frozen horizon. Others say that time grinds to an icy halt, imprisoning motion and thought in a stinging landscape of snow and despair and stifling the possibility of ever knowing what lies beneath the spectral lights of the northern sky. Out of such mysteries, myth and legend grow.

Down on the shore skirting King's Bay, the incoming tide had narrowed the beach to little more than a Woolem's width. Panting and drenched in perspiration, Edward and Willemina were running low on sand and nearly out of steam. Come hound or high water, they would soon need to stop and rest a while.

The coastline had begun to change dramatically. When they'd first jumped down from the ridge, the beach had been a blanket of soft sand. Now, the sand was being replaced by rocks and boulders of increasing size. Instead of a cooperative toehold beneath their feet, the travelers struggled to find sure footing among the shifting stones.

Obstacles crept into their path, causing them to spill momentum from their exertions like wind from a sagging sail. Boulders, uncovered by the receding tide, pushed their angular shoulders through the sand, only to stare up at the sky with vacant eyes. Driftwood, like the bones of shipwrecks long past, lay lifeless on the shore, their twisted nails rusting in the waves. The tragic history of King's Bay was strewn all around the feet of Edward, Annelyse, and Willemina. A history which included a sad chapter on Woolems.

Half-buried in the smooth stones of the shore, the bleached bones of some great creature stood as silent mourners beneath an overcast sky. A rib cage was clearly visible, curving with somber elegance, rounding the apogee of its doleful arc before plunging back into the stones from where it sprung. Edward recognized the skeleton as that of a Woolem.

Pirates peddling their prisoners to the four corners of Laprofonde often ran aground amid the many islands of King's Bay. This unfortunate, innocent creature had undoubtedly fallen victim to the fate of just such a disaster. Foundering on the rocks, the waves had pounded the ship's hull to pulp, relinquishing the captives within to the churning of the sea.

When Willemina saw the bones of her kinsman, a loud cry like the bellow of a foghorn surged up from deep within her bruised heart. This was an ancient grief, a reminder of innocence lost and the era in which the Woolems learned of the existence of such things as anger, hatred, and greed. The gentle Woolem felt all things as if for the first time. For such wounds never heal, they only ever hide their tears for a while.

Edward pressed on, unwilling to let them linger too close to such sadness for too long. They needed to maintain their focus and stay on the alert.

The further north they went, the further from the water's edge they were forced to journey. By now, the sand had been altogether replaced by boulders, so that the easiest path available to them gradually led them back up the ridgeline. The travelers were now some ten feet above the shore and steadily climbing.

Edward was eager to find a place for them to rest that was sheltered from view. The cliffs were far too exposed for his liking. Even though the rockface was pockmarked with caves of various depths and sizes, he was reluctant to choose a location with only one exit; recent events had proven that pursuers might arrive at any moment. He would seek higher ground and the cover of trees.

The irregular-shaped boulders slipped and skidded beneath their feet, as Annelyse, Willemina, and Edward struggled up toward friendlier ground. Mosses and lichens carpeted over the seams between rocks, making it difficult to determine the best place upon which to place their feet. Annelyse, in particular, experienced the worst of it. Though healed of the effects of the saw-toothed tree's poison, three days of limp paralysis had left her muscles shaky and unsure. As a result, she stumbled along behind the others, often lagging, and slowing down their progress.

Mounting the crest of the cliff, Edward paused to survey the surrounding landscape. On the left, a rocky slope plunged into the churning waters some thirty feet below, as King's Bay sloshed among the many boulders in its grip.

Directly to the west, the long, thin Windermere Islands sat just above sea level. Uninhabited, and little more than bare rock, the islands are fringed in flowing garlands of green seaweed and algae which shimmer like emeralds in a black, brooding ocean. The constant motion of their hairlike garments gives the illusion that the Windermere Islands undulate with the surging of the sea.

While their low profile and the narrow channels they form serve to accelerate and direct the westerly winds unobstructed toward the cliffs to their east. Windermere Sheer is notorious, not only for its precipitous drops, but for the wildness of the winds that unleash their bitter jealousy against the brutalized coastline.

To the right of where Edward, Annelyse, and Willemina stood, the bald heads of the Borderland Hills peeked out from the barren meadows like a clutch of eggs in an egg hunt. Each hill was identical in shape and size and stretched out toward the northeastern horizon. Bordered to the south by the burned-out remains of the Silent Forest and to the northwest by a divided river comprised of loosely crocheted strands of water, the Borderland Hills appeared to have been shoehorned into an area far too small to accommodate them.

Down below the egg-shaped mounds, the hills concealed a collection of ancient burial sites. Long before the lords of Hyland Manor held sway over the lands to their south; before ever a name of lineage or a word of lore was recorded, the people living south of the Far Reaches used this area to entomb the bodies of their own.

The methodical funerary rites yielded symmetrical hills delineating the border between the lands of the living and the shadowy realm of the dead. The borderlands were frontiers all must one day cross, and only ever from east to west, from the dawning of all days into the inevitable sunset. The hills were not regarded as impassable because of their geographical properties but, rather, because of the realities they symbolized.

According to Willemina, the Daisy Chain would have led them directly north through the heart of the Hills, had they been able to follow it that far. A passage, known only to the Woolems, would have then successfully taken them through the dense hills and the fractured rivulets to their northwest. But, without the Daisy Chain to guide them out of the disfigured wreckage of the Silent Forest, they had only the treacherous coastline for a guide.

To their north, in the direction they intended to travel, the Cliffs of Fall awaited them. Among the three travelers, only Willemina understood exactly what that meant and what they could expect. She had tried to warn them against taking the coastal road, but now there was no other option.

The hardwoods that had once been a part of the Silent Forest now gave way to a small grouping of evergreen trees overlooking the cliffs below. Into this stand of fifteen or so trees, Edward led Annelyse and the Woolem. This was the best cover they were likely to find anytime soon. It would have to suffice.

The winds racing up from the bay had become more erratic and frenzied as the day wore on, bringing with them a heavy shroud of grey storm clouds. The temperature was plummeting and, with it, the sagging spirits of the exhausted travelers. A sleepless night had turned into a fearful flight, made even more tense by the possibility of being set upon without warning by the hunter's dog. Edward had no illusions that the evergreens would shield them from Gyilkos' expert nose, but the cozy closeness of the trees was comforting, nonetheless – even if falsely so.

Desperate for even a short nap to compensate for the previous night, the three travelers made themselves comfortable as best they could. Soon, Annelyse had snuggled up in a nest of Willemina's wool, and the two were fast asleep. Even Edward, unable to will his eyes open any longer, was deep in sleep, his hunting knife in hand. Overhead, the clouds obscured the sun; rain was falling on the western horizon; and an immense silence pressed inward from all directions.

At the foot of the cliff, the face of King's Bay had changed color to match the slate blue of the sky. Like the indistinct lining of wind-whipped clouds, a wispy foam frothed and dissolved in the roiling of the waves. Scooped from the surface of the water by the hands of an errant breeze, the foam crumbled into clumps, before dropping back into the sea.

Kitebirds, like motionless, paper cutouts, glided on the breeze above the bay, never once flapping their wings, ominous in their lifeless demeanor. Hidden among the sea oats that grew like stubble between the broken boulders of the cliffs, plump quail drew their brood up into the warmth of their downy wings. Every living thing knew how to read the signs written across the western sky. Every living thing had a plan to survive the danger approaching from over the sea. Every living thing except the three who were now asleep and woefully unprepared in the path of a hurricane.

The first to awaken was Willemina. Something was wrong. Whether it was the change in barometric pressure or the sickly cast of the olive-green sky, something was off. Opening her eyes, she remained still; listening; reluctant to alarm the others without cause.

Beyond the howling of the wind as it raced among the loose stones of the cliff face, and the ponderous heaving of the bay, Willemina heard nothing. No birds singing. No squirrels chattering in the evergreen branches overhead. Not even the occasional screech of a far distant kitebird. All animal voices had been silenced. The sensation was not unlike that of awakening to find yourself on an empty train well past your stop. The three travelers had been abandoned to their own fate. It was time to rouse the others from sleep.

Before Willemina had a chance to speak, the dark clouds looming above them cracked with thunder, split open, and spilled their cold, wet wrath down on all below. The slap of the raindrops against their cheeks jolted Edward and Annelyse from slumber, casting them into the chaos of the storm. The limbs of the evergreen trees were like ermine-draped arms bobbing in the raving winds, urging any who would listen to leave the area and seek shelter of a more solid sort.

Glowering from a distance much closer than was courteous, the slowly turning mass of cloud was an inverted whirlpool. The tempest was hard at work drawing moisture from the sea to pelt unshielded eyes with stinging salt spray and rob all warmth from exposed skin. A cyclone of debris careened in the air around Edward, Annelyse, and Willemina who did her best to protect the others. Soot from the nearby forest floor; lumps of tree limbs distorted into hideous shapes by the fire; even tiny pieces of shale, like shrapnel from the cliffside, collided with the bodies of the huddled humans and dismayed Woolem.

Edward used the sleeping bags and backpacks to cover their heads and faces from harm, but the searching fingers of the wind only peeled back their defenses. All was in motion. All around them was mayhem. In a matter of minutes – no, moments – they had been thrown headlong into havoc. The only shelter they had at hand was the swaying, bending, moaning stand of evergreen trees, and these were proving to be inadequate to the task.

Holding Annelyse's forehead against his own, Edward created as much of a feeling of security as he could on the leading edge of a hurricane. By sheer force of will, Edward channeled calm into his daughter's heart. But this false sense of security was violently wrenched from their grip by the jaws of a dog plunging its teeth into the back of Edward's thigh. Gyilkos had once again found them.

Still holding the hunting knife in his hand, Edward slashed at the face of the dog whose teeth pierced deep into his quivering muscle like the tines of a fork. Catching Gyilkos across the nose, the hound released Edward's leg in an explosion of searing agony. Edward Bellamy clutched at his blood-soaked thigh, reeling with pain.

Gyilkos' own recovery was swift, spurred on by a wicked desire to avenge his earlier injury at the point of a spear. There was an ulcerous gash in his front leg, no doubt inflicted by the throw of the sharpened torch. Now, the beast's snout had been sliced open by the blade of Edward's knife. There would be no restraining the creature's attack, no waiting for Gyilkos' master. The animal was enflamed with hatred, enraged, and wounded. He would rip out the throat from beneath Edward's miserable head. Nothing less would satisfy the fiendish pride of the hunter's beast. The dog reared back, taut as a trigger, ready to give vent to all darkness.

From somewhere amid the flapping arms of the wind-blown evergreen trees, a mass of broad limbs suddenly engulfed Edward, Annelyse, and the Woolem, as if snatching them out of the jaws of peril. The three astonished survivors who had, a split-second before, been in mortal danger now found themselves sheltered by what could only be described as a thick wall of branches.

From the other side of the wall, the frantic sniffing of a confused Gyilkos could be heard. The dog was digging at the foot of the barrier, employing his injured (but still formidable) nose to locate the prey who had been inexplicably ripped from his claws. But it was no use. The barricade between them was as solid and impenetrable as if it had been made of concrete.

The darkness in which the three travelers now sat was absolute. The sun, struggling to no avail, had failed to push its face through the quilted curtain of cloud cover, and now languished in the dark along with the rest of creation. Though Edward, Annelyse, and Willemina could hear the clamor of the hurricane and feel the wall of branches sway against the buffeting of the wind, the air around them was still and close. The rain that had drenched them to the bone only added to the unpleasant humidity as it evaporated from their hot, anxious skin.

Taking a deep breath, Annelyse was the first to break the silence.

"What happened?" she asked, voicing the one question on everyone's mind.

"I think we're in the eye," Edward replied, his hands searching the darkness for some bearings.

"But… what about the branches?"

"Blown down," Willemina posited. "Trees fall down."

"On top of us?" Annelyse asked with some degree of horror.

"More like around us, I think," came Edward's response. "That would explain the darkness. It feels like we're inside a pile of tree limbs."

"Great," Annelyse added sarcastically. "How do we get out of here?"

"I'm not sure we want to just yet," her father reminded her. "That blasted mutt is still out there."

"Stay a while," Willemina echoed in agreement.

"Yes, sweet one. That's best."

Edward reached one hand over to pat the Woolem on the leg for reassurance, as he did, his fingers brushed up against a tangle of branches to his left. Using the mesh of limbs to pull himself to a standing position, Edward began feeling his way along the wall. As he did, he formed a mental image of the space in which they'd been confined.

The wall they were facing was, indeed, tightly compact. Though they could still hear the pawing and whining of Gyilkos on the other side, the dog had made no dent in the barrier whatsoever. Rather than just a haphazard pile, the limbs curved around to the left in an unbroken wall of branches.

The general shape of the space was oblong instead of circular, coming to a point at both ends. Above their heads, there were no obvious branches. They couldn't tell if there was a ceiling composed of tree limbs high above their heads, or if the eye of the hurricane had stilled the rain and so thoroughly snuffed out the sun as to give the impression of a ceiling.

Beneath their feet, Edward could discern only a rough mat of debris, like a well-littered forest floor. Pacing it out, Edward concluded that several of the evergreen trees must have been felled all at once, creating the enclosure in which he now stood. It felt large enough so as to bestow no sense of claustrophobia, but small enough that it seemed almost cozy.

The greatest point in its favor, however, was that it had effectively placed a barricade between them and the murderous dog. In Edward's mind, the darkness, humidity, and uncertainty of just how to exit when the time came were all reasonable trade-offs for their security.

At that moment, on the other side of the wall, Gyilkos let out a blood-curdling yelp. Edward, Annelyse, and Willemina then heard the padding of paws running away from them at great speed. Something had either injured or startled the dog badly enough to cause him to break off his efforts and abandon his prey. Relief and apprehension wrestled within each of them. Whatever had scared off their enemy, Edward prayed it was friendly to people and Woolems.

Moments after Gyilkos' unexpected departure, there was a subtle change. The roaring of the sea began to fade, as if distancing itself from the darkness in which the three travelers stood. Though the winds outside continued to jostle the wall of evergreen branches, the growing calm of the waters of King's Bay suggested that they were, in fact, in the eye of the hurricane or that the storm had started to move eastward. Either way, Edward decided that it was time for a look around.

Reaching into his backpack, Edward Bellamy felt for a box of matches. Striking one on the sole of his boot, he cradled the tiny flame in his hands.

"What are you looking for?" Annelyse asked, as her father squinted his eyes in the feeble light.

"An opening," he replied, "A way out."

"Willemina help," the Woolem offered, leaning her huge body against the wall of evergreen limbs.

To everyone's surprise, the branches held fast, even against the strength of a Woolem. It was clear, they'd have to use more than brawn to break free from their enclosure.

After thoroughly scouring the surrounding walls by the insufficient light of one matchstick, Edward and Annelyse could find no obvious opening to provide them with an exit. Deciding to make one for himself, Edward drew his knife and began sawing away at the branches, dulling his blade in the process and doing very little damage to the limbs. They could not push, disentangle, or cut their way out. There was one method left to try.

Reaching into his backpack again, Edward retrieved the entire box of matches. Lining up a dozen or so just below an exceptionally thick branch, Edward held one match in readiness. He reasoned that the space in which they were trapped was large enough to endure a few short burns without filling up with dangerous amounts of smoke. The plan was to burn through a few key limbs, encouraging them to loosen their grip on the integrity of the wall, and enabling Willemina to push a hole straight through to the outside world.

Handing Annelyse a blanket he'd taken from his pack, Edward instructed her to drape it over her and Willemina's heads as a mask against the smoke.

"Don't remove the blanket until I say," he added. "I need to make this burn count if we're to breach the wall."

As Edward finished his thought, a new and insistent voice piped up from somewhere overhead.

"Oh no, no, no," it said with insistence, "There will be none of that here, thank you very much!"

"Who was *that*?" Annelyse asked in astonishment.

"Fighting a lire… wighting a mire… setting my **fall** on **wire** would be prepopsterous!"

CHAPTER TWENTY-THREE

Just Holding On

In the pitter of a heartbeat, the mysterious space in which the travelers had been enclosed now revealed itself. Cold, drab sunlight, trickling in through the slowly opening limbs of Albert Prume's incomparable Tree RV, drenched the interior in soft familiarity. All along, unknown to them all, they'd been seated facing the wall opposite the front door, their backs to the living room. But now that sight had been restored, they started to recognize every detail around them.

At a small, square table near the kitchen, Annelyse spotted Albert's favorite chair, still as wobbly and unreliable as ever. There was the ladder leading up to Albert's loft bedroom, the pot-bellied woodstove in the living room, and the round porthole window through which Annelyse had first seen the Quibble Woods.

Everything that had been pushed overboard and lost in the belly of the Perigoh Fair had since been replaced. The few things that *had* been recovered from the junk heap inside the Echoing Caverns appeared every bit as tired and forlorn as might be expected.

A wooden bucket, carrying more holes than it would ever carry anything else, sat useless by the sink. A cedar chest, missing the bottom half of one leg, leaned against a corner in the living room. The crumpled arms of an umbrella, its shredded webbing useless against the rain, gathered dust in a bin beside the front door.

Everything was a shambles, and yet everything sat precisely where Albert Prume wanted it to sit. He was fastidious about his housekeeping. He liked things his way, even if his way was not always entirely clear to his own mind. Above all else, Albert Prume was agreeable, and so was his unrivalled home. Annelyse and Edward were overjoyed to be back inside Prume's Wile.

Standing at the control panel and looking as frumpy as a loaf of bread in the rain the pleasant face of Albert Prume grinned atop his disheveled body. He had one hand wrapped around a bulbous, wooden handle dangling from a cord above his head. As he pulled on the grip, the branches comprising the outer walls feathered out, letting in the evening breeze.

The world outside glided by, as Albert guided his mobile array of five evergreen trees along the cliff head above King's Bay. The distant sound of waves breaking against boulders, like the hiss of thunderous snakes, faded with each step. The travelers were now following the ridge as it climbed ever higher, exposed to the whims of the windy heights.

"Cake yourselves momfortable," Albert called from the command console. "This wind will only get whippier as we go!"

Albert offered no explanation to Edward, Annelyse, or the Woolem for how he came to be there. He didn't tell them how he'd skirted the borders of the Quibble Woods, days before, just as soon as he'd parted company with his new friends. He never did like the haunted woods, and he had been loath to step one, single tree root inside that cursed forest.

Keeping to the northern bank of the Perigoh River, he'd made his way through the lowlands of Narrow Nook, past the woods of Shatter Lake, and over the Miralette just before Edward had arrived on its southern shore. Thinking he had found a nice, quiet home among the trees of the Silent Forest, Albert Prume was soon dismayed to find the woods on fire. Forced to flee, like all the other woodland creatures, the blaze drove him northwest over the Borderland Hills and toward the safety of the sea where he happened upon Gyilkos and his three hapless prey.

Edward Bellamy had been forced to piece together the events of the last hour on his own. Rather than being buried in a pile of fallen evergreen limbs, as he'd surmised, the travelers had obviously been snatched up by the long arms of Albert's Tree RV and deposited inside. The sudden springing to life of a stand of five evergreens had so startled the hunter's dog that Gyilkos had bolted in fear for his life. Who could blame him? It's not often that two humans and one Woolem are spirited away by a bunch of trees, much less that those trees then up and leave. Edward almost felt pity for the frightened mongrel.

Annelyse had also been busy trying to work out all that had happened. Having had about as much success as her father, there were still far too many unanswered questions to be ignored. Screwing her face up into one, great question mark, she opened her mouth to commence the inquisition. "But how…" she began.

"No bime for tuts," Albert interrupted. "It's tangerous derrain out there, my dear! Must, must, must be on our guard!"

The little man tweaked and fiddled with a symphony of knobs and buttons, all the while keeping a close watch on one, tiny bubble of air as it bobbed back and forth between two lines drawn on a tube of water. Albert was trying his best to keep the traveling Tree RV as level as he could, as it made its way over rocks, around obstacles, and up and down slopes in their way.

Ever curious (and often regretting her curiosity), Annelyse popped the porthole window open to take a look outside. Down below, some one hundred and fifty feet beneath the ridgeline upon which they were trudging, King's Bay roared with white rage.

The precipitous drop, plunging headlong into a jagged slurry of saltwater, fell away at the very tips of the Tree RV's toes. With each step, loose stones rained down through the void, grasping to no avail at every ledge and shelf they passed. There were far more gaping holes and broken chasms at the feet of the nimble evergreens than there was solid ground. Ever cautious, the tree roots fanned out like feelers, testing every toehold before trusting it with the full weight of everyone they were carrying. All the while, Albert directed the trees' every move.

As if the slippery footing wasn't enough to cast Annelyse into wild panic, the winds that battered the trees broadside seemed hell-bent on toppling them all over the edge of the cliff. Westerlies blowing in from the open sea slammed against the walls of woven limbs like wide, wooden paddles beating dusty rugs.

Caught in the path of cold easterlies tumbling down the distant mountainsides, the heavy, wet sea breezes met the frigid air like wrestling cyclones. The overall effect was a dizzying dance of unpredictable motion. Annelyse quickly grew nauseous watching it all. She had seen enough to know she didn't want to see any more.

Closing the porthole window, Annelyse dropped to the floor, her eyes wide as windmills, her mouth agape.

"What is it?" her father asked, noticing the color draining from his daughter's face.

Annelyse just shook her head in wordless warning.

"Cliffs and drops and windy waves," Willemina said without emotion.

Annelyse nodded vigorously; her eyes still dilated.

"Better to lot nook," Albert stated in agreement. "Not a pretty sight. No, no, no, not pretty at all."

"Nonetheless…" Edward replied, determined to see for himself just what sort of road they'd been forced to take.

Pushing his head through the window, Edward surveyed the precarious danger over which they were traveling. Directly ahead, he could see the bare knees of the evergreen trees as they lifted their legs to clear obstacles. On the left, the earth plummeted toward the sea in one terrifying fall from a height. On the right, the cliff sloped ever-upward. Beyond that, the Borderland Hills formed a dense barrier that ran to the eastern horizon and beyond. The whole region seemed designed either to bar entry or to imprison those already inside.

As their path curved back toward the west, Edward was greeted by a magnificent sight. Rising from the ocean some two hundred feet below the cliff head, a solitary spire towered over Albert's forty-foot-tall evergreens. Like a colossal cone of white stone, the spire was the singular outgrowth of a circular island, its summit sharpening to a pinprick more than six hundred feet above sea level.

Encircled by a halo of clouds, the entire height of the great tower ran with shimmering moisture. Edward could not tell if it was rainwater from the circlet of clouds above or salt spray from the sea below that coated the bare skin of the great pillar. Whatever its source, the flow was endless and made the Spire of Lament glisten like a teardrop in the midday sun.

Calling over his shoulder to Annelyse, Edward made room for his daughter to see this amazing sight. Willemina glanced up from her place on the living room floor. She recognized the tower. She knew what it meant.

"Near the Sheer," she said, this time with a noticeable hint of apprehension in her voice.

"Time to hatten down the batches!" Albert yelled to the others. "It's about to get even more blustery!"

Edward pushed the window closed but, no sooner had he done so than a gust of wind flung it back in his face.

"Turn the latch," Albert instructed. "And bolt the front door, too!"

Edward followed Albert's directions, then gathered Annelyse and huddled down on the floor beside the Woolem. Whatever lay ahead, Edward was determined to keep them all together.

Albert Prume remained hard at work at the control console, turning dials, pushing buttons, spinning wheels. As he did, the long, gangly branches of the Tree RV began to draw themselves closed like fingers in a fist. It was now dark as pitch inside, much as it had been when Edward, Annelyse, and Willemina first arrived.

In an instant, a greenish-yellow glow was kindled in a jar hanging above Albert's ruddy head. Upon closer inspection, Annelyse saw a friendly swarm of fireflies shining their luminous backsides for the benefit of all to see. The light was scattered throughout the room by the concave sides of the glass jar, no doubt designed for that purpose. As a result, the work of the brilliant little bugs was amplified and more than sufficient to navigate by.

"That would have been helpful earlier," Annelyse quipped, with some annoyance.

"Oh no, no, no," came Albert's reply, "I did *not* want to see that hurricane. Nertainly sot! No, no, no. I was hunkered down beside the pot-bellied stove waiting for it all to blow over. It wasn't until your father threatened to set my frees on tire that I thought I'd better take matters into my own hands!"

Annelyse just shook her head.

"Now stay low," Albert cried above the wind. "Here we go!"

With the jar of fireflies dancing in mid-air above, Albert tightened his grip on the controls. A look of dire determination hardened his doughy features to stone, as Windermere Sheer approached.

The Sheer was similar to the Cliffs of Fall over which they had just journeyed. Loose, shifting stones fell through chasms of deadly descent high above the churning waters. The horizontal ground had a habit of flipping vertical in the blink of an eye. Every step had to be chosen with utmost care.

The ridge upon which they were forced to walk was only a few feet wide. In places, gaps in the path forced Albert to train his trees to leap from foothold to tenuous foothold. At all times, the cliff head threatened to give way and slide into the sea below, carrying everything it touched along with it. True, there was very little difference between the Cliffs of Fall and the terrain upon which they now walked - very little, except for the untamed currents.

Windermere Sheer stands at the violent intersection of three gale-force, atmospheric currents. Thundering down from the north, the harsh, winter winds of the Mouth of Maelstrom bite deep into the marrow of anyone caught in their grip. It is said that the northern gales are so dense with heavy cold that they strike with the force of a stone wall, leveling all in their path.

Swirling up from the south, the warm Breath of Allure carries fury from far distant isles in the form of thunderheads, hurricanes, and tornadoes. Fragrant with the perfume of exotic flowers, the tropical current tempts sailors to disaster upon the perilous sea. Its arrival often brings devastation, without ever a hint of warning. What the impassioned winds cannot shatter, their hot, arid temperatures desiccate until nothing remains but sand.

Blowing unobstructed from the western sea, channeled, and accelerated by the low-lying Windermere Islands, the Wanton Winds feed endless supplies of moisture – at times, blizzards; at times, tsunamis – into the gaping rifts of pummeled cliffsides. These vicious westerlies blow without ceasing, stripping bare everything their prying fingers grope, leaving only barren lifelessness. It was the Wanton Winds which sculpted the Spire of Lament, drawing it upward from the ocean floor, smoothing and polishing its exposed body until not a blemish remained. It will be the same winds that, over time, reduce the spire to dust.

At the point of collision, these three formidable currents wreak havoc on the sheer drops and bare ledges of the towering shoreline. Windermere Sheer is that collision point, and Albert Prume was leading Edward, Annelyse, and Willemina straight into the confluence of danger.

Inside the tightly closed Tree RV, the howl of the wind was deafening. The cozy interior echoed like a subway station at the approach of a speeding train. Even the noise of the wind insinuating itself in the spaces between branches was not unlike that of screaming brakes on steel tracks.

Outside, the three warring currents took turns broadsiding the vehicle, each attack nearly knocking the evergreens off their feet. At the point of the wind's impact, the wall of the Tree RV bowed inward, cramping the space inside. Like a child's finger poking at the side of her prize goldfish's plastic bag, the three captives felt equally vulnerable toward the prodding wind. There was no cover to be found, only courage against a hostile foe. But at the center of chaos, the best they could do was hold on tight. While Albert feverishly worked the controls, the others wrapped their fingers around the interlacing branches of the floor, trying to remain stationary in a pitching and heaving room.

The cliff face was now a vertical rockslide where once the ridgeline had proceeded horizontally. At some point in its tragic history, this part of Windermere Sheer had decided to simply let go and take its chances with the sea. Every bush and shrub had been laid flat and twisted into grotesque shapes, like a ribbon curled by the blade of a knife. The scar left behind by the ancient rockslide had never healed.

Albert's trees were now forced to clamber over the fallen stones on their hands and knees. Searching every crack and crevice for a fingerhold, the evergreens maintained as much contact with the wall of limestone as they could. At times, the hurricane-force winds struck the rocks out from underneath them, sending the Tree RV sliding down toward the ravenous sea below. At other times, the best the trees could do was to press their collective bodies against the cliff face, offering as little relief for the relentless winds to take hold of as possible. From a distance, the journey of Prume's Wile across the angry face of Windermere Sheer must have looked like the death throes of a wounded spider on a wall.

With every assault of the currents, more and more leaves were being plucked from the evergreen's branches. A cyclone of green swirled in the air above Prume's Wile, like a flurry of monochromatic butterflies. Little by little, the Tree RV's outer defenses had been stripped away, allowing the wind to wind its claws around the rafters and throttle the evergreens without mercy. Soon, everyone inside was exposed to the full fury of the Sheer.

Edward pushed Annelyse up against Willemina's side, while the Woolem turned her body windward as a screen against the elements. Albert secured himself to the command console using a length of rope around his waist, his hands a blur of activity. It was essential that he remain at his post, though wind and gravity try to dislodge him.

Without the cover of leaves, its occupants could clearly see what was taking place all around them. On their left, a swift tumble down the cliff and into the rocky jaws of the sea, the prospect of which appeared more appealing with the passing of time. The undulation of the waves had become hypnotic, and the sea seemed to whisper temptation in their ears. "Let go, fall freely, I will catch you," came the seductive call. In the deep trench of their turbulent exhaustion, even madness such as this began to make sense.

On the starboard side of the Tree RV, the open sky frowned upon the brazen climbers with disapproval. They were as off-kilter as a tacking catamaran. Indeed, all of Albert's belongings were, once again, in jeopardy of being lost, having slid up against the seaward wall of the Wile. With the increasing exertions of every root, branch, and limb, the tight weaving of the walls was unraveling. The fist of evergreens was opening against its will.

A hail of stones, picked up and thrown like buckshot through the open spaces of the RV by the vicious wind, cut the faces of everyone inside. Embedding itself in the Woolem's wool, the jagged debris irritated Willemina's sensitive skin, causing her to scratch herself raw. Annelyse felt as if she were back among the giant mosquitos of Culicidan Cave. The barrage was inescapable.

Like a sandstorm in the desert, the tiny shards of shrapnel even wore away the lacquer from the furniture

Albert's father had made with his own hands. Nothing that presented a surface against which the fragments might collide was immune. But the cloud of stinging pain in which they found themselves now blinded everyone to the presence of a new, more deadly danger.

Without a single leaf remaining on the Tree RV's branches, their protective camouflage was entirely gone. Alone and exposed on the back of the bare rockslide, Albert, Edward, Annelyse, and Willemina had become easy targets for a skilled hunter. Their predicament required that they give up stealth and speed in exchange for caution. But their slow-going had given their pursuer the upper hand. Now, standing only a few feet away from Albert, Gyilkos had once again tracked them down. The wicked beast had vaulted across the rockface and squirmed in between the loosening branches of the Tree RV. With his teeth bared, he snarled slavering hatred, a green fire in his eyes, dead set on his murderous purpose.

"Albert!" Annelyse cried, alerting their guide to the presence of the hunter's dog.

"You, again!" Albert fumed, one eye on the control panel and the other on Gyilkos.

But before another word was spoken, Edward Bellamy grabbed the umbrella from the bin by the front door and lunged toward the beast. Wielding the ragged weapon like a club, Edward landed a blow across the dog's back, collapsing its hind legs, and knocking the breath from its lungs. The great tracker had been caught off guard.

Edward stood between Albert and Gyilkos, ready to defend the kindly little man to the death, if necessary. Gyilkos was more than happy to oblige. Righting himself, the animal leapt toward Edward, landing both front paws on the man's chest.

Instead of pinning him to the ground, as he'd done when first they'd met, Gyilkos sank his claws deep into Edward's flesh, letting the full weight of his vile body drag him to the floor at Edward's feet. The gaping tracks of the dog's sharp nails burst forth in a spurt of bloody agony. Collapsing to the floor in a blinding flash of pain, Edward Bellamy lost consciousness.

It was now up to the Woolem to step into the breach left by her friend. She did not hesitate a moment. Pulling herself up to her full stature, Willemina towered over the lithe body of the hunter's mutt, ready to make her move. Faster and nimbler than the gentle Woolem, Gyilkos took a calculated risk, and leapt straight for Willemina's face. Had he been a bit slower to act, the mighty Woolem could easily have subdued the dog with one, massive foot. But, seizing the advantage, the beast clamped its jaws like a vice across the Woolem's face. Unable to open her mouth or free her nose from her enemy's grip, Willemina struggled for breath.

Throwing her enormous head from side to side, in an effort to shake loose her attacker, the Woolem staggered like a tree ready to fall. Gyilkos tightened his hold on the now lightheaded Willemina's snout, determined to suffocate his prey to death. A Woolem would make a fine feast for any predator.

From behind Willemina, Annelyse grabbed anything she could find at hand, hurling it at the dog, to no effect. The flailing Woolem made it difficult to strike her foe while leaving her friend unharmed. Annelyse was utterly unable to help.

At the control panel, Albert remained focused on the treacherous climb being executed outside. Glancing back over his shoulder, he was also aware of the struggles going on around him. Abandoning the controls would mean a perilous fall and certain death to all inside the Tree RV. But, as he'd proven before in the past, Albert Prume, when firmly at the helm of his grand evergreen trees, was a force to be reckoned with.

Reaching over with his right hand, he took hold of a joystick not far from the center of the console. With a sweep of his wrist and a flourish of the stick, Albert commanded the same two tree limbs that had reached out and pulled Annelyse, Edward, and Willemina into the safe embrace of the Wile – and away from the hunter's dog – to pick the wicked creature up bodily.

Yelping with alarm, Gyilkos squirmed against the grasp of the branches, to no avail. Had they wanted to, the powerful limbs could have squashed the creature like an over-ripe banana. Instead, they heaved the infernal animal out onto the near-vertical face of the rockslide. Unable to catch his footing at first, Gyilkos slid a dozen or more feet before digging his claws into the loose stone. Panting and straining for a better toehold, the dog stood splayed out against the rock wall, partially obscured in a cloud of dust.

Three hundred feet below, the Great Sault Sea surged with ravenous anticipation, eager to learn the fate of the hunter's dog. It didn't have long to wait for, just then, like some sort of divine retribution, the entire mass of the once-stationary rockslide began to shift.

All at once, the stones below where Albert Prume's Tree RV stood clinging to the wall gave way and slid like a solitary sheet of ice into the frothing sea below. The flattened shrubs and twisted bushes, the wind-eaten rocks and white-faced limestone, everything - including Gyilkos, the best tracker north of the Miralette - slipped beneath the surface of the waves never to be seen again. In a great gurgling gulp of foam, the sea swallowed what the earth had cast aside.

Without missing a beat, Albert released the joystick, and turned his full attention back to piloting his trees across what remained of the cliff face. Time was more pressing than ever before since the entire field of stones and boulders had become unstable. He had to usher his exceptional trees to the relative safety of the ridgeline above as quickly as their roots could take them.

While Albert kept busy, Annelyse tended to Willemina's wounds. Her face had been punctured in several places by the teeth of the hunter's dog. The deep crimson of the Woolem's blood trickled down the innocent creature's face. More distressing, the Woolem was having difficulty breathing. Whether from her injuries or from the stress of the attack, Willemina was badly shaken. All Annelyse could do was clean the Woolem's wounds and sooth her nerves with kindness.

Before Annelyse could turn her attention to her father, Edward revived on his own. His first conscious moments brought with them a flood of anguish and the reminder of the gashes still bleeding on his chest. These were but the latest in a collection of injuries he had endured in the brief time since leaving his little cabin by the sea.

He would never forget his first encounter with Annelyse's mysterious abductor and the kick he received at fireside, resulting in a cut in his forehead. Nor would he forget the burning of Gyilkos' teeth as they pierced the muscle of his thigh. These wounds, and the latest ones - which ran in two unbroken lines from his collar bones down to his navel - would be forever carved into his flesh.

"What happened?" Edward asked, struggling to his feet.

Albert Prume shot a mischievous look over his right shoulder, answering, "The dunter's hog left unexpectedly. He will not be returning."

Turning to his daughter for clarification, Annelyse cocked her head in the direction of the sea, her eyes wide with silent explanation. Edward caught her meaning, a wave of relief washing through his anxious mind.

"Almost there," Albert called. "Now, to find the way down..."

"Down?" Annelyse asked, shouting over the whine of the wind as it whipped around obstacles and slithered through cracks in the branches.

"Down through the Sheer and onto the plain," Albert replied. "But I could use a Woolem's help," he added.

Willemina lifted her head, still laboring to breathe. Annelyse had been snuggling and reassuring the Woolem in an effort to calm her. But at the mention of "a Woolem's help," the selfless heart of the sweet creature turned from her own troubles to the needs of her friends. She knew the way down from the heights of the Sheer and onto the Plain of Windermere. She would guide them.

Taking her place beside Albert at the control console, Willemina scanned their surroundings through the command porthole. She was looking for the most subtle of signs; a sign that marked what could only be seen by friendly eyes; a sign so easily missed that only a Woolem might notice it.

All around them the cliff face was crumbling and sliding into the sea. The avalanche triggered by the hunter's dog had set off a chain reaction. Everything was in a state of collapse. It was only Albert's steady hand that had managed to navigate the Tree RV to higher ground above the immediate danger. But, even now, the ridgeline they had mounted was beginning to disintegrate. They needed to get off the Sheer before suffering the same fate as Gyilkos.

In an uncharacteristic show of excitement, Willemina called out, "There!" motioning with her front leg in the direction of a large outcropping of boulders.

"Well spotted!" Albert said turning the evergreens toward the berm.

Much like every other pile of stones on the rockface, the outcropping was unremarkable to the casual observer. But, to the Woolem, it meant hope. This was the way off the perilous Sheer and down to the protection of the plains below. This was the way home.

Albert Prume seemed to recognize the outcropping, too. The moment Willemina pointed it out to him, he knew what to do. He'd been here before. He'd taken this path, long ago, and the Woolem knew it. There was more at work between Albert and Willemina than they let on. There was a story to be told, here; but it would have to wait. For now, their sole task was to get everyone to safety.

With the wild winds still throttling the bare evergreen branches, Albert did his best to position the Tree RV on the leeward side of the immense boulders. This provided some shelter from the direct buffeting, though the swirling breezes caught up among the stones still wreaked havoc wherever they could.

The side of the outcropping facing the cliff wall revealed an unexpected feature. Three separate piles of boulders, as tall and wide as a Woolem, sat - as if stacked with a purpose - behind the berm.

"Must choose," Willemina said.

"Choose what?" Annelyse asked, "A pile of rocks?"

"Doorway," came the Woolem's answer.

Albert now chimed in, "Right you are, my dear! But this is where I fet a little guzzy… let a gittle fuzzy… need your expertise. I've forgotten which one it is."

Inspecting the cairns closely, Annelyse spied something striking. Atop the middle pile of boulders, sat a small, round, yellow rock around which smaller, white stones radiated like the rays of the sun. The arrangement was no larger than the palm of her hand and, yet, to Annelyse it bore great significance.

"Look!" she cried to the others. "It's a daisy… made of stones."

"Middle pile," Willemina added, as if to affirm that the stone daisy had been placed in the right spot.

"Of course!" Albert exclaimed. "The wise man finds the middle course!"

"It helps that it's marked! I guess even a wise man needs a hand." Annelyse added, with an ounce of sass. "Now what?"

"Open the door," Willemina responded.

Stepping outside the Tree RV, the Woolem approached the three piles of boulders concealed behind the outcropping. Thinking they might be of help, Edward and Annelyse followed, while Albert remained at the controls. The wind and the shifting stones still made it necessary for Albert to react to the changing conditions. Abandoning his post would be tantamount to abandoning his evergreens to the whims of Windermere Sheer. Nothing good could come of such a situation.

Willemina began dismantling the middle pile of rocks, using her powerful legs to push the enormous boulders aside. Annelyse quickly surmised that she would be of little help to the great Woolem and decided to sit down on the first cairn in the line of three.

"No," Willemina said with great insistence. "Must not touch other piles. Too dangerous."

Annelyse hopped down without hesitation but not without question.

"How are the other piles dangerous?" she asked.

"Long falls through darkness. Sharp rocks and waves. Too dangerous. Must not touch other piles."

Annelyse's curiosity was satisfied for the time being. Of course, it might have been that her inquisitive mind was simply distracted by what was happening with the middle pile. Willemina had been laboring for a quarter of an hour, knocking boulders off the pile with a thunderous thud, then pushing them off to the side. As she worked to clear away the tremendous stones, things started to come into focus for Annelyse.

Where once it had lain hidden by a blockade of boulders, a cavern now opened up, hewn from the rockface by the strength of mighty hands. The entrance to the cave was large enough to accommodate a Woolem. The floor appeared to proceed horizontally for only a few feet before plunging at a steep angle down into the darkness.

What caught Edward's attention were the walls of the tunnel. The sides, floor, and even the ceiling were all as smooth as if they'd been polished. Like the tunnel walls of a groundhog's home, these surfaces appeared to have been formed and refined by the frequent passage of some huge creature.

"Door open, now," Willemina said, as she removed the last of the boulders. "Willemina first. Better that way," she added, and then, without explanation, the Woolem stepped inside the opening and disappeared from view.

From inside the Tree RV, the voice of Albert Prume called out to Edward and Annelyse, "You're next, you two!"

"What about you and the trees?" Edward inquired.

"We'll be along. But you, first."

Taking hold of Annelyse's hand, Edward led her inside the cave. Immediately upon entering, they both lunged forward with a jerk. They hadn't realized it, but they'd been straining their stance against the wind for some time, now. The sudden absence of the battering breezes was like the unexpected disappearance of a wall they'd been leaning against.

The new silence weighed heavily upon their fatigued ears. They'd grown accustomed to the round, howling throat of the wind so that the quiet inside the cave felt quite as tangible as if they'd been wearing a pair of earmuffs. The only sound they could hear was that of an elongated emptiness, like the breath of the sea echoing inside a conch shell.

The entrance to the cave was only a few feet away from daylight, so both Edward and Annelyse were able to see just fine. For her part, Annelyse wished it had been as dark as it had been inside the Mosquito Cave. For, there at her feet lay their next task. Oh, that she had simply stepped inside and fallen unawares down the black hole staring up at her. As it was, she knew precisely what her father was about to do, and the thought of it terrified her.

"Hold onto my hand, Leesy," Edward said. "All will be well."

With that, Edward Bellamy leapt, feet first, into the unknown, taking Annelyse with him.

They both hit the tunnel floor on their backsides and, instinctively, tucked their heads down and their knees up, wrapping their arms around their legs. Annelyse held tightly to her father's hand, hugging her updrawn knees with one arm, her face buried between them. It didn't matter if she kept her eyes open or closed, the tunnel was the very definition of blindness. But with her eyes closed, Annelyse felt less able to imagine her surroundings, so closed they remained.

The second their backsides met the tunnel floor they were in motion. Faster and faster, the floor fell away beneath them. Only in the places where gravity momentarily outstripped momentum did Annelyse and Edward feel the tunnel pushing back on them. The sensation was that of a vertical drop endured from a seated position. They could neither anticipate nor control their descent. They were tangled up in a helpless freefall and there was no end to be seen.

Until, after an eternity of weightlessness, gravity finally took over; their bodies once again had mass; and Annelyse and Edward found the bottom of the tunnel – or rather the bottom of the tunnel found their bottoms. But it was not at all as they'd expected. Indeed, their downward momentum was arrested in the softest way possible.

With a noise like that of a sighing cloud taking its ease, Annelyse and Edward sank into a fragrant bed of curly locks. The warm embrace in which they had landed wrapped its arms around them both and drew them into precisely the sort of reassurance they needed. They had traveled some two-hundred and fifty feet - at times falling, at times sliding – right into the waiting arms of a Woolem.

"Willemina first," she whispered in the dark. "Better that way."

Annelyse threw her arms around her friend, inhaling the sweet scent of wildflowers that had become synonymous with Willemina.

"Better for us," Annelyse said with a smile. "But are you ok?"

"Willemina strong. Willemina plushy, too," the Woolem chuckled.

"And I'm grateful for both," Edward added.

"Must get up now. Must make room for trees," Willemina said, as she ushered Edward and Annelyse out of the way.

From two-hundred and fifty feet above their heads, a yell could be heard like the battle cry of a maniac mercenary.

"Yippeee!" it echoed in the darkness, followed by what Annelyse later described as the sound of the wind slipping on a banana peel.

Like a subway car made of tree branches, Albert Prume's Tree RV descended through the tunnel, scraping the walls with its limbs as it went. At the helm, Albert squealed with delight, his childlike heart reveling in the excitement of unbridled speed.

Just before reaching the bottom, the evergreens expanded like an overheated piston in an engine cylinder, slowing the vehicle to a gentle halt.

"Fantastical!" Albert exclaimed. "That never gets old! Nope, nope, nope! Never!"

"You've done this before?" Annelyse asked with surprise.

"Oh yes, my dear. Many times, but long ago - oh yes, oh yes - long, long ago."

"So, where do the other doors lead?" Annelyse asked, referring to the two untouched piles of boulders.

"No place half as nice as this," Albert assured her. "Sea Chutes, they're called. Safe name for dangerous drops, I call it. But, thanks to your sharp eye in spotting the stone daisy, we chose the right tunnel!"

"Middle way is the right way," Willemina confirmed.

"Inbubid… indudibib… indubitably! But I'll take the sun on my face over a musty old cavern any day. All aboard and out we go!"

The Tree RV drew itself up and took on its old familiar shape, even if it was entirely leafless. Everyone climbed inside and, with Albert at the controls, the stand of five, forty-foot-tall evergreen trees made its way down another short passageway and into the light of day.

Even though they'd spent only a few minutes wrapped in darkness, their eyes were ill-prepared for the bright glare of daylight. Even less prepared were Edward and Annelyse for the drastic change in landscape. Exiting the tunnel, the travelers set foot upon the Plain of Windermere at last.

At their backs, the great Wall of Windermere Sheer held the tumultuous winds at bay so that only a soft breeze now caressed their faces from the east. Behind them, the cliffs through which they had descended sloped up toward the ridgeline, two-hundred and fifty feet above where they stood. A blanket of green lay across the feet of the Sheer, becoming bare stone halfway to the summit. It looked like a dam of enormous size being slowly reclaimed by the lush, green plain.

On the other side of the wall, the Spire of Lament, like the steeple of a great cathedral, rose from the unseen ocean. A watchtower battlement could not have been more imposing or encouraged greater assurance.

There was a sense that they were standing within a safe haven. All the natural barriers through which they had just passed seemed to have been constructed for the sole purpose of guarding this place, and deterring others from finding, entering, and spoiling such a paradise.

Streams and pools of clear water shone in the afternoon sun. Tufts of tall grass sprung from the ground all around them like accents in an ornamental garden. Rabbits and squirrels, birds and chipmunks tended to their homes and gathered food from the rich stores of the fertile grasslands. Wildflowers of every color and kind dotted the landscape like hard candy spilled across a carpet of green. Behind the walls of watchful refuge, all living things flourished. Shielded from the discord of a belligerent world, harmony finds its voice.

Edward and Annelyse had found something, too: a second Averlune, a land of tranquility, an untouched utopia where kindness was first nature and cruelty had not yet been learned. The Plain of Windermere was as unlike Windermere Sheer as love is from hatred, as joy is from grief. They would soon come face-to-face with all four within and without themselves, as all must do. Where better to confront such things than in paradise?

A short distance away from where Annelyse, Edward, Willemina, and Prume's Wile now stood, a garden path presented itself among the clumps of pampas grass and cattails. Meandering lazily to the left, before drifting back toward the right, the path had no particular destination in mind.

About forty feet down the ambling garden lane, on a boulder beside a stony brook, there sat a young man, his back to the newcomers. In his hand, he held a pencil. On his knee, a leather-bound journal lay open. Annelyse was the first to spy the young man and, running to meet him, she wrapped her arms around his neck in joyful recognition.

Laughing to be greeted in such a way, the young man looked up at Annelyse and softly whispered, "There you are."

No More-Foreign Country

The young man had a knack for being present. And whenever he *was* present, he was present without reserve. He arrived without notice before he was needed, and he departed in silence the moment his task was complete. He was adept at attentive, skilled in silence. It could be said that he spent himself on everyone he encountered, and he only encountered those in need. There was joy in his heart and gravity in his eyes, and from both sprung a kind compassion that enriched those he met.

He rarely spoke above a pensive whisper, but every word was buttressed by confidence. If his ways were veiled in mystery, it was the mystery of one who seeks to be unseen so as not to distract from that which is important. And what was important to the young poet was love; loyalty; the keeping of promises; the righting of wrongs; living at one with all things; and these characteristics defined him truly.

Though a man in his mid-thirties, there was a youthful quality about him. Virtue often clothes the virtuous in timelessness. A life lived with simplicity and detachment from frivolous distractions had sharpened his purpose and softened all his edges. He was kind, but he was no fool. He was understanding, but he maintained high standards for himself. Above all, he was loyal and committed to his family and friends. For, in his youth, his actions had been twisted into a grave injustice, and he would not rest until that wrong had been set right.

Annelyse Bellamy had never met anyone like this young man and, still, the suspicion she'd felt at their first meeting crept into her heart once more. He reminded her of someone she knew well. She just couldn't remember who.

"Here I am," she said in response to his usual greeting. "Right where you led me."

"Your journey to this place began long before you were born, child," the poet said with a smile to reveal nothing.

Annelyse was not ten seconds into her reunion with the Poet of Perigoh and, already, he was speaking in riddles. But she was overjoyed to see the young man, as if he were a tiny piece of Averlune, a little reminder of home come to encourage her after their daunting trek across Windermere Sheer.

Ever since their meeting on Ruhner's Beach, Annelyse had felt a connection with the young man, made stronger by the little helps he'd sprinkled along their way.

It was his words that had opened her mind to the mysteries in her mother's life. It was his poem that had first suggested the existence of Woolems. So far, everything he'd said had proven to be true. Annelyse was certain that what remained of his clues and riddles would soon be explained.

Edward drew up behind Annelyse. Raising her head, she watched with apprehension, unable to read her father's expression. Edward Bellamy had shown nothing but contempt for the young man, in all his prior conversations with Annelyse. She had no reason to believe that this unexpected meeting would be any different. Steeling herself against what was sure to be an unpleasant experience, Annelyse held her breath.

Seeing Edward approach, the poet stood to face him, equally apprehensive as Annelyse and ready for the worst. Stopping in front of the young man, Edward's eyes softened as he reached out with both arms and pulled the poet into an embrace. Annelyse's mouth fell open, as confusion muddled her freckled face. Her father's reaction to the man was just plain inscrutable. After a moment, Edward stepped back, his hand still resting on the young man's arm.

"What is going on here?!" Annelyse demanded, convinced that an explanation was in order.

Edward squeezed the poet's arm, then turned to Annelyse, saying, "How else should I greet your uncle?"

With a wink, Edward said no more, leaving Annelyse more befuddled than ever. Seething with indignation, she readied a string of questions like a barrage of mortar shells aimed straight for her father. But before she was able to launch her first volley, Willemina and Albert Prume joined the others.

"Hello, old friend," the poet said, caressing Willemina's injured face with concern. "I see Giuseppe's dog caught up with you."

"Aye, and the Sheer dispatched him to the sea," came Albert's unapologetic reply.

"Poor soul," the poet said with sympathy, "I can't help but think that his fate would have been quite different with a gentler master."

"Should've kept better company, for sure," Albert agreed.

"And how are you, Mr. Prume?" the poet asked, extending his hand.

"Bever netter, but for the loss of a lew feaves," he replied, motioning to his bare-branched Tree RV. "It's good to see you again, young sir!"

"Stop! Wait one minute!" Annelyse commanded. "You *all* know each other? And you," she now directed her impertinence at the young man, "You're my *uncle*?! *How* are you my uncle?! Somebody had better tell me what's happening around here, or I'll…"

"Mind your manners, Leesy," Edward cautioned preemptively. He knew well where his daughter's current tone of voice was headed.

"May I?" the poet asked of Edward who nodded with gratitude burdened by exhaustion. He was too tired to wrangle with his daughter alone.

The young man spoke to Annelyse, "Your mother was my sister. Beyond that, all will be explained soon, child," he said touching her on the arm. "I promise. But first," he said, addressing the others, "The evening wanes. May I invite you all to pass the night under my roof?"

"Delightful!" Albert exclaimed, hopping aboard his wandering treehouse. "Lead the way!"

With a bow, the young man bid the company follow him a bit further. The grass upon which they now walked was trimmed close to the ground and provided a spongy cushion, in contrast to the harsh, shifting stones of the Sheer. On either side of the path, tufted pampas grass rose in tall festoons out of the bare earth. Beds of white, pink, and purple flowers lounged in shapeless leisure around the feet of maple trees, their leaves casting trembling shadows on the petals below. Scattered like centerpieces of ornate silver at a garden party, ponds and trickling fountains reflected the orange of the sky with impressionist subtlety. The air itself sparkled with a million colors.

Blooming well out of season, fruit trees, berry brambles, and sunflowers – all heavily laden and irresistible - swam with activity. Annelyse imagined that there wasn't a bird, bee, chipmunk, or squirrel within miles of this peaceful place who ever went hungry. Everything appeared to have been cultivated with care. In fact, the farther they walked, the more the meadow looked like someone's well-sculpted backyard.

The walkers now approached a large garden surrounded by a border of oyster shells. Shrubs, like heaps of campfire coals, throbbed red in the diffuse light of evening. Bee balm of various colors and fragrances leapt up from the black soil like fireworks on the Fourth of July. Beans and peas, trained along trellises of rough-hewn tree limbs, wound themselves around every available branch. Tomato, squash, zucchini, and pepper plants stood in long queues, their joyful leaves bobbing in the gentle breeze. This was a paradise lost, a forgotten Eden, a secret long held by a chosen few.

Hidden in among the flowers, trees, and vegetables, stacks of wooden boxes buzzed with productivity as, inside, nectar was fanned into honey by the wings of brilliant bees. A perfect balance had been reached between work and play, and even the smallest insect benefited from the great partnership of all living things.

Not an inch of space was wasted. All was being put to good use; all was flourishing. And yet, there was no stench of mechanization, no scowl of industry. In this place, there was only the fruitfulness of care, and bountiful profit beyond all accounting.

In the middle of the garden beside a small lake, a glass bubble - no bigger than a shed - sat glistening in the green grass. Though slightly elongated in shape, the see-through shed was circular enough to be entirely without corners. Where the various panels of glass met, seamless, rounded edges preserved the overall impression that the tiny house was little more than an enormous, somewhat oblong raindrop.

On one side, a curved, glass door sat open to the dewy night air. It was to this door that the poet now led his friends. While Albert parked his wandering stand of evergreens, Edward and Annelyse examined the wonder of the raindrop house.

"Willemina stay here," the Woolem said, assuming her host meant to invite her inside his too-tiny home, too. "Willemina like the stars."

"I know you do, my friend. May I do anything for your comfort?"

Settling herself into a thick patch of knee-high grass beneath the boughs of Albert's Tree RV, the Woolem thought a moment, then replied, "Leave door open? Willemina likes poet's stories, too."

"My door is always open to you, kind heart. You will hear our voices for companionship. Rest yourself a while and eat whatever suits your taste." Leading the way through his front door, the poet smiled, saying, "Welcome, friends. My home is honored by your presence."

Annelyse followed her father and Albert Prume through the open door. Upon entering, they found themselves in a room without obvious purpose. Attached to the opposite glass wall, a small shelf with a wash basin and terra cotta pitcher seemed to float in mid-air. Next to that, there stood the only piece of furniture in sight. An old, worn wooden table with two, mismatched, three-legged stools languished in the rounded corner. There were no couches, no armchairs, no armoires, or benches. There wasn't even a larder or sink. In fact, the room in which Annelyse was standing was the only room on the ground level, and it seemed to serve as both kitchen and living room, though without the usual identifying accoutrements.

"Make yourselves comfortable anywhere you like," the young man announced.

"Comfortable?" Annelyse began. "Where's all your stuff?! Where's your living room? Your kitchen? Where are your comfy chairs?!"

"There are some seats there," the poet replied, pointing toward the mismatched stools. "Feel free to put them where you like."

"You do live here, right?" she asked with lightly veiled sarcasm.

"As much as anywhere," the man affirmed.

"How can you live without things?!"

"Far better than with them, I find."

"But you've got to own *somethings*!" Annelyse objected, trying to wrap her head around the poet's unusual austerity.

"No one ever owns anything," came the strange reply. "We can use things, but the moment we try to own them they start to own us."

Annelyse stared back with blank perplexity.

"Joy weighs nothing, child. It is free and unencumbered. But the moment we attach our joy to things, those things begin to weigh us down. Our freedom is hampered, our joy dissolves into cares and worries and obsessions. If we want to be joyful, we must say no to things, attachments, even ourselves often."

"It doesn't feel very joyful when Dad tells me no," Annelyse countered.

"That's because you have not yet learned this truth. Your father is not saying no to you. He is teaching you to say no to yourself, and there is no greater kindness than to teach another the way to happiness."

"But it *doesn't* make me happy when I have to do what I don't want to do. It must be like that for everyone," Annelyse was sure that the young man must be wrong this time.

"Nothing worth having has ever been achieved by only ever doing what you want. An athlete achieves victory only after much self-denial. Your victory must be the achievement of joy, and so you must learn to deny yourself all the many things that do not bring you joy. Everything I do not have in this house I do not have in my heart. But what I do find in this house, fills my heart to overflowing. Things clutter, joy expands. And I would gladly give the greatest possession to be possessed of joy."

To Annelyse, this – like much of what she'd heard from the poet – made no sense. But the proof was in his eyes, in his contentment, in his heart. He was a joyful soul, and he owned – or rather *was* owned by - nothing at all. Maybe there was something to this notion.

"While you rest, I'll gather some dinner for us," the poet announced. And with that, he took his leave.

As Edward and Albert busied themselves laying out blankets from the Tree RV and sleeping bags from the Bellamy's backpacks, Annelyse explored the uncluttered raindrop home of her newfound uncle.

There was little to discover beyond what she had already seen. No doors to open, no knickknacks, or photographs, only the one empty room in which her father and Albert labored to bring some comfort. There was, however, one new feature that had previously gone overlooked. A stairwell, in the far end of the room, descended almost vertically into what must surely have been a basement or root cellar. Perhaps this was where her uncle kept all his belongings.

Annelyse was reluctant to press her newly discovered relative status, so she did not dare explore this latest mystery without permission. But, standing at the top of the stairs, she peered down into the darkness at her feet, imagining what she might find below.

Maybe there were big beds overflowing with pillows, or larders bursting with hams, blocks of cheese, and homemade pies. Maybe the room in which she was now standing was just the entryway, and the real house – with all its creature comforts – was down below. She'd been far too uncomfortable and hungry for far too long, and it was beginning to weigh heavily on her body and her imagination.

Just then, Annelyse's uncle returned, his arms overflowing with fruits and vegetables from his gardens. Placing his burden on the wooden table, he noticed Annelyse in the back of the room and joined her.

"Curious, isn't it?" he asked, with a sly grin.

"Mm hm," Annelyse replied, trying not to appear too eager.

"Help me with the food and I'll show you."

Letting go of all restraint, Annelyse ran to the wooden table, picked up as much as she could carry, and returned before her uncle had time to react.

"All set!" she said.

"Indeed, you are." Calling to the others, the young man invited them to, "Please, join us."

Pausing at the top of the stairs, the poet turned to Annelyse and said, "Now you will have your answers, dear niece. Come."

Descending the steep, unlit staircase, Annelyse could barely see the pile of produce in her own arms. But, as she reached the bottom step, her eyes adjusted to the change. Immediately, she was struck by something odd. Though subdued, it was brighter down below than it should be. A light, like liquid starlight or the moon dissolved in a glass of water, drenched the subterranean room in a soft glow.

Having walked further than the width of the upper room, Annelyse could tell that they were not directly beneath the area in which their sleeping bags now lay. The basement was twice as large, and more rectangular than circular. What was more, Annelyse saw that the entire ceiling of the basement was made of glass.

Shining down through the roof, Annelyse could see the moon and stars and even the pulsing of fireflies from the gardens. The room was flooded with the same pale yellows and whites as the world above. Yet, everything she saw appeared to be somehow distorted.

Apart from the glass ceiling, this second room was as empty as the first, except for the presence of a small bookcase beside which sat a tattered, old armchair. On the shelves, dozens of leatherbound journals were stacked without any obvious system of organization. Across the back of the chair, a blanket of greens and oranges was draped, the weave of which was familiar to Edward's eyes.

"Halla made that, didn't she?" Edward asked.

"She did," the young man replied. "She is ever solicitous for my comfort, both bodily and otherwise. It's my writing blanket. I throw it over my legs when I write, and I always think of her sweetness."

"Why does the light swim so?" Annelyse asked, changing the subject while staring up at the ceiling, lost in thought.

"An excellent choice of description," the poet said, squatting down beside his niece. "That's exactly what it does. The light swims."

"I don't understand," Annelyse complained, twirling one strand of hair between her thumb and forefinger, still gazing upward.

"The head knows, but only the heart understands," her uncle whispered to her.

"That's what Halla said," Edward said in surprise. "She said the same thing to me."

"Who's Halla?" Annelyse asked, having heard the name twice now.

"She is the *one who knows,*" the poet replied, quoting his own poem.

"*... found along the Maidenhair...*" Annelyse replied, completing the line. "And you found her?" she asked, looking wide-eyed at her father.

"I did. And because of her, I found you."

Annelyse had descended the stairs with her arms loaded down with vegetables and her head overflowing with questions. She was adding more questions by the minute, too many to sort out in her own mind. She must take them as they chose to come.

Returning to her first inquiry, Annelyse repeated her question, "But *how* does the light swim?"

"The same way you or I would. It dips its toes in the water, decides it's safe to go in, then plunges headfirst into the depths."

"I still don't get it," Annelyse said, with some degree of annoyance.

"Did you notice the small lake at the center of the garden?"

"Yes."

"Good. So, now, the head knows. But what does your heart understand?"

Annelyse looked up at the transparent ceiling. She could see the moon rippling as if reflected on the surface of a pond. Its frail, white light spread out like a drop of oil on the waters of a windy lake. Each star, less like a pinprick and more like a tear in the fabric of the sky, stained the ceiling the color of buttercups in the rain.

The whole room fluttered in a wavy sea of luminous shadows, like the slow-moving ghosts of a school of fish meandering across the featureless walls and black, slate floor. Above them, held aloft by the ceiling of glass, the garden lake filtered the moonlight in an undulating arrhythmia of pearl white and translucent blue. Annelyse, Edward, Albert, and the poet stood gazing up at the silent night sky through the thin glass and crystal waters of the lake.

All at once, a feeling of dread overtook Annelyse. A chill slithered up her spine. She was certain that the ceiling would give way and the entire contents of the garden lake – water, fish, cattails, and crawfish – would coming crashing down upon her head. Her uncle noticed her cowering and moved to reassure her.

"Don't be afraid. New and strange are not always to be feared. I was once a stranger to you, myself. Though I have known you always. Did you fear *me*?"

"Tell me," Annelyse asked, with pleading in her eyes. "Please tell me about my mother."

The mention of her mother made Annelyse's voice falter. From the time she and her father had stepped foot outside the front door of their little cabin by the sea, she had hardly had time to turn her thoughts to her mother. The last time she had spoken of Silloah was after her nightmare beside the campfire. That was days ago, and now - in this moment of quiet, in this place of safety – the full fathomless terror of her grief flooded her heart once more. A tear escaped the corner of her eye, setting off an avalanche of emotion which threatened to carry her over the abyss much like the rockslide had overwhelmed the hunter's dog. At the sudden appearance of her old enemy, Grief, Annelyse responded with fear. For grief is a kind of madness, and there is nothing more frightening than discovering madness in oneself.

The poet wrapped his arms around his niece's shoulders, guiding her forehead down onto his chest.

"Let it wash through you, child," he said. "We cannot ford these rapids. We cannot avoid the whirlpool for long. Sooner or later, we must dive beneath the surface and swim through the black waters of grief to see what we can salvage. There is no other way."

"I need to know," Annelyse said, through her tears. "I followed the poem. I found the truth about the Woolems. But I need to know my own story."

"Yes. And I will tell you."

Sitting beneath the watery skylight, Annelyse pulled the poet's green and orange blanket of Woolem wool up under her chin. Beside her, Edward spread the food out within reach of everyone. In the tattered, old armchair, the lumpy, overall-clad Albert Prume sat like a burlap sack of overripe watermelons. His red face and white, unkempt hair glowed in the moonlight. Outside, within earshot of the open door, Willemina slept beneath the stars. She already knew the story the Poet of Perigoh was about to recount. Indeed, she had played her own part in the tale long ago.

The young man reclined on the floor in front of Annelyse and Edward, his blue eyes at home beneath the waters of the garden lake. With a long sigh, he began to speak.

"Your mother was a beautiful child. Though five years my senior, by the time I was old enough to know anything, I knew this truth beyond a doubt. Our parents, your grandparents, recognized it, too. From an early age, Silloah would wander the wildflower meadows and cow paths around our home in Averlune, singing to every living thing she encountered. The birds and animals saw in her a kindred spirit, a generous soul.

"It was she who first began collecting stories of the old days. *The Tale of Trinket Trove,* the story of Ruhner's Beach, all of it, she discovered on her own. When I was old enough, she shared them with me. I would never have written a single rhyme of poetry without my sweet sister's influence. She set my mind ablaze with words.

"From the glens of Goughlin Grugh to the heaths of Hyland and Orchard Knoll, wherever our parents visited with us, Silloah made new friends. The wild horses, the sleeping quail, even the dolphins of the Perigoh Fair, her gentle heart charmed them all. But none so much as the gentlest hearts ever made. The Woolems of the Greenfields.

"Your mother loved the Woolems. Even as a little girl, every drawing or fingerpainting she made was of a Woolem."

Edward reached into his backpack and pulled out the gift Halla had given him. Handing it to his daughter, he nodded.

"This?" she asked.

"Yes," her father replied.

"Kept for you for all these years by Halla," the poet affirmed. "A good and loving friend and the keeper of all memories."

Annelyse caressed the little painting in her hands, tracing the maiden name of Silloah Uhl with her finger, much as her father had done.

"So, when the pirates of the Isles of Wanton raided the Greenfields and kidnapped the Woolems, your mother and I knew we had to do whatever we could to save them. We joined the group of rescuers known as *The Ransom…*"

Albert Prume was roused from his dozing by the mention of *The Ransom*, "Yes," he said, under his breath. "And we accomplished our task, too."

"We did," the poet said, agreeing with his friend, "But not without one regrettable failure."

The young man rubbed his red eyes, took a deep breath, then continued.

"Willem Woolem was the oldest and wisest of the Woolems of Averlune. The leader of all Woolems, though not by choice, for Willem had reached the highest state of wisdom: humility. Because of his age, he had not been targeted by the pirates. Instead, he'd been left behind to witness the dwindling of his herd and experience the heartbreak of helplessness.

"A man named, Gióstou Póthou, a hunter, took advantage of the chaos wreaked by the marauding pirates, and trapped Willem for his own evil purposes. Even the man's wife had come to loathe her vile husband. Leaving him, under the cover of darkness one night, she escaped the deranged sickness that had claimed her husband and her only child. Hiding the old Woolem in his barn and forcing him to power the tools of his vicious trade, Gióstou schooled his son in the art of cruelty and malice.

"It was in the hunter's barn that your mother and I found Willem. From there, we took him to the haven of Halla's home in the Quibble Woods. With the help of some other members of *The Ransom...*"

"Whom, I suspect, I've had the pleasure of meeting," Edward interjected.

"Indeed, brother. Kendra, Pat, Isaiah, and the brave river otters all helped in secreting the venerable Woolem to safety. But even this great success was undone by the naivete of our youth. Unknown to Silloah and me, we were followed. The hunter, Gióstou, crept into the Forgotten Meadow and imprisoned Willem a second time. Left to die of exposure on the windswept Hill of Reckoning, the old Woolem was chained with a lock that could only be opened by the hunter's key."

The poet took a sip of water from the canteen he carried always at his side. Replacing the cap, he rejoined his story.

"The guilt Silloah and I felt was nothing compared to the great lament of the Woolems. Willemina had to watch her father grow feeble, unable to do anything more than sit by his side. Even this, Willem would not permit. He could not endure the thought of the suffering of the old burdening the young. He had lived a long life; they must avert their eyes from the chains that bound their beloved leader and live their lives, too.

"In an effort to right our unintended wrong, your mother and I sought every opportunity to take the hunter's key and free the captive Woolem. Try as we might, we were not successful, and Gióstou Póthou took the key with him to his grave.

"Or so we thought. Until, one day, only a few years before her marriage to your good father and the birth of her daughter, Silloah came to me bearing news. The hunter's son, more dimwitted and less cautious than his father, had mislaid the key. Your mother never told me precisely how she happened upon it, but she was now in possession of the very key that could free Willem in Chains.

"When Gióstou's son learned what had happened, he set a sleepless watch on the lands north of the Miralette River. With some dark art, he enlisted the help of creatures of a less than savory nature. River rats, giant mosquitos, even his own devil dog, Gyilkos, were all charged with patrolling the region between the river and Windermere Sheer.

"For no other reason than to satisfy his own injured pride, Giuseppe Póthou, the son of Willem's captor, was determined to safeguard the lasting effects of his father's wickedness and thwart any attempt to put the stolen key to good use. His own fear of heights prevented him from locating the entrance to the Forgotten Meadow. But, down in the wilderness of the Silent Forest, Giuseppe and Gyilkos held sway.

"The danger was enough to keep the mother of a newborn daughter from risking too much, and she would not hear of me completing this deadly task alone. So, the key remained in her hope chest. Your father rightly saw my own desire to undo the damage we'd done as a threat to his wife's safety, and so..."

Edward looked down at the floor.

"To protect his wife, I was barred from her life."

Catching his brother-in-law's eyes, the poet said, "I never blamed you. I might have done the same, in your place."

"Forgive me," Edward replied. "I had no right to keep you from your sister's side… not as she lay…" Edward's voice cracked, "Not as she lay dying, and certainly not in death. It was not to protect her from dangerous adventures that I did it. It was out of spite. And I am so sorry, brother. I am so sorry."

Wiping his eyes, Edward rested one hand on Annelyse's arm.

"And I'm sorry for having robbed you of your uncle, my child. I'm sorry for so very much."

Annelyse hugged her father with tears streaming down her face.

"Soon…" the poet softly continued, "she fell ill. The task she had hoped to complete she now lacked strength… she now lacked time enough to complete. And so, it fell to you, Annelyse."

"But why not just tell me all of this from the start?"

"Your mother wanted you to freely choose. She would not thrust such danger upon you. She wanted you to decide what you believed and to follow your own convictions born of those beliefs. The key was in your possession, but it would have been just as much of an injustice if I had simply stolen it from her hope chest as it would have been for your mother to command you to do something you did not fully understand. The key was yours, task was entrusted to you, but you had to decide in freedom."

"And I have," Annelyse said, her heart beginning to understand what her head was just now learning. "Your poem about Mom, your hints along the way, it all helped. I *want* to do this. For Mom, for the Woolems, I want to do what she couldn't. And I want your help. I want us to undo this whole thing together."

Edward looked at his daughter in the liquid light of the moon-drenched lake. There was conviction in her eyes. There was understanding, compassion, and maturity. She had become as much her mother as she was now fully herself. She had let her grief wash through her and carry away so much that was not her. Doubt, fear, anxiety, anger, none of this was truly her. These things are voids, empty chasms in our character, but they cannot be ignored. They can only be filled-in with their opposites: belief, courage, confidence, and love. And Annelyse, in discovering a purpose beyond herself, had begun to replace everything that had emptied her life of meaning.

"So much like your… self," her uncle said with a smile. "Never aspire to be anyone else, no matter how magnificent they might be. You will always be a better you than you would be anyone else."

Sifting through the scraps of questions in her mind, Annelyse brought forth a curiosity.

"Is he still alive?"

"Willem?" her uncle clarified.

"Yes," she replied, fearful of the answer.

From outside, a voice was heard, like that of a great quilted breeze on a stormy day, "Yes," Willemina confirmed. "My Daddy…"

The Woolem had awoken from her nap and had been listening to the poet's story. The young man's face now darkened, and, in a quiet voice, he said, "Willem is unwell. The years have worn thin his once joyful heart. Unwilling to burden his people any further, he insists on weathering all trials alone. Whether the indifference of the elements, or the creeping fears that steal into the hearts of all living things, Willem faces all things in profound solitude."

"When did you see him last?" Annelyse asked, her heart heavy with sadness.

"I see him every new moon, to sit with him through the darkest nights of the month. In the lengthening of his years, a fear of the dark has fractured his once courageous heart. I will not permit him to endure these moonless nights alone. Not when I am the cause of his misfortune."

The poet remained silent for a while, pondering the part his life had played for good or ill. Looking on the face of his young niece and seeing so much of his sister, the young man beheld the hope of his own redemption in her countenance. She had come so far.

Through the hopelessness of grief, she'd traveled along roads paved with doubts and questions back to belief. She'd taken the shreds of her world – like the torn-up pieces of her funeral dress – and woven something new, something hopeful. A sour note had been struck in the symphony of her young life and, instead of falling silent, she had begun to compose a new movement based on an unexpected dissonance.

Just like her mother, Annelyse was possessed of a lively spirit of adventure. It had served her well, up to this point. It would now complete the work begun by her mother's own adventurous spirit.

Annelyse gazed up through the waters of the skylight. Her eyes came to rest on the figure of a fish bobbing in the unseen currents of the garden lake. The fish did not struggle to impose its own will against the movement of the water. It did not fight to assert its uniqueness in opposition to its surroundings. It simply followed the rhythm set out for it by its environment. In its surrender, it became more wonderfully fishlike, more magnificently itself than it would have been had it chosen to rage against the world of which it was an integral part.

Then something occurred to the active mind of the fourteen-year-old. She did not know her uncle's name. This, she thought, would need to be rectified.

"Uncle," she began, her face still turned upward,

her eyes still locked on the fish.

"Yes, my niece," the Poet of Perigoh replied.

"What's your name?"

Catching sight of the fish who was so serenely a part of its surroundings, the fish his niece found so captivating, the young man raised one hand to hold her attention on the remarkable creature.

"Like that fish," he said, "I am *a child of the lake*."

Annelyse squinted her eyes, considering what her uncle might mean.

"Whereas my sister was named *the heart of the doe*… the Silloah Star, I am but *a child of the lake*, reflecting her light poorly."

Then, with a soft chuckle, Annelyse's mysterious uncle relented. He would give her a straight answer to her simple question. This time, at least.

"But you may call me Uncle Lachlan."

CHAPTER TWENTY-FIVE

Lessons from Nature

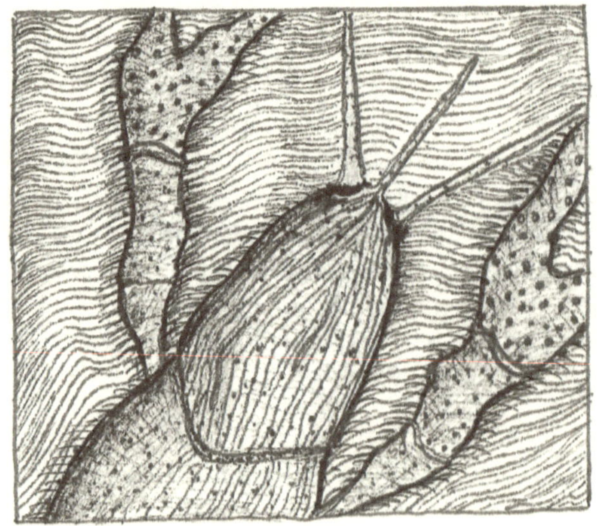

Annelyse lay on her back listening to the others sleep. The low rumble of Willemina's breathing vibrated through the glass wall, like a bow being draw across a cello's string. The Woolem was sound asleep beneath the starry sky, happy to be going home.

Slouched over in his armchair, Albert snored through loose lips. His chin lay on his heaving chest, squashing the lumpy bulk of his prodigious cheeks over his jawbones like inner tubes. Sounding like a saggy balloon releasing its gaseous contents, Albert alternated between thin whistling and rubbery sputters.

Muttering in his sleep, he let out occasional bursts

of, "Yippee," "Have at you!" or "Isn't it grand?!" between his guttural gurglings. At times, his snoring stopped altogether until, remembering the benefits of breathing, his body erupted in one great contortion, gulping air like a thirsty dog at its water bowl. Annelyse wondered that he didn't wake himself up, his was anything but peaceful sleep especially for those around him.

From nearby, Annelyse could see the silhouette of her father sleeping on his right side. She thought about the days he'd spent alone searching the Quibble Woods for her. She remembered the names her uncle had mentioned earlier that evening: Halla, Kendra, Pat, Isaiah, and the river otters. Who were they? What part did they play in her father's quest? How much more was there to know that Annelyse was unaware of?

Perhaps she'd missed out on too much for her father and her ever to feel that they'd truly shared the same adventure. Her journey had been one of helplessness, while her father's had been one of hopelessness.

Edward hadn't really wanted to leave home at all. He'd gone along only to keep Annelyse safe. Nothing more. He hadn't really believed in the existence of Woolems - or in much else, for that matter. The events of the last few years had beaten him down, reshaped him into a ghostly vapor of himself. He'd become jaded and cynical, and he felt he'd been more than justified in doing so. After all, Edward Bellamy's greatest fears had all come true. What happiness could he ever really hope to find again? Giving up on such things as hope and belief seemed the only sensible thing to do. Surrendering to his grief was as easy as letting himself fall from a great height and fall he did.

But the father Annelyse awoke to find in the hunter's barn was altogether different. He was determined, fearless, fierce, even. Somehow, in the darkness of Giuseppe Póthou's barn, Edward Bellamy had put aside his grief and rediscovered much of what he had lost. Belief in things unseen; faith in truths once held; the certainty that life is worth living, all took root in his heart once more. Even his low opinion of the young poet had blossomed into kinship and admiration. Miles away from the familiarity of Averlune, Edward Bellamy had finally come home.

Annelyse now thought about her own experience. She had set out on this quest to find answers about what her mother had believed; to discover the truth about Woolems; and to better understand some of the mysteries surrounding Silloah Bellamy. Annelyse had succeeded in holding onto everything her father had relinquished. She was determined; resolved; ready to be convinced one way or the other; open to the possibility of belief.

Over the course of events, her determination had been snuffed out like a flagging wick by the poison of the Pólcrit tree. Her resolve had been crippled by paralysis. Doubts had begun to entwine themselves like creeping vines around her heart. She'd been reduced to the same state in which her father had been mired when they'd first started their journey.

But then something happened to them both.

Face to face with the needs of his daughter, Edward Bellamy found the reason he needed to finally turn his attention outside of himself. He forgot his own inner turmoil and focused his energies on rescuing Annelyse.

She, in turn, had been compelled to rely on the help of others, in her time of weakness. She could neither cure nor free herself by determination alone. She'd become entirely reliant on Willemina and her father. And, by their own self-sacrifices, they did not let her down. In her helplessness, Annelyse experienced the healing, freeing effects of selfless love.

In this way, both their journeys – though separate, for a time – were exactly the same. They had each begun to navigate their way out of the cold, dark pit of grief and back into the warmth of hopeful sunlight by means of selflessness. In times of grief, the human heart often feeds upon itself, growing smaller and sicklier with each spoonful. The antidote to self-pitying grief is to forget oneself and focus on others, for we cannot pity what we do not recall.

The time had come, Annelyse was certain, to comfort her mother's spirit by ceasing to treat Silloah's death as the defining moment in her or her daughter's life. Lives, like all works of art, are not defined by singular moments, but by every shade of light and dark of which they are composed. Silloah's death was but one brushstroke on a canvas enlivened by a million colors.

Misfortune must not define her, Annelyse resolved. The canvas of her life must not be tarnished by the grim pigment, Death. Her life must showcase every color in the rainbow, as her mother's had, as her uncle's still did. She held the brush, and she would imitate the work of the great masters who came before her.

Staring up at the glass ceiling and into the clear waters of the garden lake, Annelyse spotted a crawfish crawling along the bottom. With equal parts scurrying and swimming, the tiny lobster-like creature alternately walked and floated its way from cattail, to reed, to fallen limb.

Never pausing to consider where it had been, the animal looked ahead – always forward – despite only being able to see six inches in front of its face. Forced by limited sight to live only in the present moment, the crawfish appeared content with its lot in life. It carried nothing, collected nothing along its way, and lived without a stain of worry.

Turning her eyes to her uncle who was deep in peaceful sleep - his back against the wall, his arms folded across his chest - Annelyse thought about what he had said when he told her his name, Lachlan.

"It means *child of the lake*," she recalled him

saying, then thought to herself, "Like the crawfish." Owning nothing; using no more than it needed; free from all cares; so filled with weightless joy that it floated as often as it walked, this is the freedom of a child of the lake. Her uncle was aptly named, indeed.

Awash in moonlight sifting through the living waters of the lake, Annelyse drifted off into the most contented sleep she'd experienced in days. She had endured so much. Chasms, caves, and caverns; mosquitos, poison, and paralysis; fire and hurricanes; deadly cliffs, and dogs, and pummeling winds; Annelyse had survived it all. Now, in this protected paradise, this far-away, forgotten place, she was safe at last.

As nighttime gave way to morning, the subterranean room in which Annelyse was sleeping began to sparkle with gold and blue. The rising sun now skipped across the surface of the water like a smooth stone, riding the ripples as they spread themselves out toward the shore. Shafts of light, like blades of tempered steel wrought from the ore of wild rainbows, pierced water, glass, and air to pool in puddles of red, orange, and yellow on the floor. Morning had reached the heart of the poet's raindrop home.

The newborn sun's warm breath caressed Annelyse's cheek, gently rousing her from her sleep. Opening her eyes, she saw no one else in the room, only the imprint of Albert Prume's misshapen backside in the cushion of the armchair, and her father's empty sleeping bag on the floor. Beside her, a plate of fruit and a cup of tea had been left for her breakfast.

Rubbing the sleep from her eyes, Annelyse chose a slice of apple, then gazed up at the ceiling as she had the night before, hoping to see her friend the crawfish. In its place among the cattails and reeds, ten fat little toes now flattened themselves against the glass bottom of the garden lake. Albert Prume had decided to begin the day with a swim.

Annelyse giggled with delight at the way the little man bobbed in the water like a chubby buoy. She watched as he pushed himself off from the bottom, wiggled his toes like a crab, then landed on one leg, giving a slight flourish with the other. Over and over again, Albert repeated his water ballet: leap, wiggle, flourish, leap, wiggle, flourish. First landing on his left, then on his right leg. If the wiggling of his ten pudgy toes was any indication, Albert Prume was in a fine state of mind on this sunny Saturday morning.

Dunking his head underwater, Albert suddenly realized he had an audience, and began waving excitedly at Annelyse through the glass. Laughing all the louder at the way Albert's enormous cheeks kept trying to float him up off the lakebed, Annelyse could not contain herself.

At that sound of her giggling, Annelyse's uncle descended the staircase, and sat down beside her on the floor, helping himself to a handful of blueberries.

"Good morning, dear niece," the poet said softly.

"Good morning, Uncle Lachlan," Annelyse replied, trying out the use of his name.

She was undecided about how it felt to have the Poet of Perigoh for her uncle. Before she'd learned that they were related, he had been merely a curiosity. Now, the mystery of it all was difficult for her to wrap her head around. All along, she'd harbored the suspicion that he reminded her of someone she knew well. Now that she knew he was her mother's little brother, it made perfect sense. Still, having such a unique celebrity for a relative would take some getting used to, she was sure.

The young man had his sister's stubby nose and her high cheekbones. His blue eyes were somewhat darker than Silloah's, but his lashes were just as long as hers. Now that Annelyse had a chance to think about it, even his laugh reminded her of her mother's. The two of them could have been twins, had they not been born five years apart. Their similarities were both striking and subtle, and Annelyse felt consoled by her uncle's company.

"Are you ready?" he asked.

"For what?"

"For what lies ahead of us this day," he replied. "It's very near. Only a few hours walk. There's no more reason for delay."

Annelyse knew what her uncle was talking about. They had passed the final barrier to the Forgotten Meadow when they'd survived the perils of Windermere Sheer. There was no other line of defense to cross, nothing to deny them entry into the land of the Woolems. Yet, here at the intersection of myth and mission, where some of the great moments of her mother's life had been played out, Annelyse was frightened.

"What is it, child?" her uncle asked, sensing her apprehension.

"I'm not her," Annelyse began. "I'm not like her, not *that* much. I'm just… me."

"And because of that, you will succeed. Only the first chapters of this story belonged to your mother," the poet assured her, "The ending is yours to write. It always *has* been, and there is great comfort in that thought. Come then. Let us be on our way. Willem has waited long enough."

Edward appeared at the foot of the stairs and walked over to where Annelyse and the poet were seated. He was holding something.

"I thought this might help," he said.

There in his hands, Edward Bellamy held a circlet of daisies. Placing it on his daughter's head, he spoke the words her mother used to say, "Arise, princess of Averlune."

Standing up, Annelyse hugged her father, with tears in her eyes.

"Where did you get this?" she asked.

"I made it. From daisies I picked along the way… when you were," Edward sighed, "When I was looking for you. They were all I had of you."

Annelyse looked at her father's face. Beneath a mask of resilience, Edward Bellamy still wore worry like an incurable wound. Scarred by all he had endured over the last few years, by all he'd watched his daughter endure, Edward was like a shattered vase, pieced together but not quite whole.

Annelyse promised herself, right then and there, never to let her father carry her as a burden ever again. She, too, was strong. She had strength to spare. She would share it with him whenever he needed her to.

"Let's go," she said, taking from her pocket the old iron key she'd found in her mother's hope chest. "It's time to… what did Mom say? Unlock *injustice and injury*."

"And so it is, dear niece," the young poet affirmed.

The party ascended the staircase to find Albert Prume waiting outside with Willemina.

"Everybody in," the little man instructed, holding open the door to his Tree RV.

"I'll walk on ahead," the poet said, "The day promises to be too beautiful to spend beneath a roof, even one so grand as yours, my friend."

With a smile and a quick bob of his head, Albert gave a show of agreement.

"I'd like to walk, too," Annelyse chimed in.

"And Willemina," the great Woolem said.

"For my part," Edward added, "I'd be happy for the ride. I can still feel that creature's claws in my chest."

"And I'll be cappy for the hompany!" Albert replied.

The group of travelers now wound its way along the garden path, holding to a course due north of the poet's home. On their right, the Borderland Hills rolled like an endless succession of tennis balls toward the east. On their left, the Valley of Enth cradled a threadlike stream in its embrace, guiding the tiny waterway past the three islands that stood in its way to the freedom of the sea.

The terrain over which they traveled was generously adorned with ponds and trickling fountains. With each step, the cultivated, backyard feel of the landscape gave way to a wild beauty like that of rich pastureland. Flower beds dissolved into meadows. Shorn garden paths became swaying sheaves of wheat. Fruit trees and berry brambles wandered among the wildflowers, lost in daydreams, forever fruitful. The sky itself seemed to dote upon the beauty of this land. She was ever partial to the pure of heart.

As they walked along, Annelyse tried to engage her uncle in conversations about everything from how similar blue jays and rusty garden gates sound, to how unlike her left thumb was in comparison to her larger right thumb and why this might be. Every bird that flew by, Annelyse asked the poet its name. Every flower in the widening meadow, she had to stop and smell. Her active mind was wide awake and eagerly devouring its surroundings.

But her uncle remained silent, deep in contemplation of not only the wonders of nature, but the wonderment of his wonderful niece. Prior to their meeting on Ruhner's Beach, he had only ever met her once before. But, even as an infant, Annelyse Bellamy had been curious beyond her years. She'd been born with an adventurous heart and an inquisitive mind, and her poet-uncle recognized a greatness in her character. Now, as they approached the Forgotten Meadow and the fulfillment of the task left to her by her mother, Lachlan wondered at what lay in store for the daughter of Silloah Bellamy. Where would this road she had chosen lead her?

Albert Prume's exceptional stand of five forty-foot-tall evergreen trees followed Annelyse, her uncle, and Willemina at a short distance. Inside, Edward sat with his back against the wall of woven branches, resting his wounded chest, his bitten thigh, and his still-aching head. At the controls, a chipper Albert hummed merrily and entirely out of tune. His was truly a joyful noise, if not altogether musically pleasing.

Walking between the Tree RV and the others, Willemina kept an ever-watchful eye on Annelyse. The Woolem's leg seemed to have recovered from the injury inflicted by the hunter's trap. There was a levity in her stride, a jubilance at being surrounded by so much that she knew so well.

Having learned from the woodland animals that Edward and Annelyse had scaled Mt. Averlune, the Woolem left the safety of her home on a quest to locate the daughter of Silloah Bellamy. Willemina knew of Silloah's promise to return to the aid of her father, she knew that the hunter's key had been found. Willemina's vigilance had become her hope.

When Silloah grew too ill to keep her promise, she confided in her brother, and he in Willemina: the key would be brought to the Forgotten Meadows in the hands of Silloah's daughter. Somehow, Annelyse would finish this task. When news had reached the Woolem of Annelyse's progress, she resolved to help her find her way. Now, they were within a mile of the Forgotten Meadow. Help had never been so near at hand.

Raising her eyes, Annelyse spied what looked like fresh snowfall on the northern horizon. A field of pure white stretched as far as she could see, east to west, blazing in the glare of the sun. The temperature had been climbing throughout the morning. The day promised to be far too warm for snow to endure. Perhaps what she was seeing was much higher in elevation or even the remnants of winter's snowpack still clinging to the Borderland Hills. Whatever it was, the nearer they drew, the larger it proved to be.

"What is that?" Annelyse asked of her uncle.

"That is our destination."

"Is it snow?"

"No, sweet niece. Not snow," the poet replied, clarifying nothing, and only intensifying the mystery.

They were now walking through the dense growth of an enormous prairie. The cloudless sky formed a dome of unbroken blue, deepening the green all around them by wonderful contrast. There were no hills, only flat expanses of fragrant wildflowers punctuated here and there with miniature trees. A constant breeze ran its long fingers through the meadow's fine hair, coaxing the scent of springtime into the air. Beneath their feet, the earth lay in leisure repose. All was at peace, attentive to the sighs of nature.

Annelyse noticed more and more daisies sprinkled in among the other flowers at her feet. What began as a scattering soon grew to become a veritable profusion of little, snowy flowers. Clinging to the breeze, a blizzard of delicate white filled the air around them – never seeming to land - until the travelers were engulfed in a cumulus cloud of daisy petals.

The field of snow Annelyse had spotted on the northern horizon lay all about, speckled with drops of yellow, and gleaming with all the brilliance of a newly bleached bedsheet. They had, at last, arrived at the southern border of the Forgotten Meadow.

From inside the Tree RV, Edward glanced up at the command porthole through which Albert had been navigating. A flash of white, like the pop of a flashbulb, stamped his eyes, and for a moment he thought it might be lightning.

Drawing the evergreens to a halt, Albert called Edward to his side to get a better look.

"Isn't it grand?" the little man asked, applying his most complimentary phrase to this unprecedented sight.

"Magnificent," came the reply from an astonished

Edward Bellamy. "It just keeps on going."

"All the way to the sea, or so I've been told," Albert said, a look of awe on his face. "I've bever neen… not yet, anyhow."

In front of the Tree RV, Willemina stood enfolded in the embrace of her homeland. With the most delicate movement of her lips, the Woolem picked one daisy at a time – stem, leaves, and flower – and savored its flavor on her tongue. These little flowers were the chosen food of Woolems, and Willemina had craved their sun-kissed sweetness for days.

"Daisies," Annelyse said thoughtfully, twirling one between her thumb and forefinger. "A world of daisies."

Her uncle knelt in front of her, an apron of white flowers reaching waist-high, "Now you see why she loved them so," he said.

Annelyse looked out over the boundless blanket of white. She felt as if the eyes with which she was seeing this unimaginable vista belonged to her mother. In an instant of beholding, Annelyse understood, and this understanding could only have come from Silloah.

She understood that this was the sanctuary of the Woolems where their rescuers had hidden them in safety. She understood that this was where the devious Gióstou Póthou had followed Silloah and her little brother, Lachlan, and imprisoned the wise old Willem. And she was certain that her mother's love of daisies was more than just a preference, it had symbolized a promise.

Every time Silloah plaited a circlet of daisies for her, she was planting within Annelyse the seeds of her promise to return the iron key to the Forgotten Meadows and free Willem. Every time she gave her daughter one of these simple, unassuming flowers, she was whispering the story of the Woolems into Annelyse's heart. And with each daisy her uncle left for her to find – from the one he'd left on the boulder on Ruhner's Beach, to the one he'd pressed into the bark of the tree in Alder's Idle, to the one he'd made out of stones atop the Sheer – Silloah's promise was renewed in the person of her daughter.

And now Annelyse stood among the mystical daisies in the mythical land of the legendary Woolems, precisely where her mother had stood decades earlier. The iron key had come home. The daisies' work was all but done.

"Which way from here?" Annelyse asked, her pulse quickening in her chest.

"I will show you," her uncle replied.

Rising to his feet, the young man motioned to the others to follow him. They were running now, the wetness of the grass staining their pantlegs as they went. Stretching out behind them, a beaten path of trampled prairie and bruised daisies - as wide as a Woolem and as broad as a stand of five evergreen trees – lay prone beneath the sky. Had Gyilkos still been pursuing them, their tracks would have been easy enough for him to follow. But, in this protected haven, they had little to fear from predators.

Soon, Willemina was outpacing the others. Her long strides made it difficult for them to keep up, and she was quickly lost to the others' view. The poet was in the lead again, guiding the company in a sweeping arc toward the eastern side of a solitary hill bulging up from the level plain. Atop the lonely mound, Annelyse could just make out the silhouette of a great tree. Strewn throughout the meadow, like a flotilla of driftwood, distant shapes drifted among the snow-white daisies.

"There," the poet said, pointing at the faraway figures. "Woolems!"

Annelyse's heart was now racing, as she neared an entire herd of the very creatures she'd set out to discover. A few feet ahead of her, the young man who had set her on this journey ran along the same paths he had taken with Annelyse's mother. Behind them, her father rode with the sweet and courageous Albert Prume in his marvelous vehicle. Annelyse was besieged by wonders on all sides, and a sense took root in her heart that she had found her place in this magical world.

Woolems of every color and hue lifted their huge heads to gape with interest at the young girl and her companions as they passed among them. The poet was known to them, but the Woolems had not seen anyone like Annelyse since a fifteen-year-old Silloah had walked these fields. Those who remembered, thought that perhaps Silloah had returned to the Forgotten Meadow, so much did her daughter resemble her.

Annelyse marveled at the diversity that existed among the Woolems. Most were as large as Willemina, but each was distinct unto itself. Their immense bodies were nearly identical in shape and size, but their individuality manifested itself in other ways.

Woolems of pastel greens and muted salmon; soft pinks and watercolor blues stood out against the white of the meadow. Some grazed along the outskirts of the herd, attentive to every rustle in the surrounding grass. Some wandered near the center of the herd, their eyes downcast, their heads bowed. Many Woolems ranged widely, exploring further afield, a glint of excitement in their intelligent eyes. And then there were those Woolems who stayed in little groups of three.

Always by the side of its mother, one baby Woolem – unexpectedly small for a species so enormous – played beneath the watchful eye of its father. Leaping and kicking its hind legs like a newborn colt, the little Woolem knew not a care in the world. No larger than a lamb, the youngster wore both hues of its parents' wool, evenly blended throughout, as an entirely new color. The child of a maroon mother and a cream-colored father would be as rosy as a sunset. The child of a lime-green mother and a purple father would be as beautifully brown as mahogany.

Among the Woolems there was only ever beauty in contrast, never conflict.

Even the character of their coats varied from Woolem to Woolem. Some had dense, curly wool, like Willemina. Others wore long, shaggy fur like a golden retriever. There were some whose coats resembled hair that had been shaved close to the skin. Nature itself seemed to revel in the richness of endless variety.

But there was another characteristic they all shared, regardless of appearance. Each and every Woolem exhibited a gentleness so at ease with their great might that it could only be called wisdom. For the fool sews discord by force, while the wise wield only peace. The Woolems were, above all else, a peaceful species. In their tranquility lay their genius. Seeing them with her own eyes, Annelyse understood how such creatures could be so easily exploited and enslaved.

As they moved through the herd of Woolems a thousand strong, Annelyse, Lachlan, Edward, and Albert approached the hill at the center of the meadow. All around its base, the flourishing field of daisies looked like a great saucer of milk. But, upon the slopes of the hill, not a single flower grew. The great mound was entirely bare, windswept, and weather-worn, but for a thin carpet of mottled grass.

Crowning the crest of the weary hill, an old willow tree stood hunched over at the waist. With angular elbows, the tree clasped its aching back in crooked hands. Dangling from twists of grizzled limbs, thin leaves curled themselves against the elements. At its feet, dry branches and twigs littered the ground. The wizened willow had seen many things in its long years. But those years were waning now, along with the Woolem whose fate had been bound to the life of the lonely tree.

Standing where the white flowers relented and the green hill rose, Annelyse's eyes came to rest on a face of such noble dignity and patient suffering as she had never known before. Shackled by a chain of tremendous weight, a grey Woolem sat amid the wreckage of the willow tree. His head rested on his folded front legs. His hind legs lounged, limp and lethargic, beneath his battered frame. The dense curls of his wool were matted and thinned by age, denuded, and made splotchy by the unrelenting wind. The outline of his recessed ribcage was clearly visible at a distance, but it was his eyes that elicited compassion.

A profound sadness pooled in the depths of his heart, overflowing his sunken eyes like limitless inkwells. He was stoic, a study in stark surrender. For a quarter of a century, his life had been lived, and mourned, and ebbed away atop that hill. The ground itself was stained to the bedrock with anguish until, even the daisies refused their joy. He was more alone than loneliness might lament, except for the love of his daughter, and the monthly visits of his new moon friend.

Beside the ancient Woolem stood Willemina who greeted the arrival of her friends with a simple introduction. Bowing her head with reverence, she said, "My daddy."

Grief is a Sort of Madness

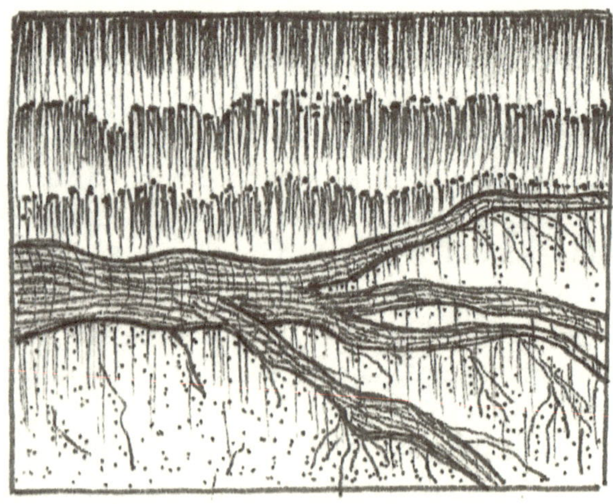

Willem lifted his head and met his guests with a frail smile. He had been told by Willemina of the approach of the daughter of Silloah Bellamy. He knew that she carried the key that would set him free. But instead of excitement or anticipation, his face bore no emotion at all. It was not hopelessness that robbed him of feeling. Rather, he had learned to accept his fate many years ago. To wish for release would have been to wish himself away. He was Willem Woolem, and that meant Willem in Chains. Without his shackles, who would he be?

Moving his mouth as if slowly chewing, the old Woolem labored to rouse what little strength he possessed and addressed himself to speak. In a thin, fragile murmur, Willem began.

"Welcome," he whispered, the pitch of his voice higher than Annelyse expected. "You have journeyed far. I thank you for your troubles."

The young poet, who knew the wise Woolem well, responded for the group.

"My friend, there is no kindness without cost, as you know. But our cost was well worth this kindness. We are happy to be here with you. Please, allow me to introduce the daughter of Silloah Bellamy."

Taking her by the hand, the poet presented his niece to Willem, "This is Annelyse."

A tear trickled from the failing eyes of the Woolem, as he recognized the image of Silloah in Annelyse's youthful face. His final memory of his young rescuer had been her look of heartbreak. Unable to free him from his chains, Silloah had spoken her promise, kissed the Woolem's forehead, then turned and walked away. Willem never saw her again. But now, there she stood. In the visage of her daughter; in the pale blue of Annelyse's eyes; in the dignity of her character, Silloah had returned to keep her promise.

"Annelyse," the Woolem spoke, setting each syllable free on the midday breeze. "Do you know what your name means?"

Dropping her eyes in embarrassment, Annelyse admitted she did not.

"Ann means *grace*. And Elyse means *oath*. Do you know what an oath is?"

"A promise?" Annelyse ventured.

"Very good. And so, you are. A *promise of grace…* the *promise of grace* made and spoken by your mother. Just as the name of Silloah is beloved in our land, the name of her daughter – the *promise of grace* – shall be, also. For you have graciously returned to keep your mother's promise."

The ancient Woolem rested his head on his front

legs again, "Forgive me," he said, "I tire too easily."

"Of course," Annelyse responded, her heart welling up with compassion.

The poet took this opportunity to continue the introductions.

"And this," he said, gesturing toward Edward, "is Annelyse's father. My brother-in-law, Edward Bellamy."

Edward made a low bow but did not speak.

"The kindness paid to me came at the greatest cost to yourself, Mr. Bellamy," the Woolem said, lifting his head a moment. "I thank you for the pains you've endured, both in mind and body."

"It was for love of my daughter," Edward explained.

"Yes," Willem replied, "And, love brings with it much heartache. But still, we love."

Albert Prume had been standing beside his Tree RV at the foot of the hill, wondering when the old Woolem would get to him. Never comfortable with emotional scenes and deep conversations, the ruddy little man with the mismatched boots and saggy overalls was always more interested in showing off his grand stand of five forty-foot-tall evergreen trees. When it was his turn at last, he stepped forward with glee.

The hint of a smile crept across Willem's face, as he took notice of his kindly old friend.

"Your leaves, Mr. Prume," the Woolem noted.

"Aye," Albert replied, "Sheared clean off, every last one. Naked as a newborn newt!"

"But no less grand," Willem assured him.

"Oh, indeed," Albert agreed, nodding vigorously. "Lothing nike my trees! True, so very true."

As they were speaking, the herd of Woolems in the surrounding fields had been drawn by curiosity to the lone hillside. Forming a semicircle around the eastern slope of the hill, a thousand Woolems of every color, shade, and hue now stood behind Edward, Albert, Annelyse, and her uncle, watching intently. Once the Woolems learned who the young girl was and what she had returned to do, whispers began spreading through the crescent-shaped herd.

The Woolems of Averlune had not seen their homeland for decades. But the Forgotten Meadow was so like the Averlune of old, that it had become a pleasant replacement. Still, the name of Averlune was like a thorn in the bruised heart of every Woolem, a reminder of not only the place of their birth, but of a time before pain. The Woolems tried to forget the events that had tarnished their innocence and cast them into exile, even naming their new home as a place of forgetfulness.

But the Forgotten Meadow could not forget the most grievous wound the Woolems had endured, for that wound still festered in the very heart of the meadow. Their leader, their wise and beloved father, Willem, still lay chained to the trunk of a willow tree. Through the dwindling shade of its crumbling branches, the sun scorched the skin of the willow's captive. Beneath the bones of its shattered limbs, the wind, rain, snow, and ice battered the tree's prisoner day and night.

Unwilling to trade the life of another creature for his own, Willem refused to let his people pull down the tree and set him free. Instead, every morning, he thanked the willow for its companionship, and every evening, he thanked the lonesome hill for supporting his weight. The gentle Woolem had learned to turn his suffering into the wisdom of gratitude. It was this wisdom that he now wanted to share with Annelyse and her father.

Lifting his head again, Willem asked his daughter to invite the Bellamys up the hill to sit with him awhile. As they climbed the slope to join the ancient Woolem, Willemina led Albert and the poet to a grassy patch beside a pond where they could refresh themselves and rest among the friendly herd. Every Woolem in the meadow wanted a chance to speak with the famous Poet of Perigoh and examine the wonder of Prume's Wile.

Holding forth like a professor of mechanical forestry, Albert delighted in demonstrating all that his trees could do. The bare branches and leafless limbs made it that much easier for his students to get a look inside the Tree RV's inner workings. Seated on the ground a little way off, the famous poet chuckled in spite of himself. He'd been eclipsed by five forty-foot-tall trees. Taking out his leatherbound journal, the young man penned a poem about his turn of fortune, while his charismatic friend held the Woolems enraptured.

Atop the hill, Annelyse and Edward were alone with the venerable Woolem who bid them to make themselves comfortable as best they could. There was, in fact, very little comfort to be found on this summit of suffering. Within the circular reach of Willem's chain, the ground had been trampled so thoroughly that nothing remained but bare, muddy rocks and tree roots. Strewn among these, sticks and branches of various widths and sizes served only to poke the soft belly of the unfortunate Woolem.

Not far from where Willem was consigned to sit, two troughs made of river stone held drinking water and a pile of wilted daisies for his meals. The Woolem hadn't enjoyed the pleasure of picking a wildflower with his own lips in time out of mind. Denied this most simple of all consolations, Willem had begun to lose interest in such fleeting things as eating. Instead, he turned his gaze outward, always outward, to the beauty of the world around him. This had become his sustenance, better suited to sustaining the soul than the body, but no less delightful.

Before his capture by the hunter, Gióstou Póthou, Willem had been old even in Woolem terms. Now, twenty years of harsh captivity had begun to steal from him even the breadth of his memories. He could recall little of his younger years and he had very little time left in front of him. His was a life burned from both ends; his past consumed by the fog of forgetfulness; his future consumed by the mortality that stalks all living things.

As she sat down in front of the legendary creature, Annelyse was struck to the heart by every distressing detail of the Woolem's body. His wool, once densely curled like Willemina's, was bedraggled, grizzled, and so infused with white as to fade his once regal ebony to pauper's grey. The nails of his four feet had grown brittle with age and poor nutrition, splintering in agony when bumped against roots and stones. He was spared no torment.

Encircling each eye, deeply wrought wrinkles, radiating outward like the spokes of a wheel, emphasized just how much Willem's body had shrunken inside his skin. Like the daisies in his food bowl, he was withering, and even the restoration of his freedom could not reverse the process.

Most pitiable, however, was the ankle around which Willem wore his shackle. The rusty manacle had worn away wool and skin, leaving only a thick band of white scar tissue where once lush wool had grown. The one mercy granted the old Woolem was that he could no longer feel the iron rub against his skin, so damaged were the nerves in his leg. Faced with his piteous state, Annelyse recoiled at the Woolem's horrid condition. Willem had suffered until he had become synonymous with suffering itself. There was no distinction to be made between the two.

"Thank you, friends," Willem said, lifting his trembling head to address Annelyse and Edward. "There is something I want to give you. Something that might be of help to you."

Annelyse watched the enormous mouth of the creature form its words with as much delicacy as if it were plucking a daisy from the meadow. His lower jaw was lined with a row of short, stout teeth which peeked out from behind his slowly bobbing lip like blooms of popcorn. There was a sense that Willem's once imposing size had simply become burdensome to him as the muscles supporting his frame shriveled to little more than rubber bands. Even so, somewhere deep inside, there was a mighty spirit still haunting the sagging rafters of the Woolem's ramshackle abode.

Willem held his guests' gaze with sorrowful eyes, as he continued.

"I, too, have suffered," he said, stating what Annelyse thought needed no affirmation. "Long ago, I lost my mother," he whispered with sadness. "Then, three days later, I also lost my wife."

It had never occurred to Annelyse before. Willem was Willemina's father, but there had never been any mention of her mother.

"These were the two great sorrows of my life," the Woolem continued, seeming to overlook his current situation. "I grieved in all the ways grief takes hold of a soul. But I did not learn the great wisdom, the great secret grief conceals, until what little I still had left was taken away. It was then, in the loss of my life's liberty, that I found freedom."

"How did you lose them?" Annelyse asked.

"The pirates took them from me," Willem said, his eyes now running red with sorrow. "And the cruel voyage across the sea took their lives from them."

Willem dropped his head into the crook of his arm, continuing his story through clenched lips.

"This is why I asked that I and my people be allowed to live within sight or sound of the sea. Because, the salt breeze ever carries their tears to me, and the wind their mournful cries. For, in the pirates callous disregard, they cast the sacred bodies of my beloveds beneath the hooves of the trampling waves."

The noble Woolem was sobbing now, his eyes

closed, his face buried in his arm.

"Lost to the cold, black, crushing depths," he whispered through his tears, "And my love did so fear the terrors of the dark."

Annelyse sat in silent heartbreak. She did not know what to say in the face of such devastation. Anything that came to mind seemed pathetic, inadequate to the task, cliched. Desperation writhed within her, clutching at phantoms of consolation, grasping at words of thin condolence.

Then it hit her, maybe that's how the mourners who had come to pay their respects at her mother's funeral had felt. They'd resorted to the playbook of futile funeral phrases, much to her dismay. But perhaps she'd been unjust toward them. Sometimes words fall far short of their intended purpose, but that does not always mean that it's better to leave them unsaid. Silence can easily be misconstrued; words, however deficient, are far less likely to be.

"I'm so sorry," she said, laying one hand on the Woolem's leg.

"Thank you, child," Willem replied, raising his head. "I tell you this not to compare our suffering, for suffering cannot be compared. It is as unique as the heart it breaks. I tell you this so that I might share with you what suffering has taught me."

Edward took his daughter's hand in his own. His eyes were fixed on Willem's face, his ears were attentive to every word the Woolem had to say.

"When I lost my loved ones, I tried to make sense of something that made no sense. When I learned of their deaths, I demanded answers to questions that had none. And at first, when my own freedom was taken from me, I allowed my enemies to imprison parts of me they would not have otherwise been able to enslave.

"My hope, my faith, my spirit, and joy… these

things cannot be seen or held in one's hand, but they are more real than wickedness which is only an absence of good. The moment I realized this I gained my freedom again.

"Recognizing that there's meaning behind each event, seeing details always within the context of the whole brought me peace. My loved ones never belonged to me; they did not live for my sake. They lived their own lives; they died their own deaths - as I live my own life, as I will one day greet my own death. All that I owned of them were the love and memories we made together. Such things never lose their meaning. Love and memories, these I still own. And I am grateful for them.

"My body can be shackled, but my spirit, my hope, my joy at reveling in every breeze and butterfly; every star and sunrise; every raindrop and wren cannot be taken captive. And for each such blessing, I am grateful.

"Under the looking glass of meaning, by the light of gratitude, the confusion and darkness of my grief were consumed. And though grief has tried to overwhelm me from time to time, the habit of thankfulness has become a way of life in which there is no room for shadows. To my everlasting joy, I have learned to find meaning, and in so doing I have discovered that the greatest wisdom is gratitude. For gratitude heals all wounds."

Willem settled himself back down. Closing his eyes, he breathed a long sigh to clear his mind. Seated in front of him, Edward and Annelyse remained silent, contemplating his words. Their own grief had begun to round a corner, days ago, with the turning of their attention outward. The magnificent newness of the landscapes and the generous kindness of those whom they'd encountered along their journey had imprinted upon their hearts a burgeoning sense of gratitude. The world pulsated with life, and life was worth living for the goodness and beauty hidden within every profoundly poignant moment. Even loss could not plunder life of meaning. Even death was but a key change in the symphony of existence.

Annelyse and her father held hands, letting these truths sort through that which still remained of the disorder inside themselves. Lying before them, and exhausted from speaking, the old Woolem dozed off to sleep.

Along the path of trampled daisies the travelers left in their wake, evil had crept into the Forgotten Meadow. Following the now drowned and lifeless nose of the tracker, Gyilkos, the unseen, bloody boots of the intruder stained the innocent daisies red with wrath. He had pursued the company down the secret sea chute from the heights of Windermere Sheer and into the Woolem's haven, armed with an axe sharpened with the whetstone of vengeance.

This evil had been there before, in the person of its fiendish father. Giuseppe Póthou, the son of Gióstou Póthou - who had long ago chained Willem to the willow tree – had been tracking Edward, Annelyse, and Willemina ever since they'd fled his barn under the cover of fire. He now lay hidden behind the western slope of the Hill of Reckoning, resolved to avenge Silloah's theft of his father's key, and his own injured pride at the escape of his prisoners.

Crawling like an insect up the opposite slope of the hill, the hunter crept in silence, his crooked nose twitching in the breeze that dribbled down from the summit. He detected the old Woolem's scent - frail and feeble and utterly defenseless - beneath the crumbling shelter of the willow. He knew that Willem's only companions were a weak little girl and her wounded father. The worthless poet and fat, doddering fool with the leafless evergreens were down in the meadow with the herd of witless beasts. He faced no opposition. There was none equal to the hunter's strength and cunning, he was sure.

This was his opportunity. This was his one chance to prove himself the victor. He would strike where his axe-fall would rend hearts the deepest. He would wound that which was most vulnerable. He would stand by and watch with satisfaction as every drop of his victim's blood drained into the greedy ground. His hatred was ravenous. His anger would have its reckoning atop that wretched hill, or he'd be damned in the trying.

Unaware of the approach of their enemy, Edward sat staring at the slumbering face of the ancient Woolem. The entire history of Averlune was etched upon Willem's majestic brow. The boundless Greenfields, the pastoral simplicity and peaceful splendor of the prairielands imbued the floral-scented fleece of the great creature like a lingering dream.

The salt breezes, the cackling seagulls, even the golden glare of Lower Perigoh Light lay tangled in the Woolem's matted wool. Willem was the best of that which defined Averlune. He was both Averlune's eldest son and, somehow, her father. Willem Woolem was the myth who came true, the legend who lived, and Edward Bellamy would never again choose doubt over belief. The irrefutable mystery lay within arm's reach.

Annelyse reached into her pocket and removed the key she'd taken from her mother's hope chest. This key had long ago been used to bind Willem to a life of growing despair. It had been found and taken at great peril to Silloah's life. Now, it would finally be used to undo Silloah and Lachlan's unfortunate error and redeem all things.

Staring at the heavy, iron key, Annelyse felt its cold weight in her hands. There was a cruel indifference about it, a remorseless lack of interest. The key was no happier in the hands of love than it had been in the hands of hatred. It exuded apathy, and Annelyse now found it repellant. The time had come to put the evil implement to good use.

From behind the sleeping Woolem, a figure now appeared, shrouded in the shade of the willow tree. In its upraised hands it held a long, stocky handle of oak fastened to the heavy weight of a furious blade. The hunter had scaled the Hill of Reckoning, axe in hand, ready to exact his retribution. Nothing now stood between him and his mark.

Sensing danger, the ancient Woolem awoke with a start to find the hunter standing over the huddled body of Annelyse. Edward cradled his daughter in his arms, frantically searching for the best defense that might save her life. Giuseppe had targeted the child of Silloah Bellamy as fitting payment for his father's stolen key. He reasoned that spilling her blood was the surest way of wounding both Edward and the helpless Woolem. His reasoning was sound, even if his mind was an upheaval of madness.

Wallowing in his moment of revenge, the hunter drew back his blade, crying, "Die now, you miserable welp!" then plunged his axe toward Annelyse's skull.

In an instant fueled by adrenaline, Willem cast the full enormity of his withered body like a ponderous projectile in the direction of the unsuspecting hunter. Without rising to his feet, the old Woolem had lunged himself into the jaws of danger, ready to receive in his own flesh the axe blow meant for Annelyse.

Instead, crashing headlong into the man, Willem knocked the hunter to the ground. The momentary distraction allowed Edward to grab Annelyse and roll a few yards down the slope of the hill and out of harm's way. But, on the summit of the Hill of Reckoning, a decades-old drama played itself out.

In the moment of his great exertion, Willem's chain had snapped taut, wrenching the trunk of the immense willow. Like piano wire slicing through a pillar of wax, the unbreakable chain strangled the trunk with such force that it severed the tree at its base. The sudden loss of balance caused the full height and girth of the great willow to topple to the ground, pinning both Willem and the hunter beneath its dry, lifeless corpse. Unseen by the others,

Giuseppe Póthou, the son of Willem's jailer, now lay dead beneath the splintered branches, impaled through his villainous heart.

A few feet away, Willem struggled to breathe under the weight of the colossal wreckage. Only his head was visible, all else being concealed by a snarl of limbs and leaves. Around his ankle, the iron shackle still clung. At his head, the chain that had bound him to the tree sat untethered, having fallen from the shattered trunk. Willem was free at last.

At the sound of the hunter's murderous cry, every soul in the meadow turned its attention to the lonely hill. Before anyone could make sense of what was happening, the tree had fallen, the enemy was dead, and the beloved Woolem was trapped. Willemina now charged up the eastern slope of the hill to the aid of her father, while Edward, Annelyse, the poet, and Albert rushed to their sides.

"Daddy," Willemina cried, dropping to the ground beside Willem's pain-stricken face. "Daddy…"

"Willie," the old Woolem whispered, with such affection as might break the heart of a dove. "Be at peace, my child."

"Willemina push tree," she said, panicked to find a solution that would spare her father's life.

"No, dear one. That would accomplish nothing. What is done must be allowed to happen. What has happened is now all but done."

"My daddy, no," the anguished Woolem wept. "No, no."

Annelyse watched in horror as the scene unfolded before her eyes. Beside her, the poet stood in utter dejection, his mind a wordless wilderness of blank pages fluttering in the winds of raw emotion.

Standing with his hands on his daughter's shoulders, Edward was numb, as if every drop of himself had ebbed away leaving only a brittle husk behind. Inside, there was nothing. No thoughts, no feelings, only the plaintive beatings of a bruised heart beneath a wounded breast. His mind was no longer able to find sense in the world around him. His heart could no longer try.

On the crest of the hill, Albert Prume was slumped over on his knees. An endless stream of tears ran from his swollen eyes over the broad curve of his red cheeks, to drip into puddles on his pantlegs. He was sobbing aloud, unable to restrain the surge of sadness bursting from inside his bountiful heart.

Willem had been his friend for ages beyond recall. The Woolem was often entertained by the tales Albert would tell of his journeys abroad. For his part, Albert had never met a sweeter soul than Willem Woolem. His humble brilliance had contributed to many of the innovations Albert made to his Tree RV over the years. It might be said that Albert's natural exuberance and constant tinkering had slowed Willem's aging, keeping him young beyond nature's reach. An energetic, inquisitive mind might very well be the definition of youthfulness. And the Woolem loved Albert's youthfulness so.

It's true that Albert Prume was not possessed of a storehouse of eloquent words, like the poet was. His was an eloquence of action. And right now, his whole being was engulfed in grief darker than anything he had ever encountered in all his wanderings.

At the foot of the hill, five forty-foot-tall evergreen trees bowed their heads in solemn respect. They were well aware that they would not be half so grand as they were had it not been for the wise old Woolem. They were the product of the magic of Halla's Quibble Woods and the wisdom of the father of the Woolems of Averlune. Adventure and courage, selflessness and daring, Prume's Wile embodied all that was best in the heart of Laprofonde.

A thousand Woolems stood motionless in the

Forgotten Meadow. Even the wandering breeze had grown tranquil, as all creation watched and waited. On the summit made flat by the feet of Willem in Chains, the dying Woolem called Annelyse to his side one last time. All ears now strained to hear the final words of a wise and noble heart.

"Annelyse," he sighed, gasping for the air needed to form each word. "The *promise of grace* who kept her mother's oath. With deepest gratitude, I thank you."

Annelyse wept openly, her quivering lip misguiding each tear along its meandering path to her chin.

"From this day forward, the name of the Forgotten Meadow will be the *Land of Promised Grace… AnnElysium.* May it always be a haven of peace. And may the Silloah star smile down upon it for all time."

Turning his gaze to Willemina, Willem smiled with all the warmth of a loving father, and with difficulty he whispered, "My child. My good… sweet… child…"

Then, closing his eyes, he breathed his last.

A cry, like the roar of the sea on the world's last night, shattered the silence and echoed through the heart of every living thing between the Wall of Windermere Sheer and the Borderland Hills. Willemina wept, cradling her father's head in her hands, kissing his face with inconsolable anguish, while the others looked on in stunned desolation.

In the fields below, every Woolem of every age and color joined in the daughter's lament. Waves of grief swelled into great storms of mourning, churning the meadow pale with despair. Even the daisies turned their faces to the ground, unwilling to look upon the cheerful face of the sun.

The Poet of Perigoh stepped forward. Kneeling beside the lifeless body of his friend, he bent over and kissed Willem's forehead as his sister had done two decades earlier. Reaching into his shoulder bag, he pulled out his leatherbound journal and opened it. Picking a single leaf from a branch of the fallen willow tree nearest Willem's face, he placed it with somber veneration between the pages of his journal and returned the book to his bag.

In a voice barely audible, the poet said, "Poor willow, this was not your doing. Every willow will, henceforth, be to me a weeping willow. And you will never be forgotten."

Laying his hand on the Woolem's head, the poet spoke his goodbye, then stood and descended the slopes of the Hill of Reckoning. Passing through the herd of mournful Woolems, he walked down to the banks of the nearby pond. Taking his place on a boulder, he sat alone in the light of the westering sun, his back to all else, his face turned toward the close of day.

Annelyse approached the fallen tree with trepidation. Resting her hand on Willemina's shoulder, she stood at her friend's side awhile. Joining her sympathy, in silence, to the suffering of the distraught Woolem, Annelyse hoped it might prove to be a consolation in some small way.

She remembered her own misery at the moment of her mother's death. All she had wanted was for someone to sit with her in her grief. Nothing more could accomplish anything of value. Nothing less was of any use. Now, as Willemina sat in the cold shadow of death, Annelyse was resolved to sit with her.

With Annelyse beside her, holding her hand, Willemina spoke through her tears.

"Where?" she asked, "Where did daddy go?"

Annelyse didn't know how to respond, though she understood exactly what her friend was saying. She recalled experiencing the same sense of confusion at seeing her mother's body, all the while knowing that her mother was no longer there. It had made no sense. Everything good and true and beautiful that had ever made her mother *present* was still visible, but, somehow, she was missing.

Annelyse had stubbornly concluded that she would not live in a universe where anything good was ever truly lost. She had been taught about an afterlife, a world of love and happiness where everything rose to wonderful newness. To her, it just made sense. If nothing good is ever lost, then this must be where it's kept. In that case, her mother and Willem would certainly be there. They had both risen to selfless heights of love in this life; surely, they didn't have far to go.

Wrapping her arm around Willemina's shoulders, Annelyse whispered her reply, "He's gone to be with your mother," she said, rubbing the Woolem's back with her hand.

"Where?" Willemina asked, "And how will he go there?"

"His spirit," Annelyse said, feeling the certainty of her words grow, "His beautiful spirit will rise to meet her. I know it."

Then reaching up with both hands, Annelyse removed from her head the circlet of daisies with which her father had crowned her before setting out that morning. With reverence, she gently placed it atop Willem's brow, in sight of his daughter.

Stepping back, Annelyse spoke with the assurance of things unseen, "Arise, prince of Averlune."

Heals All Wounds

Annelyse remained with Willemina throughout the endless hours of the afternoon and on into evening. The inconsolable Woolem refused to leave her father's side, and no one had the heart to try and convince her to do otherwise. Her loss was still too near, and she would not be parted from it.

With her forehead resting upon her father's front leg, Willemina moved seamlessly between drowsy sobbing and fits of restless sleep. Fatigue wrestled with mourning, sometimes gaining the upper hand, sometimes yielding the field. It was a tug-of-war with no victor, an effort without gain.

The young Woolem felt as if she were lost and alone in strange lands, knowing neither herself nor the now-empty world in which she wandered. Willem's only child had begun to learn that there is no greater separation than that which grief imposes. It is both a separation from the beloved lost and a detachment from one's true self. Grieving is as much an out-of-body-experience for those left behind as death is for the deceased.

A profound silence entombed the world in vague hopelessness. All AnnElysium was in mourning. Throughout the meadow, birds sat like ornaments on the bent boughs of trees, songless and sorrowful. Bees, lacking the will to spin honey on a day as bitter as this, crouched motionless among the daisies, the buzzing of their wings held in check. All those who had called the old Woolem their friend now set aside their lives for a time, in order to remember the one who had set aside his life to save another.

In the west, where the setting sun boiled the sea to vapor, thunderheads formed with stern intent. Glowering down from the heights of heaven, the dense, black clouds obscured the sunset like a flock of winged ink blots. A starless mantle draped its rumpled gown along the thin edge of the horizon. The entire dome of the sky had clothed itself in funeral attire.

For those in the meadow below, the night was spent in much the same way as the preceding hours. Annelyse remained curled up on the ground next to Willemina, both for warmth and to comfort her friend with her presence. Weariness settled itself into the recesses of Annelyse's mind, caressing her wounded heart, soothing her soul to sleep.

Nearby, Edward kept watch over his daughter, still deeply shaken by the events of the day. He now understood how his wife must have felt, and why she had been so intent upon undoing her innocent misfortune. Edward, too, wished that he could undo the calamity of this day.

He felt as if he'd let his wife down. The key he and

Annelyse had carried at great cost into the Forgotten Meadow had not been allowed to fulfil its destiny. It had not freed the captive; it had brought no resolution. This was the one thing he'd hoped to give his wife: resolution, redemption, closure. Instead, Edward was plagued by regret and a certainty that he had failed in this all-important task. Mired in gloom, Edward surrendered to merciful sleep.

Having wept until his lumpy face was so swollen he could barely see, Albert Prume descended the hill back into the cozy embrace of his trees. With no leaves to give him privacy, he drew the branches of his evergreens tightly around himself. The trees took the shape of an inverted bird's nest, huddled over-top of their master. Inside, alone in the dark, with no one to see or hear but his five closest friends, Albert Prume fell to pieces.

For the first time in his long life, he questioned fate's fairness. With freedom in sight, Willem's life had been swept away. The wicked hunter's doom was the only light of justice in a black fog of despair. Even that was of little consolation. A sharp irony had played itself out on the Hill of Reckoning that day, and it had left Albert bewildered. Within the cloister of his grand treehouse, he struggled to find his way through all the doubt and back to certainty.

Not far from where Albert now slept, the leading edge of the western meadow tumbled over the banks of a shallow chasm concealed in the tall grass. At one end of this narrow cleft in the earth, stood the same pond beside which the travelers had earlier refreshed themselves. On its reedy banks, the poet sat in solitude.

For decades, he had carried the heavy burden of hope that one day he might find redemption for his and his sister's inadvertent fault. Over the past few years, his hope had grown heavier by the addition of having to carry Silloah's own. Her illness had made it impossible for her to join in the effort to bring the key back to the Forgotten

Meadow, and she had to lay the full weight of her aspirations upon the shoulders of her younger brother. Her death only emphasized the urgency of his task. Time was of the essence, and the moment had finally arrived for Annelyse to take her mother's place.

Planting the seeds of curiosity, and fanning questions into reflection, the young poet led his niece along a path of exploration, discovery, and belief. Once belief had blossomed into conviction, action was not far behind. If she was to shoulder the responsibility of her mother's oath, Annelyse had to do so freely. And so, she did.

On the far side of grief, Annelyse became the *promise of grace* whose selflessness not only brought freedom to Willem in Chains but carried her on a journey through death and back to life again. By bequeathing Annelyse this task, Silloah's death was both the cause of her daughter's grief and the means by which her grief was cured. Destiny often finds its fulfillment along unexpected paths.

Silloah's key had restored the old Woolem's freedom without ever opening the lock. Instead, the hunter's own hateful hands broke the chains his father had fastened. But at what cost? Who could have foreseen the reckoning exacted upon that hill?

The hunter's son had paid the price of his and his father's wickedness. Willem had freely paid the price of love. Love can never be anything but a freely given gift, and it is always fruitful beyond accounting. And so, for now, the accounts balanced. Payment had been made in full. All had been redeemed, and as nighttime descended, the world looked forward to the dawn of a new day.

Strewn throughout the meadow, Woolems of every color drew their legs up beneath their bodies and surrendered to the healing hands of sleep. Beside the pond, the poet rested his head on his satchel, letting go of the grief that had gripped his heart all day. He knew too well that the heartache would return to claim him with the rising of the sun.

Atop the Hill of Reckoning, the lifeless body of the ancient Woolem lay upon a pillow of stone, beneath a blanket of broken tree limbs. Even in death, Willem was allotted no comfort. As it had always done before, the shattered willow did its best to provide the Woolem with cover from the elements. But in its mangled state, its efforts were in vain. All was now as pitiable as could be imagined. Before yielding to sleep, Lachlan resolved to find a more suitable resting place for his friend in the morning.

Throughout the night, restlessness stirred inside the troubled hearts of all those who had witnessed the day's events. The muffled chuffs of furtive, sleepless sobbing crept through the meadow like a heavy fog. But, as the sun seeped over the eastern slopes of the Borderland Hills, it found only slumbering souls among the pale daisies.

Annelyse was the first to awaken. As the sound of singing birds greeted her ears, she was appalled by how quickly nature seemed to forget the tragedy of the previous day. Seeing her friend asleep beside her, Annelyse wished she could hush the songbirds or shield the warm rays of the rising sun from laying their hands upon Willemina's shoulders. Such joyful things could only bring pain to the heart of one so tender as she.

Blinking her eyes in the diffuse light of the morning, Annelyse became aware of a scent crowding in upon the morning. The perfume was so powerful, it could not have been present the day before. Surely, she would have noticed it then. Raising herself to a seated position, she looked around for the source of the fragrance. What she saw was a scene entirely unlike that which had bid her goodnight only a few hours earlier.

Springing from the ground all around, dazzling white lilies crowned green, glossy stems, as deep and dense as water is to the sea. Peering out from within the trumpet-shaped flowers, sticky stamens powdered the creamy petals orange with countless grains of pollen. Unopened buds, like the tight-lipped beaks of birds, dangled among the blooms, nodding in the lazy breeze. Where, only the night before, all had been a vast litter of willow branches fallen among well-trodden stone, now an alpine scene of snowy brilliance capped the Hill of Reckoning.

Annelyse leapt to her feet, the thick bed of tall lilies reaching well above her waist. Wading her way over to the brow of the hill, she saw that the flowers thinned and faded where the crest started its descent. Running down to the meadow below, the steep hillside was cloaked in lush, green grass, without a single flower dotting its slopes. At its feet, the lonely hill stepped into a glade of white-maned daisies. While, on its head, it wore a crown of silver.

From a great distance, Annelyse was sure that the hill must have looked like a snow-capped mountain of diminutive proportions. From the meadow, where her friends and the herd of Woolems lay sleeping, it looked more like a mint-green birthday cake topped with vanilla frosting.

Turning back toward the summit, Annelyse noticed a clearing in the middle of the crown of lilies. As she approached the place where the willow tree had fallen, the place where the body of Willem had lain, she was taken aback by what she found. All had been transformed in the quiet of the night.

Bubbling up from the center of the twisted gnarl of willow branches, a spring of cool water cascaded in wild rivulets among the broken limbs. Encompassing the toppled tree, a circular pool gathered spring water like laughter in a lavalier. The surface of the reflecting pool was like a production of tiny ballerinas. Leaping, pirouetting, then descending to touch the mirrored sky in round, rippling kisses, water dripped from every twig in a carillon of liquid bells. The willow had become a half-submerged fountain of wood, cast in constant motion by a ceaseless flow of water welling up from deep inside the earth.

Winding its way down the opposite side of the hill, a narrow stream exited the reflecting pool. Lining its bed - and, indeed, forming the bowl of the pool itself - polished boulders of pure quartz shone like diamonds in the crystal waters. Annelyse recognized them as the muddy rocks upon which Willem had been forced to live and sleep for decades. Washed clean, the stones now revealed their true grandeur.

Wherever the wandering waters went, whatever banks they nourished, spectacular lilies grew along the shore. Following the bridal train as it spilled down the rise and over the brow of the hill, Annelyse could see the stream widen as it met the meadow of daisies. The flowing spring waters had searched out the lowlands, discovering the chasm at the western edge of the prairie.

Soon, the dry riverbed emerging from the gulley remembered its long-forgotten purpose. Ever deepening as it spread itself wide within the confines of the high, ancient banks, the stream became a running river of cool, clean water. The small pond, beside which the poet now slept, had been absorbed by the passing flood as it made its way around toward the southwest.

Awakened suddenly and astonished to find his feet immersed in a newborn river where before, they'd slumbered upon dry ground, the poet got up and started searching upstream for the source of this strange phenomenon. Reaching the foot of the hill, Lachlan followed the Lily Brook up the rise to the summit where he found Annelyse gazing down into the reflecting pool.

"There," she said, pointing toward the bottom of the pond beneath the tinkling rain of spring water that dripped from the knot of willow branches.

Dropping to his hands and knees, Annelyse's uncle strained his neck to see. Directly below the fountain of tangled tree limbs, shining as bright as a silver tea set in a lighted display case, the shackles that had once bound Willem in Chains lay upon a watery bed of quartz.

Caught among the branches above, and dangling down into the transparent waters, the iron chain was still attached to the manacle. The portion of the chain that hung beneath the water glistened like a newly minted coin. While the portion that reached above the waterline was as rusty and battered as it had been when shackled to the old Woolem.

"All things…" the young man whispered to himself in quiet amazement, "…made new."

"But where…" Annelyse hesitated. She didn't have the heart to finish her question. Still, the mystery was impossible to ignore. Willem and his would-be murderer were nowhere to be found.

At that moment, a voice was heard from down among the lilies, "With Mama, now," Willemina said, making sense of all she was seeing.

Annelyse caught her uncle's eye. Willemina might be able to understand what had happened on the hill in the secret of the night, but Annelyse was struggling.

Seeing his niece's befuddlement, the poet offered no explanation, rather, he just smiled and asked, "Where's the key?"

Removing the corroded, iron key from her pocket, Annelyse offered it to her uncle.

"It belongs here," he said, raising his hand to refuse the honor. "You know what to do with it."

Turning it over in her fingers, Annelyse recalled the moment when her mother had first shown her the key. She remembered Silloah's words, "When you're old enough and able to do what I no longer can, then it will all be revealed."

Annelyse felt the truth of the poet's assurance that the key belonged there with the shackles. In an instant of understanding, she knew what it was that her mother had meant. The full meaning of their quest was, indeed, revealing itself.

Annelyse and her father had not failed. Their one task had been to return the key to the Forgotten Meadow where it belonged. This was the one thing that had been under their control. Everything that had happened the day before had been horribly outside of their control, but the key was home. They had done what Silloah had been unable to do. They had succeeded, even if the result was not what they had expected. The key was back where it belonged, and here it should stay.

It occurred to Annelyse, that it hadn't been her mother's task to free Willem, as it had not been her intention that he be chained in the first place. Her task – and Annelyse's task - had been to do all that she could to return the key. Just as her loving efforts had been twisted to evil, Annelyse's loving efforts were all that were required to set things right. Everything else had to be left to the whims of chance, the designs of providence.

Standing beside the reflecting pool, Annelyse let the old, iron key fall from her hand. As it struck the surface of the water, every stain, every blemish, and corruption dissolved in a slow flourish of rebirth. Before coming to rest on the quartz stones at the bottom of the pond, the key had turned from rusted iron to burnished silver. Lying beside the shackles in Willem Springs, Silloah's Key could at last free the captive. For, in the coming days, as the Woolems slaked their thirst in the waters of the Lily Brook, they discovered the final, lasting gift of Willem Woolem.

Beginning with his heart-stricken daughter, anyone who drank from the spring waters experienced a loosening of the chains of grief, an unlocking of the heart. In place of mourning, gratitude sprung like lilies from once-dry riverbeds. Instead of tears, joy blossomed within the heart, spreading like embers on the breeze. Far more than freeing just one Woolem, the return of the key to the Forgotten Meadow had begun a transformation that was truly beyond all accounting, as love always proves itself to be.

Edward and Albert Prume now joined Annelyse, Willemina, and the poet beside the fountain on the Rise of Willem Springs. All were silent as, before them, over two decades of suffering and misfortune washed away. The grief that had led Annelyse and her father to ascend the rise and stand upon the summit of the Hill of Reckoning; the grief that had led them from anger and rejection to acceptance and belief; the grief that had led them from devastating loss to unexpected sorrow, now started to dissolve in the clear waters of gratitude.

Even Albert, who had begun to question fate's fairness, recognized something even more grand than his exceptional stand of five forty-foot-tall evergreen trees: the untrammeled, exponential fruitfulness of self-sacrificing love.

The generous part he had played all those years ago in guiding the wise, old Woolem through the wilderness between Halla's house and the Forgotten Meadows had been rewarded with the unfettered freedom of his enchanted Tree RV. But the generosity he'd witnessed upon that hill the day before would be rewarded with much more.

It was not simply the fair flowers growing along its banks that would continue to bloom for ages to come. The Lily Brook, or Silloah's Stream as it came to be called, springing from the place of Willem's great sacrifice would renew the whole world.

Edward wrapped one arm around Annelyse's shoulders, drawing her close. The other hand he rested upon the leg of the Woolem who, in an effort to speed Annelyse to Willem's side, had kicked Edward clear across their campsite and into the woods. Speaking with wordless emotion, Edward Bellamy simply sighed.

Beside them, the young Poet of Perigoh quietly quoted his own poem,

*"And where the Woolems wander, wild
and where the western winds did blow
there walked this wise and wistful child
who made fair wonders grow."*

"Aye," the pensive voice of Albert Prume agreed, "That she did. And isn't it grand!"

———————

Bubbling up from beneath the willow's wreckage, the healing waters of Willem Springs sputtered like flecks of molten glass in a translucent flame. Caught in the current as it slipped over the rise and down the slope, the droplets of spring water organized themselves into a stream which circled the base of the hill like a castle moat.

On the southwestern side, the stream swelled to become a river. Slowing and broadening, it crept alongside the bare branches of Albert Prume's Tree RV. With their toes in the cool waters of Silloah's Stream, the five naked trees began to bristle with feathery, green stubble which quickly grew into fully fledged evergreen leaves. Opening their long limbs to the spring breeze, the stand of forty-foot-tall trees wiggled their fingers with delight.

Continuing along its path, the river churned a white wake of lilies as it flowed through the poet's garden and past his raindrop home. Joining with the lake that formed the ceiling of the poet's subterranean room, the spring water brought a lightheartedness to every fish and frog, every swan and salamander caressed by its current. Even Annelyse's friend, the crawfish, thought it proper to spend more time swimming merrily than crawling through the muck of the lakebed. No creature proved too small to receive Willem's blessing.

When it reached the Borderland Hills, Silloah's Stream divided itself into a collection of shallow lakes before reforming on the eastern slopes. The pools of spring water so filled the valleys and concealed the feet of the Borderlands that the region would forever after be known as the Lily Brook Isles. Leatherback geese , beavers, and gangly-legged moose ventured south from the Far Reaches to make their homes among the newborn wetlands.

Undeterred, the spring-fed river pressed southward into the charred remnants of the Silent Forest. Here, the clear waters ran black with ash and charcoal, as it wiped clean the smudged face of the earth. Swirling around tree stumps and sweeping the forest floor of debris, Silloah's Stream freed the soil lying in wait beneath the burned crust of destruction. Seeds that had huddled deep in the ground, trying to escape the ravages of fire, now stretched their weary limbs. Among the sprouts of hopeful plants, the Lily Brook spread its flowery garment of snowy fragrance, as the Silent Forest became the Silent Meadow.

A week had passed by the time Silloah's Stream came within sight of the Miralette. Threading through the Fishbones and reaching the plain of Squirrel Thicket, the spring-water-river formed a shallow phalanx, claiming ground in a relentless advance of renewal.

Of the great tangles of driftwood that had once littered the shoreline like a mound of dried snake bones, nothing now remained. Even the bodies of the wicked river rats - their hides, skeletons, and yellow teeth – had been consumed by the fire they themselves had set. Nothing stood between the pure waters of the cleansing stream and the silted brown of the mighty Miralette.

As the southward flow of the cool waters mixed with the warmer, westward currents of the great river, a dense mist formed above the point of confluence. Billowing out and upward, the moisture became low-lying cloud cover. As the gentle breeze guided the gathering storm south over the Miralette, a light rain began to fall on the opposite shore.

With whiskers glazed in a gossamer of raindrops, two young river otters paddled in the brown water. The larger of the two left barely a bubble in his wake, swimming like a fish who'd popped up to take a look around. The smaller otter swam with no obvious direction, her four limbs flailing amid a chaos of frothy waves.

On the shore, the beautiful mother otter turned her eyes skyward. Licking the rain from her lips, she felt a lightening of her heart. There was something not unlike the assurance of hopes fulfilled in the taste of the clean water. With a smile, she removed the knit scarf from around her neck, then scurried down the riverbank to join her son and daughter for a leisurely swim.

The rainclouds now reached the northern woods of Shatter Lake. Moving like ghosts through solid wood, the clouds pressed themselves into every space between leaves and twigs, branches, and trunks, drenching every tree in the forest with water from Willem Springs. Off to the east, in the pastures of Orchard Knoll, wild horses whinnied and kicked their legs in jubilation, as the mist from the approaching clouds condensed upon their golden manes.

In a duck blind near a cave located at the northern end of Shatter Lake, a hedgehog sat motionless. A handmade quilt, reaching down to the ground, lay upon her lap. In her hand, she held the trigger for a box camera perched upon a tripod in front of her. Raising one hand, she rubbed a small cloth in a circular motion over the lens of her camera. The weather had turned cloudy, even though earlier she'd been assured of ideal conditions. Still, she waited, trigger in hand, for whatever wonder might wander into her camera's view.

Brushing the misty raindrops from her quills, the hedgehog paused to consider the rain's meaning. She had seen many things in her time. She had played a part in some of the greatest events of the last quarter century. Her heart was finely tuned to the significance hidden behind the seemingly mundane.

After a moment, with a look of satisfaction on her face, the hedgehog spoke to herself knowingly, "Well done, Mr. Bellamy. I do hope to meet your daughter soon. Ah, yes… that I do."

She would not have long to wait.

Just then, a hawk swooped down from the canopy of tree limbs overhead. With a flutter of its wings, the bird sent a burst of fallen leaves spiraling up from the forest floor, then bolted upward as quickly as it had arrived. But not before the expert shutter of the hedgehog-photographer had captured the hawk's impressive acrobatics on film.

Picking up a tiny teacup from a tray beside her chair, the best photographer within 100 miles of Shatter Lake whispered, "Gotcha," then sipped her tea with satisfaction.

Two weeks since emerging from Willem Springs, the clouds continued their journey, letting rain fall like a veil over every landscape and creature they encountered. Behind the advancing storm, the sunshine returned, and with it a sense of newness. Every worry seemed to vanish. Every care loosened its grip on any mind it held captive, freeing the hearts of man and beast alike, as truly as if they'd sloughed off shackles of iron.

Far and wide, over paths once trodden by the rescued Woolems being led to the haven of the Forgotten Meadow, the dew from Willem Springs descended. In place of a secret road marked by daisies – a symbol of the simplicity and ubiquity of unobtrusive faith – a sprinkling of snow-white lilies heralded faith restored, hope realized, and the redemption of all things.

Not far from the edge of the woods surrounding Shatter Lake, a tiny pair of ears popped out of a perfectly knit hat perched atop the little, brown head of a squirrel.

From inside her hollowed-out stump, the squirrel felt the refreshing cool of the rain, as the clouds moved southeast. There was more to this particular rain than might meet the eye, she was sure. Rubbing her hands together with delight, the squirrel grinned a sweet smile, then continued with her busy morning, a new and joyful skip in her already spirited step.

The Quibble Woods stood like a fortress in the heart of Hyland. Among them, trees like the saw-toothed Pólcrit and red-barked Kalósyi grew out of the fertile ground of myth and legend. Others, like the bitterwort trees, seemed more at home in nightmares.

As Halla had explained to Edward, the bitterworts echoed back to him that which they found darkest in his heart. They attuned themselves to grief, fear, anxiety, and they hurled it around like insults between the quibbling trees. Whatever sorrow was carried into the Quibble Woods, the bitterworts used it to drive the bearer mad. Now, as the misty rains of Willem Springs reached the haunted forest, a change began to work itself into every fiber of the woods.

Each raindrop seemed to magnify the care of the sun, shining light upon fears lurking within hidden places. The restless heat of anxiety cooled beneath the touch of Willem's calm and soothing clouds. Unaccustomed to the mysterious dewfall of light, liquid healing, the bitterworts began to wither and die. In their place, silent, stoic mushrooms pushed their bulbous faces out of the fertile ground. Few things know how to thrive in the refuse of decay, or how to turn lifelessness into rebirth quite so well as a mushroom.

At the southern tip of Shatter Lake, in a cabin behind a large, knotty beech tree, a grumpy fieldmouse in red breeches and black, leather boots propped his hands upon his hips with displeasure. The weather of the world had been increasingly unpredictable lately, what with forest fires, hurricanes, and rainstorms. But, instead of a string of salty expletives, the fieldmouse did something he hadn't done since long before "the recent unpleasantness." He smiled.

In the two decades since the dawn of sorrow, there had been precious few reasons for a fieldmouse to smile. But now, something in the gentle rain seemed to draw grief to the surface like spring water from the ground. Sadness and cynicism ceased to wield their influence over him, and the fieldmouse reveled in the world's reawakening.

In the weeks since Willem's death, in the parting of those who had labored to bring Silloah's Key to the Forgotten Meadow, the last of sorrow's stepchildren - the grief snipers, who lie in wait behind the commonplace and pounce upon moments of unexpected vulnerability – had also lost their power to wound. For there is no commonplace in a world flooded with wonder, and love is the greatest and most coveted vulnerability we can ever hope to achieve. In the soaking rains of Willem Springs, wrapped in the waters of the Silloah Stream, the wonders of selfless love were on display for all the world to see. Nothing harmful could prevail. Nothing hateful could stand upright in floodwaters such as these.

At last, the rainclouds arrived at a log cabin beside the Maidenhair River in the heart of the Quibble Woods. Engraved upon the red door of the cabin was the image of a cat with its tail wrapped around its shoulders. In its two front paws, it was holding a pair of knitting needles. Encircling one needle, the end of the tail became the yarn with which the cat was knitting. Indeed, she was knitting her very self into being.

On the eastern side of the cabin, the Forest of Ferns shimmered with the sheen of fresh, spring green. The sound of the falling rain upon the elephant ear-sized lobes was like the thrumming of fingers on velvet drums. With each raindrop, the enormous ferns flapped and bobbed on their unwieldy stems, until the entire sea of oversized lily pads was a wave of undulating motion.

Where the Maidenhair River skirted the southern border of the Forest of Ferns, a shaft of sunlight split the clouds, coming to rest upon the red door of the little house. Overhead, a double rainbow marked the home of Halla the Wise; the one to whom Willem had been brought by the young Silloah and Lachlan; the one who enlisted the help of the sylvan creatures. It was she who had chosen the Forgotten Meadow as the haven home of the Woolems. Hers was the wisdom that outwitted the cunning of the enemy. Inside, the tiny figure of a woman sat in her rocking chair, knitting beside the fireplace. Tirelessly she worked to turn the Woolem's gifts of gratitude into knit goods for those in need. Ever she labored in secret for the good of others.

As the rain slowed and stopped, the clouds settled in among the ferns, draping what remained of Willem Springs across the shoulders of the great plants. One by one, bending beneath the weight of the rainwater, the huge leaves tipped forward, dribbling their contents onto the forest floor.

Pooling into puddles that ran together to form eager rivulets, the spring water that had been carried all the way from where the Silloah Stream met the Miralette River, sought the fastest route down the hills, through the lowlands, and over the banks of the Maidenhair.

As it drained away, the blessed rainwater left a scattering of lilies among the ferns. Along its course to the Maidenhair, more lilies pushed their glassy green stems up through the fallen leaves and fertile ground of the Quibble Woods. Mingling with the yellow hair of the Maiden, the river of spring water ran its fingers along the shore all the way to where it joined the mighty Perigoh Fair. Everything it touched paled pure white at the meeting.

The scent of lilies overpowered that of the wet pines

and leaf tannins. All the world seemed to exhale the fragrance of flowers. Every living thing now drew breath with joy. Even the high banks of the Perigoh were lined with white blossoms, as the Silloah Stream rode along with the Perigoh Fair on its way to the sea.

After nearly a month, the crystal-clear spring waters entered the mouth of Perigoh Bay and met the salty sting of the open ocean. Even so, there remained a distinction of currents. The sea did not swallow the stream, nor did the stream lose itself among the chaos of the ocean. The great heaving, lumbering waters took little notice of the purposeful river of spring water as it cut a path around Windy Point. But, playing in the waters of the estuary, the observant dolphins sensed that some change had arrived.

Gliding high upon the thermals rising up from the Point, kitebirds and osprey had watched the gentle storm unfold. They knew the rain's origin. They'd seen Silloah's Stream flow down from beyond the wreckage of the Silent Forest. They'd seen rainclouds form over the Miralette. They'd witnessed them condense upon the lobed ferns just south of Halla's cabin. The birds now watched as the stream bathed the black sands of Ruhner's Beach like a healing balm being applied to the last remaining wound festering in Laprofonde.

Along the obsidian beach, the apathetic sea gave way to the resolute freshwater. The seagulls, who chased the tides in search of food, stood in confusion as the ocean grew calm. Bathing the beach in successive waves of spring water, all was hushed but for the movements of Silloah's Stream.

Ever adaptable to changing situations, the birds began drinking from the flow of freshwater, happy to wash the salt from their throats. But beneath their webbed feet, the sand began to shift. Seeping up between the myriad grains, Silloah's Stream turned the beach into a saturated stew of unstable shoreline.

Creeping closer to the sandstone cliff face like a slowly spreading stain, the sodden seashore was eroding away, relinquishing itself to the concerted efforts of water, wind, and gravity. The purposeful currents of Willem Springs were loosening, weakening, and prying great chunks of black beach away from the grip of the land and casting them into the rapacious hands of the ocean. The entire width of Ruhner's Beach had been reduced from a dozen yards to less than a foot in a matter of minutes. Little remained but a thin strip of sand running parallel to the cliff face.

As the remnants of Silloah's Stream lapped at the entrance to the infamous cave of Ruhner's Beach, in which the Woolems had been chained as they awaited passage across the sea, the cliff itself began to crumble. Huge sections of the sandstone walls broke free and crashed into the waves below, with splashes that would swamp a cargo ship. The sloshing seawater quickly overwhelmed the enormous boulders, rolling them like greedy trolls into hidden hordes beneath the crushing depths.

Having flowed from hilltop to sea level, Willem Springs had fed the course of Silloah's Stream until it reached its final, intended destination. Leaping from the vanishing beach below, the spring waters choked Ruhner's Cave at its full depth. Gasping for air, the wretched cavern struggled to free itself from the alarming glut of water.

The dark places that had held both the wife and mother of Willem Woolem were convulsed by tremors of bitter guilt. The whole cave frothed at the mouth like a villain poisoned by his own treachery. In an instant, the gagging beast was thrown down, its gaping mouth blasted from deep inside by the explosive force of retribution. In a silent fall from the heights of arrogance through the delicate, lily-scented air, every remaining vestige of Ruhner's Beach and its ignominious cavern were lost in the bowels of the Great Sault Sea.

Slipping silently into the hands of the insatiable sun, the clean waters of Silloah's Stream slowly evaporated, ascending to the clouds to rain again another day. All had been accomplished. Along the way it had chosen, the spring-water-stream had collected itself into life-giving caches of lakes and ponds, rivers, and brooks along which still grow a gown of lilies. Stretching all the way back to Willem Springs atop the Hill of Reckoning in the heart of AnnElysium, the Lily Brook carries blessings of freedom to captive hearts and minds even to this very day.

In a little cabin by the sea on the coast of Averlune, Annelyse sat on the edge of her bed, sewing. Off to the west, the graceful presence of Lower Perigoh Light stood like an old friend astride Watcher's Island. Annelyse could see the yellow light sweep the waves beneath a moody sky. Even from her room, the curtain of rain hanging over the bay appeared like a swarm of dense static speckling and distorting the beaming gaze of the lighthouse's powerful eye. The rain would soon pass, as these unexpected storms often did.

It had been nearly two months since the events that had taken place on the Hill of Reckoning in the land now named for her. Not a moment went by when Annelyse did not think about Willem, Willemina, Albert Prume, her poet-uncle, and especially her mother. There was so much to sort through, so much to process. Even though each day brought with it some new glimmer of light, all the answers she'd discovered along her journey still needed time to take their seat in her understanding.

She thought about Willem's words to her about gratitude. The ancient Woolem had said that "gratitude heals all wounds." Annelyse and her father had spent hours talking about this since their return, but she still seemed to lag behind his understanding. He had found some degree of peace, while her own road through grief felt less like a straight line and far more like a series of endless loops.

Somewhere along the way, her grief had moved from anger to the profound ache of empty loss, but she was still unable to find a sense of gratitude, let alone meaning, in the face of her suffering. Suffering and gratitude just seemed incompatible. As she sat there sewing scraps of fabric over holes she'd worn in the knees of her hiking pants, Annelyse let her mind wander over these latest mysteries.

Outside, the rainclouds had begun to move off to the east, leaving behind a world of dripping leaves and soggy birds. A blue sky now pushed its way through the gloom, bringing with it sunshine and the promise of a beautiful afternoon.

Annelyse looked up to see a sunbeam streaming through the windowpane near her bed and illuminating the drenched wings of a rain-battered butterfly. The unfortunate creature clung to the pane of glass, slowly fanning her heavy, wet wings. She was in a race against time. Fearing for her life, she was desperate to dry her wings and regain her ability to fly before the heat of the sun scorched her delicate body and extinguished her spark of life.

Annelyse rested her sewing in her lap, watching the drama unfold with compassion, powerless to help. At first, she was confident, assuring herself that there really was no danger. The butterfly was strong and had surely endured many rainstorms before. But as Annelyse's sense of helplessness grew, so did her feelings of indignation that suffering of any kind should be allowed to afflict a creature of such innocence.

She found herself bargaining with the situation. If only the butterfly fanned its wings a little harder, if only it didn't give up… but what? What greater motivation could there be than to regain its freedom and save its own life?

Sadness now coiled itself around Annelyse's heart, like the deadly serpent of old, tempting her to abandon all hope. There was nothing that could be done, no way to reach the grounded butterfly, no chance of a favorable outcome. Annelyse accepted these inevitabilities as simply a part of life, then turned her face away from the dying butterfly and back to her sewing. She had seen enough misery, she refused to look upon it anymore.

As the cloud cover dissipated, the butterfly's fanning accelerated to a fever pitch. But with the full intensity of the sun now bearing down on its overheated body, its strength began to wane. Struck down by the whims of cold-hearted fate, the sweet, little creature opened wide its wings and surrendered itself to death.

Then, on the edge of sadness when all seemed lost, the fierce sun proved gentler than expected. Tempered by the passing clouds, the sun softened its harsh stare, and the butterfly's wings were dried. Her freedom restored, the ecstatic butterfly caught a wisp of a breeze, and took to the sky once more.

Its suffering, though dire, had been but one stormy moment in a lifetime of both sun and rain. Its wings would bear the scars of its struggle, and it might never know the joys of flying quite so high again but, fly it would. All it had to do was spread its wings.

The butterfly's moment of suffering possessed no power to reach back into the past and mar the happiness of all that had come before. These memories were locked away within its heart; secured with the key of thankfulness; forever unchanged; and more vibrant for the darkness she'd endured. Her heart still had room to hold much, much more.

Mounting the wind, the beautiful creature flapped and fluttered with broad strokes of her majestic wings. Clouds and sunlight, flowers and fields, everything she encountered appeared brand-new and altogether wonderful.

Perhaps this had been the meaning behind her suffering, to cast all things in a new light, to make all things new. For familiarity imperils wonder, while suffering imparts worth.

Never pausing to lament the damage done to her wings, she turned her gaze outward. Looking with tiny eyes, she never failed to see the countless ways in which the world smiled back at her. Adding her own brokenness to the beauty of a broken world, she was but one in a glorious gathering of damaged goods.

Having spotted the butterfly's flight out of the corner of her eye, Annelyse watched as the thankful creature went on with its day. Smiling, Annelyse took up her sewing again. Draping the strips of fabric she'd fished-out from beneath her bed over the holes in her pantleg, Annelyse stitched the two together. It was then that something occurred to her.

Witnessing the butterfly's ordeal and the happiness that followed its healing, Annelyse thought about something her father had told her the night before, something Halla had said to him at their parting.

Halla told Edward that *"healing is often found where we least expect it. If only we are willing to see."* She had been referring to the healing wrought by the red bark of the Kalósyi tree. But now, Annelyse began to see the wisdom of Halla's words.

"It's true," Annelyse wondered aloud, "Even for the butterfly. The sun wasn't her enemy. In the end, it's where her healing, where her strength came from."

Putting down her sewing, she thought of her own suffering. Losing her mother was the worst tragedy she could have ever imagined enduring and yet, she *had* endured. Things are rarely as horrific as anticipation paints them. When the event comes, unexpected pathways open up, and we find our way through.

Annelyse's healing had begun the moment she turned her eyes outward and away from her own pain.

Then, the mother's death became the daughter's strength, and she used that strength to lessen Willemina's suffering at the loss of her father. Annelyse was living proof that true strength fortifies the weak, and that healing begets more healing.

"*Where we least expect it*," Annelyse repeated, slowly nodding, as her understanding bloomed.

Then, letting her eyes drift to the window and the glistening, green meadows beyond, she concluded, "Then there *can be* gratitude, even in suffering."

With a smile, Annelyse added the words of Willem in Chains to her new understanding, "*For gratitude heals all wounds,* and there is much to be thankful for."

THE END

About the Author & Illustrator

Matt Pelicano was born near Syracuse, New York and by age 10 was already writing poems, lyrics, music, and stories.

At the age of 17, Matt published his first compilation of poetry, followed by a second a year later. At age 18, Matt's poetry was featured with a centerfold spread in the *New York Span* and numerous inclusions in the monthly poetry journal, *Omnific*.

One of Matt's children's books, *Philbert LaRue had a Hole in his Shoe*, has been compared with the works of Dr. Seuss and Shel Silverstein. Another of Matt's novels targets a middle school-aged (and older) audience. The result of almost two years-worth of onsite research and set in Paris, France, *A Butterfly in Paris* is an adventure story, a travel guide, and a French language primer all rolled into one.

Matt's children's novel, *Tabouli: The Story of a Heart-Driven Diabetes Alert Dog,* seeks to raise awareness of diabetes alert dogs and the vital work they perform, while encouraging those suffering with juvenile diabetes to always *"follow the adventure"* and live life to the fullest. Recommended by world-renown dog trainer, Debby Kay, "*Tabouli* perfectly captures the spirit and journey of a remarkable service dog." *Tabouli* has been nominated for three awards by the Dog Writer's Association of America.

Matt has received nationwide media attention for his writing. Some of this press coverage can be seen on his website: MattPelicano.com.

From his youth, Matt has always loved the poetry of E.E. Cummings, Shel Silverstein, TS Eliot, Walt Whitman, Robert Frost, and William Shakespeare. His literary heroes include JRR Tolkien, CS Lewis, Oscar Wilde, Agatha Christie, and David McCullough.

Matt has three grown children — Andy, Joey, and Megan - and lives in South Carolina and New York.

Sandra Stanton was born and raised in Central New York. She spent her school-aged years running track, playing violin, sketching, and studying classical ballet.

Sandra graduated from The Juilliard School and traveled worldwide with Twyla Tharp's dance company.

She has taught classical ballet and choreographed at Hamilton College since 2011. Currently she works at her family's real estate business and enjoys raising her two beautiful children.

Sandra is eternally grateful to Matt Pelicano for allowing her to play a tiny part in this novel as illustrator. It's been one of the greatest challenges and honors of her career.

A Woolem

Visit Matt online at:
www.MattPelicano.com

Facebook.com/MattPelicanoWriter
Instagram.com/MattPelicano

For a Map of Laprofonde
visit www.Averlune.com